Cinema Engagé

Cinema Engagé

Film in the Popular Front

Jonathan Buchsbaum

University of Illinois Press
Urbana and Chicago

for my parents

This book is printed on acid-free paper.

Library of Congress Cataloging-in-Publication Data

Buchsbaum, Jonathan, 1946–
  Cinema engagé.

  Bibliography: p.
  Includes index.
  1. Moving-pictures—Social aspects—France.
2. Front populaire.   3. Labor and laboring classes
in motion pictures.   4. France—Politics and
government—1914–1940.   I. Title.
PN1993.5.F7B8   1988   302.2'343'0944   87-19034
ISBN 0-252-01485-5 (alk. paper)

Contents

Preface

Shortly after arriving in France during the summer of 1981 to begin research for this book, I went to the massive Bastille Day celebration of the Socialist victory at the Place de la Bastille. With the election of François Mitterand as president in 1981, France had a Socialist government for the first time since the Popular Front government of 1936. The large square was teeming with celebrants, some perched atop the monuments in the square as if squeezed upward by the press of the crowd.

As I pursued my research, I discovered that a similar and sustained elation had attended the victory of the first French Socialist government in 1936, a victory that the French Left could justly claim as its own. Studying the course of that earlier government and the disillusion that accompanied its demise, I realized that the latest socialist experiment was experiencing a similar fate, albeit for many different reasons.

During my final summer of research, in 1986, the Right was mounting its counteroffensive, flushed with its electoral victory in the spring. The mood among my friends in Paris, however, was not that of sudden disillusion. Rather, they viewed the return of the Right as a kind of inevitable slide consequent to the failure of the socialists to change French society. For them, the return of the Right was more symptom of that failure than cause.

In short, I felt that I had lived through an echo of the material I was working on from fifty years ago. The echo concluded resoundingly with the fiftieth anniversary of the Popular Front victory, the defeat of the second experiment coinciding uncannily with the great electoral wave that swept the first leftist government into power. While the Right quickly moved to dismantle the unsteady edifice patched together by the socialist technocrats, the Parisian bookstores filled their windows with reprints, revised editions, and yet additional contributions to the memory of that summer of trente-six, ironic epitaphs to the more muted hopes of the 1980s.

The parallel was indeed striking, but potentially misleading as well. Stirring as those more recent hopes may have been, in fact they bore only a pale and denatured relation to those of the Popular Front. For the Popular Front marked a stunning victory for French working people at a time when socialism had not renounced its opposition to capitalism, when it still spoke the language of revolution. The Popular Front marked a sea change, for it recognized the dignity of French working people for the first time. The exceedingly difficult historical conjuncture, however, dashed those revolutionary visions. Those visions had essentially faded by the 1980s. Despite the enthusiasm of the socialists, toppling capitalism was no longer on the agenda.

In studying the filmmaking efforts of the Left during the years of the Popular Front, I have tried to look carefully at all the extant films which I was able to locate. In order to understand what the films may have meant at the time they were made, I have looked at a wide range of contemporary sources: newspapers, revues, journals, and periodicals. I supplemented these sources with various retrospective accounts by participants, both interviews and memoirs. Finally, I consulted secondary sources on the social, cultural, historical, and political events of the period in an attempt to identify the relevant historiographic controversies that pertain to the period. Regarding these latter sources, I cannot pretend to offer any solutions to the questions they raise. Rather, I have tried to evaluate competing claims fairmindedly, recognizing at the same time that my own biases have guided me toward certain positions at the expense of others. I feel that no historian can do otherwise and to acknowledge such limitations is merely to state the obvious. Correspondingly, I leave to future scholars the opportunity to develop contending views which may further illuminate our understanding of these early essays in political filmmaking.

Many people helped me in the course of my research. During my first summer in Paris, I was summarily presented with a twelve-hour eviction notice from a *chambre de bonne* in the sixteenth arrondissement. Though a veteran of New York's housing crisis, I had never encountered such an abrupt ultimatum, but it turned out to be a fortunate delivery from the arid bourgeois ghetto of the sixteenth as Maguy Alziari offered her hospitality in the Marais. As I pursued my work, Maguy helped me in innumerable ways, not only in my work but also in introducing her Paris populaire to me. Don Siegel helped in ways which cannot be quantified, but without him I would never have had the opportunity to play polyglot baseball in the Bois de Boulogne.

Former teachers offered valuable advice during an early stage of writing, and of course their own work provided standards of exemplary scholarship: Professor Robert Sklar, Professor Jay Leyda, and Professor Annette Michelson, all of New York University.

My research often involved ferreting out material previously thought lost, and I would like to thank the many people and institutions who provided indispensable help in these investigations. The following filmmakers kindly took the time to grant me interviews and extend their hospitality to me: Pierre Prévert, Robert Talpain, Yves Allégret, Jean Painlevé, Jean-Paul Le Chanois, and Louis Joly. Among those who provided invaluable help in my research, I owe particular thanks to the late Martine Loubet. Many others aided me in various ways: Bernard Eisenschitz, Michel Marie, Claude Thibault, David Bordwell, Kristin Thompson, Dudley Andrew, Richard Abel, William Boddy, Chris Faulkner, Claude Gauteur, Bérénice Reynaud, Françoise Romand, Jean-Claude Romand, Rosette Romand, Anna Smorgull, Estelle Altman, Peter Wollen, Laura Mulvey, John Howe, Rosamund Howe, Claude Helft, Monique Vervaeke, Kate White, Eliane and Jacques Thomassin, Jan Greenbaum, Julie Guimont, Erica Warren, Elizabeth Hazan, and Royal Brown.

I would also like to thank the following people and institutions: Charles Silver and the staff of the Museum of Modern Art Film Study Center; Robert Daudelin and La Cinémathèque Québécoise; Elaine Burrows and the British Film Institute; Nicole Schmitt and the Centre National de la Cinématographie; Freddy Buache and the Cinémathèque Suisse in Lausanne; I.D. Traduction.

I would like to single out for special thanks the former Film and Television Office of the French Communist Party, UNICITE. I managed to find there the largest number of films in which I was interested, and the staff of UNICITE gave me unlimited access to their screening facilities. I could not have completed the present work without their generous help.

All of the photographs from films are frame enlargements. With the exception of the stills from *Prix et Profits*, which were supplied by the Centre National de la Cinématographie, I shot all of the stills from the films. I would like to thank Andrea Davis for her painstaking and skillful efforts in developing and printing the photographs, for the quality of the films used for the stills was poor. The head of the photography service at Queens College, Katherine McGlynne, was unstinting in her support of this work. Matthew Curtis of Corinth Films kindly allowed me to borrow *La Marseillaise*.

My editor, Cynthia Mitchell, patiently shepherded the manuscript through all its stages, gently cauterizing infelicities and consistently tightening the writing. Naturally she bears no responsibility for the affronts that may remain.

I am unable to convey sufficiently the extent of care, criticism, support, and time provided by my colleague and friend, Professor Stuart Liebman of Queens College. From the initial conception of the project to final completion, Professor Liebman combined penetrating criticism, many and specific suggestions for improvement, and encouragement to continue, all proffered with an intellectual rigor and generosity which are typical of him.

I view the present work as part of a continuing interest in film and politics which first became a serious area of study when I read the work on Jean-Luc Godard by another friend, Joel Haycock. Discussions with him over the years have helped to clarify many issues, as have his careful criticism of and comments on the manuscript. His own work and writing are models of intelligence and clarity.

Despite the somewhat specialized nature of the material covered in the book, I have tried to write for the general reader unacquainted with the politics and filmmaking of the period. I cannot gauge the degree to which friends contributed to the successful realization of that goal, but I do know that my friends Mark Jacobson and Nancy Cardozo listened and responded sympathetically to my ideas throughout the entire course of the project, sustaining me often literally with Mark's inspired cooking and always with their friendship.

Finally, I thank Simone Vittet for her patience, her support, and her injunction to work "vite et bien."

List of Abbreviations

ACI   Alliance du Cinéma Indépendent. Founded in November 1935 as the cinema section of the AEAR. Evolved into Ciné-Liberté after the production of *La Vie est à nous*.

AEAR Association des Ecrivains et Artistes Révolutionnaires. French section of the UIER. Founded in March 1932 as the Association des Ecrivains Révolutionnaires. Name changed to AEAR in December 1932.

ARAC Association Républicaine des Anciens Combattants. Founded in November 1917 by Henri Barbusse, Raymond Lefebvre, and Paul Vaillant-Couturier. Close to the PCF. Barbusse served as president, with Jacques Duclos as one of the vice-presidents.

CGT   Confédération Générale du Travail. Founded in 1895 at the Seventh National Congress of the Chambres Syndicales, groupes corporatifs, Fédérations des Metiers, Unions et Bourses du Travail. Headed by Léon Jouhaux from 1909 to World War II.

CGTU Confédération Générale du Travail Unitaire. Formed in 1922 as a result of split in the CGT; Communist directed. Represented the minority within the CGT before the split. Reunification of CGT and CGTU completed in March 1936.

FTOF Fédération du Théâtre Ouvrier de France. Formed in January 1931 as French section of the UITO. Became the UTIF early in 1936.

PCF   Parti Communiste Français. Formed as the French section of the Communist International following the split at the Congress of Tours in December 1921. PCF represented the majority at the Congress.

POUM   Partido Obrero de Unificación Marxista. Revolutionary Communist party in Spain; anti-Stalinist. Founded in September 1935.

PS   Parti Socialiste. Formed in December 1921, following the split at the Congress of Tours.

RAPP   Rossiiskaia Associatsiia Proletarskikh Pisatelei. Formed in 1928 as the Russian Association of Proletarian Writers, following the transformation of VAPP.

SFIO   Section Française de l'Internationale Ouvrière. French Section of the Labor (Second) International. Official designation of the French Socialist Party after the unity congress of April 1905.

UIER   Union Internationale des Ecrivains Prolétariens. Formed at international conference of revolutionary writers in Moscow sponsored by VAPP in 1927.

UITO   Union Internationale du Théâtre Ouvrier. Formed by Communist International in Moscow early in 1930.

UTIF   Union du Théâtre Indépendent de France. Formed early in 1936 to replace FTOF.

Introduction

On February 6, 1934, riots broke out in Paris around the Chamber of Deputies building to protest the government's implication in a financial scandal. Shouting "Down with the thieves," right-wing demonstrators hurled rocks at the police and disrupted the charges of the mounted police with razor blades attached to sticks. The same evening, the Communist party had directed its militants also to take to the streets to mount their own protest. After the violence ended in the middle of the night, several people had been killed and many on all sides had been injured. That bloody evening dramatized to the various groups on the Left the threat of fascism in France and sparked a groundswell of response that led to the victory of the Popular Front in the spring of 1936. During these two years, the Popular Front eventually gathered all of the significant political formations on the Left into a successful electoral coalition that brought to power the first Socialist government in French history.

One of the lesser-known aspects of this political and social movement is the Left's use of cinema as a political instrument for the first time in France. Over the course of several years, from 1935 to 1938, political parties and trade unions attempted both to document this mass movement and to prolong its momentum, for as an historian of the Popular Front has emphasized, "Perhaps the most important thing to remember about the Popular Front is how much it owed to a movement of the working class from below."[1] The French Communist Party (PCF—Parti Communiste Français) took the lead in the construction of the Popular Front, and at a crucial moment, just prior to the opening of the election campaign in 1936, the PCF sponsored the most important Left political film of the period, *La Vie est à nous*.

But other films of lesser scale and achievement also reveal varying attitudes toward the use of films as political instruments, and the evolution of that filmmaking reflects the shifting fate of the Left during this turbulent period. Only in the context of the contemporary political events do the meaning and importance of these films emerge fully. Therefore, the cinematic strategies and the political context of these films will be the principal concern of this study, which will consider in some detail the course of events to which these films responded and which, to a degree, the films may have inflected.

Just before the election of May 1936, having successfully led the struggle to knit together the parts of the Popular Front, the PCF took the unprecedented step of sponsoring a major film to be used for the election campaign: *La Vie est à nous*. Though several modest experiments had been produced previously for internal party use, never before had the political parties attempted to tap the power of the medium for electoral purposes. It is not surprising that the party chose Jean Renoir to oversee its first film venture: though never associated with any political organization, Renoir was a renowned contemporary filmmaker with well-known leftist sympathies. While Renoir's exact role in the production remains unclear, *La Vie est à nous* deserves to be ranked as one of the most innovative political films of the decade.

Excited by the opportunity of serving the objectives of the Left through their chosen medium, the filmmakers who worked on *La Vie est à nous* deployed an impressive array of cinematic strategies in what some have called "the first militant left-wing film made in France."[2] Central to the film is a dialectical alternation between fiction and document. In this complex dialectic, the film manifests a distrust of both the fictional form imposed by the producers on commercial films and the putative objectivity of commercial newsreels. Thus, not only does the film employ fiction and document, it also subjects both forms to transformations which require more subtle categories for adequate discussion, for it straddles several cinematic forms in its use of fiction, document, and newsreel elements. At the same time, as an election film made for a specific historical campaign, *La Vie est à nous* uses rhetorical strategies which engage many issues specific to that moment—issues which audiences at the time would have understood because of their familiarity with the political situation, even if they may not have recognized the degree of the film's formal complexity.

The PCF owed much of its popular success to its vigorous cultural efforts of the previous years. Communists understood better than other political formations the importance of public support from intellectuals and artists in recruiting the masses to their cause. In many countries this was the era when intellectuals and artists espoused political causes, and the PCF exploited this commitment to maximum advantage by presenting itself as the vanguard of the resistance to fascism. Fellow travelers assumed particular importance in this period, for their very independence from the party widened their sphere of influence over public opinion—an influence the party had seen dissipate during the sectarian "third-period" policy followed since 1928. Even before the change of this policy in 1934, the PCF had recognized the potential value of intellectuals and artists in promoting the antifascist cause as well as in refurbishing the party's image. Hence, party intellectuals organized highly publicized antifascist meetings and events, such as the Amsterdam-Pleyel Movement of 1932–1933.

The adhesion of intellectuals and artists to antifascism, then, actually preceded the official change of the PCF political line, but, even if party members did not always announce their organizing role, Communist intellectuals orchestrated the activities. Thus, the PCF was instrumental in establishing and directing the prominent Association des Ecrivains et Artistes Révolutionnaires (AEAR) in 1932. Originally, primarily through its journal (*Commune*), the AEAR provided a forum for discussion among writers of the role of the writer and literature in society. With the participation of both the most famous and highly respected French writer, André Gide, and the newest literary luminary, André Malraux (winner of the 1933 Prix Goncourt for *La Condition Humaine*), the AEAR boasted impressive credentials. The AEAR had separate sections for the various arts, including painting, sculpture, and music, and sponsored many exhibitions and lectures.[3] Furthermore, the cinema section, originally known as the Alliance du Cinéma Indépendent (ACI), played a pivotal role in the political use of the cinema by the Left in the succeeding years. The successful completion of *La Vie est à nous*, the ACI's first production, catalyzed left-wing filmmaking in the following two years.

During the production of *La Vie est à nous* the ACI changed its name to Ciné-Liberté and began publishing a magazine of the same name; it also produced a series of films. The organization agitated for the elimination of censorship; the creation of a massive union of filmmakers, technicians, and spectators to struggle against the commercial "schemers"; and the production of independent films. Ciné-Liberté did not realize all of these plans, but it did assemble in one institutional unit most of the dynamic filmmakers on the Left who shared a variety of complaints about the contemporary filmmaking situation.

However, as the political unity of the Popular Front began to disintegrate, the possibility of a nonpartisan filmmaking organization also receded. Ciné-Liberté did manage to produce some films through early 1938, always independently of the commercial industry, and pursued various other cultural activities, but the experiment evolved into a trade union group under the influence of the major trade union organization, the Confédération Générale du Travail (CGT).

Ciné-Liberté produced one major film that premiered in 1938. *La Marseillaise*, sometimes called "*the* film of the Popular Front,"[4] in fact is representative of the Popular Front only when it was on the verge of extinction, not when the turn of events truly justified optimism. This film occupies a privileged place in the mythology of the Popular Front for several reasons. Ciné-Liberté raised funds for the film with a special subscription offer sent out to the public. Jean Renoir, recent winner of the Prix Delluc (for *Les Bas Fonds*), was named to direct this project on the birth of the Republic, the French Revolution. Though not officially financed by the government, *La Marseillaise* opened at a gala première attended by all the political leaders of the Popular Front, receiving its de facto imprimatur. Despite these promising signs, however, *La Marseillaise* was a failure, both with its intended audience and as a political intervention. In only two years, the flush of unity had faded. *La Marseillaise*, fully enclosed within the confines of fictional narrative and predicated on national reconciliation instead of struggle, ended this first episode of Left filmmaking in France.

Throughout this time, however, as political unity on the Left became increasingly difficult to maintain, not all filmmakers on the Left joined the ranks of Ciné-Liberté. While not breaking formally with Ciné-Liberté, the PCF set up its own filmmaking service and produced several films. Another group representing the left wing of the Socialist party ran its own Cinematographic Service, but it did not receive any official backing from the party.

Unfortunately, not all the films have survived. Some filmmakers intentionally destroyed their copies of films before the Germans reached Paris. Others may yet be hidden away in attics or basements; some may await discovery in foreign archives. This study will investigate primarily twelve films that have been preserved. Many of the films have never been described before, and those that have been looked at by earlier researchers have received brief treatment. There-fore, this study will provide extensive discussions of the films in the context of the political and historical factors attending their produc-tion and reception.

A number of writers have looked at films made during this period.[5] Some of them have made substantial contributions to our under-standing of the period and of the role film played in the emergence of the Popular Front. There are, however, significant omissions. Perhaps most significantly, none of the studies devotes adequate attention to the films themselves. For the most part, they treat the independent political films as minor efforts taking backstage to better-known com-mercial products such as *Le Crime de M. Lange* or the works of "poetic realism." The studies do not look at how the films attempted to re-spond to concrete political concerns at a given moment. Conse-quently, these studies provide little opportunity for assessing how the political filmmmakers conceived of the project of political filmmak-ing, what ideas guided them in their work.

This study will try to remedy these gaps by describing the films and by looking at contemporary reviews which indicate reactions to the films by the people who often were participants in the events them-selves. The discussion of the films will elucidate the particular political issues raised in the films or the reasons for certain issues not being raised. The analysis will also isolate characteristics common to many of the films and consider the insights they yield in assessing initial independent left-wing filmmaking in France. While the filmmakers did not follow programmatic rules and commentators did not engage in critical discussion of the proper forms for left-wing filmmaking at the time, the films themselves reveal certain types of aesthetic commit-ments and preoccupations. These concerns revolve around the ap-proaches taken to the use of fiction and document; most of the films include both fiction and document in their search for a radical form. A basic overview of the historical and political developments of the period will help orient readers to the trajectory of the period.

The violent evening of February 6, 1934, and the public demon-strations that ensued revealed a polarization of the country that lasted for years to come, but the pressures underlying the events had been building for some time. The Stavisky scandal, involving an unsavory embezzler with connections to high government figures, broke in 1933 and touched off loud right-wing protest. This agitation, in the press and in the streets, culminated in the violence of February 6 and

forced the resignation of the head of the government, Edouard Daladier. Serious political instability persisted through the rest of the
decade.

The Communists also took to the streets on February 6 to voice
their opposition to the handling of the situation. At that time, the PCF
followed the political line decreed by the Communist International
(Comintern) at the end of the 1920s, known as the policy of the "third
period." This analysis called for intensifying the class struggle to topple the tottering capitalist regimes in the West. However, by 1934 this
tactic had failed to stem Hitler's victory in Germany and the swift
decimation of the formerly powerful German working-class movement. In France, many Communist militants demanded a change of
tack, specifically an alliance with the Socialists in a united front against
fascism, a "Front Unique" to prevent a repetition of the German
disaster.

Many Socialists supported some form of working relationship with
the Communists, but the Socialist leadership harbored deep suspicions about the PCF, going back to the 1920 split of the Socialist party
at the Congress of Tours.[6] In addition, the Socialist party had its own
internal problems and political divisions which had actually split the
party in 1933.

Nonetheless, by February 1934 popular support for unity on the
Left began to exert greater pressure on the leadership of both Marxist parties, the PCF and the Socialist party, but the PCF was the first to
respond to that pressure. In June, after having rebuffed Socialist
overtures for negotiations only months earlier, the PCF initiated discussions with the Socialist leadership. Previously, following the "third-
period" line, the PCF had thought that branding Socialist leaders as
collaborators with reaction—as "social fascists"— would somehow gain
the masses for communism. According to this position, the Socialist
party's accommodation to the capitalist order sabotaged the revolutionary aspirations of the masses. This entirely unsuccessful campaign
ceased in June 1934.[7] The next month the PCF completed a "Unity of
Action Pact" with the Socialist party, an agreement that included a
truce on attacks on either party.

Unlike the Socialist party, once the PCF had embarked on a policy
of unity, it did not hesitate or vacillate. In the fall, the PCF leaders
launched a drive to bring the Radical-Socialist party into the alliance
on the Left, a move that stunned the Socialists, for it indicated that the
PCF had evidently renounced its commitment to revolution by reaching out to the party of the middle class.[8] What the Socialist party saw
as doctrinal contradiction of the PCF, or, less generously, as outright

opportunism, the masses among all the parties tended to see as political dynamism in leading the struggle against fascism in France. While "doctrinal purity" plagued the Socialist party throughout the construction of the Popular Front, creating an image of the Socialist party as follower, not leader, the PCF experienced phenomenal growth during the period and an enhanced reputation as a responsible political party.

Of course the threat of domestic fascism would not necessarily have aroused such spirited response from the Left had not other factors contributed to a highly unstable situation in France. The French economy, initially less damaged by the world crisis, eventually suffered a more prolonged decline than the English or American economies. Successive Radical governments appeared incapable of solving economic problems, and their deflationary measures placed extremely unpopular burdens on the working class. A confused foreign policy aggravated this internal paralysis. Deeply scarred by World War I, many French people, particularly on the Left, opposed the use of force in international relations and hoped that German and Italian aggression would fade away. Some even believed that Mussolini could be enlisted as an ally against Hitler.

As was typical during this time, a mass demonstration propelled events forward. On July 14, 1935, hundreds of thousands of Parisians turned out to declare their allegiance to the idea of the Popular Front, taking an oath binding them to that pledge en masse. Though the Radical party still had not joined in an official agreement with the other two Left parties, several Radicals participated in the rally. With the obvious groundswell of popular sentiment for the Popular Front, the Radical party finally adhered to the Popular Front in the fall of 1935. Several months later, in January 1936, the three parties hammered out a mutually acceptable Programme for the upcoming April/May elections. In the Programme, the Communists blocked Socialist demands for structural reforms (such as extensive nationalizations) for fear that the non-Marxist Radicals would withdraw from the alliance. The Socialist party, again appearing ambivalent about its commitment to unity, at first resisted the dismantling of its traditional program but finally agreed to concessions.

Though all three parties endorsed the common Programme of the Popular Front, or the Rassemblement Populaire, as it was referred to officially at the time, each party waged separate electoral campaigns. In the French electoral system, elections to the national Chamber of Deputies (Parliament) were held every four years. If no candidate won a majority in the first round, the top vote-getters competed in a second round. For the 1936 elections, each party of the Popular Front ran its own list of candidates in the first round, with the understanding that the candidates of the trailing parties would withdraw for the second balloting. Before the elections, even the Right conceded the inevitability of a Popular Front victory, but few observers predicted either the magnitude of the victory or, more significantly, the distribution of the voting.

In the past, governments of the Left had been formed under the ministerial leadership of the Radical party. The Socialists on occasion had supported the Radicals in Parliament, but it was an article of faith that they would refuse ministerial participation. In 1936, for the first time, the Socialists returned the greatest number of deputies on the Left, and Léon Blum prepared to form the government. Equally astonishing was the resurgence of the PCF. At its low point in terms of membership (less than 30,000) and representation in Parliament (10) in 1932, the PCF skyrocketed to a membership of roughly 300,000 and a Parliamentary representation of 72 deputies.

Unfortunately, the euphoric unity of the first half of 1936 did not last. Political and economic realities intruded. The largest strike wave in French history swept over France in May and June 1936, even before Léon Blum took office as head of the Popular Front government. Leaders of both the Right and the Left feared the potential dangers of further instability and managed to reach a hastily arranged agreement to end the strikes. Subsequent developments aggravated the instability within the Left, first weakening its popular mandate and eventually bringing down the Popular Front government after barely a year in power. Blum returned to head the government a year later, in May 1938, but his twenty-six-day government only confirmed that the great hopes of the Popular Front had died long before.

Only recently have film historians and scholars begun to look at the early history of Left political film in the Western countries, let alone to consider them theoretically as early attempts at creating political films. The most widely read film histories tend to concentrate on commercial films. Faced with the massive numbers of such films produced, historians have isolated a rough canon of masterpieces that dominates their histories, though the criteria for this canon are not specified. When political considerations do come up, historians inevitably cite the Soviet films, for the Soviet Union pioneered in the theory and production of political film.[9] But Soviet filmmaking benefited from the active support of the government and in turn generally supported the Soviet system. The political films in the West were made in capitalist countries. Far from enjoying the support of the state, these films had difficulty raising funds even from the Left. These films were oppositional; they often expressed protests and articulated demands that governments could not ignore.

Although this study focuses on French film in an attempt to fill in one of these missing areas in the history of political film, the French production must be seen as part of a European and international surge of filmmaking activity on the Left. Filmmakers in all the major Western countries—Germany, the United States, England, and France—produced significant numbers of political films that the standard histories generally pass over. Usually, national Communist parties sparked these activities, although they did not necessarily dictate the nature of the work, nor were they always alone in this early appreciation of the potential for the cinema as a propaganda tool. In Germany, by the late 1920s, the Socialist party (SPD), the National Socialist party (the Nazi party), as well as the Communists (KPD) all used films far more extensively than is commonly known. In the 1970s, with the expansion of the field of film studies, new areas of film were opened for study, including political filmmaking. Scholars discovered whole bodies of work by politically committed filmmakers formerly neglected in earlier histories.

Germany without question produced the earliest and most sustained effort in a Left cinema. Probably the two most significant factors in this development were the indigenous strength of the two Left parties, the KPD and the SPD, and the tight cultural bonds between the Soviet Union and Germany. Actual institutional affiliation facilitated both the distribution of Soviet films in Germany and the early commitment of the German Left to filmmaking activities, largely as a result of the efforts of the "gray eminence" of Comintern propaganda, Willi Münzenberg. Münzenberg built a huge propaganda empire in Germany during the 1920s, primarily in publishing, but in 1924 he also formed a joint Russian-German film company, Mezrabpom-Russ, to distribute Russian films in Germany. Later the company produced some of the great Russian films in the second half of the decade, including *Mother, The End of St. Petersburg,* and *The Road to Life.* In 1926, Münzenberg added a German subsidiary, Prometheus Films, to make Left films in Germany. Prometheus produced a number of feature films as well as documentaries and newsreels before going bankrupt during the production of its last film, *Kuhle Wampe.*[10]

Münzenberg's ties to the Comintern, through the Workers' International Relief (WIR, set up in 1921 to channel international aid for the

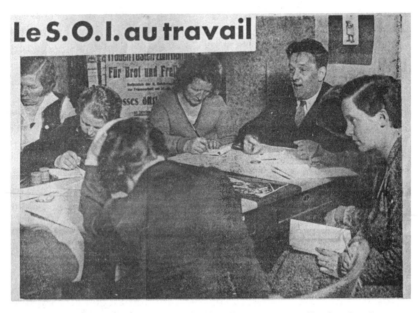

Le S. O. I. au travail

Willi Münzenberg (fourth from left), leading propagandist for the Communist International: "The S.O.I. [Socialiste Ouvrier Internationale] at work. . . . Our comrade Willy Münzenberg elaborates on the tasks of the S.O.I. at a meeting of militants" (*Regards,* March 3, 1932)

famine in Russia), also led to the first Left film production in the United States and England. Early in the 1930s in the United States the WIR supplied funds to the Film and Photo League, and their films often followed the line of the Comintern. In the early years of the decade the films—newsreels and documentaries—generally reflected the political line of the "third period" of the Comintern with its attacks on imperialism (*Bonus March,* 1932; *America Today,* 1933). This exclusive commitment to documentary work caused tension within the group, for some felt that fictional films had greater promise and also would allow them to apply certain theoretical ideas inspired by the Russian films that they saw and screened. Other Film and Photo League filmmakers wanted to continue making agitational newsreels for release in the midst of concrete struggles.

Eventually a split occurred, as the dissatisfied members formed first Nykino, and then Frontier Films. Nykino marked a transitional stage, when the breakaway group experimented with the "aesthetic of reenactment" and a pre-frontist attempt to draw in the middle class

(*Sunnyside,* 1936).[11] The politics of the Popular Front dominated the subsequent output of Frontier Films; attacks on capitalism were replaced by pleas for the defense of the Bill of Rights (*Native Land,* 1937–42). Even though the later Frontier Films often still used documentary material with re-enactment and fiction, the films no longer could claim the same immediacy of concrete ongoing political struggles found throughout the earlier work of the Film and Photo League. For its final film, *Native Land,* the Frontier group, using scripts, actors, and a long production schedule (caused in large part by the search for funding), spent four and one-half years before the release of the film.[12] By way of contrast, the feature film made for the PCF early in 1936, *La Vie est à nous,* from inception to completion and release, took two months.

While it is probably too early to offer any definitive conclusions about this international experience of Left filmmaking, certain tentative observations can be made. As a rule, groups on the Left initiated film projects in response to a deteriorating economic and/or political situation. Less expensive newsreel productions usually preceded the move to fiction films, the latter occasionally of feature length. On the one hand, the filmmakers wanted to document the plight of the workers and their attempts to remedy it. On the other hand, in their desire to build a proletarian cinema, the filmmakers also recognized the potential value of fictional forms, partially because of the undeniable popularity of commercial films, corrupted by ideological deformations though they may have been, and partially because of the success of many Soviet fiction films. Dissatisfaction with censorship and disgust with commercial cinema usually strengthened the resolve to build a Left cinema independent of the commercial industry, though distribution and exhibition strategies varied from country to country. Specialized studies have indicated the importance of these movements and the films produced by them as the Left came to discover the political possibilities of cinema.

My work on the French films is intended both to contribute to an understanding of the first Left filmmaking experience in France and to add to these earlier studies on national cinemas. Once the studies on the national Left filmmaking movements have been completed, future comparative work can proceed. However, such work must be careful to respect the multiple determinations applying in each country, lest a formalist criticism/history abstract their cinematic strategies from their intended functioning at given historical conjunctures.

In France, serious political and economic troubles did not arrive until 1934, and though several Left films were made before 1935, a

Left filmmaking movement did not begin in earnest until 1936, long after the commencement of similar ventures in other countries. As a result there is no early group of French films representing the "third-period" line of the Comintern. The PCF had supported some activity in literature and theater before the Popular Front, but its uncompromising observance of the "class-against-class" policy doomed these forays into cultural propaganda to marginality. Thus, German proletarian filmmaking of the late 1920s had no immediate influence on political filmmaking in France, and it appears unlikely that it had significant effect later either, for the writings in the Left journals of the Popular Front make no mention of it.

However, the whole question of influence is a difficult one. In French discussions of Left filmmaking from the period, the writers do not analyze the role of the Soviet films in the production of the French films. Part of this derives from the less significant role accorded film in France than in Russia, but in addition, the Popular Front owed much of its popular support to a renewal of national traditions, and attributions of foreign influence may have been avoided for fear that they might be seized upon by the Right as evidence that the Popular Front was not an indigenous French political movement. All the same, the films show signs of possible influence.

One of the reasons for emphasizing the importance of the films themselves is the relative absence of theoretical discussions of political filmmaking at the time in France. Perhaps the filmmakers gave the question of political film some thought, and perhaps the critics and intellectuals spoke of it among themselves, but they did not write about political film. They reviewed Soviet films, of course, and singled out some French and American commercial films for praise, but French political film was probably considered too marginal for serious consideration, even if some writers such as party members Léon Moussinac and Georges Sadoul were fully aware of the early efforts. The vivid exchanges among Soviet filmmakers and critics found in *Lef* and *Novy Lef* are not to be found in the Left journals in France during the 1930s. Even the critics in France who applauded *La Vie est à nous* when it was screened during the election campaign did not address its radically innovative structure. Perhaps the political pressures of the moment did not permit the luxury of theoretical investigation. But in the generative ideas behind the films one can discover the solutions worked out by the filmmakers to the challenges posed to Left filmmakers in the preceding years.

A film like *La Vie est à nous* is exemplary in this regard. It was made at the height of the popular sentiment for the Popular Front, just after the official agreement on an electoral program of the three parties (the Rassemblement Populaire). As the PCF commissioned the film to be made, one would expect it to express the position of the PCF at that moment, yet the PCF at the time was taking a decidedly nonsectarian political stand, and its political directorship did not dictate the form of the film, just as it did not prescribe conditions for writers, be they party members or fellow travelers. Thus, many filmmakers worked, with considerable autonomy, to shape parts of the film as they liked, according to their own ideas about radical film. The innovative design of the film resulted from both the first opportunity of young aspiring filmmakers to work on a film freed from the constraints of commercial filmmaking and the decision to produce the film collectively. A large part of the film's success rests on a rare formal diversity, and part of the interest that the film holds today is the formal complexity achieved in the absence of theoretical debate. A radical structure grew out of a concrete political struggle, not as an illustration of a preconceived theoretical position, which is not to say that the filmmakers involved in the project had no theoretical ideas, but rather that they arrived at a creative solution in the circumstances of the moment, in response to a specific situation.

The discussion of and search for the form of radical film depends on a thorough understanding of specific historical situations. Recent discussion of Radical film has often revolved around competing claims about what constitutes correct political form.[13] A consideration of films like *La Vie est à nous,* as well as later films made around concrete struggles, such as *Salt of the Earth* (1954) and *Ici et Ailleurs* (1974), in their formal, political, and historical complexity, can perhaps loosen the rigidity that often inhibits discussions about political filmmaking.

In this study the chapters are arranged chronologically. The first chapter considers the period before 1936. While the beginnings of the Popular Front date from 1934, the Left did not engage in extensive filmmaking activity until 1936. In the first half of the 1930s, the introduction of sound weakened the French film industry, and independent production that had flourished in the 1920s ended. As well, political censorship of both commercial films and newsreels placed additional obstacles to the possibility of Left filmmaking. In coordination with the PCF, the Association des Ecrivains et Artistes Révolutionnaires explored the possibilities offered by cultural agitation, but interest in film lagged behind literature and theater during this early period, so few political films were made before 1936.

The second chapter is devoted exclusively to *La Vie est à nous* for several reasons. First, it is the most interesting French political film from the decade and was the most important at the time as a political intervention. Second, it was the first major electoral film made by a political party in France. Third, it was the instrument for launching an experiment in Left filmmaking in the years that followed. Fourth, the film has never received either the description or the critical discussion it merits. A detailed examination of the film explains the specific references in the film to contemporary political events and issues, and attempts to account for the function of the structure of the film. After an assessment of the critical terms adequate to the film, the role of Renoir in the film and his more general relation to politics are considered.

The third, and final, chapter follows the history of left-wing filmmaking through the period from the completion of *La Vie est à nous* in April 1936 until 1938, when the Popular Front had lost not only its position of governing but also the popular unity that had catapulted the leaders to power in the first place. During this period, the cinematic experiment of *La Vie est à nous* was not sustained. The enthusiasm generated by the film led to the formation of the most important independent film group on the Left, Ciné-Liberté, but its somewhat utopian plans and goals eventually unravelled. During this time, factions developed on the Left that worked on films separately, and this fragmentation of effort led to an abandonment of the dialectic of *La Vie est à nous*. Instead of combining fiction and document in the same film, the filmmakers made either fictional or documentary films. In this context I will look at *La Marseillaise*.

The Popular Front era has excited many passions on all sides, and accounts of its successes and failures and the causes behind them vary widely. Many controversies remain about the period. No attempt is made to resolve them in what follows. Note will be taken of the existence of debates around various issues, but the discussions do not depend on taking sides. For example, one may feel that the Popular Front betrayed the revolutionary aspirations of the working class, as Daniel Guérin obviously believed and believes still, but that should not necessarily require the student of *La Vie est à nous* to reject the originality and efficacy of the film. Perhaps the activities of the Fascist leagues in France did not really represent a threat to the Republic during the 1930s. But a perception of a Fascist threat did exist, and the fear of that threat motivated a wide variety of responses. Other questions will arise in this work, but one hopes that the difficulty of answering them does not preclude a balanced examination of the films.

NOTES

1. J. Joll, "The Front Populaire—After Thirty Years," *Journal of Contemporary History* 1:2 (1966): 29.
2. G. Sadoul, *Dictionary of Films*, edited and translated by P. Morris (Berkeley and Los Angeles: University of California Press, 1972), p. 403.
3. Some of the relevant sources here, cited in the chapters and listed in the Bibliography, include Racine, Bernard, and Touchard.
4. P. Ory, "De 'Ciné-Liberté' à *La Marseillaise:* Espoirs et limites d'un cinéma libéré (1936–1938)," *Le Mouvement Social* 91 (April-June 1975): 163.
5. The earliest study, by Goffredo Fofi, provides a basic chronology, but his polemical position that the Popular Front incorrectly fought back a revolutionary movement in 1936 results in a derisive dismissal of the films. One does not learn how the films functioned or what *specific* political issues they confronted. Fofi's article is discussed at greater length below, pp. 151–54.

The scope of Elizabeth Grottle-Strebel's dissertation, written in the history department at Princeton University ("French Social Cinema of the Nineteen Thirties: A Cinematographic Expression of Popular Front Consciousness," 1974), covers commercial as well as independent production, but she tends to overlook the crucial differences and ideological distinctions among the groups on the Left, which will be a central concern of this study. In addition, she shows little sensitivity to or interest in the films themselves. For her, their importance lies in their "Expression of Popular Front Consciousness," an approach she takes from Karl Mannheim's work on the sociology of knowledge. Her sociological emphasis excludes any real engagement with the films, whether in their political complexity or their formal experimentation. Thus, for the most important (and probably best-known) film from the period, *La Vie est à nous,* she notes that "the film's structural framework is dialectical," but does not explain how this principle is applied in the film (p. 210).

The most ambitious study, by the editors of *Cahiers du Cinéma* in 1970, attempts to investigate this dialectic in the film, but their study appropriates the critical method associated with the French *Tel Quel* program articulated during the late 1960s. Essentially they show how the film illustrates these principles. As far as it goes, the *Cahiers* analysis is the best commentary on the film, but as the authors admit, the work is only a beginning. They only trace the broad outlines of the context of the film and isolate its formal and political significance in terms of their own political and theoretical commitments. Unfortunately, their approach does not confront adequately the novelty of the form, the extent of its political specificity, or its relation to any other Left films made at the time. Their study represents a theoretical intervention in the discussion of what they call "militant film" but is limited in its analytical treatment of the film itself. Their article is discussed at greater length in note 127, chap. 2.

Pascal Ory, another historian, has written a valuable article on the filmmaking organizations during the Popular Front. However, his viewpoint is overly narrow, in that he does not place the development of these groups in a wide enough political context. For example, the filmmaking activity of Ciné-Liberté, the major Left independent filmmaking organization, changed as the Popular Front changed, and the films reflect this progression. In addition, with the exception of one film (*La Marseillaise*), Ory does not describe or discuss the films. Thus, regarding the film made on the massive sit-down strikes of May-June 1936, Ory simply notes that a film was made, without commenting on what the film showed or the attitude of the film toward the strikes that brought production to a standstill.

Bernard Eisenschitz has provided an excellent overview of the period. He correctly stresses the importance of both the PCF and *La Vie est à nous*, and sketches an accurate critical chronology similar to the one indicated above. However, he also does not address the films beyond placing them in the political and critical chronology. Though brief, his study is exemplary.

Most of the biographies of Renoir make some mention of *La Vie est à nous* and *La Marseillaise*. But as will be considered in some detail in chap. 2, until recently Renoir's relation to politics was treated as an anomaly and went unexamined. Over the past decade, Claude Gauteur has explored this relation and published much relevant documentation, but he tends to concentrate on situating politically the journals to which Renoir contributed. He is not particularly concerned with the films or the importance of the Left filmmaking experience in France.

The fine study of Renoir's French films by Alexander Sesonske is the only book on Renoir to analyze the two films in detail and with any sensitivity to the historical and political context. Thus he prudently does not insist upon Renoir as the auteur of *La Vie est à nous*. On the other hand, his discussion of the film is guided by the subject of his study (Renoir), and he consequently does not place it more properly as a seminal political film of the decade, though his remarks a propos the film are perceptive.

6. For the most widely read account of the split in the French working-class movement that occurred at the Congress of Tours—still a bitter source of enmity between the Socialist and Communist parties in the 1930s—see A. Kriegel, *Aux Origines du Communisme Français* (Paris: Flammarion, 1969); also by the same author, *Le Congrès de Tours (1920). Naissance du Parti Communiste Français* (Paris: Julliard, 1964).

7. Most writers cite an article from *Pravda* reprinted in the May 31, 1934, issue of *Humanité* as the first official signal that the Comintern leadership had decided on a shift, for the possibility of joint action was raised for the first time. Part of the *Pravda* article can be found in J. Fauvet, *Histoire du Parti Communiste Français,* Tome 1 (Paris: Fayard, 1964), p. 143.

The Comintern did not adopt the "turn" to the Popular Front as official policy until the Seventh Congress of the Comintern in July and August 1935, though a great deal of ambiguity surrounds the evolution of the Comintern's attitudes to and its effects on the PCF. The debate revolves around questions of autonomy of national sections from the Comintern and the autonomy of the Comintern from the will of Stalin. The standard source for those who consider that the PCF head Maurice Thorez was entirely subservient to the orders of the Comintern is Célie and Albert Vassart, "The Moscow Origin of the French 'Popular Front,'" in *The Comintern: Historical Highlights,* edited by M. Drachkovitch and B. Lazitch (Stanford, Calif. and New York: Praeger, 1966), pp. 234–52. Further discussion can be found in F. Claudin, *The Communist Movement: From Comintern to Cominform.* Part 1 *The Crisis of the Communist International* (New York: Monthly Review Press, 1975), pp. 174–81; D. Brower, *The New Jacobins: The French Communist Party and the Popular Front* (Ithaca: Cornell University Press, 1968), pp. 48–54; P. Robrieux, *Histoire intérieure du parti communiste français, 1920–1945,* Tome 1 (Paris: Fayard, 1980), pp. 454–58. In his recent study, the late E. H. Carr, despite referring to Thorez as "pliant," nonetheless grants him a greater autonomy than the other writers. E. H. Carr, *Twilight of the Comintern, 1930–1935* (New York: Pantheon, 1982), pp. 189–200.

Whatever the real story behind the change, the PCF was given credit by the Comintern for having accomplished it. Georgi Dimitrov, secretary-general of the Comintern in 1935, singled out the PCF for special praise at the Seventh Congress of the Comintern in 1935: "France is the country where the working class sets an example for the international proletariat in the way fascism must be fought. The French Communist Party furnishes to all the sections of the Communist International the way that the 'front unique' must be made. . . . Its magnificent example will greatly contribute to the waging of the antifascist struggle in the other capitalist countries." G. Walter, *Histoire du Parti Communiste Français* (Paris: Somogy, 1948), pp. 288–89. See also Robrieux, *Histoire intérieure,* pp. 458–62.

8. The Radical-Socialist party, while considered a party on the Left, actually represented small tradesmen, craftsmen, and especially parts of the rural population. It had no strength among the proletariat.

> Radicalism is the incarnation of rationalism and of rationality in politics, of science against blind faith, of progress against tradition, the philosophy of the Enlightenment against the clerical peril. In the

1900s, radicalism is above all and almost exclusively the iron lance of anticlericalism. Anticlericalism constitutes the essential of the Radical doctrine. And after the separation of Church and State in 1905, the Radical Party finds itself disarmed, for it has lost the essential of its original program. . . .

On economic matters, there is always a firm defense of private property and almost always a firm defense against the dangerous attacks on private property that any form of collectivism represents.

J. Touchard, *La Gauche en France depuis 1900* (Paris: Editions du Seuill, 1977), pp. 46–47. Touchard presents a succinct account of the Radical-Socialist party on pp. 42–52. Following the practice of historians writing in English and translators from French, I will refer to the Radical-Socialist party and the Radical-Socialists as the Radical party and the Radicals respectively. Unless otherwise indicated, all translations from the French are by the author.

9. There is virtually no discussion of the importance of these first efforts of Left filmmaking in two books specifically devoted to politics and film. Isaksson and Furhammer mention the German proletarian cinema but discuss only two of the films. And despite the inclusion of sections on film in England and the United States, there is no suggestion that a proletarian or Left cinema even existed in those countries. See F. Isaksson and L. Furhammer, *Politics and Film,* translated by Kersti French (New York: Praeger, 1971). A more recent study restricts itself to the antipodes of left and right, the Soviet Union and Germany, omitting altogether the Left cinema of England, the United States, and France. In addition, the author claims that "today's film historians in the GDR and elsewhere tend to exaggerate the contemporary significance of the proletarian cinema in the Weimar Republic," but the author does not explain the grounds for this summary judgment. See R. Taylor, *Film Propaganda: Soviet Russia and Nazi Germany* (New York: Harper and Row, 1979), p. 148.

10. On the colorful Münzenberg, and his empire, see the following: D. Caute, *The Fellow Travelers* (New York: Macmillan, 1973) and *Communism and the French Intellectuals. 1914–1960* (New York: Macmillan, 1964); B. Gross, *Willi Münzenberg: A Political Biography,* translated by M. Jackson (Lansing: Michigan State University Press, 1974); H. Gruber, "Willi Münzenberg's German Propaganda Empire, 1921–1933," *Journal of Modern History* 38:3 (September 1966): 279–97 and "Willi Münzenberg: Propagandist For and Against the Comintern," *International Review of Social History* X2 (1965): 188–210; J.-C. Horak, "German Communist Kinokultur, Part 1, Prometheus Film Collective (1925–1932)," *Jump-Cut* 26 (December 1981): 39–41; A. Koestler, *The Invisible Writing* (New York: Macmillan, 1974); P. B. Schumann, "Le Cinéma Prolétarien Allemand (1922–1932)," translated by Iduna Schroeder, *Ecran* 73 (December 1973): 37–43; D. Welch, "The Proletarian Cinema and the Weimar

Republic," *Historical Journal of Film, Radio, and Television* 1:1 (1981): 3–18. The articles listed above, and several listed below on specific films, have attempted to reconstruct this German filmmaking activity, but more work needs to be done. The titles and sponsorship of many of the films have been compiled, but few of the films have been described in any detail. Even those films that have been discussed at some length, such as *Mother Krausen's Trip to Happiness* (directed by Piel Jutzi) and *Kuhle Wampe* (directed by the Communist Slatan Dudow, written by Brecht and Ottwald), have not been treated as political interventions in terms specifically related to concrete issues of the moment and directly related to the political strategies of the political parties backing the projects. Future work should examine the ways in which such films and others did or did not articulate the political programs of the parties. On *Mother Krausen's Trip to Happiness,* see Welch, "The Proletarian Cinema"; Horak, "Kino-Culture in Weimar Germany, Part 2, *Mother Krausen's Trip to Happiness.* 'Tenements Kill Like an Ax,'" *Jump-Cut* 27 (1982): 55–56; L. Crawford, "*Mutter Krausens Fahrt ins Glück:* An Analysis of the Film as a Critical Response to the Street Films of the Commercial Film Industry," *enclitic* 10–11 (Fall 1981/Spring 1982): 44–54. On *Kuhle Wampe,* see B. Eisenschitz, "Who Does the World Belong To? The Place of a Film," *Screen* 15:2 (Summer 1974): 65–73; J. Pettifer, "Against the Stream—*Kuhle Wampe,*" *Screen* 15:2 (Summer 1974): 49–64.

11. R. Campbell, "Radical Cinema in the United States, 1930–43: The Work of the Film and Photo League, NYKINO, and Frontier Films" (unpublished doctoral dissertation, Northwestern University, 1978).

12. Russell Campbell and William Alexander, though taking somewhat different approaches, have accumulated a great deal of material on political filmmaking in the United States, and its initial history can be considered substantially written. See W. Alexander, *Film on the Left* (Princeton: Princeton University Press, 1981); Campbell, cited in note 11. On the English Left filmmaking movement, see the following: B. Hogenkamp, "Film and the Workers' Movement in Great Britain, 1929–39," *Sight and Sound* 45:2 (Spring 1976): 68–76 and "Workers' Newsreels in the 1920's and 1930's," *Our History* 68 (1977); D. Macpherson, ed., *Traditions of Independence: British Cinema in the Thirties* (London: British Film Institute, 1980); V. Wegg-Prosser, "The Archive of the Film and Photo League," *Sight and Sound* 46:4 (Autumn 1977): 245–47.

13. Such work often involves a consideration of films and filmmakers that explore the relations in film between fiction and documentary, such as Godard, Resnais, and Rossellini. Frequently, these discussions hinge on what has come to be known, since the late 1960s, as the "critique of illusionism." See, for example, M.-C. Ropars, C. Bailblé, M. Marie, eds., *Muriel* (Paris: Editions Gallilée, 1974); J. R. MacBean, *Film and Revolution* (Bloomington: Indiana University Press, 1975); B. Henderson, *A Critique of Film Theory* (New York: Dutton, 1980).

1

To the Victory of the Popular Front

The French film industry faced difficulties throughout the 1920s. The introduction of sound and the additional shock of the depression caused severe problems, ending or restricting the careers of many filmmakers and barring entry to new talent. As the film industry declined, various other factors combined to produce for the first time a Left filmmaking movement in France. This chapter will look at the background to that development: the contraction of the French film industry; censorship; the cultural policy of the French Communist Party; early filmmaking projects; and the formation of a Left radio organization, Radio-Liberté, which served as a model for the establishment of the major Left filmmaking group of the Popular Front, Ciné-Liberté.

The French Film Industry

The decline of the French film industry had begun as far back as World War I. According to one source, French production accounted for one-third of the world market before the war,[1] but during the war it dwindled and never regained its strong international competitive position. During the 1920s the French industry functioned as a cottage industry; many small companies and independent producers financed films. But revenues from French film were not sufficient to resist the strong competition from imported American and German films, and financial problems persisted throughout the decade.[2] Of course the French reliance on small production companies did yield aesthetic returns: the absence of consolidation allowed the avant-garde to flourish with modest budgets, and many young filmmakers— L'Herbier, Epstein, Dulac, and arguably Clair—produced their best work during these years. But by the end of the decade, the film industry could no longer support their work.

In contrast to the French postwar experience, the American and German film industries thrived after the war. In America the studios succeeded in installing a vertical monopoly that guaranteed more or less steady flow of monopoly profits for over twenty years. Aided by a large domestic market, the American industry could amortize its production costs at home and then offer the same product at reduced rates abroad. The dependability of domestic revenue facilitated penetration of foreign markets.[3] In Germany, the government subsidized the film industry, promoted the export of German films, and took measures to protect the domestic industry by instituting import restrictions.[4] In France, on the other hand, "the French government did not financially support the film industry."[5]

In the late 1920s in France, the creative efflorescence of the avant-garde ended as the introduction of sound extinguished this spark of experimentation, driving many filmmakers into "retirement, or at least . . . temporary indisposition."[6] The United States and Germany held most of the controlling patents in sound reproduction equipment, and as the industrial and technological might of the American and German industries asserted itself, France could not meet the competition.[7] At the same time, because of the importance of the French market, "the great 'patent wars' between Tobis-Klangfilm and three United States studios were waged largely on French soil."[8] At first, both countries tried to raid the French industry for talent, spiriting away French directors and screenwriters to Hollywood and Berlin to produce dubbed versions of films.

But this form of production for the foreign market was inefficient. Soon, American and German companies built sound studios in France. Paramount invested considerable capital in its operation at Joinville, and its output in its first year of production indicates the scope of its ambitions: one hundred features and fifty shorts in fourteen languages. Tobis set up its studio at Epinay, but not on the same scale as Paramount, opting for quality over quantity. There, in the span of a single year, Clair directed his first sound films, all excellent: *Sous les toits de Paris, Le Million,* and *A nous la liberté*.[9]

Though the French could not compete financially with the asset- and patent-rich German and American companies, producers did not simply withdraw from filmmaking. French producers traveled to England and Germany to rent foreign studios that were outfitted for sound, completing eight sound films in 1929 (only five fully syn-chronized). The following year, French producers raised the output to nine films, but all made in Paris studios.[10] The estimates vary, but by all accounts total French production rose sharply from the fifty to sixty films made in 1929. By 1931 and 1932, the figure had climbed to about 150 French films.[11] However, the increased costs for sound equipment required larger budgets and thus significantly reduced possibilities for the more experimental films of the 1920s. Further-more, the French no longer manufactured their own raw stock. As with sound equipment, the French industry was forced to pay addi-tional tribute to foreign interests. Despite the increased production, however, Sadoul maintains that "the mere quantitative increase in film production only meant greater opportunities for second-rate work in the industry."[12]

Even though the effects of the depression soon forced the foreign companies in France to curtail their operations in France, the French industry did not necessarily reap any benefits. In 1934 the number of films dropped to about 120, and by 1936 financial adversity and scan-dal toppled two of the largest French companies, Gaumont and Pathé. The fall of Pathé was directly related to the financial chicanery of its head, Bernard Natan. As if the repercussions of these financial fail-ures on the industry were not serious enough, political groups on both the Right and Left exploited the situation for their respective partisan purposes. For the Right, the Natan affair provided addi-tional evidence that foreign Jews were cheating the French people out of their national wealth.[13] The Left viewed the Natan Affair as yet an-other tragedy inflicted on a national industry by the unpredictable chaos of capitalist production.[14]

The industry rebounded again with a greater number of films in 1935 and 1936, but quality did not improve and foreign films poured into the country. According to the major industry journal, *La Cinéma-tographie Française,* France produced 173 films in 1935, and during the same year 363 foreign films were shown (208 American, 85 German) in French theaters.[15] In 1937 the government conducted a major inquiry into the state of French film (conducted by J.-M. Renaitour) and found that all branches of the industry agreed on the weak financial condition of the industry and the inferior quality of the French product, vis-à-vis America in particular. Amid the flag-waving and hand-wringing punctuating many of the comments, no one found a solution to certain realities stressed by a number of speakers. The United States alone had 17,000 theaters, compared to only 3,000 in France. The worldwide English-speaking audience was estimated to be some 200 to 300 million spectators, far larger than the 40 to 50 million French speakers.[16] Aside from the obvious effects on gross revenues and profits, the smaller French-speaking audience limited the size of budgets, thereby reducing the production values of French films and further weakening their competitive position. At least so the industry representatives argued. In fact, it is by no means clear that comparable production values could have overcome the importance of the audience differential.

When Jean Zay, minister of education, spoke during the 1937 inquiry, he referred to a more tractable problem, the proliferation of small production companies. As total capital investment in the French industry tapered off from 17 million francs in 1935 to 12 million in 1936, the number of production companies actually increased from 158 to 170.[17] In other words, the French industry had failed to establish its own version of a studio system, and the resultant continual disorganization deprived it of financial health and stability.

However, some writers, less concerned with financial health than with aesthetic achievement, cite this very proliferation of small production companies as crucial in the creative triumphs of "poetic realism" in the late 1930s. Andrew calls it France's "greatest contribution to the history of cinema."[18] Strebel arrives at a similar conclusion in her analysis of the break-up of Gaumont and Pathé and the influx of small production companies:

> Without the framework of a big corporate structure to provide guidelines and precedents, producers had to rely more on the ideas of the film director and his team to ensure the success of a film.
> It was in such a climate of independence that more films of high artistic quality were produced.[19]

Strebel adds that the restructuring of the industry brought financial success as well, but the Renaitour inquiry early in 1937 is a catalogue of pessimistic assessments on the state of the industry, indicating that if some recovery did take place in the late 1930s, the industry representatives either did not perceive it or refused to acknowledge it.[20]

Censorship

The Left regularly bemoaned the vacuousness of the commercial cinema and was even more upset with the regime of the censor. The Left had little cause to expect that commercial producers would support progressive films, but the censor prevented the commercial exhibition of not only the few French films that the Left considered praiseworthy, but also many of the great Soviet films. As the French political and economic situation became more volatile in the mid-1930s, criticism of censorship was voiced increasingly in political terms. By 1936 censorship became the single most important issue rallying filmmakers and workers on the Left to seek an alternative Left film production and distribution system.

In France, censorship had begun on a local level. In 1909 local authorities banned the screening of a newsreel on a multiple execution in Bethune. The government took an active role during World War I, but no formal measures were taken until 1919, with the decree of July 25, which stipulated that "no cinematographic film, with the exception of newsreels, could be shown in public if the film and its title had not obtained the visa of the ministry of Public Instruction and of the Beaux Arts."[21] The censorship commission functioned as an official government body, and no film could be given commercial distribution without a visa of authorization from the commission. Before 1936 the exemption for newsreels was included in all the revisions in the system of censorship. The topicality of newsreels required that they be shown immediately, and the practical problems of instituting precensorship—that is, demanding submission of the newsreel for a visa in advance of screening—would have imposed an unacceptable delay. However, none of the decrees ever removed the absolute authority of local magistrates and prefects to ban screenings in the interests of preserving public order.

With the coming of sound, additional measures were taken to establish a more elaborate system of censorship.[22] The legal documents called for the creation of a forty-four-member Conseil supérieur du Cinéma, which never met because of its unwieldy size, and a Sous-Commission d'examen et de classement des films, known also as the Section permanente, with eleven members. The Section permanente carried out the duties of censorship, screening films daily. Its membership was divided among several branches of the government: four members from the Beaux-Arts, three from the Ministry of the Interior, one from Foreign Affairs, one from Public Instruction, and one from Alsace-Lorraine. Paul Ginisty headed this body until 1932; Edmond Sée, a drama critic for a conservative newspaper (L'Oeuvre) succeeded him. In addition, as Sée noted in an interview, recommendations by ministers were without appeal,[23] depriving the commission of ultimate independence and, implicitly at least, imposing a model for evaluation that shielded the regime in power from criticism.

Legally, then, the French film industry had no representation on the Section permanente of the Censorship Commission, and an adversarial relationship developed between the commission and the industry.[24] Understandably, the industry objected to the potential loss of revenue that might ensue from demands for changes in the final film. In addition, there were no provisions for the evaluation of scripts before the actual production of the films, a crucial precaution built into the structure of the Hays Office in the United States. Of course the American film industry, under strong public pressure, prudently circumvented the threat of federal government censorship by erecting and financing a self-censorship apparatus.[25]

Furthermore, unlike the American Production Code of 1930, the criteria for approving a visa specified in the legal decree of 1928 were vague: "The Commission . . . takes into consideration the whole of national interests, and is especially interested in the preservation of national customs and traditions."[26] This charge to the commission left wide room for interpretation and virtually insured a controversial future for the censorship group. The legal text makes no reference to political interests, but one study lists direct or indirect political considerations among the principal categories for exclusion from a visa or for demands for cuts: communist films; antimilitarist films; films that attacked the judiciary or certain state institutions; films likely to provoke incidents with foreign powers; and for foreign films, works deemed anti-French.[27]

One organization, Les Amis de Spartacus (The Friends of Spartacus), mounted an early protest against the censor, following the decree of February 1928. In March Léon Moussinac and Jean Lods launched the society for the purpose of privately screening films banned by the censor, particularly recent Soviet masterpieces such as *Potemkin* and *Mother*. Some critics claimed that the club was formed for purposes of political propaganda. However, even though Lods and Moussinac were Communists, both denied this charge. No doubt the chance to see Soviet films did draw many spectators, for most of the major Soviet films from the period were routinely denied visas. But in an article following the banning of the organization in October 1928, by which time the membership had reached 10,000, Lods clarified the club's aims: "It has been claimed that it was a society for Communist propaganda. Not at all: our goal is to shoot all cinematic works of value, that we have not had the chance to see or that we haven't seen enough.[28] Similarly, Moussinac recalled later that the club sought to attract

> all those, intellectuals and manual workers, who love the seventh art, consider it a tool of progress and civilization and not as a vulgar piece of merchandise or a vast debasing enterprise.
>
> The plan was the organization of private screenings in Paris, the suburbs, and the large provincial towns where all the new or old films,

banned or not, expressing beauty or technical, artistic, ideological or educational truths, would be screened and offered for the appreciation of the members of the Association.[29]

Whatever the sympathies of many of the members, then, the club did not proclaim any political affiliations and tried to deflect such characterizations. Rather, like other cine-clubs of the 1920s, Les Amis de Spartacus was committed to the appreciation and study of film as an art form, even if progressive films were disproportionately represented.

In the early 1930s trade journals also devoted considerable space to the question of censorship, generally opposing it. *Pour Vous* interviewed filmmakers and members of the Censorship Commission in 1933. Edmond Sée, president of the Censorship Commission, did not take his responsibilities lightly: "I find the complete liberty of theater, of the press, something indispensable. But with the cinema, we should be extremely careful. It is a means of expression so powerful, a vehicle for opinion so efficacious, that it could easily, if we don't put it in order, become dangerous."[30] But when the interviewer asked whether it was not reasonable to conclude that the censor's role in maintaining order constituted political censorship, Sée's curt response was "Not exactly." Yet a year later in the same magazine, Sée took obvious pride in his powers of political detection: "A minute of inattention on our part could have regrettable consequences. The Soviet reels notably are very well conceived. Though they are inoffensive in appearance, one discovers suddenly, sometimes in the last reel, a subversive passage which tries to take us by surprise."[31]

Evidently few lapses of attention befell members of the commission, for their uninterrupted vigilance protected the French people from the subversion of *Potemkin, Mother, The End of St. Petersburg*, and the like. But the Right did not necessarily escape the eye of the censor either, for the first major Nazi film, *S.A.—Mann Brand*, was also refused a visa on the grounds of its being "Hitlerian propaganda."[32]

Filmmakers did not share this anxiety about threats to public order. Germaine Dulac, a former member of the commission, felt that spectators' convictions were too well formed to be influenced by films, hence censorship was unnecessary.[33] Although René Clair objected to the narrowness of interests represented on the commission, he did not oppose censorship by the state in principle.[34]

As a rule, rather than banning the films outright, the censors demanded cuts in films before approving a visa, although there were some notable exceptions to this practice. *L'Age d'or* originally passed the censorship group, but the chorus of protest from the Right led

Jean Chiappe, head of police in Paris, to ban screenings in Paris.[35] After Buñuel made some requested changes and resubmitted the film with a new title, the censors ruled that the entire film was unacceptable. Sée had not seen the film in its original version, but when he saw the revised print, he said that it "was impossible to authorize."[36] Regarding Jean Vigo's *Zéro de Conduite*, also ruled unacceptable, Sée admitted the film had certain qualities, but apparently its "unhealthy tendencies" outweighed the unnamed qualities.[37] However, these films *were* attacks on French institutions—the military, the church, the educational system. One might still call for the elimination of censorship, but one could hardly contest the censor's view that these films defied the proviso concerning "the preservation of national customs and traditions." More frequently, the censor asked for excisions of dialogue or characterization that might be construed as tarring French institutions, for most films did not present such attacks as their virtual raison d'être, as did the films of Buñuel and Vigo.

Critics regularly ridiculed the hypersensitivity of the censors. One celebrated case conveys, in exaggerated form perhaps, the orientation of the censorship process.[38] *La banque Nemo* was submitted for a visa in April 1934. The film was based on a play by Louis Verneuil put on in 1931 without incident. The play related the story of financial wrongdoing at a bank. The guilty parties had ties to several ministers, however, who decided to cover up the scandal. In the relative calm of 1931, the events in the play were not taken to refer to specific historical incidents. Such was not the case in the early months of 1934. The Stavisky scandal, which broke publicly in January, centered around an unsavory embezzler who was well connected politically, and accusations of a cover-up forced the resignation of government officials and the fall of the government itself. Publicity for *La banque Nemo* sought to exploit these "striking parallels between the subject of the film and real events," and there can be little doubt that contemporary audiences would have registered these parallels. The producers had taken care to pare from the film a number of additional parallels already in the original play: the locale is no longer France; there are no jokes about foreign countries, no ironic remarks on French colonies, no allusions to the police commissioner, no caricatures of the Minister of National Education. Despite the producers' efforts, the censor demanded the elimination of fully eighteen minutes out of almost ninety in the original, including the final scene where the Council of Ministers agrees on the cover up. According to a writer who has seen both versions, "The film thus shortened became perfectly insignificant, if not incomprehensible."[39]

Sée's defense of the cuts overtly acknowledges that political considerations played a role in the responsibilities of the censor: "You would agree surely that, since the censorship commission has been in existence, it has the right, and even the duty, to take account of current events, and that a scene in the theater, applauded *a year ago,* could risk, when placed on the screen, offending *one year later* certain legitimate sensibilities! . . . What we have here is a question of timeliness! And over the course of twelve months, so many things happen!"[40] Again Sée distinguishes film from theater in its potential effect on spectators, but Sée concedes that the censor does—and should—monitor films for their possible commentary on the contemporary political situation. After the events of early 1934, as attacks on successive governments mounted in number and intensity, the censor had to contend with increasing erosion of popular support that it had more or less received before 1934.[41]

While the Left continued to condemn the activities of the censors throughout the mid-1930s, it regarded the treatment of newsreels as equally, if not more, reprehensible. All of the legal decrees since 1919 had excluded newsreels from the visa requirement, but substantial evidence supports the Left's assertions that in practice censorship extended to the newsreels as well. On the morning following the violent demonstration of February 6, 1934, the government banned any newsreels showing the events of the night before. The Minister of the Interior and the Paris police commissioner issued the order,[42] and apparently the theaters complied.[43] But the industry press protested vigorously, complaining that such an order contravened legality: "The cinema has the duty to show in France and abroad the truth about the formidable national movement of Tuesday and to deny the fallacious communiqués of the government chased from power."[44] Another trade journal indicated how the official exemption of newsreels from censorship was circumvented: "Indeed there is not official censorship, but prohibition is the rule, and police regulations are being applied severely."[45]

Some writers have suggested that technical limitations (slow film stock and lenses) hindered capturing the violence on film, but the testimony of the newsreel houses at the time contradicts that explanation. To the contrary, the newsreel companies assembled the footage with the conscious interest of restoring calm: "We shot everything, without injury fortunately. But we have projected only what we wanted. We did not want to provoke demonstrations! The reader who bought his newspapers can react afterward! It is not the same in the film theater."[46] Fox-Movietone also accommodated the wishes of the authorities: "After these riots, calm is necessary. To show viewers the demonstrations of Tuesday [February 6] would be to do something dangerous and bad. We will show on the contrary the arrival of M. Doumergue [the new prime minister appointed the following day]. We must calm the emotions and in this path we have always been on the side of the government."[47]

This rationale depends on some delicate arguments. As seen in the statements of the official censors, the film medium itself was thought to be the most powerful means of expression at the time, capable of arousing public disorder. Earlier battles had been waged in France over literature and the theater, and by the 1930s only film was subjected to censorship *before the fact* (of screening). Yet many writers, critics, and filmmakers questioned the validity of this argument, time and again insisting that newsreels on politically charged events did not trigger violent reactions in the theaters. Dulac raised a similar doubt when she observed that audiences are not susceptible to the influence of films, as they have already formed their opinions before entering the theater. However, Dulac had also said on another occasion that she had been forced to stop projection of her newsreels at times because of the furor in the theater.[48] Other commentators on the Left corroborated this experience.

Others on the Left argued that newsreels should be allowed to take different positions on the political spectrum, like newspapers. Lucien Wahl, a respected critic, said the film spectator should be able to sample a range of opinions, "just as the usual reader of a royalist paper follows the coverage in a communist paper to keep himself informed."[49]

But as support for the Popular Front swelled following the February 6 riots and their aftermath, the Left inveighed against the tacit resistance of the newsreel companies to documenting this phenomenon. The vision expressed by Wahl did not materialize, in the Left's view, because the newsreels sided with the forces of reaction, tightening the grip of capital over the media. For example, *Cinémonde* described one approach to the events of February:

> To one newsreel company which insisted last week in showing filmed coverage of the recent riots, the Prefect of Police ended by permitting the requested authorization, but on one condition.
>
> And what a condition!
>
> It was required in effect to suppress the original shouting and to replace them with the hubbub and murmurings recorded at . . . the Carnival of Nice.
>
> It is hard to get more absurd than this.[50]

In April 1934 one writer in the Communist weekly *Regards* noted, "We have seen what was shown in the cinema about the 9th and the 12th of February. And here, we know the reality. Let that make you weigh the accuracy of the filmed news." A former member of the Censorship Commission, recalling his service there, claimed that the newsreels were not censored in theory but that in practice they were. For example, shortly before the Radical party finally decided to join the Popular Front, Edouard Daladier participated in the massive rally of July 14, 1935, and demonstrated his solidarity with his more militant Socialist and Communist comrades by raising his clenched fist, a moving and unequivocal sign of allegiance. The newsreels cut out this image. Similarly, at the express intervention of Pierre Laval, then Foreign Minister, the coverage of the League of Nations meeting to discuss the application of sanctions against Italy for its invasion of Ethiopia was limited to the part dealing with Franco-Italian friendship.[51]

By 1936, when supporters of the Popular Front began to sense electoral victory as a real possibility, the rhetoric became more strident. Immediately after its electoral success the Left started to call for the abolition of the censor, even before the new government had taken office:

> The censor has no reason for being. Its supporters try to justify it with the claim that it protects the morals of little children! Hypocritical liar. . . . In fact, the cutter of films never intervenes for moral reasons: always for political reasons. It lets the worst insanity, the grossest stupidities pass. It sets aside its anger and its wrath when it considers the star-studded military films, bourgeois justice, the rapacious bosses or insincere religious people. The censor is only the administrative expression of one of the hypocrisies—among others—of the capitalist regime. It functions by whim. Its decisions are not the result of serious examinations and deep discussion. It takes two forms: a consequence of the mood or stomach of the man who, on the judgment day, represents the "commission"; servile application of an order given by a minister, the prefect of police, even the fascist press or by the archbishop. The censor is not even concerned with conforming to the official texts which supposedly govern it.[52]

Faced with this widely shared hostility to the censor, the lame-duck conservative government introduced several reforms in the censorship of newsreels. They quickly extended to newsreels the requirement of a visa! Titles and shot lists were to be submitted fifteen days prior to their scheduled showings. No post synchronization was permitted. And after fifteen weeks, the visa would expire.[53] Evidently the conservative government feared a possible leftward shift in the bias of newsreels under the Popular Front and moved quickly to legalize the de facto obstacles that the Left had been fighting for two years. The restrictions on post synchronization and the duration of the visa were redundant, strictly speaking, as denial of a visa subsumed those conditions. The drafters of these provisions knew well the manipulations to which newsreels could be subjected: they had raised no objections to reactionary newsreels. Manipulation troubled them only when the Left might take advantage of it, as it had so effectively only weeks before in *La Vie est à nous*. But before that film was made, some institutional support had been necessary. The PCF provided that support within its cultural network.

The Cultural Policy of the French Communist Party

As the enthusiasm of political union peaked in the first months of 1936, disparate cultural factions on the Left banded together in an attempt to build an alternative cinema network. The desire to preserve a somewhat fragile unity papered over various differences during the electoral drive, for they agreed on views of the commercial film industry, both the vapidity of fictional films and the political bias of the newsreels. This alienation from the commercial cinema brought together filmmakers for the production of a major work, *La Vie est à nous,* and the experience of working on that film catalyzed the formation of the most important filmmaking organization of the Popular Front period, Ciné-Liberté.

However, in contradistinction to the proletarian film experience in Germany in the late 1920s, organized Left filmmaking in France did not emerge as a propaganda strategy for rallying support until 1935–36. Münzenberg had recognized the propaganda value of film as early as 1925 when he wrote *Erobert den Film!,* and the Communist, Socialist, and Nazi parties had all engaged in political filmmaking in the following years.[54] In France, a handful of independently produced political films were made in the first half of the 1930s, but these isolated efforts were undertaken before the political parties had come to appreciate the power of modern media such as radio and film. Only with the completion of the political coalition of the Popular Front in January 1936 did a political party turn to film as a political tool for the electoral campaign.

It was hardly surprising that it was the French Communist party that decided to use film for the first time in France in an electoral campaign. Though the PCF had neglected film as a political weapon before that time, the party had engaged in extensive cultural activity previously, and filmmaking fit easily into the already institutionalized cultural apparatus of the PCF. In the preceding years, the PCF had concentrated its attention on the more prestigious domains of theater and literature in its efforts to build a large Popular Front of Culture, and it succeeded in politicizing culture itself during the period. Thus, few writers were able to evade the question of their political commitments (if not belief) for or against the Popular Front.

From its earliest days at the beginning of the 1920s, the PCF had placed greater emphasis on attracting intellectuals and artists than any other political party.[55] As a rule, this emphasis manifested itself through support, not necessarily control, of publications and organizations sympathetic to the PCF, though party members usually sat on the editorial committees. For example, Paul Vaillant-Couturier, the leading Communist intellectual/ideologue from the birth of the PCF in 1920 until his death in 1937,[56] served on the editorial board of the first of these publications, *Clarté*, with the older and more renowned Communist sympathizer Henri Barbusse (who became a party member in 1923).[57]

Even though *Clarté* adhered to the Comintern in 1921, the magazine guarded its independence through 1926.[58] Of course, to have done otherwise would have been difficult in certain ways, for the Communist party of the Soviet Union kept its own distance from cultural debates over the correct path for literature. The writings of Marx, Engels, and Lenin provided no unambiguous guide for cultural production, and the appointment of Lunacharsky as Commissar of Enlightenment resulted in a policy of cultural pluralism in the arts. The Russian Association of Proletarian Writers (RAPP), arguing for a special category of "proletarian literature," sought the imprimatur of the party in the late 1920s, but the party's few official statements retained an ambiguity that was not removed until 1934.[59] Writing in Moscow for *Clarté*, Victor Serge covered these debates around proletarian literature sympathetically, but only in the context of Russian literature. The writers of *Clarté* did not import the arguments for polemical discussion over French literature.[60]

Barbusse continued to follow an independent course even after an international literature conference held in Moscow under RAPP's sponsorship called on member groups to elaborate a program for new literature. RAPP organized the conference in 1927, at which time the International Union of Revolutionary Writers (UIER) was founded.[61] A new journal, *Monde*, was to be the French laboratory of this effort, under the direction of Barbusse. Barbusse, however, did not concur with the RAPP position that proletarian literature of necessity had to break definitively with prerevolutionary literature and art and that proletarian writers should blaze the path to this future. In one of the first issues of *Monde*, Barbusse wrote of proletarian literature that "it was not born with the revolution of 1917, but in the slow growth of the labor movement over the last 50 years. And it is in our Western countries that it has developed, and it reflects at the same time the grandeur and the weakness of this labor movement."[62]

This independent attitude earned for Barbusse a severe rebuke at the international writers conference of 1930 at Kharkov. Many delegates attacked him, including the representative of the Comintern: "We view the deviation of Comrade Barbusse as a right deviation, because this comrade maintains illusions on the possibility of a collaboration in the weekly *Monde*, or on every other terrain, between us and elements which are hostile to us, and also views with a certain disdain, I will say even with an unacceptable hauteur, the movement of the worker writers."[63] The congress passed a special resolution on the magazine *Monde*[64] in addition to one "On the Questions of Proletarian and Revolutionary Literature in France."[65] The resolution on *Monde* supported its criticisms with many citations from the magazine. Essentially, the congress found that *Monde* had not asserted its editorial prerogatives with sufficient rigor, opening its pages to reactionaries of various stripes. The tone was consistently harsh: "This program defines the weekly *Monde*, since its first issues, as a petit-bourgeois journal, reactionary at base, enemy of the revolutionary proletariat by its very nature, despite its revolutionary slogans that one finds often in its columns."[66]

Throughout this episode, however, the PCF did not comment on these so-called deviations. *L'Humanité* waited a full year before publishing the Resolution on the general situation in France and did not print the special resolution on *Monde*.[67] The party may have suspected that RAPP's pre-eminence would not last and probably also doubted the efficacy and likelihood of adopting the RAPP program in France. Eventually, the PCF pursued the policy toward literature and the arts outlined in Barbusse's message to the Kharkov conference (the special resolution on *Monde* condemned the message as "repeating diverse errors which have led to the deterioration of the journal *Monde*"): "The only way we have of clarifying the raison d'être, the meaning, and the significance of revolutionary literature which we seek to defend and consolidate here, is to search for its formula on the social level and to say that the only condition that we should require of intellectuals in order to group them in a unified movement is to support the demands of the proletariat."[68]

This resistance to intellectual sectarianism characterized the PCF policy toward cultural matters throughout the 1930s. By contrast, before 1934 the *political* line of the party accorded strictly with the narrow sectarianism of the "class-against-class" policy laid down by the Comintern, retarding the PCF's acceptance of political frontism. Nonparty intellectuals of course were not bound by such discipline, but party intellectuals had significant autonomy as well. During this period they initiated the organization of two of the most important groupings of intellectuals of the decade: the Association of Revolutionary Writers and Artists (AEAR) and the Amsterdam-Pleyel Movement.

Ironically, the AEAR was founded in March 1932 as the French section of the UIER, the hard-line sponsor of the 1930 Kharkov conference. However, RAPP's star was no longer ascendant in the Soviet Union, as the Communist party of the Soviet Union (Bolshevik) dissolved it in 1932. In these years, the AEAR represented a cultural frontism before the political fact. With Barbusse and Vaillant-Couturier occupying important posts in the organization, the AEAR was committed to attracting prestigious figures in the struggle against fascism, rather than insisting on any peculiarly Marxist or communist model for artistic production. In a letter circulated in December 1932 to intellectuals requesting their participation at a meeting in 1933 to draft a charter, Barbusse added a personal note to André Gide, probably the most prestigious French writer of the time, saying that "We attach . . . great importance to your membership."[69] Gide did not accept the invitation to join but did express his "sympathy" for the Soviet Union[70] and did lend his name and presence to the organization. His name appeared as one of the editors of the AEAR's journal, *Commune*, begun in 1933, and Gide himself presided at the AEAR's first public meeting in March 1933, which has been called "the first collective protest of intellectuals against German fascism." In a preface to the brochure published by the AEAR after this meeting, Vaillant-Couturier placed few restrictions on membership: "The AEAR is a mass organization. It is neither a cenacle, nor an open rostrum. We know what we want and where we are going. . . . And it is enough for us that those who march at our flank beside us—even if their revolutionary thought is not yet entirely clear—have chosen to be with the proletariat which still does not know them well, against a bourgeoisie which celebrates them." Nor was its name misleading, for writers were not the only figures drawn to the organization. Among the many writers listed by Vaillant-Couturier were the filmmakers Buñuel, Lods, Pierre Unik, Vigo, and Man Ray.[71]

In the first years of its existence, the literary activities of the AEAR centered on the magazine of the organization, *Commune*. In addition to reviews of plays, books, and films, the editors conducted inquiries among writers, such as "For Whom Do You Write?" to which fifty-eight writers, for the most part noncommunist, responded. The editors often commented on these responses. When one writer asked how, given her bourgeois background, she could in good conscience adhere to the AEAR, Vaillant-Couturier assured her that "without any doubt . . . you may adhere to the AEAR. . . . When you come to us, we should be sectarians and fools if we made you pass an examination in Marxism. . . . This sentimentalism [referred to in her response to the inquiry] is not so bad. . . . It is the most common path by which an intellectual of bourgeois origin can move toward socialism. It is the first element in breaking with the class from which he has come. It is the element of revolt which acts as a trampoline for the future revolutionary."[72] The magazine also carried articles on fascism, Marxist texts (*The German Ideology*), and poems (including several by Brecht).

The AEAR also spread its net over theater organizations. A marginal workers theater group, known as Prémices and directed by Roger Legris, had existed in France as far back as 1927.[73] Legris was the only professional in the group, however. Most of the actors were workers, while a few were students. Just as RAPP had tried to form a Comintern of literature in 1930, an analogous theater organization was created in Moscow early in 1930, the International Union of Worker Theater (UITO).[74] According to a UITO report, "The worker theater should become a powerful propagandist of international scope which is committed to the building of socialism in the USSR, of great progress realized in the path to the creation of a new society, of the socialist industry and of agricultural collectivization."[75] At the time of its organizing congress in January 1931, a French section of the UITO took the name of the Worker Theater Federation of France (FTOF). According to one commentator, after only one year there were 120 groups close to the FTOF, forty of them in the Paris area.[76]

Documentation on the aims and practices of the French section is sparse, but the Prémices group apparently anchored it. A split in the initial group occurred in 1932 over Legris's commitment to professionalism, and a second group set out on its own under the name of Shock Group of Prémices.[77] This name reflects the political orientation of the group, perhaps in response to criticisms voiced by the UITO (though not directed toward the FTOF in particular), which called for the introduction of new theatrical methods, specifically agitprop troupes.[78]

The FTOF encouraged a more active involvement in worker struggles. In a manifesto issued at the constitutive congress at the end of July 1931, the FTOF affirmed that the "artistic movement is linked directly to the class struggle and cannot be separated from it."[79] The organization assisted in a strike in the north of France at the time, probably with the presentation of agitational skits for the workers.[80] The repertoire included short plays printed in the official organ of the group, *La Scène Ouvrière*, such as "Aux Cheminots!"—a work protesting against new scientific management procedures. Another important theme dealt with the attempt to confront the use of media. For example, authentic photos could be juxtaposed to the official reports of health conditions among the unemployed. The photographs would expose the hypocrisy of journalists serving the interests of capitalism. Other scenes dramatize the selling of papers that only promulgate capitalist lies.[81]

The history of the Groupe Octobre, the most celebrated theater group from the period, gives the best indication of what worker theater actually was. After the split in the Prémices group, the activist wing Shock Group of Prémices needed material. They approached Vaillant-Couturier, who directed them to Léon Moussinac, a Communist writer and critic intimately and equally involved in theater and cinema. He passed on the name of "un gars très marrant" (roughly, "a very funny guy"), a relatively unknown figure, Jacques Prévert.[82]

While it would probably be impossible to overestimate Prévert's contributions to the subsequent success and fame of the group, even before meeting him the group members already had a clear sense of their needs: "We knew what we wanted: a sketch on the press, made with clippings from the papers of the time—my job then consisted of compiling a review of the press every morning—illustrating the themes of propaganda: capitalism leads to war and poverty; social-democracy has two faces (one, demagogic; the other in the service of capital)."[83] At the moment they went to see Prévert, he had been working on the preparation of a film with Pierre Batcheff and others. The day of their first meeting, Batcheff committed suicide (and the film project died with him), so Prévert asked them to return several days later. After listening to the group's presentation, Prévert read some material from one of his projects, and the future Groupe Octobre was ready to start work.[84]

Eight days later, while the group was rehearsing at a hall run by the major communist union organization (CGTU), Prévert walked in with *Vive la Presse*. Prévert read the press avidly, and the characters in the play were the papers branded as reactionary at the time: *Le Temps, Le Matin, La Croix, L'Oeuvre* (where Sée had worked as drama critic), *L'Ami du Peuple*. The play premiered at the Festival of *L'Humanité* in May 1932 and continued its run throughout the summer.[85] Part of the ending, an attack on the "rotten press," has survived:

> Look out, comrades, look out
> To die for the country is to die for Renault
> For Renault, for the pope, for Chiappe,
> For the meat merchants,
> For the arms merchants . . .
> Look towards Russia, comrades,
> Russia where there are men and children who laugh
> Men like you,
> Who are calling you and cry out to you:
> Proletarians of all countries, unite.

This excerpt expresses several constant themes from the period: appeals to patriotism only disguise the manipulation of workers in order to protect the interests of capital, in particular the munitions industry Though the PCF attacked the Socialists for voting for military expenditures in the Assembly, pacifism was the order of the day for socialists and communists alike, deeply scarred by the carnage of the First World War. This attitude coincided with the doctrinal hostility of the PCF at the time to social democracy, or "social fascism," as it was called by the party. The economic crisis had hit France by this time, and the Left glorified the successful example of socialist construction in the Soviet Union, a tendency fueled by the hysterical calumnies against the USSR spread by the capitalist press—a press vilified in Prévert's ironic title. Finally, the last line, throwing its support behind Marxism, counters the fatal nationalism of the captains of capitalist industry with the liberating internationalism of the proletariat.[86]

Prévert's fascination and dissatisfaction with the capitalist press permeated the group's productions, but clear as this political stance may be, from all accounts the surviving fragments from these plays and sketches do little to convey the impact and inventiveness of this theater. More important at the time was his phenomenal ability to compose material at a moment's notice on events that had just happened. On the Monday morning that Hitler was appointed chancellor, Prévert heard the news while working on the set of a film (*Ciboulette*). During the day he wrote a play, rehearsed it the same evening, and *The Arrival of Hitler* was performed the next evening.[87] In addition, he constantly changed scripts and improvised freely during performances. Prévert was writing at the command of events for political purposes, not for posterity. Hence written extracts may lose some of their pungency over time.

Other successes followed *Vive la Presse*. Prévert composed a spoken chorus for the defense of the jailed Communists in Germany, Thaelmann, Dimitrov, and others. One of the friends Prévert brought with him to the Groupe Octobre, Lou Tchimoukow, wrote a spoken chorus against war, in support of worker and peasant demands and in solidarity with the trial of the Scottsboro boys in the United States. The spoken choruses addressed the audiences directly, without the pretense of fiction, often dealing with current events, domestic and foreign.[88] Other groups used spoken choruses, but Prévert's wit and writing speed catapulted the Groupe Octobre to unrivalled popularity.[89]

The premiere of *The Battle of Fontenoy* at the Second Congress of the FTOF in January 1933 earned them a coveted prize. The play was another attack on war in an historical tableau of a "Theater for Armies," with roles for "guests" Poincaré, Clemenceau, Edouard Herriot, Rasputin, and others, seated together with spectators. After some speeches and funeral orations, a chaplain executes a deserter who has violated a sacred principle: "Those who live by the sword die by the sword. Those who do not live by the sword die by the sword." Later, Poincaré takes the floor: "Soldiers fallen at Fontenoy, know that your deaths have not fallen on deaf ears! (Interruptions from the audience) . . . Soldiers fallen at Fontenoy, the sun of Austerlitz shines on you. . . . War is war! One soldier lost, ten more found!!! Civilians are needed to make soldiers!!! With a living civilian we make a dead soldier!!! And for the dead soldiers we construct monuments!!! Monuments to the dead. . . ." When Schneider and Krupp announce that French and German ammunition and bombs have been mixed together, warning of serious repercussions, Poincaré silences them: "But no, it does not matter. French bombs and German bombs come from the same family. All you have to do is share."[90]

For this show, and its many other activities of the previous year, the FTOF chose the Groupe Octobre and one other group (Les Blouses Bleus, or The Workers, from Bobigny, a working-class district) to represent the French revolutionary theater at the Moscow Theater Olympics in June 1933.[91] Competing with some fifty theater companies from around the world, the Groupe Octobre carried off the first prize,[92] and *Pravda* paid tribute to their theatrical method: "The French Groupe OCTOBRE gave a revue-montage, extremely interesting, called THE BATTLE OF FONTENOY. The particular interest of this revue lies in the text being composed of newspaper clippings, parliamentary speeches, aphorisms on political leaders, etc. . . . Many caricatures of this revue were done masterfully."[93]

This same diversity of materials reappears in the independent films produced by the Left in the second half of the thirties. The desire for political involvement led naturally to an emphasis on current events, resulting in a type of alternate news coverage. The use of news documents transformed the interpretations of events given in the capitalist press through juxtaposition. The principle behind this transformation of course resembles the ideas behind Soviet applications of montage in film, and everyone on the Left had seen the Soviet films. Nor was the employment of montage unique to film. The dadaists had cut up newspapers for their collages after World War I, and John Heartfield adapted the process in his photomontages, used specifically for parodic and caricatural purposes. Heartfield often took phrases from newspapers and exposed the political distortion behind them, as in his famous photomontage on Hitler, *Millions are behind him.* The Left press in France printed several of Heartfield's photomontages after Münzenberg's *Arbeiter Illustrierte Zeitung (AIZ)*, a large-circulation, illustrated weekly, stopped publishing in Germany and Heartfield fled Germany.[94]

In terms of what *Pravda* labeled "revue-montage," it is not irrelevant that Prévert was planning a film with Pierre Batcheff when the Shock Group of Prémices approached him. For many years, French intellectuals had been passionate about film, and Prévert and his friends were no exception. The surrealists regarded film as a privileged medium, and many ties of friendship linked them to Prévert's circle. Batcheff acted in Buñuel's and Dalí's *Un Chien Andalou,* and Jacques Prévert and his younger brother, Pierre, had played in *L'Age d'or.* Jacques Prévert had already written a number of screenplays by 1932, and only several months after the formation of the Groupe Octobre, its members produced a film directed by Pierre Prévert, *L'Affaire est dans le sac.*

However, though Prévert was certainly familiar with the Soviet films, *L'Affaire est dans le sac* is completely devoid of any type of Soviet montage. It is true that the group had very little time to shoot the film, eight days by one account,[95] and had to make do with sets left over in the studio (Pathé-Natan) from other productions; but the invention and humor in the film derive from Prévert's scenario and the acting, not from the editing. The principle of montage singled out for praise by *Pravda* was essentially verbal and theatrical, but the film displays

Photomontage by John Heartfield at the exhibit of the Maison de la Culture, Paris: "The Nazis play with fire. Goering: 'When the world burns, we will persuade the world that it is the handiwork of Moscow'" (cover of *Regards*, April 25, 1935; originally published in *AIZ*, February 28, 1935, for the second anniversary of the Reichstag fire)

none of the juxtaposition of documents that was a fundamental staple of the theater work of the Groupe Octobre. Even as Prévert's fame grew, and he collaborated with the best filmmakers of the time, he did not direct any films. While thoroughly immersed in the cinema, Prévert did not extend the montage thrust of the Groupe Octobre to his cinematic work, not even in *Le Crime de M. Lange,* more overtly political and produced with ample resources.[96]

Also, despite the affiliation with the FTOF, officially the French section of the ITO, the Groupe Octobre did not have a sectarian political orientation. The members shared a resolute opposition to fascism and war, but their more specific political sympathies varied. Only a few actually belonged to the PCF, among them one of the Préverts' closest friends, Jean-Paul Dreyfus. Jacques and Pierre, perhaps more faithful to the anarchism of surrealism, had no formal political commitments. The Groupe Octobre even had room for Trotskyists like Yves Allégret.[97] As Roger Blin expressed it recently in his memoires, "In contrast to the presentations of other more militant groups, . . . those of the Groupe Octobre were more loosely directed toward the perspective of revolution, the perspective of anarcho-communism. We were in contact with the communists, but the internal tendencies of the Groupe Octobre, because of the personality of Prévert, were anarchist and communist [that is, not strictly or exclusively communist]."[98]

Consistent with its literary policies, the PCF maintained a light rein over the theater groups. At the same time its hostility toward bourgeois democracy and its internationalist perspective attracted young rebels, such as Prévert and his friends who were happy to find an organization receptive to their expressive and creative invectives. Understanding the nature of this symbiosis at that particular time makes Prévert's own comments perfectly comprehensible: "The group was affiliated with the Federation of Worker Theater [FTOF] which belonged at the time to no party but naturally the Communist party was the most important. Sometimes, the Party was not at all in agreement with our work, but the mélange was so successful, so amusing that it all worked out."[99]

During the following years of the Popular Front, pacifism and antifascism brought the Left together. A chronology and tabulation of the political positions taken by the political parties misses this rejection of dogmatism in cultural affairs. The PCF did spearhead the drive to patch together the Popular Front, but the real merit of the PCF's initiative was to take the first step in tapping the popular will that crossed party boundaries, as it did so clearly in the Groupe Octobre.

The Groupe Octobre appears to have performed primarily at Communist-sponsored events, indicating not only the group's view of the Socialist party as basically a bourgeois party but also the Socialist party's indifference to cultural organization. It is difficult to imagine the former aesthete Léon Blum rubbing shoulders with the unknown ragtag of amateurs in the Groupe Octobre, with their odes to the Soviet Union and earlier derision of social democracy. Yet Vaillant-Couturier, called by David Caute (with a touch of irony) "for seventeen years the unrivalled genius at handling non-communist intellectuals,"[100] received the young actors and directed them to his old schoolmate Moussinac, who in turn arranged the meeting with Prévert. There is no question that the PCF solicited the allegiance of intellectuals and artists for the prestige their names would confer on the party, but the party and its cultural front organizations offered in return a forum for them to make some public political stand.

Early French Political Films

During these early years of cultural agitation at the beginning of the 1930s, there was little film production, in somewhat surprising contrast to the attention paid to literature and theater. The international congresses in the Soviet Union testify to the importance accorded cultural agitation in these two fields, even if the national sections did not submit to the aesthetic discipline of the hardliners' pressure for proletarian culture. But no similar film congress was held. In part, practical difficulties prevented the realization of worker films. The transition to sound at that time raised the costs of commercial films and output fell off in the national industries. The effect on the French industry has been discussed already, but the Soviet Union's industry suffered as well, for the transition required significant investment sums. Leyda notes that "great industrial changes in the Soviet film industry" coincided with the commitment of the First Five-Year Plan to heavy industry, so there was even less likelihood of developing an amateur cinema, for the Five-Year Plan "geared filmmaking to the basic industrial programme." Under the brutal direction of Shumyatsky, this plan proposed to construct "a 'Soviet Hollywood' to be built on the shores of the Black Sea."[101] In the West, the effects of the depression hit the overextended film industries during the transition to sound, eliminating possibilities for marginal productions within the established industries. Finally, manufacturers of film equipment had never shown great interest in producing and marketing nonprofessional material, so amateur equipment was virtually nonexistent.

Nonetheless, isolated political films did get made. On March 10, 1933, in Paris, the Groupe Octobre presented an evening of their work, which now included a film in the repertoire:

> *The Battle of Fontenoy.*
> *The Knight and the Unemployed Worker,* a skit written for the dancer Pomiès by Prévert.
> *Actualités,* commentaries on the press by Prévert.
> Spoken Choruses.
> *Ça c'est du théâtre,* parody by Guy Decomble.
> *La Pomme de terre,* short film by Yves Allégret.[102]

Allégret made *La Pomme de terre* with the Prévert brothers in 1931 at the request of Célestin Freinet, a radical educator who headed the Cooperative of Lay Teaching, which funded the film.[103] Freinet wanted a film made for use in his experimental school, and the subject of the film was a short book by Marx explaining the basic principles of surplus value, *Salaire, Prix et Profit (Wages, Price, and Profit),* which was condensed to serve as an alternate title to the film, *Prix et Profits.*[104] The simple story follows the itinerary of potatoes from their planting and harvesting in the country to their retail sale in the city.

The film opens with a scene of a rural farm. A single family works the farm, shown in one of the first images, which reveals a horse-drawn plow traversing the field, followed by children running after it. In succeeding shots women are planting the potatoes, then loading them onto a horse-drawn cart. Several shots repeat this action, both suggesting the monotony of the task as well as emphasizing the quantity of potatoes they have produced. The concluding shot in the opening sequence, a picturesque view of the family returning from the fields late in the afternoon, the sunlight filtering through the branches of the tall trees in the background, establishes a picture of bucolic beauty in the life of these peasants.

Back at the farm the family weigh the product of their labor. Intertitles indicate the basic needs of the family that must be covered by the sale of the potatoes: plow, fertilizer, and clothing. As the potatoes are loaded into sacks, shots of various articles of clothing with price tags attached (coat, hat) are intercut with the labor. This straightforward intercutting clearly acts as the visual correlate of exchange value; so far no money has been introduced except for the prices of the clothing and a list on a piece of paper specifying the needed goods with the prices of each. At the end of the tabulation, one shot of money spread out like a deck of cards is shown, without comment. Presumably this shot illustrates the sum (300 francs) needed to purchase the items on the list.

A title introduces the next sequence: Leaving for the city. In shot/ counter shot, the children wave goodbye to their father as he rides away in the horse-drawn cart transporting the sacks of potatoes. At the market in the city, a merchant claims that 300 francs is too expensive, as he motions toward rows of potato sacks already in his storage. A slow pan across these sacks illustrates his contention that he has more than enough on his hands. Placing his hand on the shoulder of the peasant, the merchant informs the farmer that they will come to an understanding. The earlier shot of six 50F bills reappears and two of the bills dissolve away; that is, the merchant has paid 200F for the potatoes. Then the shopping list is shown again, now with the children's clothing items crossed off and only the plow and fertilizer remaining (at a cost now of 190 francs).

The scene now shifts to Paris, with a shot of workers entering a factory—evidently not a staged shot with actors, for the workers glance at the camera as they pass by. An intertitle identifies a wholesaler, M. Binet, who is seen leaving his house, pausing to light a cigar before driving off to Les Halles in his car. As he lights the cigar, there is a perfect movement match to a close shot of M. Binet, reflecting the care of the script but also isolating a familiar image of the bourgeois. This close shot of the capitalist with his cigar captures an image of orality commonly used in the iconography of Left artists during the 1920s, whether in the cavernous mouths of figures drawn by George Grosz or the bloated factory owners in Eisenstein's *Strike*, for example. In the next shot, M. Binet leaves in his car, in obvious contrast to the horse-drawn cart of the peasant and to the more pedestrian transportation of the workers walking through the factory entrance.

At the market Binet glances at his receipt for the potatoes being unloaded at his warehouse; we learn that he has paid 300F for them. An intertitle announces the arrival of Pierre, who is filling an order for his boss, a retailer. Binet shakes Pierre's hand and slips him a cigar as they agree to the price of 50F/100 kilos (500F/1000 kilos). At the retail store, Pierre sets the price at 0.50F/½ kilo (or 1000F/1000 kilos). Thus the price has risen by 500 percent over the price paid to the peasant for his product.

After Pierre pours some potatoes into a woman's shopping bag, the woman returns home to prepare the midday meal. At her home, while she prepares the potatoes on a small back patio in a tenement building, a clothesline of socks hangs above her as she works, another obvious mark in the film of her social station (in addition to her clothing and living quarters). When her young daughter gets home for lunch, the child removes from her book bag a book, which her

At the market, where the price of potatoes is raised: Pierre Prévert, left; Jacques Prévert, right (*Prix et Profits*)

mother begins to read to her. Intertitles reproducing the text from the book, *French History*, recount the progressive improvement in the standard of living of the workers and peasants, ever approaching the level of the bourgeoisie. The mother interrupts this edifying lesson when she sees her daughter playfully fingering a hole in her sock. Her attention shifts quickly to an advertisement in the newspaper in which the food for lunch had been wrapped, the ad proclaiming the durability of the pictured shoes. Several shots alternate then between the ad and the mother's repeated glances at the worn shoes of the girl. After this comment on the ad and the history book, another passage extols a present when the bourgeois and worker vacation at the sea or in the country, live in brighter and more spacious quarters, and so forth. Of course the immediate circumstances of the scene contradict the claim about physical living conditions, while the assertion about vacations was blatantly untrue also. Vacations by the sea were a well-known fantasy of workers before the Popular Front, and satisfaction of that wish became probably the single most powerful symbolic achievement of the working-class movement during the Popular Front period.

After the lunch scene, the film skips without transition to a dinner scene. The father is seated now at the table, and a close shot shows the father's face staring vacantly at the ground. Then a lone farmer appears in a field. This shot begins a kind of didactic coda to the eighteen-minute film: a view of a card announcing a price of 20 centimes (one-fifth of a franc, the price per kilogram paid to the farmer earlier), a series of shots of torsos of peasants working in the field, a card reading 30 centimes, the first merchant, a card with 50 centimes, then a card with 1 franc, a tilt up to a close shot of the mother's face, and back to the father as he looks in turn at daughter and wife. This sequence summarizes the augmentation of price from peasant to worker. As the peasant scene introduces the film with the representation of hard work in the field, and the factory shot shows the workers beginning their day, the merchants appear to function solely to raise the price. They are rewarded without any appreciable expenditure of labor. The peasant is forced to eliminate items from his desired list of purchases because he is given only enough money for capital expenditures to keep the farm operating.

In this analysis, the capitalists control the system of distribution, which enables them to appropriate the surplus labor. Therefore, the elimination of exploitation coincides with the elimination of these exploiters or, in the film, the middlemen. The film ends with exactly this exhortation, by intertitles alone, skirting the not inconsequential problem of how this might be accomplished. The intertitles as if exploding from the shock of comprehension just experienced by the father, conclude "They must be suppressed." The startled mother looks up to say "Who?" The answer grows larger on the screen as the title card approaches the camera: "They!" A short recapitulation of the centime chain reviews the lesson quickly before the last title: "There is only one way!" The father rises from the table in extreme low angle, a familiar emphatic device that literalizes here the power of ideas, or consciousness. The answer lies in the final synthetic intercutting between peasant and worker walking in opposite screen directions (toward each other), culminating in a close shot of their handshake before a rural hut.

In fact, the call for a worker-peasant alliance as a solution, with its attendant suppression of the middlemen, has little to do with Marx's discussion of the topic in *Wages, Price, and Profit*. A brief note on the film in *Regards* in fact does not even refer to the source of the title, nor does it mention the name of the film: "The rising costs of necessities, the misery of peasant producers, the difficulties of the workers who purchase [the necessities], all consequences of the scandalous profiteering of middlemen." Perhaps the abbreviation of the title reflects Allégret's basic unfamiliarity with Marx's economics, and his later career in the commercial industry does not betray an abiding interest in economic questions. According to Marx, different modes of production are defined by the specific mechanism by which surplus labor is appropriated by nonproducers; in capitalism, the appropriation takes the form of surplus value. The separation of direct producers from the means of production transforms labor power into a commodity, and the market mechanism treats labor power as a commodity, a characteristic unique to capitalism. As Marx considered this point to be central in the book, the absence of wage labor (the peasant is not a wage laborer) in *Prix et profits* (and the deletion of "Wages" from the title) essentially eliminates the specifically Marxist thrust of the argument. In addition, for Marx the appropriation of surplus labor derives from the capitalist's ownership of the means of production, a key premise never broached by the film. As Marx concluded, "Instead of the conservative motto, 'A fair day's wage for a fair day's work,' they ought to inscribe on their banner the revolutionary watchword, 'Abolition of the wage system.'"[105]

Nevertheless, despite these shortcomings, the film does attempt to translate an abstract economic concept into cinematic terms, and virtually all the other independent efforts from the decade concentrate on political questions, not economic analysis. Though produced during the strict "class against class" period of the Comintern, the film won first prize in a film festival held in Moscow during the Theater Olympics in 1933.[106] No doubt the relative technical accomplishment of the film, particularly the quality of the images and the clarity of the editing, compensated for its conceptual confusions.

At approximately the same time, the PCF itself made a highly orthodox political film, *La Crise*. In its present form the film lacks credits and the few sources that even mention it supply no definitive production information,[107] but its political position coincides with the position of the Comintern's "third period." First spelled out in 1928, this analysis is founded on the perceived threat to the Soviet Union posed by military buildups in the democracies. National Communist parties branded these arms expenditures obvious preparations for an imperialist war against the Soviet Union. The Soviet Union had good reason to feel anxious about such a threat—many Western powers withheld recognition of the Bolshevik regime—but in retrospect at least, disastrous consequences ensued from this policy. The extreme case, of course, was Germany, where the Communist KPD's refusal to make common cause with the Socialist SPD not only furthered the split among the parties on the Left (the refusal was unfortunately mutual) but also led to the KPD's electoral participation alongside

Hitler's NSDAP in the Prussian referendum in 1931.[108] Hindsight may render this divisiveness less defensible than it was at the moment, for the Western powers had consistently maintained a hostile stance toward the Soviet Union, and the internal power struggle in the Soviet Union probably exaggerated fears there of such a threat.

La Crise, then, refers not only to the economic hardship of the depression but also to the political crisis outlined above. The film begins with an indictment of the merchants "enriching themselves" at the expense of the peasants and workers, who must face higher prices and reduced wages. Bloated bourgeois shop at Les Halles while peasants receive foreclosure notices. A peasant family in a bare kitchen reads one of these notices, described in an intertitle as "recompense after a hard day's work." In an efficient illustration of what another intertitle calls the "solution" offered by the "exploiters," a graphic rendition of a farm and its animals and implements erases these assets one by one, as the horse disappears, then the plow, and so on, ending with a blank screen. The titles claim that there are two groups in the villages, apparently the farmers and farm workers. This first solution dispossesses the farmers.

The "solution" for the farm workers is introduced with an exterior shot of an office of the "Gendarmerie Nationale" with tricolor atop or, as the next title neatly sums it up, "War!" An effective trope follows: First, a recruitment poster for colonial troops shows a soldier in the colonial uniform, with palm trees in the background supplying the requisite picturesque touch. The reality hidden behind this idyllic poster is immediately exposed by the title "Misery," illustrated by a tilt up the tomb of the unknown soldier commemorating those who died for their country in the First World War. The next title, "The Communist Party offers you another solution," accompanies a shot showing a copy of *L'Humanité* in the hands of an unseen reader.

This sequence, then, attempts to expose the ideological function of appeals to nationalism as an answer to the travails visited upon workers by the exploitation of the merchants (not identified as capitalists). As the rest of the film argues more didactically, tapping nationalist sympathies will not arrest the exploitation of workers. Curiously, however, a long sequence of titles reproducing texts of laws submitted by the Communists in the Chamber of Deputies is the proposed response. Aside from being virtually unreadable and tedious (lasting almost three minutes), the titles evidently propose an electoral solution, implicitly accepting the legislative preconditions of parliamentarism.

Given the absence of production information, it is difficult to determine what images were shot specifically for this film. However, the lack of documentary specificity in the images, most of which show anonymous peasants or workers, suggests that these shots were taken to be used in this film. Such a conclusion is strengthened by the extensive use of obvious archival footage or excerpts from other films throughout the remainder of *La Crise*.

For example, after the lengthy texts of the Communist proposal submitted to the Chamber of Deputies, several titles repeat the earlier call to "struggle for the land, for those who work on it." A cut follows to a group of peasants dancing and relaxing at day's end. The peasants have gathered in the fields around a mechanized grain processor, celebrating their life working in agricultural collectives. The titles are intercut with this shot, instructing the audience on the strides made in the Soviet Union: "In Soviet Russia, the proletarians have taken power and the peasants are with them. The dictatorship of the proletariat has given the land to the peasants. It has given them machines, credit. The peasants are organized in agricultural collectives and march toward Socialism! It is necessary to struggle in the same path against the whites, the reds, and the greens with the Communist Party." Aside from the confusing reference to "the reds and the greens," the titles propose the Soviet model of state-run collectives for emulation. Of course the merits of Stalin's collectivization drive remain controversial, as they were at the time, but more significantly, the image used to depict this paean to collectivization is an image from Vertov's *Enthusiasm*. Thus, the filmmakers apparently felt free to extract sequences from other films for their own propaganda purposes, although they have not tampered with the original intent of the image as Vertov used it. However, the greatest moments of exhilaration in Vertov's films generally apply to the theme of industrialization, best seen in *The Eleventh Year, The Man With the Movie Camera*, and *Enthusiasm*. This sequence in fact functions as a kind of pastoral coda in the original film, which concentrates on the development of heavy industry.

The remainder of the film proceeds more directly to the foreign policy objectives of the Comintern. Military parades and entente politicians and officials pass one after the other, with a sprinkling of police attacks on leftist demonstrators to bind the association between militarism abroad and political repression at home. The Queen of Rumania, in her ornate carriage, reviews her troops, which the titles explain are troops "directed by French Imperialism, posed to invade the USSR." Next comes a sequence with British troops, with Chamberlain speaking in one shot. Mussolini preens atop his horse to the

The "pacifism" of Mussolini—Mussolini reviewing troops (*La Crise*)

delirious approval of his army. "The proletarians who struggle against war under the direction of the Communist Party are attacked in Germany." The police attacks are seen in various high-angle shots above the Kurfurstendamm in Berlin. Often, the police enter the center of the large square and begin to clear out roughly circular spaces as they rush after the demonstrators, who flee in all directions. These shots probably already had gained iconographical status by this time, for a number of films from the period reprise these types of shots. In fact, the actual demonstration footage probably was taken from Piel Jutzi's *Blutmai 1929*, a Prometheus film on a May Day rally in Germany which was broken up by the police.

As a concluding bracket to this sequence, which opened with the ironic title "English Pacifism!," a final title completes the irony: "Pacifism in Action" accompanies shots of brutal police attacks on American workers. After this long foreign tour, originally introduced by the French Tomb of the Unknown Soldier, the film returns to that site to indict French complicity in this cordon sanitaire. A title derisively cites the hollow cry of the Socialist party—"Never Again!"—referring to the First World War. The Socialist architects of this hypocrisy are named: Maginot, Tardieu, Doumer, Fernand Gouisson. Additional titles assert that only the workers and peasants, "waging revolutionary struggle, are able to prevent the imperialist war" by "unmasking the bourgeois

"We must expose the bourgeois and Socialist pacifists who hide from the masses the preparations for war" (*La Crise*)

and socialist pacifists who hide the war preparations from the masses." A map of Europe, Asia, and North America with only one country identified reveals the primary target of this belligerence: the USSR.

According to the film, the Western nations have targeted the Soviet Union as the enemy because the workers and peasants have crushed capitalism and are building socialism. *La Crise* uses shots similar to emblematic shots in Vertov films to articulate this building theme: a dam, a steel factory, leisure activities. The dam refers to the electrification campaign, tacitly invoking Lenin's electrification drive. The steel factory represents the investment in heavy industry, the foundation of the Five-Year Plan.

The focus on Socialist perfidy marks *La Crise* as a typical product of the "third period." The Soviet Union continued to fear capitalist encirclement in the late 1920s, but the Socialists bore little responsibility for those policies. In fact, since the time of the revered Socialist leader Jean Jaurès, the Socialist party consistently voiced its firm opposition to military appropriations. So the film's contention that the Soviet Union's pleas for "immediate disarmament" at Geneva proves its commitment to pacifism, while the Socialist party supports the arms buildup and distribution abroad (Czechoslovakia) does distort a fundamental French Socialist tenet. In the years of the Popular Front, the Communist party would exploit this very timidity of the Socialists to support national defense with far more justification, as the Germans and Italians were investing heavily in armaments, leading to the increasing political isolation of the Socialists and widespread public disaffection.[109]

Unlike Allégret's film, which was made outside of any party attachment, *La Crise* mobilizes archival footage for specific political ends. While Fauré places Allégret in the Trotskyist camp, *Prix et Profits* accords easily with the free-wheeling anarchist spirit of the Groupe Octobre, with its irreverent lampooning of the bourgeois and schematic concluding vision of worker harmony; in short, more a political reverie than a political program. Hence its final handshake. *La Crise* coincides point for point with the third-period line followed by the PCF. While no documentation has been found regarding this film's production and distribution, its screenings were probably limited to PCF meetings, for its sectarian line was unlikely to attract nonbelievers. The inclusion of actual footage from a Soviet and German film, furthermore, implies at least the probable granting of copyright privileges to the PCF for the use of extracts. Of course the refusal of the French censor to certify Left films for theatrical exhibition eliminated potential conflicts with commercial distributors.

But more significantly, the mixing of "fictional" (that is, filmed for a given production) and "archival" (whether documentary or excerpted) footage reflects the flexibility of the PCF in its filmmaking approach. The dominant models for political filmmaking at the time do not evidence this free interspersing of material. Esther Shub's films relied exclusively on remounting archival footage. Vertov's virulent antipathy to any acted films ("films joués") is omnipresent in his writings, and though he constructed his films according to careful scenarios. the directions never called for staging the action. Rather, the camera people followed instructions for gathering the needed shots, although the entire premise of *The Man with the Movie Camera* may belie the strict adherence to this program (that is, it is implausible to believe that Vertov did not direct his brother as Mikhail inserted himself into Russian daily life; not that this in any way compromises the essential claims of his theoretical project). And of course the films of Eisenstein and Pudovkin remained firmly in the domain of fiction, despite the critical accolades they received as "realistic." Finally, the German Left films, more directly influenced by the Soviet films, concentrated on large-scale feature film production (Prometheus). As *La Crise* appears to be the only film extant from this "third period," it would be hazardous to generalize from this film about any PCF approach to production activity, but the films from the second half of the 1930s tend to employ a similar mélange of fictional and newsreel footage.

The Formation of l'Alliance du Cinéma Indépendent

After the Paris riots of February 1934 but before the official termination of the "class against class" tactic of the PCF, cultural activity among intellectuals and artists intensified. In these early months of 1934, the Groupe Octobre performed at many soirées organized by associations close to the PCF, either frontist or sympathetic (*communisant* in French): Friends of the USSR, Committees for the Defense of *L'Humanité*, the International Red Cross, the League of Human Rights, and others. Once the PCF officially threw its support to a Popular Front after May 1934, the AEAR tried to extend its work throughout the country in a mass organization, inaugurated with great fanfare in the Left press as the Maison de la Culture in March 1935.[110] Aragon became the secretary-general of the new organization, which was dedicated to the "defense of culture" and the propagation of culture throughout the country. An impressive group of intellectuals and artists attended the founding meeting on March 14, 1935, including Gide, Malraux, Jean-Richard Bloch, Jean Cassou, Claude Aveline, René Crevel, Edouard Dujardin, André Lhôte, and Franz Masereel. The Maison de la Culture held panel discussions, with the prestigious Gide and Malraux often leading the discussions. The Maison de la Culture also housed separate sections representing the various arts: literature, plastic arts, architecture, music, theater, and cinema.

The cinema section was known as the Alliance of Independent Cinema (ACI). The ACI grew out of the cinema section of the AEAR, which seems not to have engaged in actual filmmaking, according to a chronology of independent film groups established by Louis Chavance in June 1936:

> The cinema section of the AEAR existed previously in the sphere of communist influence, but, small and without great resources, it limited its activities to ideological discussions. The communists however had already understood the sentimental power of cinema and projected Soviet films at the Spartacus Association, then, after the dissolution of that organization, in private union meetings. It is there that one was able to see the masterpieces of Eisenstein, Pudovkin, Dovzhenko, . . . it's impossible to name them all. . . .
>
> But the Communist Party did not yet envision making propaganda films in France.

> The expansion which transformed the AEAR into the Maison de la Culture transformed the "cinema section" into the Alliance of Independent Cinema.[111]

Commune, the official organ of the AEAR, reported an evening of 16 mm films at the Maison de la Culture on October 23, 1935, not political films to judge by their titles, but the note did not refer to the ACI.[112] The next month, *Commune* referred to the founding of the ACI at the Maison de la Culture on November 26, 1935.[113] That evening the ACI held its first screening, in private, in honor of Jean Vigo, "who was one of our own"[114] (his death a year earlier only aggravated the anger of the Left over the ban still in force against *Zéro de Conduite*). According to short notes in *L'Humanité,* additional screenings took place in December and January:

> January 2—"Contemporary History"[115]
> January 5—Previously unseen footage from 1934; Soviet documentary; two films made by the ACI.[116]
> January 10—*Liebelei.*[117]

The reference to the two films made by ACI is puzzling, for it is the only indication that ACI may have produced films before February 1936, the month the ACI began work on its first major project, *La Vie est à nous.*

However, more important than sorting out the precise history, desirable as that may be, is the attitude toward independent film on the Left revealed by this paucity of documentation. Despite all the calls for a revolutionary culture in the first half of the decade, the Left had neglected the possibilities of film production, preferring to screen privately films that had not passed the censor. Requiring little financial support, these screenings rallied audiences to admiration for the achievements of the Soviet Union. But the scheduling of these events was erratic, and coverage rare, for the public was not informed in advance for the most part and reviews may have already run in the papers. The ACI hoped to produce films eventually, but until that time it represented only one more niche in the administrative umbrella of the AEAR and the Maison de la Culture. Surprisingly, given the international success of Soviet films, film apparently had a low status with the party in relation to the other arts in the Soviet Union as well: "When it came to the 'cultural revolution' that accompanied the first Five Year Plan the cinema was the last of the arts to be accorded the attentions of a party conference." Only with the successful production and release of *La Vie est à nous,* with the attendant publicity and enthusiasm, did momentum build for subsequent, less ambitious projects, which attracted the active participation in the movement by prestigious figures from the commercial cinema.[118]

Actually, scattered bits of evidence throughout 1935 suggest that the ACI brought together in one body aspirations found in more short-lived organizations. On March 25, 1935, *La Flèche* ran a single article, "For a healthy cinema . . . union of spectators." At a meeting of the Syndicat Général du Cinéma, 600 people attended a screening of *Potemkin,* at which the filmmaker Jean Painlevé and the screenwriter and critic Henri Jeanson spoke in favor of forming a union of film spectators to struggle against censorship and dubbing, for the censor is "responsible for the systematic emasculation of everything that could pull the spectator out of his stagnant torpor."[119] In addition,

> The Union of Spectators will organize private screenings of films not submitted to the censor and will go beyond that, realizing a liberation without precedent; what's more, once it has gathered a sufficient number of members, it will allow independent producers and directors to make films according to their conscience, with the certainty of meeting their costs. . . .
>
> The Union of Spectators is from here on in assured of representing at least 800,000 people, through the support of the Union of Syndicates of the Confédération Générale du Travail. Its directives thus will be enforced. To all men of good will, to all those who do not consider the cinema as a joke, the Union of Spectators addresses an urgent appeal against the schemers, for a healthy cinema.[120]

This defiant appeal, with its utopian phalanx of 800,000 spectators, had no sequel as the Union of Spectators, but it does articulate a widely felt frustration with the commercial cinema. Jeanson and Painlevé had no political ties beyond their sympathy with the Popular Front, not even with any of the PCF front groups, yet they did not drop the idea of campaigning for some means of bringing spectators and filmmakers together in some fashion independent of the large commercial interests of the "combines," for a year later they had assumed leadership positions in the ACI. The projected role of the Confédération Générale du Travail (CGT) in this Union of Spectators underlines their political independence also, for the CGT was a nonpolitical grouping of unions which had resisted PCF attempts to politicize it several years earlier. In response, the PCF had pulled its members and sympathizers out of the CGT to form the much smaller CGTU (CGT Unitaire).

The Cinematographic Service of the Socialist Party

A more successful, and more politicized, enterprise started up two months later within the ranks of the Socialist party. The Socialist party did not impose the same rigorous centralized discipline as the PCF, so contending factions openly jockeyed for influence. Thus, in 1933 internecine differences resulted in a bitter split, with the expulsion of the "neo-Socialists," so named for their willingness to work with the bourgeois parties.[121] Most of the renegades returned to the fold, but the distances separating the Right and Left wings of the Socialist party remained great. Each of the major tendencies within the Socialist party conducted extensive propaganda functions for its respective position, including the publication of newspapers for internal use.[122] Blum, a centrist, edited the official Socialist paper *Le Populaire,* which made its columns available to all tendencies. On the Left, a young revolutionary group led by Marceau Pivert and Jean Zyromski continually pressured the party to militate in concert with the PCF, even if, as Trotsky sympathizers, they had few illusions about some of the less attractive features of a Stalin-aligned PCF. In the same year that the Socialist party voted to exclude the reformists on the Right, the Socialist International (SI) refused to approve the participation of left-wing Socialists in the first major expressions of antifascism by the Left, the Amsterdam-Pleyel Movement, the SI being reluctant to endorse what it viewed as a propaganda move stage managed by the Comintern.[123] Such a charge was certainly true, but for the Left Socialists fighting fascism was more important than accepting an obsolete policy, and many Socialists defied the SI by attending the two conferences in Amsterdam and Paris. While fundamental doctrinal considerations played a role, organizational problems hampered swift and forceful action by the Socialist party throughout the years of the Popular Front. Thus, when Marceau Pivert decided to extend the propaganda activities of the party into film production, establishing the cinematographic section of the SFIO,[124] he was not acting under the auspices of the leadership of the Socialist party but as the leader of the largest and most militant electoral unit of the party, the Federation of the Seine (essentially the Paris region, heavily working class).

This group produced two films in the middle of 1935: *Le Mur des fédérés* and *14 juillet 1935.* Chavance calls Pivert's group "the first to use film seriously in France," and describes the films as "direct propaganda, certainly, which did not waste its time recounting a scrawny love story in the manner of bourgeois films—rather, in an urgent manner, they recall to the workers their force, their memories, their future. . . . Their work is a remarkable utilization of ingenious and intelligent resources which compensates for the lack of material resources."[125] The writer applauds the exertions of the filmmakers under difficult conditions and approves their rejection of commercial films. In the fall of 1935, several months after the films were shot, Pivert toured parts of the country with them before the first screenings in Paris.[126]

In the film that survives, *Le Mur des fédérés*, Pivert's militancy pervades the film. In the Popular Front era, mass demonstrations assumed great importance, and they were held on days commemorating certain historic dates. The Communists had staked out their claim to the memory of the Commune of 1871 with annual marches to the Mur des fédérés, where many leaders of the uprising had been shot. In 1935, with the improvement of relations with the PCF, the Socialist party as well turned out in large numbers, as Thorez and Blum raised their fists in solidarity with the Popular Front. The film, however, takes a more militant line than the more cautious positions of the two parties, specifically on support for national defense.

The Left's commitment to national defense changed during these years, again following the lead of the PCF. During the years of the "third period," the party had refused to vote for national defense measures in the Chamber, claiming that such expenditures would be used to threaten the Soviet Union. Stalin, however, had responded to Hitler's consolidation of power and the growing strength of Germany by signing a mutual defense pact with Pierre Laval (foreign minister) in May 1935. Stalin left no ambiguity about this shift in a well-publicized French-Soviet communiqué on France's military strength: "The first duty incumbent on them [France and the Soviet Union] in the mutual interest of maintaining peace, is to allow no weakening of their national defense. In this regard M. Stalin understands and approves fully the policy of national defense taken by France to maintain its armed forces at the level necessary for its security."[127]

Virtually all the Socialists reacted with astonishment, to say the least. The party leader, Blum, wrote two days later: "I am still in a daze. The more I think about it the less I understand it. How is it possible that the representatives of the Soviet government had signed this communiqué?"[128] But Blum, like most Socialists, had never rejected categorically the concept of French national defense under a capitalist government. Marceau Pivert, however, had consistently and unconditionally espoused the doctrine of revolutionary defeatism, a position he did not relinquish even in the most optimistic days of the Popular Front. Pivert's intransigence over this issue caused a split with

his allies in the Left wing of the party, as Pivert broke with the other
leader of this tendency, Zyromski, who declared his approval of the
new tactic.[129] Pivert's commitment to revolutionary defeatism was
unchanged: "There is *never* any case, under a capitalist regime, when
the duty of national defense has an international meaning or any
virtue."[130]

Le Mur des fédérés does not dilute Pivert's categorical rejection of
national defense. After an introductory song, the first voice-over
notes that the "Fédération Socialiste de la Seine has taken the initiative to put on the screen the principal stages of the cortège of the
procession." This first voice-over briefly reviews the history of the
Commune, when "the Parisian people . . . organized for the first time
in the world a worker government." The only other voice-over, toward the end of the fifteen-minute film, addresses the audience directly with a final inspirational message: "Workers of France. Look
and awaken to your magnificent and invincible force, which is like a
river current flowing to the sea." The Left constantly cited the size of
the crowds at demonstrations throughout the period as proof to the
workers themselves of their power, and one of the functions of the
political films was to document these impressive demonstrations of
the will of the masses.

But the images, more than the sound track, convey the militancy of
Pivert's position, particularly in the choice of banners and signs. Many
of these signs were chosen to illustrate the broad support from many
organizations on the Left, for the sound track points out that in
addition to the appeals of the Socialist party and the PCF ninety-two
other organizations took part, many of them close to the PCF: CGTU,
ARAC (Association Républicaine des Anciens Combattants, a com-
munist-led veterans organization), Friends of the USSR, the AEAR,
Socialist Youth. But the most prominent signs in terms of numbers
and specific political demands proclaimed opposition to the recently
proposed law to increase the term of military obligation to two years
and the repudiation of national defense under capitalism, as in the
following texts:

> Jeunesses Socialistes. Down with the two years. Down with the national
> defense of the Capitalist Regime.

> Struggle proudly and without weakness for the unity of all the workers
> of the world, for the proletarian dictatorship, for the universal Com-
> mune. Against the war. Against the two years. No National Defense.
> Bring down Capitalism. Power to the workers.

This internationalism and rage against capitalism were no longer the order of the day for the Communists, nor even for many of the Socialists outside the Revolutionary Left in the Socialist party. The other signs displayed more general slogans for unity (No division. Everything for unity.—H. Barbusse) without more specific demands that could provoke disagreements. Noticeably absent is the tricolor in the images and the "Marseillaise" on the sound track. Pivert's internationalism, unlike that of the PCF (or the Comintern two months later), made no overtures to the concept of *patrie*.

In other respects, *Le Mur des fédérés* is competently made, if not particularly distinguished. Its linear structure begins with a brief prologue of sketches and drawings of the Commune, accompanied by some photographs of historical figures, including Blanqui and Courbet. The voice-over recounts in summary fashion the short rule of the "worker government" and the terrible repression that crushed it. After a drawing of the massacre at the Mur des fédérés in 1871, surrounded with flags from 1792 and 1848, the first moving images reveal the worker response in 1935, as the camera moves past a flurry of raised fists. A flag of the Jeunesses Socialistes rises from this sea of arms. To the singing of the "Internationale" and revolutionary songs, marchers file by, carrying the assorted banners. At the Père Lachaise cemetery, the honored survivors of the Commune arrive. Pivert himself took an active part in the filming, suggesting that his filmmaking section numbered only a few members, for Pivert can be seen in several shots clearing sight lines in the crowd for the camera to record unimpeded several medium shots of Léon Blum and later the old communards. The crew did use at least two cameras, however, for several of the shots capture a cameraman in the mid-ground cranking away at the procession. As the film began, it closes with the accent on youth marching in the uniforms of the (socialist) Red Falcons, with several titles superimposed before the last image fades out behind the last title:

> 200,000 demonstrators
> And now . . .
> Forward for Organic Unity
> Forward for
> The Conquest of Power.

Grand Rassemblement

In the weeks that followed this rally, popular sentiment for unity virtually drowned out Pivert's calls for revolutionary defeatism. Negotiations between Socialists and Communists, begun more than a year earlier, culminated in an informal agreement in June 1935. Once agreement was reached, plans began immediately for a mass celebration on Bastille Day. When half a million people turned out, this "gigantic antifascist meeting" became the virtual icon of the Popular Front.[131] Fortunately, filmmakers recorded the events of the day.

Apparently, two films were made, though more than two titles appeared in the newspapers.[132] A short article in *Le Populaire* (the Socialist paper), announcing the screening of *Le Mur des fédérés* and *14 juillet*, warned against confusing the Socialist film with one made by the Committee of the Rassemblement Populaire, official sponsor of the July 14 demonstration. The article asserts that the other film was made "in part with film loaned by our service, and [is] of a totally different nature." The PCF archives hold a copy of the film that bears the credits of the Rassemblement Populaire, and that film does not conform to the following description given in *Le Populaire* of the Socialist film: "Beginning with the evolution of the Revolution of 89 . . . the views of the huge, joyous cortege give with poignant realism the atmosphere of the magnificent energy of the masses which we witnessed. And at the end, one sees the shadows of Guesde, Jaurès, Lenin, and Marx fall on the crowd which marches endlessly, with the symbolic flag of victorious socialism, with what emotion and hope is the triumphant Internationale taken up."[133] The other film, under the title of the *Grand Rassemblement du 14 juillet*, does not begin with the reference to the Revolution of 1789 and does not have the somewhat dramatic ending described above. These particular sequences, however, would not contaminate in any way the *Grand Rassemblement*. But there are other differences that may have motivated this warning, specifically the strident nationalism of the film.

Throughout the years of the Popular Front, the Left waged an ideological battle with the fascists (in France) for traditional patriotic symbols. In the past, factions on the Left had claimed assorted occasions for their symbolic resonance, such as May 1 and the day honoring the memory of the Commune. But these dates bore heavy internationalist associations of a worldwide proletarian movement. When the fascists staked out their ideological terrain, they naturally turned to the wellsprings of French patriotism, such as the "Marseillaise" and the Tomb of the Unknown Soldier. Thus, as the Popular Front emerged as a formidable political force, the Left consciously moved to retrieve the revered symbols of the Republic as their own, putting an end to what they viewed as the shameless desecration and sullying of these symbols by the enemies of the Republic. *The Grand Rassemble-*

Cover of *Regards*, July 11, 1935

Cover of *Regards*, July 18, 1935

ment is suffused with this outpouring of nationalism and may very well have irritated Pivert, leading him to distinguish the film made under his supervision from the more festive but less militant spirit of the *Grand Rassemblement*. In addition, the film features the PCF representatives more prominently than the figures of the other parties, which may not have distorted the historical record but could leave the impression that the PCF was the real driving force behind the Popular Front, which Pivert may not have appreciated either. After all, he had been calling for unity on the Left for several years; the PCF had dropped its bitter sectarianism only recently.

The film opens with a man (probably Victor Basch, president of the Rassemblement Populaire) calling the people to the event and reading the oath that was drafted as a pledge to the spirit of the Popular Front: "We take the solemn oath to remain united to disarm and dissolve the factious leagues, to defend and develop the democratic liberties, and to assure the peace of man." Before he finishes the speech, various shots of a crowd assembling (presumably preparatory to marching) are inserted. After the oath, a new speaker begins, "We Communists," still over the shots of a small crowd milling about, and then the speaker, Jacques Duclos, is seen on the dais at the demonstration reading his speech. In the brief sentences heard, Duclos invokes the historic role of the French tricolor in the past, reserving the responsibility of the future for the red flag. He takes care to embrace the veterans present as defenders of liberty, in another bid to recover the symbolic contribution of the veterans for the Popular Front, for the Fascist leagues also recruited among the veterans for their own purposes. The cut to Duclos occurs just as he refers to the veterans. Several other speakers succeed Duclos, progressing through Socialists, Radicals, and then Léon Jouhaux, head of the CGT. This prologue ends with the oath again as the panning camera shows the crowd raising fists in unison to take the oath en masse. Duclos's priority at the head of the list of speakers in the film establishes this ordinal priority of the PCF throughout the film, suggesting the sympathies of the filmmakers. They place the communist references at the head of a series (*L'Humanité* precedes *Le Populaire*).

The prologue section immediately announces the joint sponsorship of the event; recognizing its responsibility to bury its factional differences in the common cause of defending the Republic against the provocations of the fascists, the Left has finally assumed direction of the popular sentiment. The role given to the leadership is significant here, for the leaders had been slow to react to calls for unity from the base. Unity at the top was essential to marshalling and cementing the strength of the masses. Nor was this alliance at the top ever definitive, as later events proved, hence the importance of promoting it whenever possible. This prologue was probably meant to encourage the aspiration to unity and to efface the still-visible lines of division.

During the formal recitation of the oath concluding this section, a subway/metro sequence begins. As a voice-over observes "From all parts of Paris . . . ," the people converge on the metro stations. The narrator identifies some of the quarters out of which the people are pouring: "Boulevard Richard Lenoir . . . La Rue Lafayette." The crowds mount the stairs of metro stations, a train pulls into an empty station, a train passes filled with demonstrators, passengers leave the train, they turn back toward the camera to salute with raised fists. The shot changes flow smoothly here as the formal panning of the camera enforces a continuity over these disparate shots. A pan may be extended across a cut, or the camera will pan left in one shot then pan left in the next shot. The narrator remains in the background, his commentary restricted to naming some of the sites, reinforcing the sense of scope of the events, implying that all of Paris is in attendance. The restrained commentary yields to various songs from the crowd, as well as constant cheering, ending with the "Internationale," which fades out to be taken over by the cheering.

At this point, the film tends to lose direction, for the rest of the film simply presents a succession of shots of the crowd, obviously trying to focus on banners and standards bearing inscriptions of participating groups. As these groups numbered more than two hundred in all, the filmmakers probably did the best with the footage they found, although toward the end there is a series of shots of uniformed youth groups, the Jeunesses Communistes and the Faucons Rouges (Socialists). As in *Le Mur des fédérés*, references to youth often came at the end of the Left films, for the Communists in particular sponsored an extensive network of youth activities as part of their effort to construct their own subculture. Of course the sectarianism of this practice was muted for the Popular Front, but not the motif of renewal, as the PCF experienced unprecedented growth in the period leading up to the elections in the Spring of 1936.

While the technical quality of the film certainly does not compare with the seamless product of the professional newsreel organizations, it nonetheless evidences care in its construction, particularly after the actual filming. The editing attempts to organize the footage into sequences, and shots were selected to build a rough continuity from one shot to the next, most often through camera movement. The sound track mixes the three tracks of speeches, crowd noises and singing, and commentary. However, there seems to be a conscious effort to keep the commentary to an absolute minimum, allowing the actual tracks recorded at the time to accompany the images. The filmmakers resist excessive tampering with the images and sounds. To a certain extent, the filmmakers had every reason to expect that audiences would approve any scraps of documentation commemorating their own participation in the historic event, but other factors probably account for the form of the final film.

The Left consistently voiced its violent dissatisfaction with the news-reels shown in theaters. They objected to the distortions normally contained in these films and saw in their tacit, if not overt, support of the bourgeoisie ample grounds for assuming direct collusion between the newsreel organizations and large capital formations in the society. At the same time, these newsreels often anchored the meanings of the images through a "Voice of God" narration, intervening in the images to impose a predetermined analysis or interpretation. Subsequent criticism in documentary study has confronted this issue at length, usually maintaining that such voice-over reflects a fear of ambiguity at best and, more pointedly, a fear that worker audiences would under-stand the images all too well as indictments of a repressive state apparatus (since these discussions often revolve around footage of confrontations). From this view, the Left can more easily refrain from controlling these images than the large organizations whose financial stability may rest more clearly on endorsement of forces of order in any given confrontation.

The co-existence of the tricolor and the red flag in Duclos's speech signaled the resurrection of nationalism in the political thrust of the Left. Marceau Pivert obviously renounced this betrayal of the Left's hopes for a revolutionary toppling of the bourgeois regime, but his doctrinal purity did not win broad support among the masses that flocked to the Popular Front. The municipal elections in May 1935 produced some dramatic victories for the Left, but, more significantly, informal agreements among the parties made those victories possible, a success that encouraged more extensive electoral agreements. At a time when the PCF was tapping these nationalist sympathies with great success (between June and October 1935 the PCF signed up 25,000 new members, and its growth *rate* rose even higher in the first half of 1936)[134] and the Socialist leadership remained cautious about the turn of events but could not consider withdrawing from the Pop-ular Front, Pivert's extremism had no future. In fact, Pivert's dissatis-faction became so great that he eventually left the Socialist party with his followers to found his own party.

The two films on the July 14 demonstration prefigure the future path of Left filmmaking. Pivert's cinema unit worked independently of any official (or even unofficial) Popular Front mandate. While the Left press expressed its unanimous outrage at the attack on Léon Blum in February 1936, only Pivert's group produced a film about it. Its advertisements in 1936 for film screenings always specified the responsibility of the Cinematographic Section of the SFIO (Socialist party), run by Pivert, and the filmmakers accompanied him when he formed his own party. To judge from the film made by the Committee of the Grand Rassemblement, with its Communist sympathies and its embrace of nationalism, the filmmakers associated with the *Grand Rassemblement* constituted the core of the ACI several months later.

The Struggle of Radio-Liberté

That the ACI was to be housed in the administrative shelter of the AEAR, itself within the cultural orbit of the PCF, indicates the growing interest of the PCF in film as a propaganda tool, but not a tool to be used as a wedge for dividing the Popular Front. And the ACI had no administrative link to the PCF. When the ACI claimed a membership of 20,000 in May 1936, there was no implication that the majority of this figure were Communist, for the large majority probably were not members of the PCF. A cameraman who worked with Pivert remarked casually recently that the first film made by the ACI, *La Vie est à nous,* was made in Moscow,[137] but this derisive attitude toward the ACI reflects an important distortion of the role of the PCF during the period. For the workers and, in this particular case, for intellectuals and writers, the PCF provided the opportunity to manifest their political opposition to fascism and their support of the Popular Front by enlisting in organizations set up with the aid of the PCF but not bound by party doctrine or discipline. In such circumstances cultural workers had every reason to be sympathetic to the PCF. Accusations of coercion fail to appreciate this reality.

But even though backed by the structure of the AEAR, the ACI did not produce films for several months. In that hiatus, another group waged a spirited campaign for the other modern media which was controlled even more strictly by the state than the cinema: radio. Only after the success of this experience did the ACI expand its activities to film production and make a conscious effort to broaden its popular base.

By the end of 1935 political obstacles to the final union of the Popular Front had been eliminated for the most part. In September

1935 the CGT and the Communist-controlled CGTU had completed an agreement on procedural matters leading to reunification the following spring, thus repairing a serious rift in the labor movement. The Programme of the Rassemblement Populaire, a program that the three political parties agreed to as the basis of an electoral alliance, was completed early in January. The Socialists had balked at removing planks on the nationalizations of key industries and a pledge not to devalue the franc, but the Communists, eager at all costs not to risk losing the Radicals, held firm, and the Socialists gave in. A compromise which conformed on the whole to the wishes of the Communists and the Radicals was reached on January 10, 1936.[138]

Furthermore, pressures driving the elements of the Left together had not abated. Mussolini's invasion of Ethiopia in October 1935 and the indecisive reaction of the French government (and the League of Nations) fanned the fears of fascism in France. Laval had courted Mussolini as a possible ally against Hitler, so the Left was already suspicious of Laval, and when the details of his discussions with Mussolini for resolving the Ethiopian crisis were disclosed, awarding Mussolini two-thirds of Ethiopia, the Left was furious. Aside from rewarding Mussolini's aggression, Laval's plan represented an unquestionable departure from the position of the League of Nations. Domestically, the Fascist leagues continued to grow, and Laval was seen as "the friend and secret protector of the Croix-de-feu [the largest of the Fascist leagues]."[139]

In this atmosphere, the Left opened its campaign for access to the radio. One of the regular features on the state radio was a review of the press.[140] On November 14, 1935, R. C. Radi wrote an article in *L'Humanité* calling for the inclusion of the PCF paper in this review of the press.[141] Radi described it as the fourth largest paper in France. The party placed great importance on its circulation figures and the distribution of the paper, and many attacks on *L'Humanité* vendors by French fascist thugs further dramatized this aura of militance around the diffusion of the paper. Radi implored readers to write letters and sign a petition demanding *L'Humanité*'s rightful representation in the press reviews. By December 7, *L'Humanité* claimed ten thousand signatures.

Several weeks later the drive escalated. On December 18, Paul Campargue, the radio correspondent for the major Socialist paper, *Le Populaire*, wrote an article supporting the PCF's demand.[142] He also explained the root of the problem. The minister in charge of radio, Georges Mandel, a Radical who prided himself on the responsiveness of his administration to complaints, maintained that such policy decisions were left to the individual management boards of the stations.[143] But Campargue retorted that the members of these boards owed their positions to Mandel, resulting in an illusory autonomy. After a month of sporadic protests, the Left settled on a typically frontist strategy: "We will gain satisfaction only by a common action led by the wireless listeners themselves. To unite them, we must group and organize the listeners who are pledged to the member formations of the Front Populaire. This is a project to which a number of our friends are committed. The creation of a free and impartial radio transmission will depend on the success of this endeavor."[144]

Announcements the following day in both *Le Populaire* and *L'Humanité* revealed that Campargue's words were not empty rhetoric. The two papers printed an official program of a new organization, Radio-Liberté, dedicated (in a subheading from *Le Populaire*) to a "free, impartial, and humane radio."[145] Below the program *L'Humanité* listed an impressive honorary committee with leading figures from each of the Popular Front parties: Daladier, the leader of the Radical party (first on the list); Pierre Cot, another Radical and former minister (and later appointed by Léon Blum as minister of the Air Force in the Popular Front government); Paul Campargue and Socialist Georges Monnet (also a future minister in the Popular Front government); Vaillant-Couturier for the PCF; and other prominent figures identified with the Popular Front (Victor Basch, Paul Langevin, Jean-Richard Bloch).[146] The manifesto itself, like the Programme of the Popular Front agreed upon only weeks later, was more of an ode to republicanism than a set of firm demands for a radical change in the structure of radio:

> The Radio, this magnificent means of expression of thought, this speech which triumphs over space, this peaceful weapon linking man and civilization, is the press and book of tomorrow.
>
> Radio, which should carry each day joy, diversion, culture and instruction into the humblest homes, should have only one goal: to serve truth.
>
> Unfortunately radio is not that now. Like radio in the fascist dictatorships, it is too often still in our country a means of perversion of taste and of "brainwashing." The forces of money, on which it depends, give it a unilateral partisan form, which revolts all Frenchmen with a love of liberty.
>
> Radio is ruled by censorship unworthy of the French Republic. . . .
>
> Radio in France is censorship of political, economic, social, and historical discourses.
>
> In the time we are living through, there can be no liberty of thought, no liberty of the press if there is no liberty of the radio.
>
> Heirs of those who waged the difficult struggle for public liberties,

committed to defending and extending them, we have decided to launch an appeal to all wireless listeners to form an association whose program is contained in the title itself: Radio-Liberté.

RADIO-LIBERTÉ which places the highest priority on liberty of the microphone, is the organization which must group all over France without party distinction or denomination, the hundreds of thousands of listeners eager to see developed in France a free and honest radio.

RADIO-LIBERTÉ is the great voice which defends the wireless listeners, technicians, authors, speakers, artists, who pressure the public powers to respect the will of the listeners, who demand varied and quality programming, news honestly reported not only on France but also on the entire world, educational and cultural transmissions.

RADIO-LIBERTÉ is the organization of wireless listeners with a love for progress of which radio should be the constant expression.

RADIO-LIBERTÉ is yours [est à vous]. Join it. Make it an organization which will confer on radio transmission the role that one expects of it, the mission that falls to it, in the service of true French interests and human unity, of which it should become the best and most powerful messenger.[147]

While the exclusion of *L'Humanité* had motivated the initial protest, the Left clearly recognized the political possibilities offered by this most recent mass medium in Germany and Italy. The fear of radio being controlled by French fascists and their financial backers had led the Left to close ranks here also in a defense against fascism. To this threat the organization counterposed the French heritage of republicanism.

Unlike earlier abortive efforts in film to build a mass organization such as the ephemeral Union of Spectators to protest against the control of the film industry by commercial industries, Radio-Liberté shortly articulated specific demands and mounted a publicity campaign to build a popular base. In the first week of January Radio-Liberté issued a formal set of demands, printed in both *Le Populaire* and *L'Humanité:*

The Association *Radio-Liberté*, grouping the listeners of radio who seek a national transmission free, sincere, and interesting for ALL, will lead an incessant action to achieve the various objectives of its program, in particular:

LIBERTY OF THE MICROPHONE
Suppression of the censor, which is intolerable in a democratic form of government.
Impartial review of the press, in which all papers will be cited.
Right to speak for all the leaders of the major political parties and economic and social organizations.

PROGRAMS
Reorganization of children's programs (schedule and content).
Creation of an hour available for listeners.
Transmission of important sessions of the Chamber and Senate.
Rebroadcast or reporting of major meetings of political, economic, and union organizations.
Rebroadcast of courses given at the Sorbonne which are educational, scientific, or social.

MANAGEMENT COMMITTEES
Radio-Liberté will lead the effort in any occasion to assure the true representation of listeners on management boards and to insure that their prerogatives are respected: Artistic, administrative, and financial committees, program planning, etc.
Annual elections of listener representatives will enable *Radio-Liberté* to present its own candidates and to develop its own program of the defense of the interests of the listeners.[148]

Campargue envisioned a membership of 50,000 listeners, a figure Mandel would be unable to ignore. In the following months, the two papers ran almost daily membership figures, always accompanied by bold-faced reminders to join. The figure reached 11,500 by the beginning of March, when Radio-Liberté held its first constituent assembly. By that time, Radio-Liberté had already claimed victory on its demand for all the political parties to have access to the radio in the coming elections. Council president Albert Sarrault announced on January 28 the new policy, the first time that radio was to be available to all political parties during an election campaign.[149]

The use of radio for political purposes was still a sensitive and debated issue in France at that point. Various heads of government had availed themselves of it. In discussing Gaston Doumergue's radio speech of March 24, 1934 (when he was head of the government), François Goguel observed that "the first appeal by radio to all the French people appeared in political circles a disquieting initiative, destined to relegate the parliamentarians to the background, and without doubt imitative of fascism, national socialism, or, to put it more favorably, the American presidential system."[150] On April 1 Mandel outlined the conditions for the radio speeches, each party receiving one date for a national speech and three dates on regional radios of their choice.[151]

In February the organization published the first issue of its magazine, *Radio-Liberté*. On the first page the magazine congratulated the group on attaining a membership of 8,300 after only forty days of existence. Otherwise, the magazine more or less repeated the information already reported in the newspapers, with a catalogue of the demands, principles, and the illustrious Committee of Honor. Although the four-page periodical promised monthly publication, its next three issues came out erratically, the fourth issue appearing six months later dated June/July. When the next issue appeared in October, its format had changed considerably, with fifty pages and weekly publication. However, success blunted its political edge, for thirty-five of the pages were devoted to program listings, and the remaining space was filled with industry news; the crusade had ended. On March 1, 1936, the constituent assembly fixed its identity with the Popular Front, naming three figurehead vice-presidents representing each of the political parties of the Popular Front: Léon Blum (Socialist); Paul Vaillant-Couturier (PCF); Peytral (Radical).[152] After the electoral victory of the Popular Front in May, Blum appointed Jardiller as minister of the PTT (postal services, telegraph, telephone), replacing Mandel. As Jardiller was already a member of the administration council of Radio-Liberté, Radio-Liberté evolved into a trade organization, and the magazine became a trade journal.

In those first months of 1936, however, the early popular success of Radio-Liberté provided an organizational model for a similar struggle mounted by Left filmmakers. The ACI actually antedated Radio-Liberté, but in December and January it broke no new ground, limiting its activities to private screenings with sporadic calls for a breakthrough into production, which came to nothing. Radio-Liberté cleared the path for the ACI's subsequent transformation, not in terms of production, but in isolating a core of demands and rallying popular support around the struggle for satisfaction of those demands. For Radio-Liberté's program read more or less like a taut summary of complaints filmmakers had been making for years: abolition of the censor, liberation from the control of reactionary financial forces, elimination of the political bias in news reporting, freedom for the medium to realize its true potential as the highest expression of human values.

But this congruence of common interests was not sufficient to dynamize the ACI and mold it into a militant mass organization like Radio-Liberté. It took the spark of the PCF's initiative to catalyze this transformation. Once the PCF entrusted the ACI with the responsibility of producing a feature-length film for the imminent elections, the ACI discovered a sense of its own mission and its potential for developing a filmmaking weapon in the battle against the commercial cinema. In acknowledgment of its debt to Radio-Liberté, the ACI abandoned its original name and adopted the designation of Ciné-Liberté, the name given shortly to its journal as well. But before Ciné-Liberté established organizational identity, the filmmakers in the ACI banded together to produce the film ordered by the PCF: *La Vie est à nous.*

NOTES

1. R. Armes, *French Cinema* (Cambridge: Oxford University Press, 1985), p. 19.
2. P. Monaco, *Cinema and Society* (New York, Oxford, Amsterdam: Elsevier, 1976), makes a number of pertinent observations on the state of the French film industry during this period: "In the 1920s the family firm, 'with its attachment to entrepreneurial independence,' still predominated in France" (p. 23). "Small, independent, and 'one-shot' producers characterized the French cinema of the 1920s" (p. 25). "Block booking and blind booking . . . did not exist in France" (p. 25). "In France, there was great concern during the period over that country's lack of large-scale production firms" (p. 33). See also G. Sadoul, *French Film* (London: The Falcon Press, 1953; rpt. New York: Arno Press and The New York Times, 1972), p. 33; and Sadoul, *Histoire Générale du Cinéma* (Paris: Denoël, 1975), Tome 5, pp. 7–50.
3. On the monopoly and economics of the American studio system, see, among many other books and articles, M. Huettig, *Economic Control of the Motion Picture Industry* (Philadelphia: University of Pennsylvania Press, 1944); M. Conant, *Antitrust in the Motion Picture Industry* (Berkeley and Los Angeles: University of California, 1960).
4. On postwar German film, see Monaco, *Cinema and Society;* G. Huaco, *The Sociology of Film Art* (New York: Basic Books, 1965), pp. 25–91; and Sadoul, *Histoire Générale du Cinéma,* pp. 405–42.
5. Monaco, *Cinema and Society,* p. 26.
6. "The advent of the new technique resulted in the retirement, or at least the temporary indisposition, of rising directors of the impressionist movement or the *avant-garde*—Marcel Carné, Jean Rouguier, Claude Autant-Lara, Luis Buñuel, Cavalcanti, Germaine Dulac, Jean Epstein, Marcel L'Herbier. Such successful productions as emerged seemed to happen by chance, isolated achievements whose promise was never sustained." Sadoul, *French Film,* p. 64.
7. On the introduction of sound in Europe, see D. Gomery, "Economic Struggle and Hollywood Imperialism: Europe Converts to Sound," *Yale French Studies* 60 (1980): 80–93; Gomery, "The Coming of Sound to the American Cinema: A History of the Transformation of . . . ," unpublished doctoral dissertation (University of Wisconsin-Madison, 1975).
8. D. Andrew, "Sound in France: The Origins of a Native School," *Yale French Studies* 60 (1980): 96.
9. Ibid., pp. 100–102.
10. Ibid., p. 105–10.

11. I have gathered production figures from several sources, but exact figures rarely agree. However, trends do appear to be consistent in various sources: F. Courtade, *Les Malédictions du Cinéma Français* (Paris: Editions Alain Moreau, 1978); Sadoul, *French Film;* J.-P. Jeancolas, *15 ans d'années trente. Le Cinéma des français* (Paris: Stock, 1983); E. G. Strebel, "French Cinema of the Nineteen-Thirties. A Cinematic Expression of Popular Front Consciousness," unpublished doctoral dissertation (Princeton University, 1974).

12. Sadoul, *French Film*, p. 63.

13. "The arrest of the thief and pornographer Tannersaf called Bernard Natan is the best news of the cinema year." *Action Française,* December 30, 1938. Talon notes that the Right constantly referred to Natan by his real name, Tannersa(p)f, which was a Jewish one. Cited in G. Talon, "Regards critiques sur la production et la réalisation des films au temps du Front Populaire," *Cinéma 75* 194 (January 1975): 38. According to Jeancolas, his original name was Natan Tanenzapf, born in Roumania and naturalized as French citizen in 1921; he officially changed his name to Bernard Natan in a French court. Jeancolas, *15 ans d'années trente*, p. 31.

14. In an article bearing the title "Les gangsters du cinéma" in a Popular Front weekly, J. C. Marie wrote that "The Pathé-Natan swindle is three times more important than the Stavisky swindle. It extends to 35 companies and branches whose deficit exceeds 900 million over six years." *La Flèche,* March 7, 1936. Also cited in Courtade, *Les Malédictions du Cinéma Français,* p. 129.

15. *La Cinématographie Française,* January 25, 1936.

16. *Où va le cinéma français* (Paris: Editions Baudinière, [1937]), pp. 100–101.

17. Ibid., p. 117. In addition, many of the companies were formed for the purpose of producing only one film, and the company often bore the same name as the film. Hence aside from the large number of companies, there was no continuity built up over time which might reduce the instability. "An examination of the credits for the 10-year period [1929–1939] yields the following results: 285 French companies produced only a single film apiece; 76 produced two; 32 produced three; 17 produced four; 16 produced five. . . . These figures confirm the fragility and dispersion of the French film production system." R. Borde, " 'The Golden Age': French Cinema of the '30s," in *Rediscovering French Film*, Mary Lea Bandy, ed. (New York: The Museum of Modern Art, 1983), pp. 67–69.

18. Andrew, "Sound in France," p. 114.

19. Strebel, "French Cinema of the Nineteen-Thirties," pp. 121–22.

20. *Où va le cinéma français.* It should be pointed out that most of the speakers at this inquiry represented the industry; as they were seeking financial support from the government, they had a vested interest in pleading a pessimistic case.

21. P. Léglise, *Histoire de la politique du Cinéma Français* (Paris: Film Editions, 1970), Tome 1, pp. 29–32, 63.

22. R. Pithon, "La Censure des films en France et la crise politique de 1934," *Revue historique* 258 (1977): 109.

23. *Pour Vous,* May 11, 1933.

24. Strictly speaking, the film industry was represented on the Conseil supérieur, but as this body never convened, industry input was effectively meaningless.

25. On the history of American censorship of film, see G. Jowett, *Film: The Democratic Art* (Boston and Toronto: Little, Brown and Company, 1976), pp. 233–59.

26. Cited in Pithon, "La Censure des films," p. 110.

27. Ibid., pp. 110–11.

28. Jean Lods, in an interview with Jacques Brissac, quoted by Brissac, *Paris Midi,* October 19, 1928.

29. *Cinéma 74* 189 (July-August 1974); Moussinac, "Les Amis de Spartacus," pp. 73–74.

30. *Pour Vous,* May 11, 1933.

31. *Pour Vous,* June 7, 1934.

32. Pithon, "La Censure des films," p. 111.

33. *Pour Vous,* May 11, 1933.

34. *Pour Vous,* May 18, 1933.

35. *Pour Vous,* April 27, 1933.

36. *Pour Vous,* May 11, 1933.

37. *Pour Vous,* June 7, 1933.

38. Pithon, "La Censure des films," pp. 118–22.

39. Ibid., p. 120.

40. Ibid., p. 123.

41. Ibid., p. 112.

42. Ibid., p. 116.

43. "Certain theaters saw fit to suppress from the newsreels all the coverage of the events so well that when viewing the films one was able to believe that the great facts of the week in France had been the flower contest in Villefranche and the carnival of Nice." *La Cinématographie française* 800 (March 3, 1934), cited in Courtade, *Les Malédictions,* p. 102.

44. *La Cinématographie française* 797 (February 10, 1934), cited in Pithon, "La Censure des films," p. 116.

45. *Cinémonde,* February 22, 1934.

46. Ibid.

47. *La Cinématographie française* 797 (February 10, 1934), cited in Pithon, "La Censure des films," p. 117.

48. *Pour Vous,* May 11, 1933.

49. *Pour Vous,* June 14, 1934. "The socialist Germaine Dulac . . . worked as a supervisor at France-Acutalités, the newsreel firm of Gaumont and MGM. She was often requested to water down the newsreels, to make cuts, etc. . . . in November 1933 the unemployed from the North of France on their Hunger March to Paris sang 'The Internationale' at the passing of every village and made incendiary speeches for the micro-

phone of a great newsreel firm. This firm was discreetly requested to make cuts in the newsreel that would tone down the message, and it gracefully consented." R. Jeanne and C. Ford, *Le Cinéma et la Presse 1895–1960* (Paris: Armand Colin, 1960), p. 220, cited in Hogenkamp, "Worker's Newsreels," p. 22. Hogenkamp also notes that two months after the February events, Dulac lectured on "the illegal censorship of newsreels," according to *L'Humanité*, April 10, 11, 1934.

50. *Cinémonde*, March 1, 1934.
51. S. Priacel, "La Presse Filmée," *Regards* 13 (April 13, 1934); P. Allard, "Ce Que les Français ne Doivent pas voir," *Vu*, November 27, 1935.
52. *Le Peuple*, May 25, 1936.
53. *Comoedia*, May 28, 1936.
54. See note 10 in Introduction.
55. D. Caute, *Communism and the French Intellectuals, 1914–1960* (New York: Macmillan, 1964), p. 11.
56. Ibid., p. 43.
57. J. P. A. Bernard, *Le Parti Communiste Français et la Question Littéraire. 1921–1939* (Presses Universitaires de Grenoble, 1972), p. 72.
58. N. Racine, "Une revue d'intellectuels communistes dans les années vingt: 'Clarté' (1921–1928)," *La Revue française de science politique* 18:3 (June 1967): 486.
59. E. J. Brown, *The Proletarian Episode in Russian Literature, 1928–1932* (New York: Columbia University Press, 1953).
60. Bernard, *Le Parti Communiste Français*, p. 56.
61. Ibid., p. 57.
62. *Monde*, June 23, 1928, quoted in Bernard, *Le Parti Communiste Français*, p. 59.
63. Speech by S. Gopner, one of the representatives of the Comintern, reproduced in *La Littérature de la révolution mondiale* (November/December 1931), cited in Bernard, *Le Parti Communiste Français*, p. 63.
64. "résolution sur la revue *monde*," *La Littérature de la révolution mondiale* (November/December 1931), pp. 106–11.
65. "On the Questions of Proletarian and Revolutionary Literature in France," in Ibid., pp. 102–6.
66. "résolution sur la revue *monde*," p. 107.
67. Bernard, "Le Parti Communiste Français et les Problèmes Litteraires (1920–1939)," *La Revue française de science politique* 18:3 (June 1967): 521, 527n. See also more extended discussion in Bernard, *Le Parti Communiste Français*, pp. 71–77.
68. *La Littérature de la révolution mondiale* (November/December 1931), cited in Bernard, "Le Parti Communiste Français," p. 531.
69. N. Racine, "L'Association des Ecrivains et Artistes Révolutionnaires (A.E.A.R.). La Revue *Commune* et la lutte idéologique contre le fascisme (1932–1936)," *Le Mouvement sociale* 54 (January-March 1966): 29–30.
70. Ibid. Racine refers to Gide's declarations of "sympathy" from issues of *La Nouvelle Revue française* from July to October 1932. Caute, *Commu-*

nism and the French Intellectuals, p. 238, quotes two of these journal entries: "But above all I should like to live long enough to see Russia's plan succeed and the states of Europe obliged to accept what they insisted on ignoring. . . . My whole heart applauds that gigantic and yet entirely human undertaking (May 13, 1931). [Two months later he wrote] I should like to cry aloud my affection for Russia; and that my cry should be heard, have some importance."

71. Racine, "L'Association des Ecrivains," pp. 34, 32.
72. Ibid., pp. 38–39. This is a standard story in discussion of the PCF's cultural tolerance, often treated derisively. Caute, *Communism and the French Intellectuals,* p. 115, calls it "adroitly stage managed."
73. M. Fauré, *Le Groupe Octobre* (Paris: Christian Bourgeois Editeur, 1977), p. 79.
74. C. Amey, "L'Expérience Française du théâtre d'Agit-Prop," in *Théâtre Années Vingt. Le théâtre d'agit-prop de 1917 à 1932,* Tome III (Lausanne: La Cité/L'Age d'Homme, 1978), p. 131.
75. *La Scène Ouvrière,* no. 11, cited in Ibid., p. 132.
76. Unfortunately, the author does not cite his sources, hence one should accept these figures only provisorally. P. Razdac, "Un théâtre d'agit-prop," *Critique Communiste* (Summer 1982): 56–57.
77. Fauré, *Le Groupe Octobre,* pp. 82–84.
78. *La Scène Ouvrière,* 11.
79. "Manifesto" of Le Congrès Constitif de la FTOP, *La Scène Ouvrière* 2 (February 1931), reprinted in Amey, *Thèâtre Années Vingt,* Tome IV, pp. 61–62.
80. Amey, "L'Expérience Française," p. 138.
81. Several of these plays appeared in issues of *La Scène Ouvrière,* and the following have been reprinted in *Théâtre Années Vingt,* Tome IV, pp. 165–85. *Democratie, Tu N'est Qu'un Mot!* pp. 165–71; *Les Trois L Liebknecht Luxembourg Lenine,* pp. 172–75; *Aux Cheminots!* pp. 176–78; *Chômage! Misère! Fascisme!* pp. 179–85. A short excerpt from the latter gives some sense of the ideas and methods employed:

> The Professor (in the tone of a showman giving his patter).— Millions. The most magnificent achievement of the capitalist regime. Millions of human beings who live without working. Who said that they are dying? Certainly, people die. No one can live forever! But the fact is that millions of men are freed from working. You doubt it? Here are some figures. 2,500,000 in England. 5 million in Germany. 10 million in America. Hurrah! Hurrah! 10 million without work. In our country alone! Under the capitalist regime, the countries of the avant-garde only. Total liberation of humanity. Suppression of the humiliating necessity of working. Look at these photographs. Regard them. Men stay in fresh air for hours, conforming to the needs of hygiene. (Some unemployed on the bench in a park.) They play sports, they race. (Dispersal of demonstrators by the police.)

(Show, preferably, some real photographs. If that is impossible, replace them by large tableaux or place beside the rostrum a frame with a cloth for slides. It goes without saying that the subject can vary according to local conditions.)

82. Fauré, *Le Groupe Octobre*, pp. 84–90. Chardère notes that "Outside his circle of friends, Prévert was only slightly known by the poem 'Description d'un diner de têtes à Paris France' published in the review *Commerce* (directed by Paul Valéry, Léon Paul Fargue and Valéry Larbaud)." B. Chardère, "Jacques Prévert et Le Groupe Octobre," in *Jacques Prévert. Premier Plan* 14 (1960): 72.

83. Fauré, *Le Groupe Octobre*, p. 87.

84. Ibid., p. 88.

85. Ibid., p. 127. Also Chardère, "Jacques Prévert," p. 72.

86. Extract from Ibid. On the specifically German applicability of the epithet "social fascism," see Edward H. Carr, *Foundations of a Planned Economy, 1926–1929*, Vol. 3, pt. 2 (New York: Macmillan, 1977), pp. 638–43.

87. Fauré, *Le Groupe Octobre*, pp. 139–41.

88. Ibid., pp. 173–90.

89. In a recent book, one member of the Groupe Octobre distinguishes the work of the Groupe Octobre from that of other groups: "We also did spoken choruses on occasion, but we were not particularly serious compared to certain groups in the FTOF, which we belonged to also. These groups put on mostly spoken choruses, they made demands according to job category, but they also did presentations based on political slogans giving a historical view of the Revolution, presentations drawn from Russian texts, with many parts sung. Our presentations were more of a poetic sort." R. Blin, *Souvenirs et propos recueillis par Lynda Bellity Peskine* (Paris: Gallimard, 1986), pp. 35–36.

90. Fauré, *Le Groupe Octobre*, pp. 134–35.

91. Ibid., p. 190.

92. Most accounts accept the fact that the Groupe Octobre was awarded first prize in the competition, but Raymond Bussières claims that there was no first prize. Bussières, cited in *Jacques Prévert et ses amis photographes* (Lyon: Fondation Nationale de la photographie, 1981), p. 66. In an article on Prévert, Susan Spitzer claims that the prize was never awarded: "According to Marcel Duhamel, editor of Gallimard's well-known detective novel branch, 'La Série Noire,' and former Groupe Octobre member, the play was adored by the audiences and the judges at the Olympiad, as the festival was called, but at the last moment Stalin's more rigid officials intervened to prevent the presentation of the award to the company, which had apparently displeased them. Duhamel feels certain that the Groupe Octobre's work had a distinct Trotskyist flavor, that it was, from the official communist point of view, full of 'deviations.' Indeed, the French CP's representative to the selec-

tion committee of the FTOF, prior to the Moscow festival, was strongly opposed to the Groupe Octobre and its play *La Bataille de Fontenoy,* in particular." S. Spitzer, "Prévert's Political Theatre: Two Versions of *La Bataille de Fontenoy,*" *Theatre Research International* 3, no. 1 (October 1977): 65. Whether accurate or not, this claim is entirely plausible. Fauré does identify Allégret as a Trotskyist, and Prévert resisted the yoke of any dogma. Thus, when the PCF later reversed course and draped itself with the tricolor of French nationalism to the tune of the "Marseillaise," Prévert apparently refused to march. Spitzer's article is an interesting examination of Prévert's eventual disillusion with the Soviet Union.

93. Cited in Chardère, "Jacques Prévert," p. 76.

94. For example, the French illustrated weekly, *Regards,* modelled after *AIZ,* carried the Heartfield cover, "The Nazis Play With Fire," on April 25, 1935, originally published in *AIZ,* February 28, 1935, for the second anniversary of the Reichstag fire. For Heartfield's photomontages, see *Photomontages of the Nazi Period: John Heartfield* (New York: Universe Books, 1977); D. Kahn, *John Heartfield: Art and Mass Media* (New York: Tanam Press, 1985).

95. Heinreich, "Une Vie dans le Cinéma," in *Jacques Prévert. Premier Plan* 14 (1960): 52.

96. Hence Sadoul's evaluation of Prévert as "more of a dialogue writer than a script writer." Sadoul, *French Film,* p. 73.

97. Fauré, *Le Groupe Octobre,* p. 104.

98. Blin, *Souvenirs,* p. 35.

99. Jacques Prévert, cited in *Jacques Prévert et ses amis photographes.*

100. Caute, *Communism and the French Intellectuals,* p. 43.

101. J. Leyda, *Kino* (New York: Collier, 1960), pp. 278, 339.

102. Fauré, *Le Groupe Octobre,* pp. 146–47. Production dates for this film vary in sources, from 1931 to 1933. I have accepted the early date given in the most recent and, I believe, most comprehensive filmography of Jacques Prévert, in *A la rencontre de Jacques Prévert* (Saint Paul: Fondation Maeght, 1987), p. 149.

103. Chardère, "Jacques Prévert," p. 51. Also author interview with Yves Allégret, August 19, 1981. Freinet was a radical teacher who was fired from his position as schoolteacher in 1933 and founded an alternative school in Vence (just outside of Nice) where he put his pedagogical ideas into practice and from which he promulgated his beliefs. See E. Freinet, *Naissance d'une pédagogie populaire* (Paris: Maspero, 1979). Freinet himself rejected political labels, claiming that "we are pedagogues and not politicians," in E. Freinet, *Naissance d'une pédagogie populaire,* but at the same time, he did write in the July 1930 issue of his paper,

> At this end of the year, we are more than ever inclined to continue our cooperative action in complete agreement with the groups who struggle for the school liberation through proletarian liberation.

Cited in E. Freinet, *l'Itinérarire de Célestin Freinet* (Paris: Payot, 1977).

Again, from statements of this sort, one can see clearly the widespread sympathy felt for revolutionary sentiments of the anarcho-communist variety referred to above by Roger Blin, and which animated the Groupe Octobre. Hence cultural activists such as Freinet and Prévert shared an antipathy to bourgeois values and sought venues which were undoubtedly marginal in any statistical sense, but seminal in the political/cultural production of the period.

104. K. Marx, *Wages, Price, and Profit* (Peking: Foreign Languages Press, 1964); Yves Allégret, interview with author.

105. "Pour un cinéma d'enfants proléteriens," *Regards* 10 (October 1932), cited in R. Grolier, ed., *Mémoires d'en France, 1936–1939* (Paris: Editions AIMO, 1986), p. 115; Marx, *Wages, Price, and Profit*, p. 78. In his book on the French Left, Jean Touchard points out that in the late and early 1920s, "the study of Marxism . . . was virtually neglected, not only by the universities, but also by the Communist party itself. One must emphasize this prolonged ignorance of Marxism among the Communists until 1939." J. Touchard, *La Gauche en France depuis 1900* (Paris: Editions du Seuill, 1977), p. 199.

In a critical study of the history of the PCF by dissident members, the authors assert that the theoretical study of Marxism was intentionally avoided during the 1930s in order to discourage criticism of party leaders in a French variant of the cult of personality. According to the authors, the party leaders "gained the support of the weakest new members of the party, knowing that these new members would accept more easily—lacking a solid political formation—what the older militant refused." However, this assessment applies to the years after 1934 when the membership of the PCF began to increase with the abandonment of the "third period" tactic. See collective work edited by Unir, *Histoire du Parti communiste français*, Tome 1 (Paris: éditions Veridad, 1960), pp. 208–9.

106. Interview with Yves Allégret.

107. Bernard Eisenschitz, an excellent researcher, writes that "one doesn't know on what initiative this film was shot, but the accent placed on the situation of the peasants leads one to think that it did not come from a central initiative, but from a production of a Federation of the Party." B. Eisenschitz, "Front Populaire et Idée de Cinéma Militant de France (1928–1937)," paper presented at an FIAF conference and published by the International Federation of Film Archives and Bulgarska Nacionalna Filmoteka, Varna, 1977.

108. The Prussian plebiscite of August 9, 1931. K. Bracher, *The German Dictatorship* (New York: Praeger, 1970), p. 187. Also F. Claudin, *The Comintern. Part I* (New York: Monthly Review Press, 1975), p. 163.

109. On the Socialist party and pacifism, see J. Colton, *Léon Blum: Humanist in Politics* (Cambridge and London: MIT Press, 1966), pp. 80–86; J. Lacouture, *Léon Blum* (Paris: Editions du Seuil, 1977), pp. 240–41; and

J. Marcus, *French Socialism in the Crisis Years, 1933–1936* (New York: Praeger, 1958), pp. 6–11.

110. For example, *Regards* 62 (March 21, 1935).

111. L. Chavance, "Cinéma au service du Front populaire," *La Flèche* 19 (June 27, 1936).

112. The note listed the following films: *"L'eau qui danse* and *La Route* by R. Bricon; *Trois petits tours* by P. Boyer (first prize of the competition of Paris); *Les foules de Lourdes,* by J. Lemare, actualités." *Commune* 27 (November 1935).

113. *Commune* 28 (December 1935): 510.

114. Ibid.

115. *L'Humanité,* December 29, 1935.

116. *L'Humanité,* January 5, 1936.

117. *L'Humanité,* February 7, 1936.

118. R. Taylor, *The Politics of the Soviet Cinema, 1917–1929* (Cambridge: Cambridge University Press, 1979), p. 155. To judge by its journal, *Commune,* the AEAR did not initially appreciate the mobilizing potential of film; the first issue of *Commune* appeared in July 1933, but it was a year and a half before *Commune* 16 carried the first film reviews in December 1934.

119. *La Flèche* 19 (March 25, 1935).

120. Ibid.

121. N. Greene, *Crisis and Decline: The French Socialist Party in the Popular Front Era* (Ithaca, N.Y.: Cornell University Press, 1969), pp. 6–10; Marcus, *French Socialism in the Crisis Years,* pp. 3–40.

122. Marcus, *French Socialism in the Crisis Years,* pp. 15–16.

123. Ibid., pp. 33–34.

124. SFIO was the acronym of the official name of the French Socialist Party, Section Française de l'Internationale Ouvrière.

125. Chavance, "Cinéma au service du Front populaire."

126. *Le Populaire,* October 7, 1935.

127. The full text of this communiqué is printed as an Appendix in G. Lefranc, *Histoire du Front Populaire* (Paris: Payot, 1965; 1974), pp. 469–70.

128. *Le Populaire,* May 17, 1935, cited in Marcus, *French Socialism in the Crisis Years,* pp. 121–22.

129. Ibid., pp. 127–29.

130. M. Pivert, *Révolution d'abord* (1935), quoted in Greene, *Crisis and Decline,* p. 59. Note that after the Molotov–Ribbentrop Pact of 1939, Comintern policy verged on this position.

131. Marcus, *French Socialism in the Crisis Years,* p. 144.

132. In September and early October, *Le Populaire* listed the film as *14 juillet.* On November 15, 1935, *Le Populaire* carried an advertisement for *Les Bastilles, 14 juillet 1935.* In another advertisement in *Le Populaire,* June 24, 1936, the title had changed to *Bastille 1789–Bastille 1935.* Yet another

name was used in an advertisement run in *Le Populaire*, May 16, 1937: *Les Bastilles (1789–1935)*.

133. *Le Populaire*, October 7, 1935.
134. A. Kriegel, "Le Parti Communiste sous la Troisième République (1920–1939). Evolution de ses effectifs," *Revue Française de science politique* (February 1966): 5–35.
135. "After the horrors of this first world conflict, *La Marseillaise*, sung in the first socialist revolutions, will rouse, this time among French people, the worst repugnance for having been covered with mud and blood in the trenches, for having been intoned to the limit by the civilian population in so-called patriotic demonstrations." F. Robert, "Genèse et destin de *La Marseillaise*," *La Pensée* 221/222 (July-August 1981): 75.
136. Jacques Prévert in *Jacques Prévert et ses amis photographes*, p. 69. In his memoires, Roger Blin offers a similar account:

> The Groupe Octobre did not survive the political turn of the Party in 1938, following the Laval-Stalin pact [actually 1935, see text pages 57–58]. What the Groupe Octobre vomited: the motherland, the slogans such as "long live the army," "we extend our hand to the priests," "let's get to work," etc., everything it had fought against had become sacred. Our whole program, all that we believed in, was fucked up. Some members of the group, those who were in the party, wondered if we could continue in spite of everything. But we could not turn 180 degrees from one day to the next.

R. Blin, *Souvenirs et propos recueillis par Lynda Bellity Peskine* (Paris: Gallimard, 1986), pp. 36–37.

137. Mr. Robert Talpain, interview with author, August 18, 1981.
138. The Socialists, with the CGT, had proposed nationalization of various industries: railroads, insurance, distribution of electricity, credit, banking. In addition to the nationalizations, the joint program failed to include all of the following proposals by the Socialist party: right to vote for women, suppression of the Senate, creation of a "national public service of education," paid vacations, retirement at sixty years of age. See Kergoat, *La France du Front Populaire*, pp. 73, 74.
139. E. Bonnefous, *Histoire Politique de la Troisième République*, Tome 5 (Paris: Presses Universitaires de France, 1962), p. 352.
140. In France, private and state radio coexisted. However, the private radios depended on the state for their licenses to operate and were less likely to tread on sensitive political turf in their news programs; thus, for their news reports they relied to a large degree on large-circulation newspapers with no particular political affiliation. See Pierre Miquel, *Histoire de La Radio et de La Television* (Paris: Editions Richelieu, 1972), pp. 51–60.
141. *L'Humanité*, November 14, 1935.
142. *Le Populaire*, December 18, 1935.

143. J. Sherwood, *Georges Mandel and the Third Republic* (Stanford: Stanford University Press, 1970), pp. 150–60.
144. *Le Populaire*, December 18, 1935.
145. *Le Populaire*, December 19, 1935.
146. *L'Humanité*, December 19, 1935.
147. Ibid.
148. *Le Populaire*, January 6, 1936.
149. *Le Populaire*, February 3, 1936.
150. F. Goguel, *La Politique des Partis sous la IIIe République* (Paris: Editions du Seuil, 1946), p. 497.
151. *Le Populaire*, March 4, 1936.
152. Ibid.

2

La Vie est à nous

When the PCF decided to commission a major film to be used in the election campaign beginning in April 1936, the party only extended to another cultural domain the initiative that it had seized and maintained in the first half of 1934, following the violence of the February events. Since that time, the PCF had continued its lead in putting together the pieces of a Popular Front that could achieve concrete results in the election of 1936. Beginning informally with the joint demonstration with the Socialists and the CGT on February 12, 1934, the PCF pursued this tack with formal political agreements to secure unity on the Left. At the same time, the party waged a parallel campaign on the cultural front. Following the priorities of the Comintern, the PCF first turned its attention to theater and literature and founded French sections of Comintern organizations. Recognizing the appeal that nationalism exerted on French working people, early in 1935 the party formed one large French cultural organization, the Maison de la Culture, entirely autonomous from any foreign affiliations. However, the participation of artists and intellectuals in these political activities was a two-way process. The threat of fascism mobilized the cultural community; the party did not create that momentum, nor did it control it. Hence the Maison de la Culture, soon spreading thoughout the country in many Maisons de la Culture which still exist today, received immediate support from a wide spectrum of political sympathies.

Perhaps the very importance accorded to culture in France explains the delay in vigorous filmmaking activity in this movement, for film did not have the same prestige as literature and theater. The Alliance of Independent Cinema did not appear until months after the formation of the Maison de la Culture, and even then the ACI did not cross the threshold into production. Though in place institutionally, the ACI lacked a project to break this inertia. The PCF ended this impasse when it ordered a film for the April election campaign.

The successful completion of *La Vie est à nous* transformed the hopes of the ACI into reality, leading to the creation of a functioning alternative independent production company, Ciné-Liberté. The experience of making *La Vie est à nous* demonstrated the potential of filmmaking in the political struggle and provided the impetus for the production of a series of independent political films during the Popular Front. This chapter will consider that experience—the film's production and exhibition; its formal intelligence, inseparable from its responsiveness and fidelity to the immediate problems of French working people at that historical moment; its critical reception—and also Renoir's role in the production and subsequent critical reputation of the film and his political identity at the time.

Production of *La Vie est à nous*

Early in 1936 Jacques Duclos, head of the agit-prop section of the PCF,[1] summoned Jean-Paul Le Chanois, a PCF member who held an important administrative position in the FTOF, to suggest the idea of making a film for the elections in April.[2] For the first time in France, a political party had commissioned a major film for electoral purposes. According to Jean-Paul Le Chanois, Aragon had passed on the idea of a film to Duclos and had also recommended that Jean Renoir direct the film.[3]

While Renoir had no overt political affiliations at the time, he was a logical choice for a number of reasons. Renoir's working method was always of a collaborative nature, retaining the same crew in film after film. He was not comfortable with studio interference and bristled at commercial pressures. Furthermore, he had just completed a political film, *Le Crime de M. Lange*, which brought him into contact with Jacques Prévert and other members of the Groupe Octobre.

Apparently Duclos entrusted the writing of the script to Le Chanois and Pierre Unik,[4] and Le Chanois maintains that Duclos did not interfere in the writing of the script.[5] Renoir took part in the writing also, but the final form of the film tends to support Le Chanois's assertion that Renoir did not offer major contributions, as he was not involved in politics. While such an observation is reasonable, Renoir's political activity during the period of the Popular Front cannot be dismissed so easily, and his relation to *La Vie est à nous* will be considered at greater length below.

Again according to Le Chanois, the film was financed partially by collections at PCF meetings.[6] These contributions in small coins amounted to some 50,000 or 60,000 francs, which is the figure usually cited for the cost of the film—about one-tenth of the average feature-film budget at the time. However, Le Chanois claimed that the contributions did not cover the production cost and that the PCF used some of its own funds.[7]

Although the film originally identified the production as a "film d'équipe," most accounts have assigned credits to the following filmmakers: Jacques B. Brunius, the newsreel sequences in the first two reels; Renoir, the school sequence, the story of the *ingènieur*, and the closing sequence; Le Chanois, the factory sequence; Jacques Becker, the episode on the farm.[8] A fuller consideration of the credits will be given after a discussion of the film.

The first public references to the film appeared in several publicity boxes in *L'Humanité*, but they were not particularly informative:

> La Vie est à nous
> La Vie, les luttes, et les aspirations du Peuple![9]

The following day, a larger box provided more information, and indicated the themes stressed in the film:

> La Vie.
> Les richesses et les beautés de la France
> La vie, les luttes et les aspirations du peuple
> La malfaisance des 200 familles qui divisent
>   la nation et oppriment notre pays.
> L'influence grandissante et la force du Parti Communiste.
> La vie
> La *beauté* de ses prises de vue.
> La *perfection* de sa technique.
> L'*excéllence* de jeu des artistes.
> Le dynamisme de son action
> en font un *événement cinématographique*.
> La Vie
> Votre vie
> Vos luttes
> Votre espoir
> La voie vers une
> France libre, forte, et heureuse.
> Un film parlant que vous devez voir.[10]

An unsigned review of the film, published the next day in *L'Humanité*, begins by referring to the curiosity aroused by this cryptic publicity campaign of the previous several days.

In several reviews of the film, critics cited the record time in which the film was made, between two to four weeks. Renoir said that he worked fourteen days on the film, and Le Chanois recalls that it was shot in fourteen days.[11] Other reviewers put the record time at three or four weeks, but these estimates, all given after the screening of the film, undoubtedly include the editing period. Hence, regardless of the exact time, they certainly were justified in praising the speed (some chose the comparison with a "shock brigade").

The premiere of the film took place at the Bellevilloise theater, a theater purchased by the PCF after World War I.[12] Located in a working-class district in Paris, the Bellevilloise specialized in Soviet films—which meant many denied visas by the censor for public screenings. The film opened on April 7 at the Bellevilloise, before 700 people, of which "most were militants of the party,"[13] as well as Marcel Cachin and André Marty, members of the Central Committee. *L'Humanité* described the enthusiastic reception given by the crowd: "Repeated applause greeted the most powerful sequences of the film, and a triple hurrah erupted at the end, to honor the brilliant crew which, in less than one month, to the rhythm of a shock brigade, has made this first French film populaire."[14] The article, written only two days after this screening, concludes with the promising note that the film had been ordered in fifty towns throughout the country, "and soon the whole world will be able to applaud it." The film was shown several days later at the Pantheon cinema, April 10 and 11, with party leader Maurice Thorez present as well.

However, the ambitious plans for distributing the film were frustrated by the censor. Accounts of the role of the censor in the life of *La Vie est à nous* vary somewhat. Contemporary reviews and discussions of the film consistently decry the denial of a visa. Louis Chavance claimed that the formation of Ciné-Liberté was facilitated "by the censor, which has had the idea of forbidding *La Vie est à nous*."[15] Sadoul stated outright that "the visa of the censor was refused" but was even more outraged that Guichard (a member of the Censorship Commission) and Sarrault (then prime minister and interior minister) had not permitted a private screening at the Salle Pleyel.[16] Normally, denial of a visa prevented commercial exhibition but did not apply to private screenings; hence Sadoul's anger at the refusal of authorization for even a private screening on the grounds that the theater was a public building (available for rental) and thus would not constitute a private event. Sadoul attacked the hypocrisy of subsequently allowing film screenings at the same Salle Pleyel during a meeting for the Fascist league l'Action Française:

> Thus one of the major French political parties has not been authorized, during the election period, to project in private screening *La Vie est à nous*. But a gang of men who wield the kitchen knife to slaughter the working class,[17] an illegal organization has every right to project antidemocratic and antiparliamentary films, this not only in Paris, Salle Pleyel [a public auditorium], but also, as "l'Action Française" and "The Royal Courrier" announce, in sixty towns in France, the group has been given authorization [for the screenings]. Already since December a number of these screenings have taken place. They were "private" but announced by posters. Mr. Guichard and Mr. Sarraut have authorized these screenings.
>
> And the same week when the dissolved Action Française announced their sixty royalist and cinematographic meetings, the police commissioner of the 20th arrondissement requested, against all legality, the interdiction of the projection of *La Vie est à nous* in a private hall, in private meeting.[18]

Apparently the film was submitted to the censor and denied a visa. In addition, screenings that did not qualify as strictly private were also rejected on the ostensible technicality Sadoul attacked. Finally, under the law individual mayors had the authority to forbid private screenings when they judged them to be potentially threatening to public order. It is easily understandable that the Left objected to the array of measures available to prevent screenings of films.

On the basis of information in the National Archives, Pascal Ory specifies that the film was submitted to the censor only after the installation of the government of the Popular Front on June 6.[19] Francis Courtade, relying primarily on Ory's research, accepts this version also.[20] However, while the records preserved in the National Archives are unfortunately extremely incomplete regarding the activities and decisions of the censor, a letter that Ory undoubtedly used as his source in fact contradicts his version. The letter is in the form of a memorandum, addressed to the minister of education, in response to a telephone inquiry from a Communist deputy, Louis Mercier, requesting a visa for *La Vie est à nous*:

> The film was submitted for a visa during the election period and M. Albert Sarraut, Prime Minister, was of the opinion that it could not be authorized to be screened publicly, for it was foreseen that in their turn, "L'Action Française," "Les Croix-de-Feu," and in general, all the politi-

cal parties would present propaganda films which would naturally provoke disorders in the Paris cinemas and the rest of the country.

Thus, it is a question of principle that M. Louis Mercier is raising, that of determining if the commercial theaters are able to show films of political propaganda. The answer can be given neither by the Minister of the Interior (National Security) nor by the Ministry of National Education, but only by the Council of Ministers. The question is, indeed, to determine the policy of the new government regarding film screenings.[21]

No explicit answer exists among the available documents, but a letter from the minister of national education, dated September 2, 1936, states that the ministry refused to reconsider films that have previously been denied a visa.[22] Le Chanois has stated on various occasions that the film was not submitted to the censor at the time, for a refusal would have made all screenings more difficult.[23] On the basis of contemporary evidence, Le Chanois's version appears the least likely.

Given the history of censorship throughout the 1930s, La Vie est à nous's difficulties with the censor were in no way anomalous or surprising. What makes it noteworthy is its timing, on the eve of the victory of the Popular Front at the polls. Mercier no doubt wanted to use La Vie est à nous as a test case, for numerous critics hailed the new government as an opportunity to abolish, or at least revise, the institution of the censor. On June 4, Sadoul demanded that "the government of tomorrow must authorize soon, very quickly, La Vie est à nous. This film is the voice of millions of French people, a great voice which should not be banished to the chambers of private screenings."[24] The previous week, Sadoul had been even more categorical in his remarks on the censor: "One of the first tasks of the government of tomorrow must be to . . . suppress the scandalous rule of the censor."[25]

The film never did receive a visa, either before or after the elections, and its screenings were limited to private meetings, generally PCF gatherings, although Sadoul does refer to a private screening attended not only by PCF dignitaries such as Thorez and Cachin but also representatives of the Socialist party (Georges Monnet) and the Radical party (Albert Bayet and Jacques Kayser). However, this event occurred weeks after the election; since the three major parties of the Popular Front coalition all ran their own candidates in the first round of elections, they would not have lent their presence before the election to partisan campaigning events of another party. In contrast to all the other major Left publications, most of which were formally independent of any political party, Le Populaire, the Socialist party paper, did not even review La Vie est à nous.

The Conception and Design of *La Vie est à nous*

The film itself can be approached in a number of ways. As it was made at the express request of the PCF, one would expect to find the themes and emphases chosen by the party for the electoral campaign. These ideas of course must conform to the Programme of the Rassemblement Populaire published on January 10, 1936; however, the relative vagueness of that document fails to indicate the nuances of interpretation adopted by the separate parties that finally subscribed to the Popular Front. Since these parties had specifically rejected agreement on the choice of individual candidates running on a Front ballot, the election campaign was not simply a contest between the Popular Front and the other parties but also a competition among the Socialists, Radicals, and Communists. Losers in the first round would withdraw in favor of the leading vote getter in the coalition. Hence, the parties had a clear interest in differentiating themselves each from the other.

At the same time, as the later critics noted, the film is a historical document pervaded with the spirit of the time—an optimism that actually reached its highest point in the months immediately preceding Blum's assumption of power as head of the Popular Front government. What critics have not indicated, however, is the remarkable degree of historical specificity contained in the film. Beyond a dry litany of PCF propaganda, the film addresses itself with great precision to the issues of the time and even foreshadows unforeseeable future developments. Such foresight—more than merely fortuitous—provides powerful evidence that the PCF did speak for the working people, did understand their concerns, and thus confirms its claims to have been the prime animator behind the creation of the Popular Front in response to an inchoate popular will that the PCF was uniquely placed to translate into concrete action.

And finally, again in the vanguard, only the PCF saw the mobilizing potential of film and made its resources available for the production of an ambitious first effort whose success, deserved in its own right, becomes that much more admirable when compared with later political films made during the government of the Popular Front. In this view as well, *La Vie est à nous* expresses the people's attitudes toward film, rethinking standard film practice current at the time, formulating novel solutions to a widely shared popular frustration.

Unfortunately, the conditions of the film's production—the PCF's sponsorship for electoral purposes, the speed with which it was completed, the multiplicity of authorship—have deflected commentators from a close investigation of the film. Their praise disguises an implicit patronization that the film does not merit in fine or more globally in its conception and structure, for a careful consideration of the film reveals a complex and impressive array of strategies for political filmmaking.

The film opens with a shot of the sea and a coast covered with trees and shrubbery, immediately followed by a similar shot. These shots evidently illustrate the accompanying commentary, "The geographical situation of France, surrounded by the Atlantic Ocean and the Mediterranean," even though one cannot identify the two seas from the shots. The following shots continue the geographical description, each shot matched with a new feature listed in the commentary:

SHOT	COMMENTARY
3. wheat field with thresher	the even distribution of fields
4. mountains	and mountains,
5. rich vegetation	the fertility of the soil and the mildness of the climate,
6. boats on river	the existence of great waterways,
7. large ship on river	the system of communications,
8. wheat field	the industriousness of the people
9. wheat (close shot)	have made of our country one of the richest and most beautiful in the world.

The opening of the film focuses exclusively on rural images which establish a sense of open space, the grandeur of the country of France. They present a France not usually seen in films and, more significantly, not experienced by the urban population—especially the sea, the very first images, for as Grelier says in *Mémoires*, "the image which stands out from all the others of the time is that of The Sea for the First Time." Thus, from the start the film identifies itself with a picturesque France unfamiliar to the mass of urban workers. Only two months later, French workers had the chance to see their own country for the first time. After the strikes of May and June, workers won the right to paid vacations—perhaps the single most important victory of the working class. Virtually all contemporary and subsequent accounts stress the importance of this innovation.

In opening with a sequence reminding viewers that France is an agricultural country, the film tries to include the rural population, the peasants, in the audience. Like most Communist parties and certainly including the Bolsheviks, the PCF drew most of its strength from urban, industrial workers. As a rule, the PCF paid lip service to the peasant population but had little representation in that sector, which was traditionally more conservative, lower middle class. In France, the

"The Riches of France": schoolteacher (Jean Dasté) revealed as the source of the voice-over (*La Vie est à nous*)

Radicals received support from the peasants. By acknowledging the importance of agriculture in the economic life of the country, the PCF obviously hoped to avoid an indifference to the agricultural population traditionally associated with the party.[26]

The opening sequence proceeds with a recitation of production figures cataloguing the diversity of crops cultivated in France—wheat, oats, barley, rye, corn, buckwheat, wine, cider—each crop illustrated with a different image or images. In this opening section the film takes the form of a documentary film, the images subservient to a Voice-of-God discourse, offscreen and unidentified. In the twenty-ninth shot, however, the speaker, a teacher, is directing his discourse offscreen. A long shot reveals the teacher giving a lesson to a classroom of schoolchildren. Three shots of the teacher serve as a transition to the second part of the lesson, then the camera pans across some cows, pushed offscreen by a horizontal wipe to a steel foundry, as the teacher says, "France, an agricultural country, has also become a great industrial country."

The sequence of shots accompanying the figures of industrial production are more familiar, for they are evidently modeled on industrial sequences in Vertov films. Thus, after the initial view of iron production, we see a miner hammering out coal with a pickaxe, trams passing by loaded with coal, then a dam, an electricity plant, an electrical stanchion, a transformer, and a blast furnace. Production clearly means first of all heavy production, iron and coal, as well as electrical energy, which Vertov often used as a visual trope for Lenin's famous maxim that "socialism + electricity = communism." The sequence concludes with various shots of an automobile factory and a warehouse full of new cars, the only consumer goods shown in this celebration of French industry.

The teacher has not mentioned the PCF once in this openly nationalistic introduction, and the choice of profession would deflect suspicions of partisanship for a particular party or political formation. After this evocation of the agricultural and industrial wealth of the nation, the next section extends the lesson not only to the realm of cultural production but, more significantly, to the cultural heritage of France dating from the Middle Ages: "The centuries have accumulated in France magnificent artistic treasures. A multitude of anonymous architects, sculptors, and builders in the Middle Ages built cathedrals, like those at Chartres, Rouen, Reims, Sens, Amiens, like Notre-Dame in Paris, whose beauty is a tribute to the genius of our country." As the camera tilts up the imposing facades of Chartres and Notre-Dame, the party, barely fifteen years old, attaches itself to this cultural history reaching all the way back to the twelfth century to support its claim of patriotic allegiance to France. Even the fabulous public works of the Sun King take their place in this French pantheon: "The Renaissance, the century of Louis XIV have left us castles and palaces, several of which are magnificent jewels. The Palace of Versailles is a dazzling display of grandeur." The lesson ends with a tribute to Paris, whose "artistic and intellectual influence has no equal." However, the teacher concentrates on Paris as a center of haute couture, "the capital of luxury and elegance," drawing couturiers, milliners, shoemakers, jewellers—a town where one can marvel at the coats and furs worn at Longchamp, the Bois de Boulogne, the Champs-Elysées.

The views of Paris—of the Eiffel Tower, the Louvre, the Arc de Triomphe, boutiques—disappear when the teacher is seen again in the classroom, speaking now of the "haute-mode," and none of these fabled adornments of the haute-bourgeoisie nor their gathering spots is illustrated. The reason for this denial of images becomes clear as the teacher looks over the classroom with a sad expression, as if registering suddenly a certain disparity between the magical world evoked by his discourse and the immediate reality of the children, and concludes, "Of course, you have not had much of a chance to notice it."

This opening sequence, then, introduces a number of themes that will be pursued later in the film. First, the commentary stresses that France is a rich country economically, endowed with impressive agricultural and industrial wealth. This was in certain ways a difficult claim to make in France at the beginning of 1936, for France continued to suffer from enormous economic difficulties. The policy of deflation practiced by the succession of Radical governments had not solved the persistent currency crisis. Unemployment at the end of 1935 had reached a record level of 460,000. Purchasing power and the standard of living had plummeted disastrously. Yet the film excludes any images witnessing this economic paralysis, of which there could be no question at the time.

In fact, the film adopts quite literally the rhetorical strategy used by Maurice Thorez in his speech to the PCF Congress at Villeurbanne at the end of January 1936, just before the production of the film. The commentary spoken by the teacher takes passages verbatim from the opening section of this speech, "L'Union de la nation française."[27] This section, "Les Richesses de la France," has subsections devoted to Agriculture, Industry, Communication Routes and Means of Transport, and Population.

The film eliminates entirely the partisan comments in the speech, which for the most part extol the wisdom and prescience of the party. For example, Thorez begins his assessment of the riches of France by reminding his listeners that "the Communists were the only ones to foresee the economic crisis which has shaken the capitalist world for more than six years, at the same time that the politicians of the bourgeoisie were celebrating the prosperity and stability of the capitalist system."[28] Thorez then distinguishes this prescience of the party from the errors of the Socialist party. On the other hand, he counters Trotsky's charge from 1931 that France was a "backward country" with the invocation of the riches of France. Thorez, then, situates the perspicacity of the PCF between the latent bourgeois sympathies of the Socialist party and the disparagement of French stature found "in this sampling of Trotskyist thought." After this assertion of the wisdom of the party, he takes up the report on the economic situation in France, beginning with "The geographic situation of France . . . ," the paragraph reproduced verbatim at the beginning of the commentary in *La Vie est à nous*. In the speech, Thorez makes no further partisan comments until the last paragraph of the section, noting that "it is appropriate to note in particular the growth of the industrial proletariat, the increase in the importance of the class which constitutes the determining factor in the final evolution of society." None of this is included in the commentary either. In short, the film's commentary has excised all political references in the speech, such as socialist, proletariat, even class.

The commentary adds three parts not in the speech: the cultural heritage, Paris, and the luxury industries. From the earliest days of the Popular Front, the party had actively recruited intellectuals and artists. The very choice of Renoir to direct *La Vie est à nous* bears witness to the flexibility of its cultural overtures. Aside from their prestige value, intellectuals also represented a section of the middle class, arguably the most sought-after group in the elections and the film. The reference to luxury industries is somewhat anomalous, even in this context, in that these products hardly benefit working people, middle class or working class. Precisely because they are beyond the reach of these classes, the dresses and furs are not shown. For this concluding section of the commentary, the filmmakers resort to a classical découpage, intercutting shots of the teacher with various shots of the students, listening attentively, leafing through books, playing pranks. As the instructor himself realizes, the children have no experience of these products. Hence, the sequence ends on the contrast between the conspicuous consumption of the rich and the modest, if not poor, lives of the children. The decision not to show these clothes signifies a contrast which the next sequence will develop.

An examination of the status of the shots in this sequence shows that what began as a straightforward series of documentary images has now been incorporated into a fictional situation of a schoolroom. The fiction dissolves the authority of the Voice of God. In addition, Jean Dasté plays the role of the teacher, just as he played the role of a teacher in Jean Vigo's *Zéro de Conduite,* a film the censors found too realistic at the time and banned outright, a decision volubly protested in the Left press. Although these opening images are revealed to be embedded in a fiction, they nonetheless retain at least some of their status as documentary. Furthermore, the lecture of the teacher is even more difficult to categorize, for it is at once a document—the speech of Thorez, already delivered—and the invention of the filmmakers. This sequence, then, confounds the boundaries between documentary and fiction, a central strategy followed throughout the film.

After the teacher dismisses the class, the children walk home through a deserted, rubble-strewn suburb, exchanging stories triggered by the lesson. As one marvels at the figures for the French production of silk, another tells about raising silk worms once, feeding them lettuce and mulberry leaves, after which they turn into butterflies. Obviously he has no idea of what silk clothing is, let alone its value. Another expresses his preference for chicken over rabbit, as a companion says that he never eats any. After they walk past some empty store fronts, one with a notice of bankruptcy attached, one of the children opens a dialogue that leads into the next sequence:

> "Yes, old man, France is a very wealthy country."
> "But at home, my mother often tells me we're poor. How come?"
> "Your father out of work?"
> "No, but we never seem to have much money at home."
> "Same with us."
> "Well, at home, there's as much money as you need. Only yesterday my mother said, 'Thirty sous left to finish the week.' Get that."
> "Thirty sous, you must have fun at home."
> "But those four billions? Whom do they belong to?"
> "To the rich."

Here, in a poor suburb, the children speak the absence indicated in the schoolroom sequence, the plight of the poor: hunger, reduction of wages and purchasing power, unemployment. The dialogue and setting articulate the contrast between the riches described by the teacher and the daily realities of the economy. Here, again, the fiction, spoken by uncomprehending children, comments on or reflects an immediate reality. Its status as fiction is not in question here, but the entire discussion dramatizes a lived reality.

As soon as the child answers casually that the wealth belongs to the rich, the film cuts to a medium shot of a woman who recites formally to the camera that "France does not belong to the French, she belongs to the 200 Families." This phrase, the "200 Families," had a specific meaning at the time and became a rallying cry for the Left. Its precise meaning designated the two hundred largest stockholders in the Bank of France, which was privately owned and run.[29] These stockholders voted for the bank's board of directors, who determined its policies.

Daladier was the first to invest the phrase with more insidious overtones in 1934: "Two hundred families are masters of the French economy and in fact of French politics. They are forces that a democratic state should not tolerate, that Richelieu would not have tolerated in the French kingdom. The influence of the 200 Families weighs on the fiscal system, on transportation, on credit. The 200 Families put their representatives in power. They interfere in public opinion, for they control the press."[30] Apparently, Daladier coined the term to designate a scapegoat for the breakdown of the Cartel des gauches in 1926, but its arrival on the political scene in 1934 served as a powerful propaganda weapon seized upon and exploited by the Left. Its currency peaked at the very beginning of 1936 when two Leftist publications, *Le Crapouillot* and *La Flèche*, brought out special issues detailing the conspiracy. Explicit proof of nefarious machinations hidden in the web of interlocking directorships is notoriously difficult to establish, but even an historian who finds the "myth" of conspiracy "absurd" admits at the end of his study that "the myth makers draw attention to an indisputable fact. A financial and industrial oligarchy of a sort with considerable political influence has existed."[31] Whatever its real import, the Left used the phrase to name the traitorous villains in France bleeding it of its riches (and in more literal terms, capital flight was an incessant problem during the 1930s in France and was illustrated in a political film made by Germaine Dulac several months later: see below pp. 214–17).

The woman proposes the term in exactly this sense in response to the bewilderment of the children, but she addresses the spectator directly. A chorus, seen outside atop a hill, reinforces this direct address in an openly didactic appeal to the spectator: "France does not belong to the French, she belongs to those who plunder her. Ladies and Gentlemen, come with us, all of you, young and old, please, follow us. We are going to show you who your enemies are. You are going to see the enemies of your country at work. Comrades, look." The chorus espouses the position of the film on the causes of the economic crisis. In answering the question of responsibility posed spontaneously by the children—Whom do they belong to?—the chorus interrupts the flow of the fiction and guides the reading of the return to fiction. Placed outside both the fiction and the documentary, the chorus comments on the action. Even if its observations are not extensive, it introduces yet another element not usually found in films, "spectacles" or documentaries, though its function in classical theater, the same function as in the film, is well known. Although the performance of the chorus in *La Vie est à nous*, not enclosed within the narrative, may be unique in the films of the period,[32] choruses were an integral part of the Left culture of the Popular Front. Various choruses took part regularly in Leftist soirées during the period, singing, of course, but also mounting spoken choruses relating to political events. They often shared the stage with groups like the Groupe Octobre and Regards.

During the speech of the chorus, the camera cuts to a caricature of the 200 Families, signed by Jean Effel, a well-known political cari-

Jean Effel's design for the cover of the "Album of the 200 Families" (*La Vie est à nous*)

caturist whose work appeared often in Left publications. He has rendered a representative group from the 200 Families sitting for a formal portrait, a veritable cross-section of reaction: a bemedalled Army officer, a fat capitalist with cigar, an old veteran wearing his medal, a woman with a French flag stuck in her hat, a dog with a dogbone medal, a priest and a bourgeois matron bearing a cross. The various themes knotted together here are militarism and nationalism, but the cross also implicates the church in this camarilla, the only such religious reference in the film.

Traditionally the church, in alliance with conservative forces, had considerable political influence in defending French morality from the assaults of the atheistic Left, led by the archfiend Communists. This mild attack on the church in *La Vie est à nous*, then, would not be surprising, were it not for the astonishing change in the party attitude toward the church. In its efforts to build support for the Popular Front, the party had progressively and consistently reached out to the Socialists, the Radicals, and their middle-class constituents. The title for Thorez's speech of January 1936, "L'Union de la Nation Française," conveyed perfectly the spirit of this policy. But even the detractors of the PCF during this phase were unprepared for the famous "extended hand" offered by Thorez in his radio speech of April 17:

"We extend our hand to you, Catholics, workers, employees, artisans, peasants, we who are laic, because you (tu) are our brother, and you are concerned with the same cares as we."[33]

The almost total effacement of attacks on the church in all likelihood reflects this change and contrasts radically with the anticlericalism of *Le Crime de Monsieur Lange,* which was released only months earlier during Christmas. Prévert and Renoir shared an antipathy to the church, with its strictures on moral probity, and mocked its hypocrisy in the person of Batala in the film. Batala runs a printing firm with a charming but absolute lack of scruples, stealing the royalties from authors and studding their writing with references to the virtues of commercial products sold by his advertisers/investors. He is the sort of man who sends his secretary off to seduce an impatient creditor and himself seduces an innocent laundress who delivers his change of linen. Finally forced to flee the creditors, Batala survives a train accident and dons the clothes of a priest, but not his character. His first act as a priest is to exploit his new attire to swindle a newsdealer. Returning to his business, now run successfully as a cooperative by the workers, he blithely reclaims ownership, carrying off this latest effrontery in his priestly garb, waving his omnipresent cigarette in blasphemous arabesques all the while. Monsieur Lange/l'ange, head of the cooperative, acting to protect its interests, shoots Batala, the priest, and is acquitted of wrongdoing by a workers' jury, thus allowing him to flee across the border to escape French law. This caustic and irreverent treatment of the clergy drew little notice in the press and apparently had no trouble with the censor. Perhaps it was felt at the time that Batala's impersonation of a priest was final proof of his depravity and that his punishment fit the crime.[34]

La Vie est à nous bears none of the traces of this irreverence, even if it does not go so far as to extend its hand to the church. One critic has indicted the film, and Renoir, for this political expurgation and suggested that this regimentation to party discipline may have had something to do with Prévert's nonparticipation in the *La Vie est à nous* project.[35] The contrast between the films is certainly evident and plausibly attributable to the evolving position of the party. The wisdom of this evolution is a political question, however.

Effel's design has a caption of "Album des 200 Familles" below, and the cover turns on to a series of pages in a photo album to show Guy and François Wendel; Schneider, Marchand de canons; Laurent, forty-one seats of administrators; Renault, de Billancourt; Un des Neuflize; André Lebon; Louis Marlio. Yet another type of document,

Standing before a sign reading "Buy French," an industrialist (Jacques B. Brunius) lectures executives on the need for cutting back production and lowering wages (*La Vie est à nous*)

the family photo album, is used here to literalize the idea of family, to underline the family connections of this network of the powerful.

The last page, with the photo of Louis Marlio, turns like the others, unveiling a long shot of a corporate boardroom where the director is speaking to the board members. The transition of the turning page and the setting incorporate this scene into the Album of 200 Families, now a fictional representation of one of their inner sanctums, with a poster on the wall: "Buy French." The director, played by Brunius with grave resignation, reviews the situation of the economic crisis. With the shrinkage of the market, production cutbacks must be made. One of their companies has had to destroy some of its equipment.

As the director reviews the experiences of the crisis in other countries, the "Buy French" sign becomes a projection screen, showing first an industrial girder toppled on its side. The camera then tracks in on the screen within the screen to fill the frame with two shots of workers, one with a sledgehammer as if effectively dismantling the industrial edifice. The commentary observes that this destruction of material has brought excellent results and has even necessitated the dumping of food stuffs, such as milk in the United States, wheat elsewhere, and coffee thrown into the sea. Newsreel images are used to illustrate this lecture, including one with Dutch and French subtitles ("wheat is burned"). The director returns to the screen to remind his listeners that the company has had to take harsh measures, laying off many workers and forcing the retirement of devoted employees: "It is essential that our personnel understand and adapt to the circumstances. They must accept the inevitability of such sacrifices. We have foreseen some new reductions in this sector. . . ."

Abruptly, the scene shifts to a spacious interior of a casino, where the director is seated, in evening clothes, at the gambling table. Two women walk by and stand in the doorway long enough for one of them to say, "But, my dear, I buy only American cars. I hate French cars." As they pass offscreen, two men arrive, and one asks the other, "Social insurance, then, what does social insurance mean?" The director then proceeds to lose two million in his Banquo game and calmly gets up to leave, totally unconcerned with the sum involved.

Just as abruptly as the scene opened, it shifts back to the boardroom, where the director is finishing his speech: "New procedures, Gentlemen, urgent ones, will lead to a new temporary reduction of personnel and to a readjustment of wages."

In this sequence the short episode of the casino has been constructed to contradict the rationale shifting the hardships of the crisis onto the workers—the rationale of deflation, cutting back on expenditures by the government and industry, laying off workers, driving up unemployment, reducing wages and prices, balancing the budget. Government and industry had pursued this policy consistently since the beginning of the crisis in France. Worker discontent with these measures was only aggravated by the imposition of the so-called decree laws in 1935, a prerogative of the head of the government when the legislature is not in session. In the film, as soon as the director calls for new sacrifices, the casino sequence mocks the reality of these sacrifices, for the rich impose no sacrifices on themselves.

The gambling metaphor is particularly apt, for it shows not only that the wealth of the rich has not been affected but also that the industrial leaders are content to leave the solution of the country's problems to chance, a profoundly indifferent and irresponsible attitude which exposes the hypocrisy of their grave calls for sacrifices. Nor is the man's ignorance of social insurance a dramatic exaggeration of this irresponsibility, for reactionary representatives had proposed reductions in social insurance benefits in the legislature.[36] Even though these measures were not passed, they reflect a real callousness of industry to the deepening misery of the workers. Finally, the remark about buying American cars, juxtaposed to the call to "Buy French" in the boardroom, unmasks the solemn appeals to patriotism, so often sounded by the Right, as an ideological tactic camouflaging a serious destabilizing flight of capital.

The use of the newsreel footage also engages the issue of film as an ideological practice. In the opening sequence of the film, the appearance of the teacher, set in the fiction of the schoolroom, suddenly transforms the status of the documentary images. They no longer rest as incontestable facts attached to a rhetoric of objectivity. Of course the spectator is never obliged to accept the documentary's claim to objectivity, but one of the enduring distinctions from fiction associated with the documentary is that there is some extra-film reality against which the claims of the documentary can be tested.[37] By continually blurring such distinctions, *La Vie est à nous* tries to expose the ideological functioning of this objectivity, though more specifically as it concerns newsreels. During the director's speech in the boardroom, he enlists the unquestionably newsreel images to support his arguments for the necessity of deflationary measures. As discussed above, the Left repeatedly attacked the bias of the newsreels, all controlled by large commercial firms, for supporting the foreign policy of Laval, for its respectful coverage of Mussolini and Hitler, and for ignoring the mass demonstrations by the Left so crucial to the image of unity in the Popular Front. The Left realized, then, that newsreel images were not innocent. At all times one had to interrogate the uses and interests that these images served. This is not a question of simply producing Left newsreels to contest the monopoly and distortion of images by the Right. It was important to combat the conception of the newsreel image's supposed affinity with truth, its authority as fact. When the casino sequence rejects the argument of the director, it also rejects the discourse of the newsreels, which have been incorporated as objective evidence in the rhetoric of the necessity of worker "sacrifices." Logically, this position excludes all authority of newsreel images, even if used in Left newsreels.

Already in the film, there have been three speeches, with each speaker identified first in a close shot. Obviously, the filmmakers were sensitive to the status of cinematic discourse. First, a schoolteacher speaks to children, an audience particularly susceptible to ideological deformations, as they are unequipped with experience and knowledge to discover a reality, and their dialogue after the lesson manifests this incomprehension. Like so many other domains at the time, the classroom was politically contested territory. The Right saw the teaching ranks infested with perfidious Communists: "We must give the children a national education. Certainly this does not mean discrediting some excellent teachers, but freeing them from the influence of 80,000 Communist teachers who, in the system of committees, control advancement and the distribution of favors. . . . The syndicate of schoolteachers must be dissolved, the consulting committees eliminated, the teachers' colleges reformed." [38] In the film, the fictional teacher is not meant to deny the accuracy of the images but only to pose the first term of the question, completed by the sequence with the children: If France is a wealthy country, how can these children be so poor? The film accepts that these images are open to question, ultimately accepting their reality at the very end of the film.

The woman who answers the question of the children and introduces the chorus advises the audience directly to take a critical stance by announcing what is to follow and openly controlling the interpretation of the sequence, even though the sequence and interpretation need no explication. On one level, the chorus is redundant. But at the structural level of the film, its constant oscillation between fiction and document, the chorus provides one more encouragement to view the screen—to view cinema—critically, just as the classical theatrical chorus abstracts the lessons from the fiction.

By the time the voice of industry speaks, the spectator has been warned against a passive submission to the sounds and images on the screen. Hence, the director's recourse to newsreel images, actually projected on a screen behind him, should be viewed critically as a cinematic device employed for political purposes—in this instance, the need to burden workers with additional economic hardship as an unfortunate consequence of the economic crisis afflicting the country.

Following the director's call for reduction of wages and after the casino sequence, the other members of the board take up the chant for "Reductions. Reductions. . . ." The chant dissolves to a crowd of workers demanding "Du travail et du pain. Du travail et du pain," and the crowd is seen from above. Slowly the camera descends behind the gate of a factory, succinctly indicating that these workers have been denied employment by the factory. This slogan of "work and bread" was a common one during rallies at the time, and its call for these most basic necessities underlines the severity of the crisis.

Before this demand ends, the film cuts to a country setting with a woman looking toward the camera; she then runs offscreen as the demand on the sound track fades out. In the next shot another woman is merrily firing a type of Gatling gun. A long shot still in the country follows: the woman from the first shot runs into the frame to place a worker's cap on a flat cutout of a human figure, which turns

Gentry at target practice, firing at a maquette of a worker, which they call a *salopard*, or "bastard" (*La Vie est à nous*)

The following shot, the gentry now transformed into uniformed French fascists (*La Vie est à nous*)

De nombreux journaux ont déjà reproduit cette photographie particulièrement édifiante sur l'activité des bandes fascistes en France. Ceux-ci, sont les francistes de M. Buccard, s'exerçant au pistolet au camp de Breuil en Seine-et-Oise. Mais ce qui n'a pas encore été révélé au public, c'est que l'un des personnages qui s'entraînent ainsi à l'assassinat des ouvriers, c'est M. ITALO SUGLIOTTI, directeur de la « NOVA ITALIA », organe officiel du Fascio italien de Paris. On le reconnaît au dernier rang debout ; il porte une chemise noire et est tête nue, alors que les autres francistes sont en chemise bleue (claire) et portent le béret. Nos lecteurs tireront facilement les conclusions qui s'imposent : Liaison du fascisme français avec ses modèles italien et allemand, liaison financière sans doute ; enfin preuve éclatante de la complicité des pouvoirs publics qui tolèrent la participation des fascistes étrangers aux exercices de guerre civile des fascistes français.

"Numerous papers have already printed this particularly instructive photograph of the fascist gangs in France. . . . Our readers will easily draw the obvious conclusions: the ties of French fascism with the Italian and German models, a financial tie without doubt: final striking proof of the complicity of the public powers which tolerate the participation of foreign fascists in the civil war exercises of French fascists" (*Regards*, October 5, 1934)

out to be a target. A group of men and women dressed in hunting outfits, readily identifiable as hauts bourgeois, take aim and fire on this human target after the woman runs out of range. A waiter holding a tray offers the group drinks as they practice. The next shot shows several of the group, kneeling and standing, firing offscreen left. A shot of identical composition immediately replaces this shot, but now the group is wearing military-style uniforms, which an intertitle explains: "The French Fascists exercise." After a cut back to the same group, another intertitle: "We have already seen them at work." Then a dark shot, taken at night and hard to see, with a tram and people moving in and out of the shot. Another intertitle: "6 February 1934." Then a series of shots of apparent street battles taken that night. Thus, the demands of the workers in the film are answered by the bourgeois amusing themselves with some target practice, firing on a worker. Across a cut the bourgeois are transformed into French fascists, who are then placed historically by the intertitle as the instigators of the events of February 6, 1934, shown in newsreel footage from that seminal date.

The newsreel footage is of extremely poor quality. A study of the film coverage of this event indicates that the censor intervened immediately to prevent any screenings of this footage, even though it appears that it was well covered by newsreel crews.[39] By the time *La Vie est à nous* was made, good footage of this night was probably difficult to locate, if it even still existed. Or the filmmakers may have intentionally taken only footage that had passed the censor in 1934 to avoid any problems of their own with the censor. What is curious is that the murkiness of the footage corresponds to the difficulty of establishing the meaning of those events. The official inquiry into the events gathered many of the relevant facts, but the motivations and real objectives proved more difficult to establish.

Demonstrations by the various Fascist leagues had taken place throughout January 1934. Their immediate cause was the Stavisky scandal and the charges implicating members of the government in its cover-up. Alexandre Stavisky, with the aid and/or knowledge of several government figures, had swindled the government out of tens of millions of francs. After discovery of the fraud, Stavisky disappeared and was found dead several weeks later, officially a death by suicide, but accusations were rife that political figures had conspired to have him murdered.[40] The leagues took to the streets with cries of "Down with the thieves" and "Down with Chautemps," the prime minister. On January 28, the Chautemps government resigned. Demonstrations continued.

The Left was dismayed at the passivity shown by the guardians of order in the face of activities of the leagues. They accused the Paris Prefect of Police, Jean Chiappe, of partiality and sympathy in granting permits to the leagues for their demonstrations and refusing the same to requests by the Left. They demanded his dismissal, which the new premier, Daladier, finally asked for. Chiappe resisted, though the interpretation of his response is still unclear. Daladier claimed that Chiappe said he would be in the streets, presumably with the leagues, if he were forced to resign. Chiappe asserted that he had said the dismissal would throw him into the street without a penny, a reference to his financial rectitude as prefect. Thus, some writers have seen the demonstration of February 6 as a call for returning Chiappe to his post, but the importance of February 6 extends far beyond the immediate fate of the reactionary Chiappe.[41]

"The night of the 4th [February 4, 1934] . . . or the great evening of [Paris Prefect of Police] Chiappe" (*Regards*, February 9, 1934)

A more serious and troubling question is the antiparliamentarism of the leagues.[42] Ministries had come and gone with great frequency in the preceding years, with three in 1933 alone, and the fall of the government certainly appeared to be the objective of the January activities of the leagues. Without doubt they wanted to see the installation of a strong right-wing government which would take any necessary steps to stabilize the political and economic situation, but it is far from clear that their appreciation of the successes of Mussolini and Hitler went so far as wishing to reproduce those models in France. Instead, the leagues benefited from a vagueness in their programs, most noticeable in the experience of the most important organization, the Croix-de-Feu, led by Colonel de la Rocque.

The Croix-de-Feu was an organization of veterans from the First World War. It had begun in 1927, but only after de la Rocque took over its leadership in 1931 did it grow into a significant force, with some 700,000 members at its height. According to one of his followers, Colonel François Casimir de la Rocque "did not speak well, wrote badly, but he inspired confidence and his troops believed in him."[43] A subsidiary group, the Volontaires Nationaux, was formed to accommodate members who were not old enough to have served in the war. The Volontaires Nationaux, less imbued with the blind obedience and discipline to de la Rocque observed by the older veterans, tried to pressure de la Rocque into defining a concrete program. When de la Rocque could evade these pressures no longer, he published a small volume, which the Volontaires Nationaux found full only of empty phrases. When they approached him to insist on the urgency of drafting a program, he reportedly replied, "You absolutely want a program. Well, then, propose one to me. I'll see."[44] Thus, in the most important of the leagues, one does not find a clear antiparliamentarism (other leagues did support that path as the only solution, though without agreement on the form of its replacement).

An additional complication in understanding the evening of February 6, not always remarked on, was the presence of the Communists. The "third period" policy still reigned in the PCF, and during the stormy session of Parliament in the evening of February 6, the Communist deputies chanted "The Soviets! The Soviets!" The secretariat of the Central Committee issued a directive the same day: "All the party meetings [closed to nonmembers of the party] of sections, cells, fractions, etc. planned for the evening are cancelled. The place of all Communists is at the head of the masses in the battle, following the line fixed by the party."[45] André Marty, in *L'Humanité* of February 6, sets out this line more concretely:

Colonel François Casimir de la Rocque, leader of the fascist Croix-de-feu (*La Vie est à nous*)

The Volontaires Nationaux, the youth organization of the Croix-de-feu (*La Vie est à nous*)

One cannot struggle against the fascist bands without struggling at the same time:
—against the government accused of having let them develop, even of having aided them.
—against social-democracy.
One cannot struggle against the fascization of the regime without at the same time denouncing the attitude of the Socialist party for supporting fully the government which develops it.[46]

Despite these inflammatory texts of the PCF, there is no reason whatsoever to suspect that the PCF envisioned a seizure of power. The same disclaimer cannot be made for all the representatives of the Right, but there is no definitive evidence that the leagues planned a coup d'état, and certainly not in concert. In any event, the Left described the events of February 6, which left some twenty dead and 500 wounded, as a fascist attempt to take power.

The Left immediately decided to stage a counter demonstration as a public riposte to this fascist threat. However, the divided Left could not so easily agree on the response. The Communists adhered to their violent opposition to the leaders of the Socialist party, for they still sought to win over the Socialist masses from their reformist leadership. The Communists proposed a demonstration for February 9, but the CGT, with the agreement of the Socialist party, decided on a general strike for February 12. Ignoring the government interdiction, the PCF demonstration took place on February 9. Violent confrontations left sixteen police wounded and fifty civilian casualties. Four of the wounded died the following day.

La Vie est à nous follows the historical account of February 6 as Thorez related it in his speech at Villeurbanne—an account which omits any mention of the fact that the Communists were also on the streets on February 6. Instead, the film presents an elaborate argument to identify the leagues with Hitler and Mussolini. After the footage of the night of February 6, an intertitle precedes several shots of "Dawn of February 7." In one of the shots, de la Rocque, wearing his military medals, speaks with several colleagues. The next shot is a low angle of fascists marching, the Arc de Triomphe looming above in the background. Then a high-angle shot of the Croix-de-Feu marching, de la Rocque several paces to the side, marching in a ludicrous, mincing stutter step to the tune on the sound track: "Quand un vicomte rencontre un autre vicomte."[47] (It seems that Brunius doctored this shot to caricature de la Rocque.[48]) An intertitle introduces the foreign association: "The French Hitlerians march in military fashion." The trick shot of de la Rocque then alternates with other

Hitler speaking, his words replaced on the sound track by a dog barking (*La Vie est à nous*)

shots of the Croix-de-Feu marching, including one with uniformed youth carrying the banner of the "Sons and daughters of the Croix-de-Feu." After the fourth trick shot, the direction of the marchers changes, so that the composition and direction of movement will match perfectly the succeeding shot of Nazi soldiers passing in crisp military formation, a swastika superimposed over the soldiers. Then Hitler appears at a podium, about to address a crowd. As he speaks and gesticulates, the sound track, well synchronized to Hitler's lip movements, substitutes a dog's barking for Hitler's words. In the next shot the crowd roars its approval; then there is a shot of soldiers advancing in battle, presumably during World War I (to judge from the uniforms), with a military insignia superimposed.

To summarize this part of the sequence, de la Rocque surveys the still-smoldering damage the morning after February 6 and appears in command of his followers, as an intertitle refers to them as French Hitlerians. After additional shots of the Croix-de-Feu, the French Fascists are replaced on the screen by Nazi soldiers. A crowd shouts its approval of Hitler's barking, and the last shot shows the soldiers at war.

Thus the film—following a line taken by the Popular Front, not exclusively by the PCF—links the French Fascists in paramilitary uniforms with Nazi soldiers in full battle gear. They follow, without comprehending, the gibberish of their leader directing them into a war. The identification with Germany is important: throughout the period the PCF waged a vigorous campaign to recapture the traditional symbols of French patriotism, which meant wresting them from the grip of the Right. As the PCF sought to shed its own image of marching to the step of Stalin's orders, it launched a similar accusation against the Right's claim to be the sole guardian of French traditions. In reality, French fascism developed as an indigenous phenomenon. If some Frenchmen did seek an authoritarian solution for France's problems and if some saw Hitler as a model, on the whole the Right was not sympathetic to Hitler.

However, the Right did not see clearly and protest against the real potential for war that Hitler represented. The folly of appeasement had a long way to go before the debacle of Munich, but once the PCF abandoned the "third period" position and identified fascism as the primary enemy, it was the most consistant among the currents of the Popular Front in warning against Hitler. Neither the Radicals nor the Socialists were as convinced of the inevitable danger of Hitler. The contention in *La Vie est à nous* that Hitler meant war should not be taken as one more sign of its Frontist orientation but as a polemical point conforming to the analysis of the PCF, though of course widely shared within the Popular Front and certain to be approved by a wide spectrum of the electorate. Although this sequence does not contribute a novel political analysis, it does advance an argument which was not accepted as self-evident at the time. Its ultimate correctness, whatever the reasons, should not be allowed to obscure this absence of consensus.

Again, as earlier in the film, this sequence uses newsreel images but in this case bends them to its own Left interpretation. The trick shot of de la Rocque is used four times, suggesting that the filmmakers were particularly pleased with the idea but also indicating the care given the film. As critics remarked at the time the film was made, certain montage sequences exhibited lessons taken from the Soviet filmmakers. The shot juxtapositions impose readings not legible in the individual shots, such as Hitler ordering World War I soldiers into battle.

The trick shot of de la Rocque shows that the filmmakers experimented not only with montage but also with individual shots. This shot demonstrates perhaps better than any other shot in the film their radical refusal to see images—even, or perhaps particularly, newsreel images—as possessing an inviolable integrity. If all images served some point of view or, alternatively, if no image was innocent and incontrovertibly true, the most dangerous images were those of newsreels and documentaries, for their images were preferred and often accepted as true. Tampering with the image, through superimpositions and trick footage, breaks this circuit of reception and ideally elicits reflection on the implicit claims of these images to objectivity.[49]

Another set of images in the sequence can be considered similarly: the shot of the smartly dressed bourgeois taking target practice matched closely with the next shot of black-shirted Fascists engaged in the same activity. The second shot is modeled exactly on a photograph of French Fascists that appeared in several Left publications and must have gained some notoriety, for it was reproduced also in the PCF annual, *Almanach Ouvrier Paysan*.[50] This is the last shot before the newsreel shots begin. With no knowledge of the photograph, one understands that these bourgeois firing on the target of a salopard are the same paramilitary Fascists who seek to overthrow the Republic.

When one realizes that both fictional shots are based on a news photo, it becomes clear that there is another intentional interpenetration of fiction and documentary. The second shot functions as a bridge between the fictional country estate and the newsreel coverage of February 6. The reproduction of a documentary photograph insists on the incorporation of a certain extra-film reality into the fiction. This assertive slippage between documentary and fiction seeps retrospectively into the country shots, changing their status from fiction pure and simple to a fiction revealed as disguise for a fascism infecting the wealthy French bourgeoisie. The film's constant "work" on the fiction/documentary oppositions reflects a conscious rejection of either category as a controlling one for the film.

The same cinematic strategies are employed as the sequence continues with Mussolini. After the shot of the soldiers sent into action by Hitler, Mussolini prepares to speak. An air raid siren on the sound track prefaces his remarks, followed by bombs exploding as he opens his mouth. He inspects his troops, the Coliseum visible in the background of one shot. To the sounds of machine gun fire, Mussolini, on horseback, begins to turn his head. Cut to the charred remains of a lone soldier in a trench. Return to Mussolini as he completes his turn. A pan of crosses in a cemetery. Mussolini again at a speaker's stand. A warship's heavy guns rise, fire in a second shot, and the explosions follow. A single plane drops its bombs, then many planes release theirs. Tanks, cavalry, and infantry engage in ground combat, with strict alternation of screen directions. The sounds of warfare punctuate these shots and fade out as the screen dissolves to a trench littered

Mussolini "speaking" the sounds of war (*La Vie est à nous*)

with bones. Superimpositions of war insignia, Italian and German, fade in and out, the last one of a skull that rises quickly from the head of a dead soldier to fill the screen before a fade to black. An insignia with a skull in the middle is superimposed over an armband and disappears as the armband moves away from the camera, and several longer shots of marchers take the action back to France, where people on balconies salute the fascists filing by on the street below.

The sequence obviously portrays Mussolini as far more war-thirsty than Hitler. Hitler's barking leads to war, but Mussolini's speech is the literal sound of war—specifically the war in Ethiopia, which still raged during the production of the film. On October 3, 1935, Mussolini had invaded Ethiopia with 200,000 troops with modern arms. The sequence emphasizes the presence of these arms with a virtual inventory of a modern army: navy, air force, tanks, cavalry, infantry, artillery, as well as the decaying victims of poison gas.

The Left was outraged at Laval's handling of the situation. The secret discussions between the British foreign minister, Samuel Hoare, and Laval early in December became known; the news that they had agreed on a plan to deliver two-thirds of Ethiopia to Mussolini caused a sensation. Hoare resigned under pressure, for England had strategic interests in the Middle East that they were not eager to have threatened by an Italian presence in Ethiopia. Laval remained in office, but his inept policy alienated England, France's closest ally, and Italy, which Laval had hoped to win over as an ally against Hitler. The failure of Laval's policy only tightened the unity of the Popular Front: "The Italy-Ethiopia conflict and the reactions that it drew in public opinion, in showing the danger that fascism posed to peace, only reinforced the current which led all the forces of the Left to the Popular Front. Henceforth, misunderstanding was no longer possible. Not only did M. Laval appear abroad, in the eyes of opinion, as a partisan of the dictatorships to the detriment of the Franco-British alliance, but even internally as the friend and secret protector of the Croix-de-Feu."[51]

The return to the French fascists closes the bracket of domestic fascism that opened the sequence, cementing the bond in the film between the German and Italian fascists and the French leagues. A worker pushes through the crowd looking on at the fascist spectacle to ask, "Nothing to be done?" verbalizing a sentiment felt by at least part of the crowd. As he answers, "Yes, there is the Communist party," there is a shot of the facade of the PCF headquarters, decorated with a hammer and sickle and the injunction "Proletarians of all countries, unite." A headline from L'Humanité of February 9 calls for a demonstration for "Front Unique" that evening. Six *still* photos then are used to represent the violent encounters between the demonstrators that night.

While it is probably impossible to know at this point whether footage of this event was available to the filmmakers, the absence of footage, the only example in the film, testifies to both the importance of this event to the PCF and its relatively limited public support—so limited that it may not have been covered at all by news cameras. In his Villeurebanne speech, Thorez did not temper his partisanship in recalling the date:

> Our party, *alone*, knew how to summon people to the struggle. *Alone*, addressing itself to the Communist workers and their Socialist brothers, it has called them to the unforgettable demonstration of February 9. Ten proletarians fell at the Place de la République. Ten martyrs of the worker and antifascist cause, who have written with their blood on the pavement of Paris; *No, fascism will not succeed in France.*
>
> The demonstration of February 9 was, for all workers, for all antifascists, a signal and an example. Three days later, four million workers stopped work.[52]

At all costs, then, even without any film footage, the film had to present February 9 as the *first* response to the fascist threat. Without the support of the Socialist party or the CGT, the number of participants and likelihood of success were inevitably reduced. The film, like Thorez and the PCF, acknowledges the numerical superiority of the February 12 demonstration, which the PCF hesitated in supporting, but uses the historical anteriority of February 9 as the basis of the PCF's claim to have been the generative and animating force behind the birth and growth of the Popular Front. Despite the hesitations and doctrinal modifications, such a claim was not undeserved.

The film recounts this growth more or less chronologically, always with ample footage. A *L'Humanité* headline announces the large February 12 rally, the day of a general strike called by the CGT; another headline of "Six Workers Killed in Six Days" precedes several shots of a funeral cortège organized by the Communists to honor those dead, with Thorez and (*L'Humanité* editor) Marcel Cachin side by side in one shot. An intertitle, "Unity of action. Front Populaire," serves to cover the year and a half's momentum toward unity, for the next images are of the July 14, 1935, rally—that of the Rassemblement Populaire, in which Communists, Socialists, and Radicals participated together for the first time. The first shot displays the monument at the Bastille festooned with the simple garland, "1789–1935." The "Marseillaise" begins on the sound track as this shot appears on the screen.

One of the battles waged by the Popular Front was for the reclamation of the symbols of French patriotism from the ideological arsenal of the Right. In his radio speech before the election, Thorez refers to this reconquest when he says, "We have reconciled the tricolor of our ancestors with the red flag of our hopes."[53] Though not a Communist, Albert Bayet, one of the founders of the League of Human Rights, expressed this sentiment more expansively and evocatively but in a way which highlights the significance of these symbols for the PCF: "We have suffered three thefts: we have lost Joan of Arc, the tricolor, the unknown soldier. But in the ardent awakening of the Popular Front, the great memories have come back. July 14, 1935, the tricolor has flown above the immense rassemblement of republicans. Paris, the real Paris, has felt the breath of '89. So, let us not despair. As it has retaken the flag of liberty, the people will retake Joan of Arc. Then it will proceed, in countless numbers, to proclaim at the Tomb of the Unknown Soldier its unshakeable desire for peace. And that day the Republic will finally be the Republic."[54]

The film proceeds directly to this battlefield with an intertitle: "The Fascists have exploited the Unknown Soldier. They wanted to make use of the veterans." Then de la Rocque, standing solemnly before the flame at the Tomb, steps forward to pay hommage with a ritual sword.

The film responds first with an intertitle "But November 11, 1935 . . ." and then with a *L'Humanité* headline: "The Unknown Soldier has refound his comrades." On that date, veterans demonstrated at the Tomb of the Unknown Soldier to assert their claims, but this time the veterans represented the Left, no doubt led by the Communist-directed Republican Association of Veterans (Association Républicaine des Anciens Combattants, ARAC). Crippled veterans lead this procession, propelling themselves in a wide variety of wheeled vehicles. The Arc de Triomphe dominates the last two shots, as if the French people have retaken possession of it visually after its earlier sullying by de la Rocque.

After the demonstration, a title awards credit to the PCF for beating back fascism:

> The Communist Party has forced back Fascism. To ward off this threat for ever, to abolish poverty and war, let us follow the example of the workers of
> Title: The USSR.

Again the facade of the PCF headquarters is shown, probably at a later date, for it is now covered with all the major slogans to be used by the PCF in the electoral campaign: Bread, Peace, Liberty; For a France Free, Strong, Happy; The Rich Must Pay; Long Live the Union of the French Nation Against the 200 Families Who Plunder It. The PCF, in other words, openly proposes following the inspirational example of the Soviet Union, even if it makes no allusion to its relative allegiance to or independence of the CPSU and the Comintern. The shots of Communist political figures do trace such an affiliation, however: Lenin, Stalin, Dimitrov, Marty. Dimitrov was head of the Comintern at the time and delivered the major address approving the line of the Popular Fronts at the VIIth Congress in 1935. Marty was the former French representative to the Comintern and a member of its executive committee until the dissolution of the Comintern in 1943.

Each of these figures is identified by an intertitle, a device which is used freely in the film and which could be seen as a vestige of the silent film and a consequence of the limited resources at the disposal of the filmmakers. Such an explanation, however, is not consistent with the considerable cinematic sophistication evidenced in the film. The images have been chosen and edited with great care, with many optical superimpositions used for rhetorical emphasis. The sound track arrays an impressive variety of sounds: speech; outdoor dialogue; songs and crowd noises recorded at demonstrations; sound effects of pistols, machine guns, airplanes, bombs falling, explosions,

L'Humanité facade during the April-May 1936 election campaign: VIVE LE FRONT POPULAIRE. BREAD. PEACE. LIBERTY. FOR A FRANCE FREE STRONG AND HAPPY. VOTE COMMUNISTE. THE RICH MUST PAY (*La Vie est à nous*)

a dog barking. Sound and image combine in voice-over, synchronous direct address, postsynchronized sound effects, and asynchronous counterpoint of sound and image. Given all this counter-evidence to a poverty of means, or a lack of technical facility, the titles appear to be a conscious choice to exclude voice-over. The only voice-over in the film occurs with the first images. The sudden cut to the teacher reveals the source of the discourse, and the subsequent long shot of the classroom widens the space of the speech, now implicated in a fiction. Having begun with the standard Voice-of-God narration of documentary, the film progressively dismantles its authority, first by personalizing it in the dramatic actor Dasté then by situating him visually in a fictional scene. Voice-overs could have replaced all of the titles in *La Vie est à nous*. The filmmakers rejected that option, refusing a cinematic strategy no doubt associated for the Left with the distortions of newsreels.

The next section of the film is composed of four fictional episodes: an attack on a *L'Humanité* vendor by fascist thugs, a factory protest, a farm foreclosure and auction, and a saga of an unemployed engineer. After the shots of André Marty, an intertitle announces Marcel Cachin, director of *L'Humanité* and one of the founders of the PCF. Instead of cutting to a shot of Cachin, as it did with the other figures, the film cuts to several shots of vendors on the street selling *L'Humanité*. Then Cachin, seated at his desk presumably in the offices of *L'Humanité* (under a bust of Marx), reads aloud the latest circulation figures of *L'Humanité-Dimanche: 360,000.* The PCF placed great emphasis on the dissemination of its publications, of which *L'Humanité* was its pride—"the major paper of the Popular Front, one of the best weapons of the working class and our Communist party."[55] After Cachin nods his approval of the figures, other vendors distribute their papers to passers-by in an open-air marketplace in Montreuil, a worker suburb which was part of the "red belt" encircling Paris. Three black-shirted Fascists—members of the Bucard gang, the "fachos" admirers of Mussolini—see and hear a vendor and run up to seize his papers and knock him to the ground. In several one-shots workers nearby see the struggle and rush to chase off the Fascists, a demonstration of the sympathy of working people for the PCF and their antifascist solidarity. The sequence is not particularly noteworthy, but it does place the PCF among the people, the vendors being indistinguishable from the workers who come to their aid. Ever since the split into the PCF and the Socialist party at the Congress of Tours in 1920, both parties had claimed to speak for the proletariat. With the serious decline of membership in the PCF during the "third period," plummeting to less than 30,000 in 1933, the credibility of this claim by the PCF was seriously compromised. With the formation of the Popular Front, membership figures rocketed, approaching (and later surpassing) those of the Socialist party. But whereas attacks on the Socialists as "social fascists" and collaborators with the bourgeois enemy were patent distortions, the Socialist party had acquired an image more recognizably bourgeois than the PCF, at least in its leadership. Blum, a man of letters and cultivated taste, was unmistakably bourgeois. Even the Revolutionary Left tendency of the Socialist party, led by Marceau Pivert, lacked authentic identification with the proletariat, according to Guérin, who, as a member of the Revolutionary Left, had great esteem for Pivert: "Among the pivertists . . . I suffered from their nonworker origin, from the relative distance which separated them from the real proletariat and its problems."[56] The PCF tried to exploit this "distance," which is implicit in the sequence, for overt attacks on the Socialist party were out of the question.

The sequence ends with a shot following the *L'Humanité* sound truck to the *L'Humanité* offices. Inside, Cachin reads the mail that has just arrived, starting with a letter from a metalworker, dated March 27, 1936 (less than two weeks before the first screening of the film). After a shot of the opening lines of the letter, in which the worker mentions a problem with a "chrono" (a time and motion expert), the scene shifts to a factory interior, where a woman is working at a machine. A man approaches her and proposes a date that evening. When she rebuffs him somewhat rudely, he takes out a stopwatch to time her performance and warns her that she is not working quickly enough. The chrono then passes to an older worker (Gustave), times his work, and asks him to stop by his office after work. Another worker asks Gustave what the chrono wanted, and Gustave replies that "he wants . . . he wants . . . that I'm too old." The chrono meets the shop foreman on the stairs and tells him to prepare Gustave's last paycheck. The foreman points out that Gustave is only two years away from retirement, having worked there for twenty-three years. The chrono retorts that Gustave's early dismissal will save money: "After twenty-three years, a man is finished." He waves the foreman away with the reminder that production will not rise with such sentimentality. That evening on the street a couple embraces, but the man is distracted, thinking about Gustave. The woman says it is no concern of theirs; they have better things to do.

The same evening a meeting of a factory cell takes place. One of the workers, Victor, is named president and sets the agenda for the evening: an examination of the situation in the factory, the factory journal, response to the violation, the dismissal of Gustave. The recorder Tonin notes the recent reduction in the piecework rates and the release of Gustave at the last moment, giving the cell no time to react. A militant impetuously cries that he will break the chrono's neck, but the others convince him that his rashness would not restore Gustave's job. They agree instead to put out a flyer to inform other parts of the factory of developments, then to "examine the possibilities of a work stoppage to defend old Gustave and have the stopwatch withdrawn. Or at least to make the boss modify his methods. Then, we will demand the restoration of the former piecework rate."

As the meeting breaks up, Gustave's daughter arrives, carrying an infant, and tells them she fears Gustave is about to do something foolish, which would be ruinous, for Gustave is their sole source of income since the death of her husband. The workers find Gustave in the factory, about to destroy some of the machines with a crowbar. "You're crazy. A few machines, they'll just order other ones. Then you'll serve time. And then, seriously, it's not the machines. Look at Russia. They have succeeded in shortening the work day and raising

The efficiency expert (Max Dalban) surveying the workers (*La Vie est à nous*)

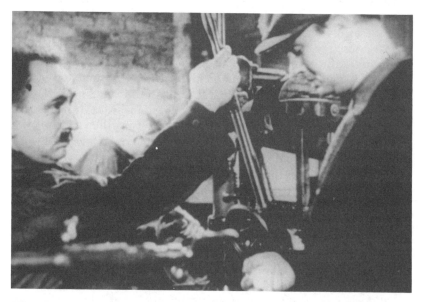

The efficiency expert timing the elderly worker Gustave (Emile Drain) (*La Vie est à nous*)

The union meeting to discuss job action: Communist Tonin (Charles Blavette) has the floor (*La Vie est à nous*)

wages, thanks to the machines. But here, the big shots, they would prefer to let us die of hunger rather than lower their profits."

The next morning, at nine o'clock, the cell members leave their machines. The chrono tries to stop one but is knocked to the ground by a comrade. The other proceeds to shut off the power to ensure a work stoppage. The workers assemble at the stairs, decide to present their demands and extend the work action to the whole factory if they are not accepted. One timid worker cautions, "No politics, especially, no politics," but a delegate responds, "But it is politics, it's politics for all of us, Hitler."

Before the workers confront the management, the director of the factory discusses the situation with his aides. The chrono blames it on the Communists. The foreman recommends granting the demands. When the assistant director adds that they have to buy time, the director concurs and goes to speak to the workers outside his office, affecting an air of surprise. A delegate pleads Gustave's case almost apologetically, sure that there must be some mistake. The director listens sympathetically and assures them that he will take care of it, but he sees no reason to stop work for such a trivial matter. The delegate then raises the question of the chrono, but the director interrupts him to say he will arrange that also and sends them back to

Marcel Cachin, editor of *L'Humanité,* reads a letter from a worker in a metal factory (*La Vie est à nous*)

work. The delegate is taken aback by the ease of the concessions. As the workers shuffle about in confusion, the Communist Tonin, already shown to be the most forceful and articulate cell member, intercepts the director, who has turned his back to return to his office, and reads the demands set down by the cell, including the threat to continue the strike throughout the factory if satisfaction is not given. The director is not pleased with this turn of events and retires to his office. The first delegate thanks Tonin for rescuing him from being duped. The assistant director emerges from the office to convey acceptance of the demands but promises sanctions for any future work stoppages. The committee returns to the waiting workers with the good news, and all applaud the victory. The end of the worker's letter is shown, before Cachin picks up the next letter: "My comrades in the factory thank the Communist party whose action was successful in the case of old Gustave. They know that this action takes place every day in all situations where their life and work conditions are involved."

There are several reasons for considering this sequence in some detail. First, as Borde concluded after an exhaustive study of several hundred films from the 1930s, the world of the worker did not exist on French screens.[57] Only *La Vie est à nous* offers a glimpse into that world. *Every* shot in this fictional sequence is set in the factory and relates to work. That is, the work situation is not just a pretext to a fiction of the workers' private lives that renders work a tangential background, such as in *Le Jour se lève,* where there is a rare shot of Gabin at work with an industrial tool. In *La Vie est à nous* the problems of the workplace are the sole concerns of the fiction.[58] The rarity of the workplace alone makes it worthy of a careful look.

Second, the story revolves around a work stoppage. Only about a month after the film was finished, the largest wave of strikes in French history broke out. The strikes came with no forewarning, erupted spontaneously, and took the union leadership entirely by surprise. The work action in *La Vie est à nous* does not follow this pattern, but its conception of worker militancy before the fact (of the real strikes) admits of many interesting points of comparison.

Finally, the PCF took an extremely controversial position during the strike wave. As the party sponsored *La Vie est à nous,* it is reasonable to search in the film for indications of the PCF's conception of militant action before the fact. In his January speech to the party congress, Thorez had stressed in particular the "mass political strike" of the working class. As the film conforms rigorously to the specifics of that speech, it should be an accurate representation of the PCF line and a basis for an evaluation of the consistency of that position faced with the unforeseen spontaneous "social explosion"[59] of May and June. However, consistency or divergence in itself has nothing to do with correctness, which is another question, and one still contested by historians.

The choice of a metal factory is significant. The Popular Front was "essentially an urban phenomenon," and the PCF drew most of its strength from the urban proletariat, concentrated in the Paris region.[60] The strikes began in the metallurgy industry, with protests against the dismissal of workers. On the one hand, the choice of the metal industry was a logical one, for the Communists exercised a dominance in the worker organizations. On the other hand, the metal industry workers were among the least affected by the economic crisis, for they were assured of stable orders for war matériel.[61] As well, it was a private industry, not one of the public services where the power of the less political CGT was dominant.[62]

According to a number of authorities, the role of the public services was crucial to the question of there being a revolutionary moment.[63] Had there been a concerted plan to seize power, the public services would have been one of the first targets to neutralize, bringing a paralysis of the government during the spread of the strike movement. In Paris there were no strikes of public facilities owing to the nonrevolutionary position of the CGT.

The metal workers were industrial workers, subjected to modern forms of industrial management such as the assembly line and piecework wages. The film shows a remarkable sensitivity to these issues by organizing the sequence around the cold calculations of the efficiency expert. Nor was the chrono who aroused such hostility in the sequence just a symbol chosen for dramatic reasons. During the strikes workers lynched effigies of chronos, and photographs of these rituals were published in the press.[64]

The sequence also deals with the issue of procedures used in the designations of worker representatives. The Leninist conception of the party entailed strict discipline to the political analysis by the party, and at the time of the Congress of Tours in 1920, Lenin had singled out the danger in France of anarchism's defiance of order, hierarchy, and authority.[65] In the film, the cell takes upon itself the responsibility of formulating the demands, though the demands—for restoration of former piece rates and the rehiring of Gustave—are all economic. At the close of the cell meeting, the film deflects the nihilistic Luddism of Gustave, who is about to destroy the machines. The machine as enemy was not a new idea in the cinema, Fritz Lang having turned it into a nightmare in *Metropolis* and René Clair into a prison in *A Nous la Liberté*. *La Vie est à nous* avoids this metaphoric approach, substituting the ostensible experience of the Soviet Union, where machines at once raise salaries and shorten the work day. The film may make the point polemically with this utopic image of work in Russia, but the pervasive hostility to machines can be gathered from Blum's remark in his radio speech before the election that "socialism wants to make the machines a servant, not an enemy."[66] It might be noted here that laudatory reports on the Stakhanovite movement in Russia were just beginning to filter into Communist papers and speeches about this time, creating a somewhat contradictory juxtaposition to the film's references to piecework.[67]

When work is halted on the morning of the stoppage, the film shows the workers assembling at the stairs to choose a strike committee. The degree of worker support for the cell, which decided on and executed the action, cannot be determined from the film. But the designation of the workers to serve on the strike committee is accomplished by acclamation, on the spot, with no real elections. This method is perhaps not strictly democratic, but neither is it a prearranged affair.

The Communists were often accused of such stage managing and manipulation of the workers. During the actual strikes, the Right hurled these charges continually, and the film puts that charge in the mouth of the chrono. The film, then, takes care to include this scene at the stairs to rebut such criticism, which did not come from the Right exclusively. Apparently, during the strikes, strike committees were formed similarly to the fashion depicted in the film: "In the great majority . . . the strike committees are most often formed by the meeting of the most dynamic union and political militants, those who gave the signal to stop work or toward whom the workers turn, after the stoppage, because they are known as belonging to a worker organization."[68]

The confrontation with management, however, leaves no doubt about the importance of the party. The first worker gets flustered by the director. Only the party member Tonin keeps his head and formally presents the demands, which presence of mind prompts the metal worker to write to Cachin thanking him for the aid of the party. This written coda, the only mention of the party in the sequence, not only attributes the victory to the party but also implicitly endorses the tactics and values disseminated by the party: the importance of discipline, order, and planning.

By all accounts, order and discipline did prevail during the strikes, but not planning. The strikes began spontaneously and spread with an irresistible momentum: "In more than one business, work stopped without any demands having been formulated, and the demands were presented to management sometimes only after several days of occupation."[69] Lefranc, contemporary witness to the events and later their historian, relates a telling personal anecdote on the degree of worker preparedness: "Disoriented or lost in the CGT building, the strike delegates knocked at my door. What have they come to do? Register at their professional federation. Yes, without doubt. But especially to find out 'what they should demand' now that they were on strike. And why did they go out on strike? 'Because they're going out on strike everywhere.' The collective contagion was obvious, and they did not hide their disappointment when a militant explained to them that it was they who first had to determine what they were demanding."[70]

This spontaneity and the sheer scope of the movement obviously caught the entire union leadership off guard, the CGT and the Socialists as well as the Communists. It would have probably been impossible for them to check the strike fever even if they had wanted to, but they were understandably loath to oppose this mass expression: "It was clear that everywhere the militants were unable to direct the strikes, to limit their spread, to foresee the consequences. The Communists themselves, who tried to appear more at ease than others, did not hide, in private conversations among militants, the fact that in their demands the workers didn't follow any orders. They said that the best thing to do was to let the popular wave carry you so as to give the impression that you directed it. It is quite accurate that the leaders followed the troops without knowing where this adventure would lead them."[71]

The unpredictability and rudderlessness worried the union leadership, for they feared that their electoral success would dissolve in their powerlessness to govern the very people who had voted the Popular Front into office. No one knew for sure whether a truly revolutionary situation was present, or imminent. Whatever the reasons, the combined efforts of the union leadership succeeded in stemming the immediate danger, with the intervention of Thorez's "One must know how to end a strike" probably being the most conclusive, and, certainly, then and since, the most controversial, the veritable "smoking gun" of the PCF's betrayal of the working class.[72]

Just as the PCF had resisted Socialist proposals for structural reform in the final draft of the Programme of the Rassemblement Populaire, so in June it opted for an economist solution to the strike crisis, although it did not rush to apply the brakes. The strike in the film is triggered by the same action as in the initial May strikes. Its modest demands and work stoppage, however, give no hint of the breadth, militancy, and mass support that accompanied the occupation of the factories, an unprecedented form of union struggle in France.

The film also provides no insight into what Thorez may have meant by the expression "mass political strike" in his Villeurbanne speech. The film does not broach questions of ownership or worker representation in management councils, whereas during the occupations Blum characteristically tried to split a nonexistent hair to deny the incontestable illegality of the occupations: "No factory was occupied by outsiders; it is a question rather of installation, in the factory, by the workers staying there even after work has ended."[73] Léon Jouhaux, head of the reformist CGT, spoke directly to the political fears and hopes implicit in what was effectively a seizure of management property when he characterized it as "neither political nor insurrectionary, but strictly professional."[74]

The factory sequence, then, offers a remarkable insight into the attitude of the PCF toward union activity. The events in the sequence foreshadow with surprising accuracy many of the issues and developments central to the sit-down strikes that stilled production only weeks after the first screenings of the film. Those strikes began in response to the dismissal of workers, as in the film. Additional pressures referred to in the film hardened the militancy of the workers: the imposition of rationalization, the resistance by management to the forty-hour week, the reduction of wages. In the film, the party assumes a leadership role democratically, that is, with the support of the workers; it is a role other workers are unable to fill. For the success of the strike, the party demands absolute discipline and specifically argues against any destruction of factory (private) property, checking nascent Luddite tendencies among some workers. During the strikes the workers took great care to protect that property. And perhaps most significantly, the demands in the film, as in the real strikes, did remain "professional," as Jouhaux stressed in his speech after the Matignon agreement. While certain elements among the Socialists, a party far less centralized than the PCF, did envision the seizure of the factories and the possibilities of a "revolutionary moment," the PCF pursued a strictly economist policy, in the film and the later strikes. Some writers have criticized the Thorez injunction that "it is necessary to know how to end a strike," but they usually fail to complete the sentence accurately with "once satisfaction has been obtained."[75] This nuance suggests that the PCF did not oppose worker militancy per se but did want to limit it to the arena of concrete, economic demands. At the same time, to have advocated anything less would almost certainly have been ineffectual and perhaps would have marked an irrevocable break with the sentiment of the great mass of workers.

The sequence ends with a shot of the letter seen at its beginning, forming a type of coda. The letter thanks the PCF for its aid in orchestrating the successful work action, adding that the workers are aware that the PCF engages in such defenses of worker rights throughout the country "every day." In contrast to the PCF's earlier propaganda strategy, before the "turn" to the Popular Front, the sequence contains no attacks on the Socialists, nor does it make direct appeal to the Socialist workers. The effectiveness of the factory story depends on the particularity of the references to real conditions, implying rather than asserting the intimacy of the understanding between the PCF and the interests of the workers. None of the Socialist films shows a similar sensitivity to the immediate problems of industrial workers. In the competing claims of the PCF and the PS to be the real representatives of the proletariat, this sequence makes a far more compelling case for the PCF, especially when one recalls Raymond Borde's observation that *La Vie est à nous* is the only film from the decade in which one finds the French working class.[76] The workplace and working conditions, moreover, are not merely colorful background to another drama. The working class and their economic situation itself constitute the drama.

The following sequence, about the farm, also confronts the real issues facing farmers at the time, but the film does not arrive at a practical resolution of these problems. Several factors were responsible for the difficulties besetting French agriculture. During the early 1930s, when the world financial crisis reached its height, the French government instituted deflationary measures such as laying off workers and cutting wages. Prices fell and demand dropped. At the same time, in the worst years of the crisis, wheat production increased, putting a downward pressure on market prices. To protect agricultural revenue the government moved to set minimum wheat prices, which were above the market price. But as demand was not sufficient to absorb the large harvests at the official price, the farmers were forced to sell at prices below the official minimum, creating a large black market in what was called "gangster wheat." Some farmers tried to stock wheat in the hope that a smaller crop the following year would drive the market price up to the vicinity of the minimum price. But this option was not available to the smaller farmers, for they did not have the facilities to withhold their wheat. According to Sauvy, the government had not understood the lessons taught by the past 2,000 years, that setting prices means nothing without a corresponding control over production.[77] Farmers received less income, but because of the relative downward inelasticity of fixed costs such as transportation, their production costs did not fall off proportionately. Therefore, the crisis affected them more gravely than the industrial population.

Caught in this squeeze, farmers were threatened with foreclosures, and the farm sequence in *La Vie est à nous* is organized precisely around this danger. Despite having a barn full of wheat, indicating the problem of overproduction, the farmer cannot meet his expenses. As the auctioneer takes an inventory of the farmer's possessions, the farmer's nephew (played by Gaston Modot) enters the house. He expresses his displeasure at the state of affairs, and the farmer tells the auctioneer to pay no attention to him, for the cousin is a Communist. This comment acknowledges the hostility farmers felt toward the Communists, who had little success in agricultural areas.

Undeterred by this rebuff, the nephew organizes his friends to save the farm for his uncle by physically intimidating prospective bidders to remain silent, but his method has an ambiguous relation to the official position of the PCF. In effect, the film proposes illegal resistance to the foreclosures. However, the very decision of the PCF to support the Popular Front represented a commitment to work within existing legal structures. At the same time, the schematic program of the Popular Front did call for a "suppression of foreclosures," and in fact between October 1933 and October 1935 there had been thirty-seven incidents of the sort shown in the sequence.[78] The question of foreclosures was a central concern and, as so often in farm crises, perhaps the easiest to dramatize. The foreclosures were a micro-economic problem confronting many individual farmers; prices and the size of the crop could be dealt with only through a more general policy for the agricultural sector.

The farm sequence, as well as the factory sequence, contains three generations of families with the same missing member, a father. In the first, Gustave's daughter appears at the end of the cell meeting to warn the others that Gustave may be considering some rash action after his dismissal. She is carrying a small child in her arms while she relates that Gustave is the family's sole source of income since the death of her husband. She gives no indication of the cause of the death. In the farm sequence, as the auctioneer proceeds with his inventory, he inquires about the picture hanging on the wall. The mother explains that her son died some years after the war as a result of his exposure to gas in battle. The Communist (Modot) enters the house at that point.

Even though none of the critics noted it at the time, the absence of these two fathers may represent another contemporary reference: a declining birthrate in France. With the loss of so many young soldiers during World War I, the birthrate dropped, resulting a generation later, in the mid-1930s, in a smaller labor pool of young males. Suddenly, natality became an important subject of public concern. The immediate problem was manpower available for military service. Germany's re-arming resurrected the question of France's military preparedness, and Laval proposed lengthening the term of military service to two years to compensate for the numerical reduction. During demonstrations of 1935, the Left objected vigorously to this measure, and footage from those demonstrations in *Le Mur des fédérés* shows great numbers of placards calling for a refusal of the "two years." In the same years, the number of deaths exceeded the number of births, threatening a long-term manpower shortage which would have far broader consequences than shrinking the armed forces manpower. Hence, while politicians had avoided this unpleasant topic despite its imminence, the shock of the natality figures forced it into the public arena during the Popular Front years.[79] Given the wealth of other contemporary references throughout the film, this unstressed detail adds yet another element to the film's fidelity to the issues of the moment.

The third fictional sequence, the longest of the three, aims at a part of the electorate probably most susceptible to propaganda influence—the unemployed and the middle class. In all likelihood the PCF did not expect to make great inroads on the Socialist voters or on the agricultural electorate. But the Radical party was in disarray. A succession of Radical governments had failed to improve the economic crisis, and the polarization of the country into hostile political camps did not abate. As the deflationary strategy followed by this series of governments appeared only to aggravate the social and economic conditions, support in the Assembly for the Radical government began to erode. Increasing numbers of deputies from the left wing of the Radical party voted with the bloc of Socialists and Communists. Fearful of being relegated to a position of relative political marginality and reassured by the concerted moderation of PCF overtures, the Radicals eventually joined the Popular Front. The identity of the Radical party had always been a more amorphous amalgam of political beliefs than that of the Socialist party and the PCF, for its supporters came from the unorganized middle classes, the petty and middle bourgeoisie (the strata, that is, that were perceived at the time to have been responsible for the ultimate victory of Hitler). Hence, the defection of part of the Radical party entailed less doctrinal difficulty than the changes in the positions of the Socialist party or the PCF.

The sequence traces the economic descent of René, a young, unemployed *ingénieur* (the term in France has a broader meaning than in America; to call him an engineer would exaggerate the extent of his training, that of a lighting technician). As the sequence opens, René is packing a suitcase, preparing to leave his girlfriend. He is frustrated by his inability to find work, for he cannot provide for the girl; without him, she could move in with her sister. She tries to dissuade him, but as she prepares his favorite meal in the foreground, René sneaks out in the background. He finds work washing cars in a garage where an Algerian is working already, but loses that job the same day when he does not finish washing a car in time. The furious customer then drives up to the disconsolate René on the street, commiserates with him over the loss of his job, and offers to help by giving him a membership application to the Volontaires Nationaux. As he drives off, the car splashes dirt on René, who uses the application to clean his

After failing to find work, René (Julien Bertheau) slips away while his girl-friend, Ninette (Nadia Sibirskaia), prepares his favorite meal (*La Vie est à nous*)

trousers and then tosses it in the gutter. Wandering the streets, René comes to a soup kitchen—as in the United States, a ubiquitous sign of the times—but the food runs out before René reaches the front of the line. Hungry and homeless, René collapses in a doorway. A bourgeois couple see him and rush by quickly. Some young men pass by then and carry him to a meeting of Young Communists, who feed him. Amidst the activities at the gathering, René repairs a flood lamp used to light the chorus that is rehearsing, thus finding a place to apply his training in the supportive environment of the PCF.

Once again, the events that unfold are embedded in the reality of the time. Exacerbated by deflationary policies of wage reductions, unemployment persisted at high levels yet not necessarily in the most heavily industrialized sectors, such as metallurgy. The middle classes as well suffered from the economic crisis. Many workers like René—new entrants to the labor force and for the most part offspring of a middle class either apolitical or sympathetic to the pragmatic conservatism of the Radical party—had no particular political affiliations. René, however, does have sufficient political awareness to reject the option of the Fascist leagues, in this case the Volontaires Nationales, the youth organization of the Croix-de-Feu. And finally, the PCF, highly organized at all levels, maintained a wide network of Young Communist groups.

Although René's material cares fade away when he discovers refuge in the party, party membership meant much more than mere amelioration of material circumstances. The party offered and insisted on a whole way of life, an alternate culture. By weaning members from the traditional French culture, the PCF sought to extend its influence over consciousness itself, in what Kriegel describes, in a passage on the appeal of the party to intellectuals, as "the dynamics of a *spiritual conversion.*"[80] In trying to convey some sense of the "strangeness" of membership in the PCF, Kriegel gives the following description: "The Communist party is not in fact a party like other parties. . . . In the last analysis, it conveys the overriding fact that the party's place is fixed outside of established society. Given its nature, the party tends to reach beyond the strictly political domain of traditional majority or oppositional groups. It keeps its distance from other parties whose purely political theories it challenges. It also keeps its distance from a society whose very foundations it calls into question. In short, it is of and by itself a party-society, a party that is also a social model."[81]

Thus, when René opens his eyes at the Young Communist club, he glimpses a new way of life. The camera lingers on a close-up that captures his wonder and amazement at the world before him. The immediate images and sounds that make up that world are the Communist chorus singing the most characteristic song from the years of the Popular Front, "Au devant de la vie." Several months after the elections, in *Vendredi*, André Chamson wrote of the special status this song had already acquired: "If one had to give a face to the Popular Front, as the artists knew how to give one to Liberty, it would be that of a young man tanned by the sun, lithe, a seasoned hiker, honest in spirit but not naïve, singing as he marches alongside other young men, with the resemblance and difference of brothers. 'Allons, au devant de la vie . . . Allons au-devant du matin.'"[82]

The song, virtually a theme song for Communist youth (though its popularity was not restricted to Communists), evokes images of youth and the future. One verse enjoins "comrades" to "share . . . our plans, our work, our cares." The refrain expresses the joy that "toward the rising sun Our Country Goes." Youth is marching toward a new future to the rhythm of "factories and trains whistling in the town," clearly an urban image. The song, then, deepens the sense of material rebirth, of food and shelter, René experiences in the care of the Young Communists, for it implies a spiritual rebirth as well. In the

The "rebirth" of René, rescued by the Communist party (*La Vie est à nous*)

two preceding sequences, the PCF led the struggle for economic demands at the factory and the farm. The target audiences in both these cases were clearly defined: factory workers and small farmers. But in neither situation was there any attempt to insist on party allegiance. In fact, the farm sequence ends with the Communist nephew gracefully deflecting the thanks of the farmer and withdrawing from the scene with his friends. René's specific trade has little importance beyond establishing his background as middle class. Otherwise, as he walks the streets without direction, he enters the life of despair afflicting so many others. This sequence attempts to respond to that malaise, hence its overt strategy of stressing nonmaterial needs and a reassurance that working together as comrades will be the foundation of a new, hope-filled future.

When René asks who the singers are, he is told, "Some workers who come here in the evenings to rehearse. There are even some professionals." This remark accurately testifies to the recent re-organization of the former workers theater network to include professionals. This was yet another sphere in which the party wanted to widen contacts between workers and artists, so it was natural afterward to be proud of the participation of professionals. After this brief comment, the chorus, alternating ensemble and solo parts, recites the essential mes-

Standing before a portrait of Stalin, an audience listens to speeches by Communist party officials (*La Vie est à nous*)

sage of this sequence: "Comrade, you are not alone; in the depths of your misery, you are not alone. The future appears black to you, life seems hopeless. Comrade, take heart once more. You are not alone, you are not alone. Life for all will be beautiful because we wish it so. Life will cease to be cruel. Peasants, workers, unemployed, boys and girls, friends, comrades, the Communist party calls you. Peasant, worker, unemployed, boys and girls of the people, do you hear the voice of the party? Come take life by the hand. Don't wait, time is short. The Communist party calls upon you to take the future in hand. La vie est à nous. Comrades, come with us." The two earlier sequences appealed to those segments of the electorate in which the PCF already had an identifiable presence, and the episodes concern the efforts of the PCF to defend the interests of the factory workers and farmers against any assaults on those interests, whether jobs, wages, or property. But many others had no interests to lose, having been long out of work or even unable to find a first job. To these dispossessed, who have no political influence, the party reaches out with the promise of comradeship.

The importance attached to this group, as a potential electoral support, is reinforced by the ending of the sequence. Unlike the two other fictional sequences, the scene at the hall of the Young Commu-

Paul Vaillant-Couturier, leading PCF liaison with intellectuals and artists and co-founder of AEAR (*La Vie est à nous*)

nists does not have a formal closure of a letter of appreciation to Cachin. As René looks on in several close shots and attends to the direct address of the chorus, presented as a simple alternation of shot-reverse-shot point-of-view structure, suddenly a shot of a large audience standing in a room replaces the expected close shot of René in the alternation. The new shot, displaying a large picture of Stalin on the wall, introduces a new space, yet the implication is that this audience is also listening to the chorus when it says that the "Communist party calls you." This shot actually functions as a transition to the final sequence of the film, recorded at the Pathé Studios at Francoeur—a series of short statements directly to the camera by various members of the Central Committee. After the shot of the audience, a title announces the speaker in the following shot, Vaillant-Couturier. Thus, the story of René blends smoothly, without closure, into the ending of the film, which tries explicitly to gather all the preceding material into a unity.

The film achieves this unity through both the discourses of the party officials and the formal organization of the conclusion. The first three speakers had specific functions within the party, and each spoke to different groups. Vaillant-Couturier was probably the most popular and best known among the leadership of the party. With his back-

Union leader Renaud Jean (*La Vie est à nous*)

ground and friendships in the literary and artistic circles, he directed the liaisons with Communist front and fellow-traveler groups. As a wounded veteran of the first World War, he was active in the ARAC and a constant champion of peace. Finally, he promoted the cause of youth through the youth organizations of the PCF and projects for health care and education of children. Thus, in his speech he pledges to struggle for the defense of the rights of veterans: "We don't want to pay with our pensions after having paid with our lives." He promises also to struggle so that young people will no longer be unhappy. He ends with one of the electoral slogans of the PCF, "Make the rich pay."

As with each of the speakers, a title next identifies Renaud Jean, who dealt with agricultural questions.[83] As he was to do no doubt in the radio speech he delivered from the Toulouse-Pyrenées station,[84] he advances the rescue program for agriculture designed by the PCF. During his discourse, there is a cut to the crowd seen earlier listening, but this time Modot (the nephew), the farmer, and other actors from the farm sequence are in the middle of the frame, recalling that earlier sequence.

A woman, Martha Desrumeaux, then launches an appeal to the "women of France, married, mothers, engaged, who dream of a better future. Struggle with the Communist party to obtain immediately for your children and your family, bread, liberty, peace, and a better life." Even though women did not have the right to vote in France at that time, the PCF took care to recognize them. Tiersky points out that "the PCF, of all French political parties, has traditionally had the most open policy regarding the participation of women,"[85] and Desrumeaux's position as a member of the Central Committee indicates that this reputation was not merely empty rhetoric.[86] Another insert appears here of members of the Young Communist chorus seen earlier, with male and female members. In this case, however, there is no attempt to imply some diegetic link to the insert as listeners. The shot was taken straight out of the previous sequence, unmistakable from the lighting and camera angle and clearly a nondiegetic insert.

The last four speakers are the most powerful heads of the PCF: Cachin, Gitton, Duclos, and Thorez. They do not represent particular constituencies among the population as the previous speakers do (youth and veterans, peasantry, women), and they sound the central points of the PCF position within the Popular Front. Cachin stresses the party's stand against the external fascism of Hitler and Mussolini, which is why the Communists voted for the Franco-Soviet Pact and approved the sanctions imposed by the League of Nations against Italy "to end the shameful butchery of Ethiopia." Faced with such dangers, workers of the world must unite "to fight as brothers against fascism and war, side by side with the Red Army of the Soviet Union." The one cutaway shows the actors from the factory sequence at the center of an attentive crowd, apparently in the same hall as the actors from the farm sequence seen in an earlier insert.

In the shortest speech, Gitton pays tribute to the size of the party, with "tens of thousands of men and wonderful women. This is our strength, a formidable creative force. Our party, which strives for a better society, the happiness of the working family, is the warm house in which one wants to live." As he invokes the image of "our party," the scene shows a crowd listening—none recognizable from another part of the film—as if illustrating the idea of the nameless thousands that make it a "great party."

Duclos places the Popular Front in the familiar revolutionary tradition of the French Republic, beginning with the French Revolution, when the young people of France "were in Valmy, standing against the monarchy of Europe, the old feudal society. . . . Young people of France, you were on the barricades during the Commune in Paris. Young people of France, you were fighting in the street in February 1934. You were there on February 9, Place de la République, where one of your own fell and died. . . . Walk hand in hand in the conquest of life, in the conquest of happiness." Before this lyrical call for the

Jacques Duclos, one of the leaders of the French Communist Party (*La Vie est à nous*)

appropriation of the future, René and his girlfriend find each other again among the crowd of listeners, embracing briefly before returning their attention to the end of the speech.

As leader of the party, Thorez has the last words. He calls on French Communists "to follow the example of our brothers in the Soviet Union," adding that "we are internationalists." As in his speech at Villeurbanne, he argues for "the union of the French people, for the reconciliation of the French nation against the 200 Families and their fascist agents. In other words, what we want is to ensure the salvation of the country." He concludes as he began, with another homage to the inspiration of the Soviet Union: "Forward under the great and beautiful flag of Marx, Engels, Lenin, Stalin. Forward for the success of the Popular Front, of work, of freedom, and of peace. Forward for the triumph of the French Republic of Soviets. Long live a strong, free, and happy France, the France that the Communists want and will bring about. We care deeply about the number and the health of its children, about the abundance and the quality of its material and intellectual production, about the diffusion of its culture."

In these speeches, then, one hears the major slogans used by the PCF for the electoral campaign, all of which had been worked out

Party leader Maurice Thorez before portraits of Lenin and Dimitrov (*La Vie est à nous*)

already in the Villeurbanne speech in January: the identification of the PCF with the *French* revolutionary tradition; the importance of youth and the peasants; the attribution of the cause of the crisis to the catch-all phrase of the 200 Families; the deep commitment of the PCF to the pre-eminence of *French* culture; the defense of benefits for veterans; the urgency of the struggle against fascism. In short, the PCF proclaims and appeals to French nationalism, a self-conscious maneuver to deflect charges of taking its orders from Moscow. Jean does make an isolated reference to capitalism, but he does not call for its abolition. At the same time, the texts clearly refute Fofi's charge that references to the Soviet Union are nonexistent in the film. In fact, it is curious that Thorez allows such effusive praise for the Soviet Union and even surprising that he goes so far as to encourage the "triumph of the French Republic of Soviets," for it is difficult to think of a more inflammatory vision to fan the fears of their enemies and allies alike.

Once again the filmmakers use inserts to take advantage of the opportunity to blend fiction and document. Even though the political figures have been enlisted as performers, they do not belong to the fiction(s) represented in the film. But the actors from those fictional parts appear now as members of an audience listening to the speeches

René and Ninette re-united, listening to campaign speeches (*La Vie est à nous*)

through the simple principle of synthetic editing, the point-of-view structure of the eyeline match. These actors no longer portray the characters that they played in the fictional parts. Yet they still retain associations from within the fiction, for the filmmakers specifically show the farm actors during the speech of Jean on the peasants and the women from the chorus when Desrumeaux speaks. An insert even implies that the separation of René from his girlfriend, unresolved in the fiction, is repaired when they meet again as members of the audience. Here, the fiction literally spills over into the sequence of documents (the campaign speeches).

In addition, the film extends the strategy of typicality or representativeness contained in the fictional sequences. As indicated above, those sequences construct the anecdotes around specific, easily identifiable situations drawn from the contemporary reality. Regardless of the composition of the audience—factory workers, farmers, members of the middle classes—viewers would recognize references to their particular problems—assaults on the apparatus of social security, efficiency experts, job dismissals, farm foreclosures, unemployment, soup kitchens, recruiting by the leagues. When the characters from these stories reappear in the audience for the speeches, they are part of a large group of listeners, implicitly amidst anonymous countrymen sharing their problems, frustrations, hopes. The actors are always framed in the center of these group shots, so that one can see them immediately in the inserts, but they are always surrounded by others in a crowd. Thus, the film takes care to insist on the typicality of the stories, not only in the fictional scenario, but also by exposing the artifice of the stories themselves. The actors portray roles of working people, but when they join the crowd later in the film, they are workers as well, equally interested in hearing the program of a political party reaching out for their support.

After Thorez finishes, the film gives the screen over to the actors and the anonymous crowd. In a scene shot at the Knoll in Morel, separate groups singing the "Internationale" march across the screen, the synthetic cutting drawing them together into a large mass of people, a straightforward cinematic device enlisted for political purposes, as in the end of Pudovkin's *Mother*, which the filmmakers had undoubtedly seen. In *La Vie est à nous,* however, the crowd not only grows numerically but also accumulates various segments of the population, marked by the actors from the three fictional episodes. Modot, the Communist seen earlier, carries the child of the farmer and leads one group marching in one direction. René and his girlfriend head another group, moving in the opposite screen direction. The size of the groups in the shots increases, and not all the groups can be associated with political interests by the actors among them. Eventually the groups meet in one long shot, their numbers swelling to fill the screen in a mass of marchers.

Following this symbolic union, the film returns to a series of images from the beginning of the film, their meaning now transformed. The opening of the film posed the question of the existence of want and poverty in a country rich in resources. The images review these riches: first a shot of wheat, then a river (transport and communications), connecting rods in a factory (industry), a forest. According to the argument of the film, this wealth now belongs to the people, for they have finally achieved unity in the Popular Front, and on the screen at least, the people have seized control of what is rightfully theirs.

The last images literalize the metaphor of the wave of humanity that is the Popular Front. Recalling another finale in a Soviet film from the heroic period, when the battleship Potemkin rushes through the water past the Czarist fleet, *La Vie est à nous* cuts in several shots of the water surging past the side of a boat, conveying a sense of the power driving the masses forward. And this thrust is directed toward the future, emphasized aurally in the refrain of the "Internationale,"

> C'est la lutte finale
> groupons-nous et demain
> l'Internationale
> Sera le genre humain,

and presented visually by the recurring shots of the farmer's child borne aloft, advancing ever closer to the camera, as his face gazing off into that future provides the final image of the film. Despite the assimilation of the groups into the anonymous mass, however, the film's vision of the future is not that of a classless society. Having accepted the premise of an electoral coalition, the PCF has tried to separate or differentiate discrete interest groups and assure each of them—the proletariat, the peasants and farmers, and the middle classes—that the PCF understands and is working for all of them.

The conception of *La Vie est à nous* went beyond the more modest efforts of the other films to document the vitality of the Left. *La Vie est à nous* systematically questions the authority normally invested in newsreel images and sounds; it proposes a critique of the mode of newsreels themselves. The film openly tampers with the newsreel segments on multiple levels: editing, sound/image relations, and the images themselves. These deformations of newsreel documents overtly propose new meanings for the documents, interpretations that coincide with the position of the Left.

The assertiveness of these formal interventions makes no attempt to disguise the deformations of the original material. The exaggeration of these techniques demonstrates the power of film to create meanings according to the viewpoint of the filmmaker(s), even when the sounds and images were not produced for the sole purpose of being recorded. This "work" on newsreel does not propose simply a substitution of Left newsreels for the reactionary newsreels then monopolizing the theaters. All newsreels have these means at their disposal, and knowledge of these rhetorical possibilities should help viewers to develop a critical stance toward newsreels. In other words, whether intended or not, the newsreel sequences didactically illustrate the power of cinematic techniques to distort, and caution spectators about accepting claims, associations, arguments as accurate or true by virtue of their inclusion in purportedly objective newsreels.

As well, in various ways, the fictional material aspires to document the lives of French working people by dramatizing real situations. The situations are historically specific to the years of the mid-1930s, not timeless situations found in most fictional films of any period. The abundance of contemporary references in these anecdotes is astonishing, suggesting that the filmmakers rejected any dramatic idea that would not have immediate contemporary resonance. As the documentary sequences are invaded by fiction, so the fictions also activate a wealth of documentary material.

In this mixture of fiction and document, *La Vie est à nous* is unlike any other film from the period. Its discursive method does interrogate the forms of both fiction and documentary films, aided in this enterprise by its polemical premise as a partisan electoral film for one of the political parties. The film offers an analysis of the political and economic situation and an optimistic view of the future, both of which correspond to the historical reality of the Popular Front. That reality grew out of the enthusiasm on the Left and the hope for change, an élan not to be found in the great films of poetic realism cited as representative of the period by film critics and historians.[87]

Critical Reception

As Sadoul pointed out in support of the film's qualification for a visa, the reviews "from publications of the most diverse opinions have been unanimous in their praise of the great artistic qualities" of the film.[88] Sadoul exaggerated here, but not flagrantly. Most of the reviews were favorable, but the variety of emphases struck in the reviews was revealing of Left attitudes toward film in France at the time.

On the most basic level, all paid tribute to the simple fact that the film was made, "this first courageous effort for a free, authentic cinema."[89] "On the whole, the film has great scope, which gives the greatest honor to the talent of all the collaborators."[90] Only the reviewer for *Commune* explicitly exploited the occasion for partisan political advantage: "It is significant that the first film made in France by a political party is made by the Communist party. And what other party was better prepared to make it and what film would be able to show us the danger of a restoration of the monarchy in France . . . ?"[91]

But while commentaries generally acknowledged party sponsorship, they did not necessarily exempt the film from criticism. Even Vaillant-Couturier, a powerful public spokesman for the party and co-author of the film, admitted that "certain aspects of the scenario" could be criticized.[92] He did not specify these aspects, but Le Chanois recounts that the first screening of the film was held before the Central Committee of the PCF, and although it was well received, strong criticisms were voiced. Benoît Frachon, head of the CGTU, found fault with the factory sequence, objecting that the union did not play a strong enough role. After some time of criticism, during which Le Chanois and Renoir were understandably nervous, Thorez, "who was not an idiot," closed the discussion by concluding that nothing is perfect and that the film would serve admirably for their purposes.[93]

Most reviews accepted that the film was a propaganda film and therefore took the view that it should not be faulted for that. Chavance chided his colleague, Georges Robert, for making that criticism two weeks earlier in *La Flèche:* "One might as well reproach a painting for being a painting or a play for being performed on a stage."[94]

Probably the most common response was to emphasize the encouragement for the future offered by the realization of *La Vie est à nous,* rather than to praise particular virtues of the film. The commercial industry itself was virtually unanimous about the malaise of the French film industry, in both its quality and its weak competitive position vis-à-vis American films. This pervasive attitude only strengthened the criticisms from the Left, which was predisposed from the start to reject the products of the commercial industry. Vaillant-Couturier adopted this relatively doctrinaire stance when he wrote that *"La Vie est à nous . . .* gives already an idea of what the French cinema could be like when it is liberated from the servitude of money and it becomes a film of the people."[95]

The first issue of *Ciné-Liberté* called it "not only a Communist film, but a grand film *populaire,* a date in the French cinema."[96] The importance of the term *populaire* was underlined in *L'Humanité,* which also referred to it as a "grand film *populaire,* but this time, truly *populaire,* that is, destined to serve the people and not put them to sleep." Implicit in this qualification is the recognition of a distinction between so-called films of the people, seen as ideological distortions concocted by the commercial industry, and a film made by working people, working collectively toward commonly shared goals. This antipathy toward the hierarchical organization and concomitant alienation normally found in the commercial industry was expressed clearly and pointedly in *L'Humanité:* "Working on this film has been for them a magnificent revenge on so many other films, on which they had to work individually, in seeing their intelligence, their expertise and their talent sacrificed to the appetites of the capitalists of the cinema."[97]

Certainly, in retrospect expectations for any radical transformation of the commercial industry appear utopian, but they do reflect widespread frustration with the commercial cinema. The production of *La Vie est à nous* coincided with the final heady days when even the reactionary parties were conceding the inevitability of the Popular

Front victory.[98] When *Ciné-Liberté* succeeded in publishing its first issue at the end of May, it was by no means chimerical to envision opening a fissure in the commercial monopoly, to be filled by a popular alliance of spectators and technicians who had joined forces to forge this first militant left-wing film in France: "It is a great hope that this film gives to honest and free filmmakers, a route that it opens toward the production of tomorrow."[99]

Such were the general outlines of the criticism that greeted the completion of *La Vie est à nous*. Serious analyses of the film itself, as opposed to the phenomenon of its production and distribution, were less frequent. Most concentrated on plot descriptions interspersed with enthusiasm for its successful completion. It must be kept in mind, though, that film criticism in general was still at a relatively primitive stage at the time.[100] None of the journals, be they industry journals or intellectual reviews, devoted extensive space to reviews. Even in the left-wing press, long reviews were virtually nonexistent. Film was not even always thought to be an obligatory subject for coverage. When the cultural weekly *Regards* began publishing in 1933, there were no film reviews. And when film was allotted regular coverage, the reviews were no longer than several paragraphs, and most were devoted to Hollywood films.

Sadoul's writing during the period illustrates these tendencies. In the second half of the 1930s, Sadoul was the regular film reviewer for *Regards*. At the same time, he wrote long book reviews for the more serious intellectual monthly *Commune* as well as comments each month on twenty to thirty reviews/journals. Although Sadoul did not write the major review of *La Vie est à nous* for *Regards*, he did comment on it: ". . . a propaganda movie, but at the same time a film of considerable artistic value. Renoir and his collaborators have made with this film one of the best French products of recent years. The faith, the enthusiasm, the élan which animates this group of skilled technicians pervades all the action and the breath of fresh air that runs through it is truly unique."[101] One senses a certain defensiveness here in the dichotomy between propaganda and art, a legacy no doubt from the earlier critical reception given the Soviet films, whose defenders wanted to ensure their value through artistic justifications, and esthetes pointed to the artistic inventiveness that could be abstracted easily enough from their political rhetoric.

Some two years later, Sadoul stressed the well roundedness of the film: "*La Vie est à nous* . . . is certainly a film of propaganda, but a propaganda human and alive, which touches deeply and lacks neither emotion or humor."[102] Here Sadoul revealed a humanist thrust that the PCF was eager to identify with at the time, as if the attachment of the film to universal values would exonerate it from charges of simplistic propaganda.

This humanistic emphasis derived directly from the conscious strategy of the PCF at the time, and Sadoul's comments clearly echoed, if not paraphrased, the words of Vaillant-Couturier at one of the first screenings: "Everything in this film is rendered with such sensitivity, such a delicate touch, a manner so profoundly human, and such a powerful force of truth, that it avoids what could be the principal danger for a film of this sort: crude agitation, oversimplification, melodrama which repels rather than leads."[103] Le Drimeur, who wrote the official review for *Regards,* sounded the same chords but went slightly further in accounting for the structural explanation behind its success:

> This film . . . explains why life is cruel to the mass of men and how this life is able, through a will for unity, to become beautiful. It explains this neither by oversimplification nor by phrases, but by the convincing force of its images and its rhythm.
>
> Communism appears in it not as an imaginary hope, but in its brotherly and human face, set among our daily activities.[104]

Other critics went beyond the promise for the future justifiably raised by the film. Several commentators saw in the film the first appearance on French screens of the working people: "*La Vie est à nous* is a simple, clear film, leaping directly from life. It presents to spectators some essential aspects of the lives of the French people today, at their most typical, most fundamental."[105] For years critics had protested against what they called the puerile and sentimental melodramas shown in the theaters and also against the double standard of the newsreels, which were filled week after week with footage of Hitler and Mussolini but systematically suppressed images of the people during the endless mass demonstrations that followed the events of February 1934.

Yet the critics did not speak only of the superior quality of *La Vie est à nous.* They pointed out that it was the first opportunity for French working people to see their own lives on the screen. It was the fidelity of that representation that would inspire the working people with the possibilities of the cinema, not the normal practice of commercial cinema which sought to efface that reality: "The workers of our country will recognize themselves in *La Vie est à nous,* because they act in it and struggle in it as they do every day of their lives."[106] Monnerot in *Commune* evokes the "wonder, joy, confidence of the spectator who sees himself in the play as he is, of the man who recognizes himself in the play finally, worthy of occupying the screen and being an example."[107]

Only a few critics tried to explicate the structure of the film and account in concrete terms for its success. Le Drimeur lauded the "convincing force of its images and its rhythm," but gave no examples, hence it is difficult to know what images he found convincing.[108] Monnerot singled out the newsreel images and named them:

> Certain images represent some facts which actually took place: the march of the Croix-de-Feu to the Arc de Triomphe, the chaotic battle between the police and the demonstrators the night of February 9, acquire, as we well know—with all our heart—of what they speak, an unexpected degree of intensity. They propose a reality, incite strong reactions. Thus the Colonel de La Rocque dragging his feet in a bizarre fashion on the Champs-Elysées, a bouquet of violets in his hand, and followed by his staff, this image of self-righteous complacency and paramilitary ataxy,[109] assumes in April 1936, the value of an urgent call to the people of France. Thus a striking face of a dead Ethiopian soldier, a negro version of the valley of death [the title of a Rimbaud poem], is only a question posed to men in the most direct way possible. Thus the massive and *populaire* cortège of workers killed by the police while fighting on February 9 indicates proudly that the Communists have no cowardly and unconditional horror of struggle and of death. . . . Each of these images brought to mind an idea of immediate relevance, of first importance, a meaningful idea; nothing less than a question of life and death.[110]

Many of these images were drawn from events more than two years earlier, yet Monnerot not only argued that each image names an idea but also suggested that the images take on a new meaning with the passage of time—that is, the reality of the Popular Front and its repudiation of fascism.

For someone who did not write on film, except on this one occasion, Monnerot displayed considerable perception in isolating the newsreel sequences of the film for their legibility. This legibility was defined not by the clarity or technical quality of the images but by the specific meanings that the workers would immediately recognize from either their own presence and participation in the events or the pictorial reports in the newspapers. Although he did not discuss the importance of shot juxtapositions, his review did not ignore theoretical questions entirely: "This means of expression, if it fails completely to translate according to its own laws and possibilities, virtually limitless, the highest human values, leads to confusion in the hands of those who use it in the defense and illustration of an unacceptable world, of an old-fashioned vision of man, and finally, of their own mediocrity. Too often it is spectacle that cinema gives us, but this art is so modern and so much our own that the worst reel sometimes protests against what it is meant to say and reclaims the content of human aspiration which was taken from it. It is exactly the reverse that is produced in *La Vie est à nous.*"[111] Film's "own laws and possibilities" were not laid out, but the subsequent criticism of "spectacle" and the lengthy consideration of the newsreel images propose a conception of film whose natural vocation is to capture a reality normally disguised in the camouflage of spectacle.

Not until the end of the review did he address the fictional sequences, for which he had a lukewarm appreciation: "These true stories . . . assume for us a place among the most immediate and decisive justifications of cinema as art."[112] Like Sadoul and others, Monnerot felt compelled, almost reluctantly, to claim the film's qualification as art, even though the entire review to that point had based its analysis on other criteria. The film's dichotomy between fictional and newsreel footage evidently posed a problem for Monnerot, who was unable to theorize a model of film that might accommodate their coexistence.

One critic did think through this dichotomy for the film as a whole. Pierre Bost was the regular film reviewer for *Vendredi,* a publication J.-P. A. Bernard has called "perhaps the most representative journal of the spirit of the Popular Front . . . an organ which existed only by and for the Popular Front."[113] Its years of publication corresponded roughly with those of the existence of the Popular Front: it appeared first on November 8, 1935, and ceased publication exactly three years later, with issue number 158 on November 10, 1938. A front-page editorial in the last issue explained that the paper was born with the Popular Front, and with its dissolution the paper could not continue. The list of principal contributors supports the paper's claim of independence from political parties: Gide, Julien Benda, Jean Guéhenno, as well as the Communists Paul Nizan and André Wurmser. The final editorial reaffirmed that original independence.

Following common practice, Bost reviewed commercial films for the most part. Conforming with the stance of the paper, he did not adopt a dogmatic tone of condescension or derision toward films according to their politics. Thus, he maintained a sober, reasoned attitude toward *La Vie est à nous.* For him, PCF sponsorship did not guarantee the worth of the film. His analysis, which appeared after the elections, had none of the polemical urgency found in some of the commentaries discussed above, and perhaps that very political distance prompted reflections that transcend historical interest in their formulations around political film.

Rather than approaching the film through its discrete images, Bost is more interested in the structural organization of the film and its theoretical implications:

> What is remarkable here is the ingenuity of the construction, the intelligence with which the "chapters and images" come together and balance each other. The film is at the same time a documentary, a montage, a series of sketches, and a succession of persuasive speeches. The group which has constructed the scenario has imbued these diverse elements with real accuracy and judgment; some images hit hard, with others the humor loosens a dialectical rigor which would become fatiguing; there is satire, joy, emotion (a little facile at times). Rarely has a film in France succeeded "without story" as coherent, as intelligent, and which shows as clearly what the cinema could do in illustrating and expanding on ideas. In sum, while the films we see are always, more or less, plays or novels, *La Vie est à nous* is the first *film-essay* offered to us.[114]

What distinguishes Bost's review is his sensitivity to the discursive possibilities of film, which depend crucially on the intercalation of disparate cinematic elements. These elements derive from identifiable practices, such as documentary or fiction, but their dialectical interrelations defy categorization in any one of these rubrics. Hence Bost reached for some term that could convey this synthesis of construction and found a perfectly apt phrase in *film-essay*. Nor did he use this term solely as a formal label demanded by the heterogeneity of the film. The film-essay is a legitimate cinematic form in its own right in its purposive exploration of ideas.

Of course the most articulate theory of a discursive film practice was expounded during this period and earlier by Eisenstein, but other passages in the review cast doubt on Bost's familiarity with Eisenstein's ideas: "One sees how the film is constructed: alternation of documentary and story: a method inspired evidently by the Russian cinema, and of the art of montage, of which Ruttmann's *Melody of the World* remains the masterpiece."[115] One would have expected Eisenstein's *October*, which Eisenstein certainly viewed as the apogee of his work on the intellectual cinema, to be named the unquestioned masterpiece in a cinema of ideas. It is true that Eisenstein was in official disfavor in the Soviet Union after his return from the West (if not before), but there is no reason to think that Western critics—certainly not the nonpartisan Bost—tailored their appreciation of his films and writings to fit the vicissitudes of Soviet film politics. Furthermore, the alternation of documentary and fiction is not a characteristic of Eisenstein's films, nor of Vertov's. Vertov and Eisenstein disagreed about the priority of document and fiction, each working exclusively with one, an opposition that *La Vie est à nous* obviously rejects.

Finally, Bost observed that the film was made by a crew of technicians, artists, and workers and that Jean Renoir was the principal author, "but the film's choice of anonymity is appropriate for this film, which is made to speak to the masses and which is a film of Communist propaganda."[116] For Bost, even if the film was not entirely a collective effort in actual fact, the decision ("parti pris") to release the film with no individual credits bore remarking, for such an approach stood out in contradistinction to film practice everywhere. As part of a movement dedicated to collective activity, the film departs from normal industrial hierarchization, which the French film industry, with its own star system, observed as diligently as did Hollywood. Even among the political films of the Popular Front, Ciné-Liberté products included, *La Vie est à nous* remains unique in this respect.

To summarize, then, reviewers responded favorably to the film. They applauded the effort and energy of all who surmounted adversity to produce it and hailed it as a harbinger of promising future work on the cinematic front, of a truly independent cinema of the people. For the first time, French workers could see themselves on the screen, not subjected to the falsification of commercial interests pursuing a return on investment. And *La Vie est à nous* opened a new path to political filmmaking in its interweaving of document and fiction, a cinema of ideas.

After the film disappeared during World War II, there was no further writing about it for some thirty years. Its rediscovery and commercial release elicited a new round of critical comment in 1969. By that time various histories of the Popular Front had been written, but with one major exception the later critics failed to engage the film in its historical specificity, a somewhat surprising lapse given the events of May 1968.

The greatest obstacle in the later analyses was the participation of Renoir. With auteur theory still being practiced, many critics sifted through the film in search of the Renoir gold, consigning the remaining flotsam to the bin of historical curiosity. Marcel Martin, for example, writes: "Certainly, it is first of all a historical document, but it is much more than that, a work marked with a human quality where we must see the subtle and profound sign of Renoir."[117] Even Sadoul, an excellent film historian, if not a brilliant critical exigete, calls it "unarguably a brilliant work of art, stylistically characteristic of Renoir during his best period."[118] The Renoir deity looms even larger in reviews destined for a less specialized public: "It is naturally when Renoir is at work that a film-tract takes its true dimension . . . the images swell with a generous lyricism which touches and inspires us."[119] It is true that the PCF proudly celebrated Renoir's participation at the time the film was made, but their motivations were more political than aesthetic. Renoir was one more cultural figure to be added to the party's conquests on the cultural front. Over the years, however, Renoir's participation on the film has both explained and obscured critical examination of the film, and his role will be considered in more detail below.

Even when, in the later commentary, the Renoir aura does not eclipse the politics of the film, it does reduce them to a general outline, recalling contemporary remarks: "If *La Vie est à nous* is so perfectly successful, this is due to the particular climate of the time it was made, to the fact that the crew was deeply allied with the working masses, inspired by the same socialist ideals."[120] Fair and accurate as this judgment may be, it glosses the specific functioning of the film, its specific intervention at a crucial historical moment. There is no question that the film reflects the time of its conception and execution. What is at issue are the particular questions posed, the perceptions of the political situation and the economic circumstances, the proposed solutions, and, no less significantly, the cinematic strategies developed.

Most of these later commentaries followed one or both of the lines enumerated above, as either a masterful Renoir production or an historical document. Hennebelle, a specialist in political film, attacks the film, unfairly in my opinion, for being "simplistic" and worthy of interest "mostly as a fetish or token," but as he also ignores the specific historical situation in both politics and the cinema, his rationale never goes beyond simple assertion.[121]

The seminal article by Fofi demands more serious response, for his study of the politics of the films of the Popular Front unequivocally applies informed political judgments. This first article on the subject of Left films during the Popular Front remains in many ways the best treatment. It is based on copious and careful documentation, traces multiple interrelations in the politics of culture during the period, and bristles with an aggressive polemical tone. According to the introductory note accompanying the English translation, an untranslated introductory section deals with the Italian Left at the time the article was written (1966), when "the right wing of the Italian Communist Party was waging a determinedly opportunist campaign to try to swing the rest of the Communist Party and groups to the left of the Party into an alliance with the Socialist Party."[122]

Fofi wants to expose the inevitable reformism of Frontist ideology, in the specific instance of the French Popular Front, but he announces quite openly his corollary agenda in returning to the Popular Front: "Studying it, even just studying specific aspects of it, may help us to clarify our ideas about the present. Our view of the past should not be gratuitous, and I for one am not a detached observer" (p. 8). For Fofi, reformism is always a betrayal of revolution. Once the decision is taken to collaborate with the bourgeois parties, revolutionary potential evaporates. Thus, the films made by the parties and the unions "necessarily reflected the confusion typical of every reformist movement and of the Left's participation in and support for a government. The workers will no longer be exploited and rebellious. They will collaborate in the national effort for the nation's progress" (p. 18). This unqualified indictment of reformism characterizes the ultra-Left position that Lenin warned against in *Left-Wing Communism*, for it disregards possible tactical advantages of short-term collaboration in building strength for revolution in the longer term. It seems difficult to question this caution in principle, so Fofi's belief that there was a "revolutionary moment" during the strikes of May-June follows from his general view of reformism more than from an analysis of the reality of the political situation. Fofi himself points out that studies of the period were still unavailable in 1966, so his endorsement of Guérin's study and that of Danos and Gibelin cannot pretend to a thorough and balanced examination of the historical evidence.[123] At the same time, subsequent historical investigation has not resolved the question definitively. The problem with Fofi's approach, then, is his refusal to admit the possible efficacy of Frontism at the time—a problem aggravated by his concern to advance his research for political purposes relevant to the resurgence of Frontism in the Italian Communist party in 1966.

Given that the PCF proposed *La Vie est à nous* as an electoral weapon for the Popular Front, Fofi's judgment is more or less predictable:

> A political propaganda film must be judged, first of all, on political grounds. The slogans also demand comment. And here one cannot but note its oversimplistic schematization. . . . This is not analysis but an ideological operation of the most cursory kind. . . .
> Capitalism is reduced to a series of remarks which explain little. . . .

> This film is typically Frontist in the sense that it illustrates perfectly the Communist party's meagre revolutionary outlook at that time (and since . . .). It is also a significant fact that the direction of the film was, in large part, entrusted to allies who, like Renoir—the fiery declarations of the period notwithstanding—were putting forward essentially bourgeois demands for a sincere, but hardly extreme, adjustment. (P. 23)

Fofi's claims here are perfectly accurate. But even if one were to concur with Fofi's political judgment, the film's bias should not disqualify it from consideration on its effectiveness as a political intervention, unarguably an "ideological operation." Fofi may want to criticize the PCF during the Popular Front for its desertion of the Revolution, but to dismiss a film sponsored by the PCF for propounding the line of the party cannot possibly result in a fair hearing for the film.

Throughout, Fofi's article suffers from a split vision. He unearths a wealth of material, chronicles the political filmmaking activity, and traces the cleavages and fault lines of artistic movements and participants. Praise is given generously and fairly. But when the terrible hour of judgment arrives, no one and no film can be found to brave the tide of Frontism.

Another difficulty is that Fofi apparently analyzes films he has not seen, though he is not consistently forthright about this unfortunate oversight. He quotes at length from passages of *La Vie est à nous*, but the citations are riddled with inaccuracies. He speaks of the difficulty of seeing the film and attributes part of this difficulty to the fact that the only copy is held by the PCF. Nor does Fofi say that he has seen the film. He is equally silent on many of the other films he mentions, relying often on written accounts or scripts. This tendency only reinforces his political bias, which reduces the sensitivity to cinematic structures and culminates, at the end of the article, with the one film that satisfies his political criteria:

> If we want an overall "class" assessment of the cinema in this period we must look to the only existing example, *Contre le Courant* (1938), a documentary made by Pivert's Parti Socialiste des Ouvriers et Paysans, *which unfortunately I have not seen. . . .* [my emphasis]
>
> A single sentence from the text, which refers to June 1936, seems to me relevant to the whole experience: "The proletarian revolution was within our reach: we were not able to grasp hold of it." (P. 43)

A revealing epilogue: not seeing is believing.[124] Despite this outrageous conclusion and the suspicion cast on Fofi's preceding commentaries, his work remains invaluable. However, the danger of his reliance on written texts lies in not seeing the complexity of the film text.

After the first public release of the film in 1969, only the editors of *Cahiers du Cinéma* tried to address the film in its structural and political complexity. In 1970 *Cahiers du Cinéma* produced the first detailed analysis of *La Vie est à nous* in an excellent collective text.[125] As *Cahiers* was "close to" the PCF at the time, their reading of the film differs markedly from Fofi's piece in its evaluation of the party.[126] *Cahiers* does not quite defend the PCF's position during the Popular Front, but the tally of crises threatening France at the head of the article can have no other interpretation, implying that the PCF had no realistic choice but to rally to the defense of the Republic. The *Cahiers* text offers *La Vie est à nous* as an exemplary model of the "militant film."

In their collective text the *Cahiers* editors imported a new critical vocabulary and procedure from a current literary criticism found in the writings of members of the *Tel Quel* group to produce a deconstructive reading of the film. Despite a somewhat obfuscatory reliance on *Tel Quel* terminology, their discussion remains the most perceptive and sensitive treatment of the film, even if its observations are understandably schematic.[127]

For thirty years after the production of the film, then, there was little critical comment on it. Its disappearance during the war and afterward contributed to this neglect but does not explain it, for even when Fofi discussed the film in 1966, he displayed little appreciation of its importance or value as a political film. Fofi mentions in his article that a copy of the film was held in the PCF archives, but if that were true, the PCF apparently had no interest in resurrecting it, and it is not clear why it was rediscovered only in 1969.

With the development of auteurism by *Cahiers du Cinéma* during the 1950s, that magazine made a concerted effort to salvage and reestablish the critical reputation of Renoir after his stay in Hollywood. This enterprise necessitated a prudent suppression of Renoir's political activities during the 1930s, of which his participation on *La Vie est à nous* would have been the most damning.[128]

Another factor, however, probably applied also: the originality of the film. As noted above, Pierre Bost was forced to coin a new term for the film in his 1936 review. As he was evidently unable to classify it within contemporary critical rubrics, he called it a "film essay."[129] The film did not fit conveniently into the categories of documentary or fiction. On the simplest level the co-existence of both types of filmmaking in the same film confounded this critical dichotomy. As well, production circumstances did not conform to normal procedures, for it was made collectively and shown only privately. The film displayed no "stars" from the commercial industry, nor was there even a hero of the fiction, for there were several fictions. The only actor who could arguably be considered a "proletarian" hero from the commercial films of the period, Jean Gabin, did not participate.

The Role of Renoir

A related factor in the critical neglect of *La Vie est à nous* has been the reign of auteurism in film studies and the particular reputation of Renoir. As has been seen, value was attached to the film to a large degree because of Renoir's association with it. At that time, Renoir had already achieved the status of the greatest French filmmaker in the prewar years on the basis of his work in the 1930s, and since that time more than ten book-length studies—not to mention numerous articles and interviews—have been devoted to his films. Hence, it seems relevant to consider to what extent *La Vie est à nous* should be or can be thought of as a Renoir film and, more importantly, whether an auteurist approach is even relevant to an appreciation of the film.

Part of the question revolves around the importance the critic attaches to the principle of coherence or consistency. One Renoir scholar, Claude Beylie, proclaims his view quite explicitly at the beginning of his study: "Our intention . . . [is to] resituate this oeuvre in the current of universal art, to disengage it from certain questionable contingencies in which some have tried to enclose it, to prove finally that it proposes, as he would say himself of his father, 'one of the rare witnesses, so rarely formulated in the history of the world, of the transformation of material into spirit.' "[130] Obviously, *La Vie est à nous* is composed of virtually only such contingencies, so Beylie sees the film as an aberration in Renoir's career, forcing him to account for several of the most productive years of Renoir's life with the observation that "Renoir encountered French socialism only in the enthusiasm of a day, and adopted its theses only very provisionally." Yet, from the end of 1935 until the beginning of 1939, Renoir directed or worked on eight films, received the Prix Delluc, and served on the editorial board of a Left film journal. Even Sesonske, in his excellent book on Renoir's French films, is not immune to this type of rescue operation: "However central the politics of the thirties may have been in the genesis of [*Le Crime de M. Lange*], or however important political references may have been to French audiences at that time, the film transcends the politics of the moment, for its characters represent more than just the clash of political ideas." To his credit, however, when he reaches *La Vie est à nous,* Sesonske makes no attempt to foreground these universal, transcendent values. He accepts the marked differences between this commissioned film and Renoir's own projects and in fact sees the differences as evidence of Renoir's rejection of dogma: "Viewed within the context of Renoir's work, the film confirms, above all, his openness and flexibility, his unwillingness to be wedded to a single style, not even to his own."[131]

Other critics, more sensitive to these so-called contingencies, place less weight on isolating *the* Renoir signature. Singlehandedly, Claude Gauteur set about reconstructing Renoir's political involvements during the second half of the 1930s, exhuming scores of articles and interviews from these years in editing *Ecrits* (1974). Astonished at finding such a wealth of material ignored by Renoir exegetes, Gauteur gathered the material into one volume in the hope that it would fill in gaps in the critical treatment of Renoir: "The only merit that we claim is to present to the public for the first time an approach to Renoir—and an approach to Renoir by himself—which is a total one."[132]

Furthermore, Gauteur wanted to correct what he feels to be a critical imbalance in the literature of Renoir, resulting from demands for unity: "Renoir is not one, but . . . many. Or, if you wish, in the image of Proteus, his unity is his very multiplicity."[133] Gauteur pursued this task himself some years later with his *Jean Renoir, La Double Méprise,* in which he starts from the same premise, verbatim, about Renoir's multiplicity. The later book essentially fills in the contours of the literary politics of the journals in which Renoir's writing and interviews appeared, selecting and juxtaposing excerpts to highlight Renoir's political stance.

Still, despite all this material and annotations, Renoir's specific contributions to *La Vie est à nous* remain unclear. His own remarks on the film are sketchy. A year after he worked on the film, he said in a Communist youth magazine, "Still *La Vie est à nous* is a great joy of my career and in it I truly became aware of cinema and its role."[134] Over forty years later, in his autobiography, Renoir has little to say of the film: "*La Vie est à nous,* which I supervised, was shot principally by my youthful assistants and technicians. I directed a few sequences but had nothing to do with the editing."[135]

Whether out of modesty or political disillusionment, Renoir distances himself from the production. In other retrospective comments he refers to himself as the "producer, in the American sense of the term," implying that, with the exception of the sequence of René, he did not direct day-to-day operations. Furthermore, he strips the political associations from these memories in his autobiography when he recalls his work with the collective: "They were warmhearted realists. Their views might differ, but they were still Frenchmen. I felt at ease in their company, enjoying the same popular songs and the same red wine."[136] Although it is true that the majority of the group that made the film were not Communists, members of the party, they had all responded to the partisan call of the PCF because of their political sympathies and not because of their appreciation of "the same popular songs and the same red wine."

However, Jean-Paul Le Chanois, who also worked on the film, disputes this version of the production, although his recollections are not entirely consistent.[137] According to him, Renoir directed most of the film, though Jacques Becker and he took several of the shots. In this version Le Chanois follows the line taken by the PCF at the time the film was made, which Cachin laid out on the evening of the premiere, as recorded by *L'Humanité*. Cachin thanked Renoir, calling him the "principal artisan" of the film, at which point the audience erupted in "endless applause." Cachin then added that "we hope that this warm tribute has been well appreciated for this brave fighter for art and the cause of the people."[138] The next day, Vaillant-Couturier seconded this praise in similar terms: "We must be pleased that [the film] has provided the great director Jean Renoir with a theme on which his talent has expanded magnificently."[139]

However, the PCF's campaign during these years to attract intellectuals and artists makes this acclaim inconclusive evidence. Through the Association des Ecrivains et Artistes Révolutionnaires and numerous other Communist frontist organizations, the PCF reversed its previous sectarian course by stressing its image as a party with its roots deeply implanted in French culture, as its chief cultural spokesman, Vaillant-Couturier, put it.[140] Hence, it was important that the roster of its sympathizers include many illustrious names who were not members of the party. No one could say that the organization of film workers that formed during the production of *La Vie est à nous* was a Communist organization. The Communist Moussinac may have been a member of the editorial board of the group's journal, *Ciné-Liberté*, but Jeanson was an outspoken anti-Stalinist and Renoir's contacts with the PCF were recent and fraternal rather than doctrinal. The PCF, then, was eager to surround itself with prominent fellow-travelers, and its effusive praise of Renoir may not reflect his actual degree of responsibility.

With little primary documentation to rely on, most writers follow Renoir's account, which Le Chanois's published statements support.

Le Chanois shot the factory sequence, and Becker directed the farm episode. As Le Chanois was a member of the PCF, he would have been a logical choice for the factory sequence, for he could have consulted with militants and party officials while working on the script. Unik also collaborated on the script, as he did on the later Le Chanois-directed PCF election film, *Le Temps des cerises* (discussed in the next chapter), but Le Chanois does not emphasize his role. In his 1952 book, *En Marge du cinéma français*, Brunius relates that Renoir asked him to assemble the first two reels of *La Vie est à nous*, an opportunity he welcomed as a chance to experiment with his ideas on the construction of films from a variety of cinematic and aural objets trouvés:

> The montage film appeared to me the perfect place to experiment in this domain. My idea was to conduct the experiment with the greatest possible number of 'ready-made' elements: newsreel images, sounds from the film library, prerecorded music. Several years passed without the occasion presenting itself and I feared that someone else would have the same idea and do it before me. Fortunately, nothing happened until the day when by chance in 1936 Jean Renoir, to whom I had never spoken of my idea, asked me specifically to edit in several days the first two reels of his film *La Vie est à nous* in the conditions close to the ones I had envisaged. There was even one additional constraint: the text of the "commentary" for the first sequence was imposed in advance. All that was needed was to search for the images. Thus the experiment was not entirely conclusive. At least I had the chance to attempt in detail what most interested me: how to associate the rhythm of the word and thought to the rhythm of the image.[141]

Brunius says nothing of whatever political leanings he may have had at the time, and as the book deals primarily with the avant-garde, he leaves the impression that he saw Renoir's offer as a chance for formal experiment. Brunius also makes no reference to any interference in his work on the project, for he pronounces himself satisfied with its reception by audiences. It seems probable, then, that Renoir did not exert strong directorial control over the film. For whatever complex reasons, whether political naiveté or professional largesse, Renoir delegated responsibilities for a large part of the film to younger film-makers who had never had the chance previously to direct on their own. In fact, Becker quarrelled with Renoir himself over that very problem when the choice for director of *Le Crime de M. Lange* had to be made.[142] When Becker was passed over in favor of Renoir, Becker walked away from the project, though in all fairness to Renoir there is no reason to think that the producers of *M. Lange* would have agreed to Becker, precisely because of his inexperience.

Turning to the film itself, one can easily find several Renoir touches which establish its artistic pedigree. The one most remarked upon is the deep focus shot at the beginning of the story of the engineer. As his girlfriend tends to the cooking in the foreground, René slips out of the apartment in the background, charging the foreground-background opposition with dramatic significance. The girlfriend continues her conversation with René after he has left, and several moments pass in dramatic tension before she discovers his flight. The presence of Nadia Sibirskaia in the role of the girlfriend also suggests Renoir's hand in this sequence, for she had just finished working with him in *Le Crime de M. Lange,* and she explained later that she acted in the film at the express invitation of Renoir.[143] Sesonske, among others, observes that two sequences in the film, Brunius at the casino and the auctioneer taking the inventory, will be expanded in fuller treatments in two similar scenes from *Les Bas Fonds*.[144] No one appears to have commented on the scene of the country gentry at target practice—an obvious precursor, in miniature, of the famous hunting spectacle in *La Règle du jeu*.

The editors of *Cahiers* adopt a different tack in arguing for the omnipresence of Renoir. While granting the existence of various local Renoir touches, they decry the ideological bias of such criticism:

> Idealist criticism reveals here most clearly its presuppositions and methodological foundations: analytic empiricism (incapable of thinking a whole, historically determined in the complex and dynamic unity of its elements, it dissects and atomizes it into particles, which it places in relation with other particles, all as arbitrarily placed somewhere else) and the very tenacious "prevision of the past." Double process of recognition and not of cognition, production of a pseudo-knowledge, description of surface (which can be perceptive) and not analysis of a specific functioning. The first, sometimes, wears the makeup of structuralism, the second will gladly take the form of an absolution.

For them, the structural principles governing other Renoir films from the period are simply put in the service of a "political discourse": "For example, the alternation dear to Renoir of strong moments and weaker moments, his dialectical principle of equilibrium, of well-regulated stresses or relaxations of the various dramatic elements, find here just as easily their application to the dialectic progression of a political discourse; this other Renoir principle of the division of the film into large unities which send back to one another fits in perfectly here with the didactic care of breaking up the political material into shots which will have to mutually complete and clarify each other."[145]

Renoir himself corroborated part of this method in an article written shortly after the completion of *La Vie est à nous:* "Certain auteurs of film, and I am one of them, consider that the best approach to a shooting script [découpage] consists in dividing the film into several principal scenes or sequences, each of which, forming a little portion of the action, could be considered as a whole."[146] And his films bear out this analysis, filled as they are with set pieces that gather together central themes of the films, such as the meal scene in *Le Crime de M. Lange* or the fête de La Colinière in *La Règle du jeu.* This conception of the scenario may have also led him to his celebrated use of long depth of field, which he wrote about in an article published just before he began working on *La Règle du jeu:* "The farther I advance in my profession, the more I am inclined to shoot in deep focus. The more I work, the more I abandon confrontations between two actors neatly set up before the camera, as in a photographer's studio. I find it convenient to place my characters more freely, at different distances from the camera, and to make them move."[147] But Renoir's commitment to composition in depth and autonomous scenes contradicts the position of *Cahiers* mentioned above. Perhaps Bazin exaggerated when he wrote that "this conception of the screen assumes . . . the almost total disappearance of montage,"[148] but editing has never been one of the strengths associated with Renoir's work. Critics speak of his direction of actors, his sympathy for all his characters, the integrity of filmic space, his belief in direct sound, a nonliterary dialogue, action unfolding on multiple planes, but not editing. Nor do the "large unities" referred to without examples in the *Cahiers* analysis clash stylistically with one another in Renoir's films.

Yet this clash of modes of filmmaking is precisely one of the strategies and strengths of *La Vie est à nous.* The young filmmakers around Renoir had not settled into a recognizable style, as had Renoir by that time. Some of the Renoir "touches" possibly did not even originate with Renoir. His films must have impressed directors-to-be like Becker and Le Chanois. No one has remarked on the elaborate camera movements during the cell meeting in the factory sequence (usually attributed to Le Chanois), but there Le Chanois may have been copying a technique learned from his mentor; Renoir's influence may also explain the similar camera movement during the farm inventory. Similarly, the dress and manner of the factory owner in his confrontation with the workers' council seem modelled on the Jules Berry interpretation of Batala in *Le Crime de M. Lange.* But these archaeological finds are not what make the film interesting. Efforts of such recuperation under the sign of Renoir can lead to ludicrous assertions—for example, Beylie's learned judgment that the shot of René parting quietly from his girlfriend "bears witness to a science of depth of field, which only the auteur of *Le Crime de M. Lange* was capable of."[149]

The problem with the *Cahiers* discussion of Renoir is that they propose a homology which is not substantiated. For them, the principles of construction are the same in Renoir's other films of the time and *La Vie est à nous,* but only in the latter film are the principles applied to a political discourse. They do not specify, however, what they mean by "his dialectical principle of balancing." They do enumerate some of the ways that *La Vie est à nous* employs a dialectic principle, between document and fiction, but the multiple levels on which that principle operates in the film, with its transformations of meanings through a consistently assertive form of editing, bear little similarity to the other Renoir films of the period. In both cases there may be "autonomous blocks," but the mere existence of *relatively* autonomous segments does not justify the logical leap of saying that the relations among the blocks are analogous. This is not to belittle Renoir's importance in the making of the film but rather to suggest that while one can isolate and identify certain Renoir touches, these are not the main virtues of the film nor of particular interest in the functioning of the film as a political intervention, which was the stimulus for the film.

At the time Renoir was identified politically as a fellow traveler. He earned the designation of leading "filmmaker of the left"[150] on the basis of his many activities in the struggle against fascism. No other filmmaker of the period compared even remotely with Renoir in the public visibility of his stance as supporter of the Popular Front. From the time of his working with Prévert and members of the Groupe Octobre on *Le Crime de M. Lange,* Renoir signed manifestos, gave interviews in the Left press, wrote many articles, and served on the editorial board of *Ciné-Liberté.* For example, when *Commune* printed a letter of support to the Soviet Union, among the illustrious names found in the list of signatures that included Gide, Le Corbusier, and Picasso, Renoir was the only filmmaker.[151]

Renoir was also the only filmmaker to respond to a "grand inquiry" announced in the first issue of *Cahiers de la Jeunesse* (July 15, 1937), on "Cinema and Youth." In an unsigned call for response, the magazine laid out its areas of interest: "The cinema is far from giving youth what it had every right to expect. Too many films without value are offered to the public, to the young for whom the cinema, in many cases, takes the place of intellectual nourishment. The inquiry of

Cahiers de la Jeunesse will uncover the reasons for this debasement of cinema, will denounce the men and the practices which are responsible."[152] In his reply, Renoir sketched a modest and not particularly militant outline for the mission of film, but he does express his dissatisfaction with the failure of the established film industry to encourage the entry of new talent:

> Like all the arts, cinema should contribute to youth a single thing: aid in the knowledge of man, of man and nature. . . . Thus, cinema should reveal human characters, personages—that is to say that it should be true, uniquely true (without being novelistic if possible). . . . Only, this is a difficult thing, because the large companies do not like the truth. The naked truth is considered as a revolutionary element. . . .
>
> The producers should be young themselves. Here we have the problem of the access of youth to a profession where it is difficult to enter. The "producers" have some proven men, whose "devotion" they can count on and in whom they can depend for this. They fear the young.[153]

Renoir had experienced his own share of troubles with producers, and in his own work he always sought independence from producers and encouraged young filmmakers.

Renoir, however, was not always as mild as this in his observations on the film industry. Seven months earlier he took a harsher tone:

> The business people in film are bastards. They are only business people and nothing else. They reject all that is new; they fear always not making enough profit. . . .
>
> In the USSR, the filmmakers do not undergo these business hindrances. They are free. They can shoot films. And then, they don't have the worry of tomorrow, the fear of ruin.[154]

This idealization of life in the Soviet Union was standard fare in the vocabulary of the fellow traveler, and there is no reason to single out Renoir as uniquely ignorant of certain realities, even if Renoir had managed to complete nine films under the adverse conditions in France, while Eisenstein had not completed one film in more than seven years and Vertov only three in that time.

Possibly Renoir was basing this vision of the Soviet industry on what he experienced during a visit to the Soviet Union. He does not mention this trip in his autobiography, and critics attach no importance to it (neither Beylie nor Sesonske refer to it in their carefully documented studies). Actually, Renoir himself alluded to it only rarely in his many articles from the 1930s. In his only article in *L'Humanité*, Renoir recounts the story of a special morning screening of *The Youth of Maxim* when he was in Moscow: "It is the great step forward, it is progress, it is truth. It is possible that in the USSR all our comrades do not appreciate the real importance of this film; it doesn't matter; the tree is planted, it will yield its fruits, and Stalin, in awarding the authors of this work the Medal of Lenin, knew what he was doing."[155] In the "Souvenirs" article from 1938, he calls the applause after a Moscow screening of *Nana* "one of the greatest joys of my life."[156] But aside from these few examples, Renoir did not use the Soviet film industry as a foil for the malaise of the French industry.

However, he did take a great interest in the situation of the French industry. On one occasion, influenced no doubt by his ties with militant Leftists during the production of *La Vie est à nous*, Renoir unleashed a virulent, dogmatic attack on the commercial industry:

> These bourgeois authors are not to be ranked in the category of creators, but rather as streetwalkers, and I look forward with impatience to the moment that this mass that they think they have conquered will finally have its say and will sweep out this whole elegant riffraff.

> Film directors are the children of the bourgeoisie. They bring to this profession the weakness of their decadent class. The public of the first-run theaters, who often decide on the success of a film when it opens, is also a bourgeois public. . . . Thus the cinema, this art essentially populaire, is made and run by people who, we see it year in and year out, distance themselves more and more from the people. For the gap which is opening between the Paris of the beaux quartiers and the Paris which works, between the Etoile on the one hand and the Bastille on the other, becomes each day wider. Soon it will be unbridgeable and the capital of France will be divided into two enemy camps. . . .[157]

Apparently Renoir adapted his style to the journal he was writing for. He wrote this last astonishing piece for an issue of *La Flèche* in May 1936, before the outbreak of the Spanish Civil War, at a moment when the Popular Front was still riding the crest of popular enthusiasm, which evidently carried Renoir along with it. Of course, the organization, Ciné-Liberté, never came close to accomplishing this vision of an ideological housecleaning, and perhaps this very powerlessness abetted these visionary tendencies in Renoir: "We will pass perhaps through many vicissitudes before arriving there, but we will see certainly one day the coming of this society without classes where men will no longer shoot each other and where the problems of production and distribution will be easy."[158]

But as his films evidence a diversity of styles and interests, so Renoir assumed various voices in his writing. While there is no denying the stridency of the pieces written during 1936, and occasional pronouncements later, on the whole he was more restrained. Before 1936, Renoir had written only several short articles; after 1936, as he wrote more frequently, his tone softened, and a more mature style emerged—less acerbic, softer, and more self-assured. He developed this style during his tenure as regular contributor to the Communist daily, *Ce Soir*, edited by the Communist Aragon and the prominent fellow traveler Jean-Richard Bloch. Aragon had suggested Renoir to the PCF as the director of *La Vie est à nous*, and given its success it is not surprising that he invited Renoir to write for the new paper. It first appeared on March 2, 1937, and Renoir's first Wednesday column came out two days later. In all, of the sixty-nine articles Renoir wrote between 1936 and 1939, fifty-five were for *Ce Soir*.[159]

The author of these Wednesday columns turns out to be an essayist, and most of the articles are not about film at all. He writes about his films from time to time and offers his opinions on measures for the improvement of the industry on occasion. He praises the quality of the French workers in the film industry and endorses the controversial forty-hour law, citing the efficiency and enthusiasm of the crew that worked on *La Bête Humaine*. But on the whole he tells anecdotes from which he extracts an antifascist moral.

In one of his first efforts, he takes a theme that he returned to several times, beginning with some random incident:

> In rummaging about in my attic, by chance I came upon a book that I had not opened certainly in a good 25 years.
> It was the rulebook of the cavalry. This moved me a little, because I am a former cavalryman. I leafed through it, then read with more attention. It is a remarkable work; the riding is taught in it with a precision and conciseness which would be the envy of some modern technical works. But what struck me—and we enter here a domain purely moral—is the insistence that the author takes in recommending the avoidance of affectation and rigidity, not only in the exercise pure and simple of the art of riding, but even in all facets of military discipline.

He proceeds to note that the French "salute very badly and are very far from this rigidity" but that the fascists Hitler and Mussolini dress very badly: "Amuse yourself by looking at a photo of Mussolini or Goering. Where the devil have they unearthed these pea jackets which squeeze them and these boots which yawn with boredom at each step? If I were running a hotel and I had bellboys as badly done up, I wouldn't keep them a moment in my employ. I'd have too much fear that they would chase away the clientele." Renoir sprinkles this caricature with argot, as he did in his films, but the last sentence abruptly shifts from frivolous to serious: "What is serious is that there are millions of men who are not laughing and that the flip side of this farce is an appalling tragedy."[160]

Mocking the pretensions of the fascist dictators was one of his favorite themes, but he never let the sarcasm obscure the denunciation of their barbarism. When Renoir learned that Mussolini had banned *La Bête Humaine* (for the Italians, that is; Mussolini reportedly braved the ordeal in private screenings), he wrote that this news initially filled him with great pride, as well as his sentence to a single dose of castor oil pronounced by the Fascist party.

> Alas! a closer look at the situation quickly showed me that this honor was less flattering than I had believed at first. If the dictators busy themselves so willingly with affairs that seem so trivial to simple mortals, it is simply, I am now firmly convinced, because they have nothing better to do and they are bored to death during their utterly empty days.
>
> What do you imagine, for example, that Mussolini and Hitler talked about during their last interview, which terrified the world? I am sure that they did not risk a word on the questions troubling our unfortunate planet: not a word on China, and still less on Japan; let's not even mention Spain or the copper mines! Total silence on oil, unemployment and rearmament.[161]

The innocent dictators are simply following orders decided upon by others, in Amsterdam, London, or Paris, "clothed in modest, well-tailored suits, discreetly and silently carving up the world among them. . . . They send their orders to the dictators, and all they have to do is have them carried out, which is not very tiring and gives them free time."[162]

Renoir did not try to write serious political analysis in these articles. He did speak of the workers at times, but rarely the proletariat. For the most part, he rejected the political rhetoric of the articles from 1936 for that of satire. Not once did he voice support for the PCF, even as first among equals as *La Vie est à nous* had done. His most partisan statements were several brief endorsements of the government of the Popular Front. His antifascism was firm and constant: opposition to fascist expansionism in Europe, Africa, and China and an unequivocal repudiation of racism (particularly in Germany).

It is unlikely that anyone will establish conclusively Renoir's exact role in the making of *La Vie est à nous*, but the evidence of his films, writings, and interviews does not warrant primary attribution of the film's strengths to Renoir. Renoir's realism exfoliated in many directions, formal and thematic, and his films deserve to be called experimental. But through this period of his greatest films, he did not question the premise of narrative. And regardless of normative judgments one might draw from his use of depth of field and camera movement, these techniques do preserve the integrity of diegetic space. Though not a necessary consequence, Renoir's use of depth of field does eliminate assertive, synthetic montage. Formally, *La Vie est à nous* represents a departure from both of these constants of the contemporary Renoir films. Furthermore, Renoir's antifascism was not yoked to a strong identification with the PCF or even, by the standards of the time, to the USSR. Yet partisan advocacy of the PCF was the raison d'être of the film. Renoir's writings from the time are filled with little narratives, and perhaps what he said of his writing to the readers of *Ce Soir* may apply as well to the extent of his concerns with both politics and its implications for film theory and practice: "I am not a writer. I am simply a guy who doesn't know how to resist the desire to tell a good story."[163]

NOTES

1. Robrieux, *Histoire intérieure*, 1:439.
2. Jean-Paul Dreyfus, a Jew, changed his name when the Germans occupied France, taking the new name of Jean-Paul Le Chanois. To avoid confusion, I refer to him always by his adopted name. Sources on the production history of the film indicate that Jean-Paul Le Chanois provided most of the material. I interviewed Le Chanois on July 22, 1981, in Paris, and his remarks then conformed, on the whole, to the material found in other published sources. See B. Eisenschitz, "Front Populaire et Idée de Cinéma Militant de France (1928–1937)," publication of the International Federation of Film Archives and Bulgarska Nacionalna Filmoteka, Varna, 1977; C. Faulkner, *Jean Renoir: A Guide to References and Resources* (Boston: G. K. Hall, 1979), pp. 92–96; interview with Guy Broucourt, "Jean Renoir et Jean-Paul Le Chanois. Petite Histoire de *La Vie est à nous*," in *Les lettres françaises* (November 19, 1969); *L'Avant-Scène Cinéma* (January 1970): 51–53; M. Maurette, "Les Jours se Lèvent," in Grelier, *Mémoires*, pp. 91–93. Renoir's own brief remarks on the film will be discussed below.
3. Le Chanois, interview with author. Le Chanois claims that Renoir was flattered by the offer, that he enjoyed the chance to associate with the likes of Thorez, Duclos, and Vaillant-Couturier. Perhaps there is some truth in his assertion, but it is more likely that Renoir shared the same attraction that so many fellow traveler intellectuals and artists felt for the popular wave that was the Popular Front. In addition, Le Chanois

himself was a party member, and it is at least plausible that the attitude attributed to Renoir in the presence of the PCF luminaries belonged more properly to him.

4. The group worked on the script at the apartment of Le Chanois, who adds that his wife participated also.

5. "There were only one or two conversations with Jacques Duclos, who indicated to us the position of the Communist Party in the Popular Front and in the election campaign." Broucourt, "Jean Renoir et Jean-Paul Le Chanois."

6. Ibid.; *L'Avant-Scène Cinéma* (January 1970).

7. Le Chanois, interview with author.

8. Aside from the sources listed in note 2 above, see also, J. Brunius, *En Marge du cinéma français* (Paris: Arcanes, 1954), pp. 122–33.

9. *L'Humanité,* April 1, 1936.

10. *L'Humanité,* April 2, 1936.

11. Renoir worked fourteen days on the film, according to an interview with Renoir with *Le Canard enchaîné,* cited in *L'Humanité,* April 10, 1936.

12. E. G. Strebel, "French Social Cinema of the Nineteen Thirties: A Cinematographic Expression of Popular Front Consciousness" (Ph.D. dissertation, Princeton University, 1974), p. 189. According to one source, La Bellevilloise "was the first theater populaire founded by a worker cooperative which was committed to projecting only special films, known as 'noncommercial' by the majority of businesspeople." Jeander, "Les Ciné-Clubs," *Le Cinéma par ceux qui le font,* présenté par D. Marion (Paris: Fayard, 1949), p. 383.

13. *L'Humanité,* April 9, 1936.

14. Ibid.

15. L. Chavance, "Le Cinéma au service du Front populaire," *La Flèche,* June 27, 1936.

16. *Regards,* May 28, 1936.

17. This is a reference to the inflammatory article by Charles Maurras in *L'Action Française,* October 13, 1935: "You have somewhere an automatic pistol, a revolver, or even a kitchen knife? This weapon, whatever it is, should serve against the assassins of peace, whose names you have." Maurras used the paper as a forum for his virulent antisemitism, and the "kitchen knife" gained notoriety following the attack on Léon Blum on February 13, 1936. The incident prompted enforcement of the law of January 10, 1936, calling for the dissolution of the Action Française. Cited in L. Bodin and J. Touchard, *Front Populaire: 1936* (Paris: Armand Colin, 1972), p. 33. Maurras was sentenced to jail for his journalistic irresponsibility. See E. Bonnefous, *Histoire Politique de la Troisième République,* Tome 5 (Paris: Presses Universitaires de France, 1962), pp. 376–77.

18. *Regards,* May 28, 1936.

19. P. Ory, "De Ciné-Liberté à *La Marseillaise,*" *Le Mouvement social* 91 (April 1975): 155.

20. F. Courtade, *Les Malédictions du Cinéma Français* (Paris: Alain Moreau, 1976), p. 136.

21. Unsigned memo within Ministry of National Education to the Minister of National Education, June 17, 1934, Archives Nationales, F21 4695/3d.

22. Letter from Minister of National Education to M. Roger Lefevre, Deputy of Charente-Inférieur, September 2, 1936, Archives Nationales, F21 4695/4a.

23. Broucourt, "Jean Renoir et Jean-Paul Le Chanois."

24. *Regards*, June 4, 1936.

25. *Regards*, May 28, 1936.

26. The sources consulted do not disagree on the importance of agriculture to the French economy during the period, both statistically and psychologically. In addition, the role of agriculture in France was far more significant than in the other industrialized countries. An early historian of the Third Republic, for example, noted "the social crisis of French agriculture, a direct consequence of the economic crisis, owed its gravity to the fact that the peasant world had retained in France an importance relatively more significant than in the other industrialized countries." F. Goguel, *La Politique des Parties sous La IIIe République* (Paris: de Seuill, 1946), p. 378. Thirty years later another political historian claimed that this special role of agriculture had not entirely disappeared: "There existed, and exists today, in France, a mystique of wheat and bread, for which it is always dangerous not to take account." Bonnefous, *Histoire Politique* 5: 311. More specialized studies point out that the large agricultural population and its failure to adopt efficiency measures slowed the rate of industrialization in France. See G. Wright, *Rural Revolution in France* (Stanford, Calif.: Stanford University Press, 1964); A. Sauvy, *Histoire Economique de la France Entre les Deux Guerres. (1931–1939)* (Paris: Fayard, 1967); J. Christopher, "The Dessication of the Bourgeois Spirit," in *Modern France,* ed. E. M. Earle (Princeton: Princeton University Press, 1951), pp. 44–57.

27. M. Thorez, "L'Union de la nation française," in *Oeuvres Choisies,* Tome 1: *1924–1937* (Paris: Editions Sociales), pp. 190–296.

28. Ibid., p. 191.

29. Lefranc, *Histoire du Front Populaire,* p. 80.

30. Edouard Daladier, speech at the Radical Party Congress at Nantes, October 28, 1934, quoted in Bodin and Touchard, *Front Populaire,* p. 49.

31. M. Anderson, "The Myth of the 200 Families," *Political Studies* 13:2 (1965): 168.

32. While the appearance of a spoken chorus itself may not have been unusual, Eisenschitz specifies that the one used in *La Vie est à nous* is "not integrated" in the fiction. Eisenschitz, "Front Populaire et Idée de Cinéma."

33. Thorez, "Pour une France libre, forte et heureuse," in *Oeuvres Choisies,* pp. 309–21.

34. In fact, I was surprised to find such a mild response to the anticlericalism of *M. Lange* upon its release. I believe such surprise is the result of a failure to appreciate the strength and even respectability of the anticlerical tradition in France. From the nineteenth century on, the eminently bourgeois Radical party drew its inspiration from that tradition.

35. G. Fofi, "The Cinema of the Popular Front in France (1934–38)," *Screen* 13:4 (Winter 72/73): 5–57.

36. Inspired by certain employers' organizations, "the suspension of the social security laws was proposed in Parliament, unsuccessfully. . . . Unemployment benefits themselves were criticized: in spite of their very modest rate, it was argued that their existence was an obstacle to the necessary reduction of the level of salaries." Goguel, *La Politique des Partis*, p. 379.

37. N. Carroll, "From Real to Reel: Entangled in Nonfiction Film," *Philosophical Exchange*, Fall 1983.

38. Quoted in Bodin and Touchard, *Front Populaire*, p. 47 (no source given).

39. Pithon, "La Censure des films en France et la crise politique de 1934."

40. Alain Resnais made a film called *Stavisky* (1974) based on these events.

41. All the standard histories discuss the seminal role of February 6, 1934, which Bonnefous calls "one of the most serious dates of the Third Republic between the wars." Bonnefous, *Histoire Politique* 5: 213. A consideration of whether "the riots themselves were part of a deep-laid plot against the Republic" can be found in M. Beloff, "The Sixth of February," in *Decline of the Third Republic*, ed. J. Joll (London: St. Anthony's Paper No. 5, 1959), pp. 9–35. On the particulars of the dismissal of Chiappe, see Bonnefous, *Histoire Politique* 5: 226–27; S. Berstein, *Le 6 février 1934* (Paris: Gallimard, 1951).

42. For discussion of the leagues, see Berstein, *Le 6 février*, pp. 56–81; Bonnefous, *Histoire Politique* 5: 186–91; Lefranc, *Histoire de Front Populaire*, pp. 62–66.

43. Bonnefous, *Histoire Politique* 5: 188.

44. Ibid.: 206.

45. "The Soviets! The Soviets!" Ibid.: 209; Fauvet, *Histoire du Parti Communiste Français*, Tome 1, p. 133.

46. Lefranc, *Histoire du Front Populaire*, p. 25.

47. Jeancolas, *15 ans d'années trente*, p. 199.

48. C. Beylie, "Jean Renoir," *Anthologie du Cinéma* 105, in *l'Avant scène Cinéma* 251/252 (July 15, 1980): 149.

49. In its use of newsreel images, the film probably benefitted from the tutelage of Vertov's films, especially in the formal match on screen composition and direction of movement to construct the conceptual congruence of French and German fascists. Eisenstein's manifesto on sound may have influenced the filmmakers in the original idea to separate the sound and image of Hitler, an effective use of contrapuntal sound proposed by Eisenstein in 1929: "*Only a contrapuntal use* of sound

in relation to the visual montage piece will afford a new potentiality of montage development and perfection. *The first experimental work with sound must be directed along the line of its distinct non-synchronization with the visual images.*" "A Statement," in *Film Form*, edited and translated by J. Leyda (Cleveland and New York: Meridian Books, 1957; 1967), pp. 257–59. In a recent account by a participant, Marc Maurette relates that an apparent newsreel shot was actually carefully planned and taken by the filmmakers: "In *La Vie*, Renoir does a montage of newsreel footage on a march of the 'Croix-de-Feu,' de la Rocque at the head. Renoir needed a shot of bourgeois, on the balcony of a nice building, giving the fascist salute; the City Hall of Montreuil is just such a large modern building, with a balcony which was perfect: Marguerite Renoir, Suzanne de Troye, and I got on the balcony and were filmed saluting." Maurette, in Grelier, *Mémoires*, p. 93.

50. The photograph appeared earlier in the illustrated weekly *Regards,* October 5, 1934.
51. Bonnefous, *Histoire Politique* 5: 352.
52. Thorez, "L'Union de la Nation Française," p. 247 (emphasis in original).
53. Thorez, "Pour une France libre, forte, et heureuse," p. 321.
54. A. Bayet, "Jeanne d'Arc, les trois couleurs et le Soldat inconnu," *L'Oeuvre,* May 25, 1936, quoted in Bodin and Touchard, *Front Populaire,* p. 73. His remarks clearly echo the declaration read by Jean Perrin at the July 14 demonstration of the previous year:

> They have taken Joan of Arc from you, this daughter of the people abandoned by the king whom the popular élan had just rendered victorious, and burned by the priests who have since canonized her. They tried to take from you the flag of '89. . . . Finally they tried to take this heroic "Marseillaise" from us, this revolutionary and un-flinching song which made all the thrones of Europe tremble, at the same time, which must not be forgotten, that our great republic called, for the first time, all people to liberty, this "Marseillaise" which has been for a half century the song of oppressed people, and of Russia herself, this "Marseillaise" of Rude who sculpted its taking off on this Arc of Triumph which shelters your unknown brother, and where you do not have the right to pass.

> Kergoat, *La France du Front Populaire,* p. 64.
55. Thorez, "L'Union de la Nation Française," p. 289.
56. Guérin was a member of Pivert's Revolutionary Left wing of the Social-ist party at the time. D. Guérin, *Front Populaire Révolution Manquée* (Paris: Maspero, 1963; 1976), p. 109. Wall supports the claim about Pivert's limited following: "His following consisted for the most part of intellectuals and was most extensive, with the exception of Paris, where the party was weakest." "The Resignation of the First Popular Front Government of Léon Blum, June 1937," *French Historical Studies* 6:4 (Fall

1970): 549. For retrospective comments by participants, see Grelier, *Mémoires*, p. 92. Maurette reports:

> We were shooting in the worker suburb of Montreuil, an important link in the "red belt," these hamlets or towns in the ever-expanding industrial suburb just next to the "zone." The zone was the open land bordering the forts which encircled Paris where the Périphérique is today. Construction was forbidden here in order to leave the land open for cannon from the forts. Little gardens, kitchen gardens, were rented at low rents to retired railway workers, streetcleaners, and retired civil servants who loaned them or sublet them to others, just as poor as they. And some poor people were allowed to build cabins there. I visited one during the shooting. . . . After a mix-up, *L'Humanité* was not delivered. . . . Disaster! A little man, some forty years old, obviously unemployed, coat ragged, old cap, said timidly that he could lend us some. I accompanied him to his hut in the zone, a primitive lodging about 8 feet 2 by 5 feet; an old mattress on a clay floor, a chair with a candle on a saucer. On a packing case, a kerosene hot plate, a wash-basin; a pitcher on the ground, windows covered with oil paper, no glass. And in one corner, next to an old leather suitcase, carefully arranged in a large pile, some dozens, hundreds of *Huma*, the oldest on the bottom, already completely yellowed, the latest at the top, one year, two years of *HUMA*.

57. R. Borde, in an untitled article in "La France des années trente vue par son cinéma." Catalogue of Exposition organized by the Cinémathèque de Toulouse, la Bibliothèque de Toulouse, et le Musée des Augustins, May-June 1975, p. 13. See also F. Garçon, *De Blum à Pétain*, pp. 57–58.

58. "Gabin, for example, plays a melancholy sandblaster worker in *Le jour se lève* or a tainted/sick railway worker in *La Bête humaine;* however, while remaining professionally in contact with his coworker, he separates himself little by little and becomes a character without real relation with his milieu. As the tragedy progresses, the social context is wiped out, thus losing its social import in the story." Ibid.

59. Subtitle of Lefranc, *Juin 36* (Paris: Julliard, 1966). Lefranc draws on the expression first used by Lucien Romier in *Figaro*, September 1, 1936.

60. Bodin and Touchard, *Front Populaire*, p. 133.

61. Goguel, *La Politique des Partis*, p. 383.

62. In further pursuit of unity of the Left, the PCF had entered into discussions with the non-Communist unions to repair a rift in the union movement dating from the policy of the "third period." Communist-dominated unions had broken away from the large Confédération Générale du Travail (CGT), forming the CGTU (CGT Unitaire). This move corresponded to the attempt to build a strong Communist nucleus among organized workers, but the CGTU never approached the numerical strength of the CGT. Part of the problem derived from the

commitment of the CGT, particularly under the firm leadership of Léon Jouhaux, to refrain from any political affiliation.

An agreement on procedural matters was completed in September 1935, and a congress of unification took place in March 1936. One of the central obstacles to unity was the reluctance of the ex-Unitaires (i.e., Communists) to support the CGT demands for structural reforms, for fear of damaging relations with the Radicals and endangering the Radical party's crucial adhesion to the electoral push of the Popular Front. But the tactical importance of successful reunification tempered the PCF's resistance.

Before the reunification of the CGT and the CGTU, the CGT controlled the unions of civil servants and the CGTU/PCF directed the noncivil servant unions, and the metal workers were the largest of the CGTU unions. As the degree of unionization tended to be smaller in the non-CGT unions, the PCF benefitted at the expense of the CGT during the strikes, for it was able to mobilize large numbers of previously nonunionized workers within the non-civil servant industries. Thus, as Jouhaux himself estimated regarding the metal workers, before the strikes of June 1936 the CGTU enjoyed a 6 to 5 advantage; after the strikes, the figures shifted to 9 to 1. Kergoat, *La France du Front Populaire,* p. 132.

63. Goguel, *La Politique des Partis,* p. 384.
64. *Regards,* June 18, 1936.
65. Thorez cites Lenin's remark in his *Fils du peuple* as part of his justification for the position of the party during the strikes in June 1936: "Our party had supported the strike. . . . This active solidarity required us to take on new responsibilities. There was a risk of dislocating the Popular Front. . . . We recalled the teaching of Lenin: not to yield to impatience. He wrote to the French workers in 1920: 'What has always caused problems in France is the anarchist phrase.'" Quoted in Danos and Gibelin, *Juin 36,* Tome 1, p. 114.
66. Blum, radio speech, April 26, 1936, cited in Bonnefous, *Histoire Politique* 5: 414.
67. On June 3, 1935, Georges Friedman spoke on the problems of mechanization, according to a note in *Commune* 23 (July 1935). Later the same year, on December 19, Friedman spoke on the Stakhanovite movement, reported in *Commune* 29 (January 1936).
68. Danos and Gibelin, *Juin 36,* p. 37.
69. Goguel, *La Politique des Partis,* p. 384.
70. Lefranc, *Histoire du Front Populaire,* p. 148.
71. Delmas, quoted in Danos and Gibelin, *Juin 36,* p. 49.
72. Most writers view the speech of Thorez as the single most decisive act in ending the actual threat to social order posed by the occupations of the factories. The question of the existence of a revolutionary situation during the strikes of May and June is one of the most controversial ones for commentators. The key problem in answering the question is the

use of the term "revolutionary *potential*." That is, *if* revolutionary elements had seized the opportunity and led the masses in a struggle for
power, would the masses have followed? Would such action have provoked not simply civil unrest, but actual civil war? The earliest historians of the period believed there was a revolutionary situation: "In
reality, the movement itself, seen in its entirety, is a proletarian revolutionary movement responding to the precise definitions that we have
given of this word [all acts and attitudes of the working class which
reveal the intention to question the right of property of capitalists for
their businesses, p. 44] . . . this strike is truly the classic beginning of a
revolution." Danos and Gibelin, *Juin 36*, p. 49. A more conservative
historian, Bonnefous, refers to the strikes as taking on "a character
clearly revolutionary," though he does not elaborate. Bonnefous, *Histoire Politique*, Tome 6, p. 3. Guérin was a member of Marceau Pivert's
"Revolutionary Left" tendency within the Socialist party and believed in
Pivert's call to action at the time of the strikes: "Everything is possible,"
the title of an article by Pivert that appeared in *Le Populaire* on May 27,
1936. Guérin criticizes himself and the other Pivertists (Guérin's word)
for their failure to exploit the opportunity: "Thus, our task was to help
the workers pass from unconsciousness or semiconsciousness to full
consciousness. In June 1936 we missed the [passing] ship of history. As
Marceau Pivert will say: 'The proletarian revolution passed within arm's
reach: we didn't know how to seize it.'" Guérin, *Front Populaire*, p. 124,
and discussion, pp. 116–34. In a more recent book, Jean Lacouture
dismisses the hypothesis of there being a revolutionary situation as
"dreams of leftist intellectuals such as Daniel Guérin." Lacouture, *Léon
Blum* (Paris: Editions du Seuil, 1977), p. 279. The literature on this
question is fairly extensive by now, and though there is hardly a consensus on the role of the PCF, my own sense is that the film presents a
surprisingly accurate sketch of the situation, though there is certainly
no suggestion that the party would try to apply the brakes to the movement as it did with the real strikes once it gauged their amplitude and
feared a possible rupture in the Popular Front coalition. For further
discussion, consult Badie, Hainsworth, Kergoat, and Schwartz in the
Bibliography.

Thorez delivered his speech on June 11, 1936, at the gymnase Jean
Jaurès, and excerpts from it were printed the following day in *L'Humanité*, June 12, 1936.

73. Blum, address to Chamber of Deputies, June 6, 1936, quoted in Danos
and Gibelin, *Juin 36*, p. 31.

74. At the suggestion of Annette Michelson, I have translated *corporatif* as
"professional," which should be understood as Jouhaux's attempt to
enclose the demands in the rhetoric of trade union demands. Lefranc,
Juin 36, p. 137.

75. The speech of Thorez reads as follows: "If the aim now is to obtain
satisfaction for the demands of an economic nature while at the same

time raising progressively the consciousness and the organization of the mass movement, then it is necessary to know how to end a strike once satisfaction has been obtained. It is necessary to know how to agree to compromise if all the demands have not been accepted yet, but if one has obtained victory on the most essential and most important demands." Thorez, "L'Union de la Nation Française," p. 342. Claudin distorts and even changes the text: "While it is important to lead well a movement for economic demands, it is also necessary to know how to end it. There is at present no question of taking power." Claudin has eliminated phrases and re-arranged the order. Claudin, *The Communist Movement*, p. 203. Colton also elides the qualification, "once satisfaction has been obtained." J. Colton, *Léon Blum: Humanist in Politics* (Cambridge, Mass.: M.I.T. Press, 1966), p. 154.

While historians of the Popular Front and of the Communist party have mocked this speech of Thorez for years, one historian has located a strikingly similar passage from a Thorez article of 1932 which at least suggests that the PCF line during the strikes of 1936 was not as abrupt an abandonment of the workers as other historians have maintained:

> To know how to end a strike may be more important than starting one; one must know sometimes how to reach a sort of truce, to not insist on all the demands before returning to work with a movement conscious of its force and prepared for other struggles.

M. Thorez, "Pour un travail bolchevik de mass," in *l'Internationale communiste*, no. 23, Dec. 1, 1932, cited in S. Wolikow, "Le PCF et le Front Populaire," in *Le PCF, étapes et problèmes*, ed. Bourderon et al. (Paris: éditions sociales, 1981), p. 120.

76. In his study of the strikes, Wall notes the organizational weakness of the Socialists in the union movement, which goes a long way toward explaining the success of the PCF in gaining control of the CGT after the unification of the CGT and the CGTU: "The sudden need for skilled personnel to organize new recruits also worked to the advantage of the communists. The socialists, in contrast, found themselves almost totally unable to exercise any influence on this development, however alarmed they were to see it take place. They maintained no anxiliary organization in the factories, having long since abandoned the 'terrain of class struggle' to the communist cells; they were committed to respect the armchair dogma of the political independence of trade unions (an absolute absurdity from the standpoint of communist doctrine); and a rigid separation was maintained between SFIO [socialist] and CGT leaders." I. Wall, "French Socialism and the Popular Front," *Journal of Contemporary History* 5:3 (1970): 8–9.

77. Sauvy, *Histoire Economique* 2: 379–91.

78. Kergoat, *La France du Front Populaire*, p. 31.

79. Throughout his book, Sauvy indicts the French politicians for their ignorance and/or indifference to relevant economic realities, including

the problem of natality: "The deficit of deaths over births, once reported, should have attracted comment by its seriousness. However,
when the figures are known, in the Spring of 1936, they draw hardly
any attention. Hypnotized by the immediate situation and by their
material riches alone, the French firmly shut their eyes." Sauvy, *Histoire
Economique*, p. 180. See also Bonnefous, *Histoire Politique* 5: 321. Thorez
commented on the problem in his speech at the Villeurbanne Congress
of the PCF, in a section called "Le problème de la dénatalité." Thorez,
"L'Union de la Nation Française," p. 218.

80. A. Kriegel, *The French Communists* (Chicago: University of Chicago
Press, 1972), p. 176.

81. Ibid., p. 140.

82. *Vendredi*, August 21, 1936.

83. Renaud Jean had founded a Confédération Générale des Paysans Tra-
vailleurs (CGPT) in 1929, "but despite the unrest produced by the
depression, the results were disappointing." After the electoral victory
of the Popular Front in 1936, Jean was appointed chairman of the
chamber's committee on agriculture. G. Wright, *Rural Revolution in
France* (Stanford, Calif.: Stanford University Press, 1964), pp. 55, 66.

84. Renaud Jean, radio talk delivered on April 14, 1936. Walter, *Histoire du
Parti*, p. 302.

85. R. Tiersky, *French Communism, 1920–1972* (New York: Columbia University Press, 1974), p. 200.

86. Robrieux includes Desrumeaux among a group of officials in the
CGTU who had the closest ties to the worker base. He also notes that
she worked with the textile union. Robrieux, *Histoire intérieure*, p. 435.

87. In contradistinction to *La Vie est à nous* and the other films discussed
here, the masterpieces of poetic realism end tragically, as did the Popular Front perhaps, but it was the hope for change that brought the
people together in that political coalition. In two films, *Le Crime de M.
Lange* and *La Belle Equipe*, worker co-operatives assume control over
businesses. In Renoir's film, the law's protection of capitalist ownership
causes the failure of the venture. The lottery winners in *La Belle Equipe*
experience internal pressures, bordering on the melodramatic at times
(a romantic rivalry for the same woman), which dissolve the partner-
ship. In both films an initial optimism turns to tragedy, ending in pessimism for the success of the collective. Carné presents an even bleaker
vision in *Quai de Brumes*, though one more representative of the para-
dox in the term *poetic realism*. The realism refers to the recreation of a
milieu, overlaid with a rich aesthetic texture, as the "poetic" stylization.
When the paradigmatic social outcast, Jean Gabin, in the role of an
army deserter, arrives with his lover (Michèle Morgan) at the Marseille
docks, the beauty of the dawn mists hovering over the harbor forms an
image of their idyllic love as well as a premonition of its inevitable
doom. In contemporary reviews of such films, Sadoul repeatedly seeks
to legitimate the artistic success of these films as descendants of the

literary forbears from the pantheon of the nineteenth century: Balzac, Flaubert, Zola. This project of artistic justification has enshrined the admirable works of poetic realism as the signal contribution of French cinema to film history during this period. But these terms of analysis have no relevance to an evaluation of the political films produced during the 1930s in France, which certainly deserve their place in the French film history of the period even if they call for different critical criteria. Some of the important Sadoul reviews have been reprinted in Sadoul, *Chroniques du cinéma français,* ed. B. Eisenschitz (Paris: 10/18, 1979), pp. 11–56.

88. Sadoul, *Regards,* April 30, 1936.

89. M. Hilero, *Ciné-Liberté* 1 (May 20, 1936): 2.

90. Chavance, "Le Cinéma au service."

91. *Commune* (May 1936): 1155.

92. Vaillant-Couturier, *L'Humanité,* April 10, 1936.

93. Le Chanois, interview with author.

94. Chavance, "Le Cinéma au service."

95. Vaillant-Couturier, *L'Humanité,* April 10, 1936.

96. *Ciné-Liberté* 1 (May 20, 1936).

97. *L'Humanité,* April 3, 1936.

98. In an article written by the reactionary journalist Henri Kerillis under the title "Battez-vous! Battez-vous!" he asks whether a victory over the parties of the Popular Front is impossible and then responds:

> No, certainly, it is not impossible. But in the end, figures are figures. With the national deputies numbering only some 180 out of 615 in the outgoing chamber, it seems very fanciful to hope that they will reach 308 next April, while the Popular Front benefits this time from the total participation of the Communist votes, which it did not have four years ago.
>
> There remains only, instead of arithmetic victory, the possibility of achieving a psychological victory.

Echo de Paris, March 5, 1936, cited in Bodin and Touchard, *Front Populaire: 1936,* pp. 40–41.

99. Hilero, *Ciné-Liberté* 1.

100. Jeancolas, in a recent book, calls the theoretical discourse on film at the time in France "most insubstantial." Jeancolas, *15 ans d'années trente,* p. 107. In a personal communication, Richard Abel, author of *French Cinema, 1919–1929,* takes issue with this characterization of writing on film in France. Though I have not examined the writing on film during the 1920s which Abel writes about so thoroughly and authoritatively, my impression from the contemporary material that I have looked at from the 1930s is in accord with the judgment of Jeancolas. Certainly there was writing on film, but no theoreticians of note emerged from that decade, and one just does not find debates over cinematic topics engaged in by writers with a common set of references. The same the-

oretical output simply does not match either that from French theoreticians produced during the 1920s or the ongoing debate that one can find in both *Lef* and *Novy Lef* in the Soviet Union of the 1920s. Thus, articles of interest turn up from the 1930s, as Abel has demonstrated in his forthcoming anthology of French writings on film, but I question whether there was truly a community of writers participating in a shared debate rather than a scattered group of writers expressing their occasional ideas about film. Borde seems to support this view as well when he writes that "the active cinéclubs of the end of the silent period disappeared little by little, as did the intellectual journals (*Cinéa, La Revue du Cinéma*). The cinema press was limited to specialized weeklies, of which one was very well informed (*Pour Vous*) and the others more popular (*Cinémonde, Mon Film, Mon Ciné, Ciné-Miroir*). The cinéphile had become an anachronism." Borde, " 'The Golden Age,' " p. 70.

101. Sadoul, *Regards,* June 4, 1936.
102. Sadoul, *Almanach Ouvrier-Paysan,* 1937.
103. Vaillant-Couturier, *L'Humanité,* April 10, 1936.
104. Le Drimeur, *"La Vie est à nous," Regards,* April 9, 1936.
105. Review in *L'Humanité,* April 3, 1936.
106. Le Drimeur, *"La Vie est à nous."*
107. J. Monnerot, *"La Vie est à nous," Commune,* May 1936.
108. Le Drimeur, *"La Vie est à nous."*
109. I have translated the French word *ataxie* literally by the English word *ataxy,* which means "lack of order."
110. Monnerot, *"La Vie est à nous."*
111. Ibid.
112. Ibid.
113. J.-P. A. Bernard, *Le PCF et la question littéraire. 1921–1939* (Grenoble: Presses Universitaires de Grenoble, 1972), pp. 195–96.
114. Pierre Bost, *Vendredi,* May 16, 1936.
115. Ibid. Regarding the familiarity of French viewers with Soviet films, Eisenschitz notes that

> up to 1939, it is mainly the major Soviet fiction films which are seen, for obvious reasons (lack of interest of the industry in documentary films of questionable commercial value) and less obvious reasons: absence of reflection (if not of information, as the books of Marchand and Weinstein and Moussinac bear witness to) on the propagandistic use of documents; . . .
>
> Vertov, Shub, and the others are unknown or not well known; . . . *Enthusiasm* was shown only once, during Dziga-Vertov's trip to Paris (November 1931).

Eisenschitz, "Front Populaire et Idée de Cinéma."
116. Bost, *Vendredi,* May 15, 1936.
117. M. Martin, *Cinéma 69* 141 (December 1969): 110–11.

118. G. Sadoul, *Dictionary of Films* (Berkeley: University of California Press, 1972), p. 403.

119. De Baroncelli, *Le Monde*, November 18, 1969.

120. P. Haudiquet, *Image et Son* 235 (January 1970): 127.

121. G. Hennebelle, *Cinéaste* 9:3 (Fall 1979): 61.

122. G. Fofi, "The Cinema of the Popular Front in France (1934–38)," *Screen* 13:4 (Winter 72/73): 5–57.

123. D. Guérin, *Front Populaire Révolution Manquée* (Paris: Maspero, 1963; nouvelle edition, 1976); J. Danos and M. Gibelin, *Juin 36*, vols. 1 and 2 (Paris: Maspero, 1952; 1972).

124. I have seen a truncated version of this film in the possession of one of Pivert's camera operators, Robert Talpain. According to Talpain, parts of the original forty-five-minute film were later removed for use in other films. I am not discussing the film above for two reasons. First, the extant film is missing a considerable amount of footage. Second, according to Guérin *(Front Populaire Révolution Manquée,* p. 121) and Talpain (interview with author), the film was made in November 1938, long after the Popular Front had expired as both a mass movement and a formal government. In addition, the ending of the present film contains a passage from May 1939 (the first congress of a new party formed by Pivert). But it should be recalled that Fofi's praise for the unseen film is merely for the political position of the film, which claims that the Popular Front betrayed the interests of the workers. In any other respect, the film merits no more than passing mention as a political film. Aside from an opening speech to the camera by Pivert, explaining the events of 1934–38, the film subsequently simply selects documentary material (shot by his own Cinematographic Service of the SFIO) from those years and arranges it chronologically, opening with footage from February 1934 and concluding with the first congress of the new party, the Parti Socialiste Ouvrier et Paysan (PSOP), established by Pivert and the Gauche Révolutionnaire tendency of the Socialist party after the expulsion of the former from the PS in 1938. Pivert set up the PSOP in protest against the replacement of internationalism and opposition to imperialist war by nationalism and the union sacrée within the Socialist party. The film uses the images to illustrate the demonstrations of the Left during the period (Le Mur des fédérés, July 14, 1935, the strikes of May/June 1936, etc.) and to present various speeches and articles of Pivert calling for a renewal of the revolutionary tradition and a repudiation of nationalism. The film has little interest as a political intervention beyond the articulation of Pivert's position, which can be found in greater detail in Guérin's book, as Guérin followed Pivert to the PSOP.

125. *"La Vie est à nous,* Film Militant," *Cahiers du Cinéma* 218 (March 1970): 44–51.

126. In a subsequent editorial a year and a half later, the *Cahiers* editors explained at some length their reasons for refraining from criticizing

the party at that time—reasons which were based on theoretical questions regarding the relationship between the political line and the cultural line of the party. Essentially, the *Cahiers* editors confessed that they had not sufficiently recognized the fundamental importance of the political line and the impossibility of supporting a cultural line which was the product of a political line with which they had serious disagreements:

> Thus, rapprochement with the PCF, whose culmination is marked by a collective analysis of *La Vie est à nous* taking up word for word in an uncritical fashion the thesis of the film (the theses of the PCF during the period of the Popular Front, and today, *on* the Popular Front).
> Note: It is symptomatic that this text is practically the only article from *Cahiers* . . . to have been cited approvingly by the Party press.

Cahiers du Cinéma 234–235 (December 1971/January-February 1972): 6.
127. Regarding the adoption of *Tel Quel* terminology, their article does not refer to these sources by name, but their use of terms such as *production of meaning* and *deconstruction* identifies the literary influence. Their analysis has two central points and a third which I will return to.

First, for *Cahiers*, *La Vie est à nous* qualifies as a "militant film" partially because of its success in "thinking . . . its own process of exposition":

> Instead of being only its utterance, it reflects on the very conditions of its process of uttering: it poses not the question of meaning (given at the beginning of the film, unique and unchangeable), but that of its "effects of meaning." (P. 48)

The film achieves this form of deconstruction through the "dialectization" of the modes of documentary and fiction. *Cahiers* cites the opening documentary images as an ideological operation, fixed as it is within the "closed" discourse of the institution, "the School," characterized as "connoting a particular, traditional, dead knowledge." The dialogue of the children on their way home from school reveals that those opening images are "lying images" because of what they leave unsaid—the poverty of these particular children (*Cahiers* claims that the initial images themselves are not untrue, for France is a rich country, only that they "lie by omission, dissimulation, abbreviation"). That is, the sequence with the children exposes the ideological nature of the opening documentary, one that lies about the real situation. Because of the filmmakers' distrust of newsreels at the time, the film uses the fiction "to criticize the document."

Second, the *Cahiers* article praises the film for its care in organizing its message according to the particular "addressee of the message." *Cahiers* argues that the last fictional sequence (the *ingénieur*) is more complex than and different from the preceding two sequences (the work stoppage and the resistance to the farm foreclosure) because its intended audience ("the principal addressee of the political discourse of the film") is one that has not yet been converted to the PCF. The earlier sequences could assume the adherence of industrial workers and poor farmers because "their adhesion to the party is the logical consequence of their class being." But for *Cahiers*, the material circumstances of the middle classes, the crucial audience for the film, would not dictate a similar recognition and consciousness of the same class identity. Hence, the story of the *ingénieur* must

> substitute for the demonstrations and analyses of the first two fictional sequences a rhetoric of "conversion," of providential chance, of "grace." . . .
>
> Thus, for the [*ingénieur*], the path to Communism is truly a wrenching [*arrachement*] from his class, a wrenching which cannot be based on recognition . . . but on the much more difficult and ambiguous leap of consciousness [*prise de conscience*]. (Pp. 50–51)

However, this sequence is distinguished from an ordinary "idealist" fiction, which would resolve the final leap with a "fantasmatic closure," by the documents/discourses of the real PCF leaders. Presumably, *Cahiers* is claiming here that an idealist film would accomplish the leap through some deus ex machina, whereas *La Vie est à nous* offers a concrete solution that audiences could avail themselves of, just as the protagonist of the episode does: join the PCF.

It should be clear from the earlier discussion of these sequences and issues that, on the whole, I am in substantial agreement with these parts of the *Cahiers* argument, though I have not used the same critical terms. Formally, the film does reject and even criticize a single ruling discourse of fiction or documentary, for the film as a whole. In this double rejection the filmmakers expressed their distrust of the two traditional, dominant modes of filmmaking. I have tried to indicate that the complexity of this rejection and critique is more extensive throughout the film than the *Cahiers* writers show. Politically, the sequence of the *ingénieur* is crucial in the solicitation of the middle classes, and the lack of formal closure (that the two letters effect in the previous sequences) does acknowledge and respond to the difference in the itinerary (leading to the PCF) of the middle classes.

However, without retracting any of the foregoing, I feel that the *Cahiers* presentation at times forces a theoretical apparatus on the analysis of the film by isolating several examples and ignoring many details. The film does work at questioning modes of filmic discourse, and one might even concur that some sequences "deconstruct" the documentary mode, but is this equivalent to "reflecting on the very conditions of its process of uttering"? I do not believe that this terminology borrowed from *Tel Quel* necessarily contributes to the understanding of *La Vie est à nous*, or, more generally, to the problems of militant film. After all, *Tel*

Quel uses these terms polemically to argue *against* privileging any one reading, yet *Cahiers* has produced *an* excellent reading of the film. On the other hand, their use of "dialectization" seems not only appropriate but necessary to the film's double refusal of fiction and documentary.

Furthermore, much as I agree with the *Cahiers* comments on the *ingénieur* sequence, their summary description of the other two sequences oversimplifies the reality of the film's relation to the political situation of 1936. First, even if one accepts that the industrial worker audience and the poor farmer audience would have already acquired proletarian consciousness as "the logical consequence of their class being," one should not equate that consciousness with adherence to the PCF. More workers belonged to the Socialist party and/or the CGT than to the PCF. These sequences were meant not just to hold on to those workers already Communist but as well to draw adherents from the other parties. Second, it is curious to term the "class being" of small farmers or peasants "proletarian."

To summarize briefly, the *Cahiers* article is the first to have attempted a reading of the film, but the authors bring to it an already elaborated theoretical framework. Placing that grid over the film generates incisive and pertinent observations but at the same time yields an incomplete reading of the film and potential distortions. Perhaps a longer discussion of the film by *Cahiers* would have clarified some of these problems, but I suspect such an effort would have required some modification or at least explication of the overly schematic theoretical machinery.

I think it is also likely that Godard exercised an additional influence on the formulations of the *Cahiers* writers. Godard followed these developments in literary criticism and inserted references to various texts of such criticism in his films (e.g. Derrida in *Le Gai Savoir*). While Bost had no examples from contemporary filmmaking which might have helped him to think through his concept of "film essay," Godard's work throughout the 1960s may have mediated the *Cahiers* elaboration of this concept, as a look at several deep, recurrent concerns in Godard's work clarifies. On many occasions Godard has referred to himself as an essayist. From early in his career, Godard consistently rejected as facile the widely held distinction between Meliès and Lumière—the former founding the tradition of narrative filmmaking, the latter responsible for the documentary line. Godard's films themselves increasingly interrupt the smooth flow of a fictional narrative, sometimes isolated by intertitles as separately numbered segments. After his break with commercial filmmaking, he radicalized these tendencies toward disparateness with the assertion that film is merely a collection of sounds and images.

La Vie est à nous, of course, does not take these ideas as far as Godard, but the issues engaged are similar. The film presents a variety of documentary shots. The opening sequence, on the riches of France, was probably shot for the film and organized into a minidocumentary on

France. The accompanying voice-over, however, reproduces part of a pre-existent text by Thorez, an historical document. Parts of actual newsreels, stock footage, are cinematic documents. The speeches by the party leaders are more ambiguous, in that they were shot specifically for the film, but they are perhaps the only filmed records of the campaign speeches delivered before the Popular Front elections. All of these documents interact with the fictional sequences to mount arguments, to investigate ideas, to constitute a film essay.

While these interactions in and of themselves would be sufficient to qualify potentially as a film essay, the film not only juxtaposes fiction and document but also actively works at dissolving the boundary between the two modes of filmmaking associated with each. Thus, meanings of images and sounds undergo transformations, rendering the distinction between document and fiction problematic.

These striking similarities in the films of Godard and *La Vie est à nous* may very well have guided the *Cahiers* writers in their approach to the earlier film and should earn for *La Vie est à nous* a more important place in the history and theorizing of radical film.

128. I owe this observation to Professor Annette Michelson.

129. Regarding possible precedents, *La Vie est à nous* does resemble some of the Prometheus films made in Germany several years earlier, though there is no indication in the French periodicals of the Popular Front period that anyone had seen these films in France, let alone noted their political and cinematic strategies. And more significantly, none of the films (which I have seen) could be described accurately as a "film essay." Those films were financed by a Left political organization in opposition to the reactionary commercial films of UFA and other companies, whose depiction of the working class outraged the Left. But of the known feature films by Prometheus, none was made specifically for electoral purposes. Also, at the end of an article on *Mother Krausen's Trip to Happiness*, Horak writes that it "seems to be no coincidence that the Prometheus's period of greatest achievement (1926–1929) corresponded to a momentary trend in Comintern policies, whereby the CP openly supported alliances with other nonsectarian left-wing organizations." J.-C. Horak, "*Mutter Krausen's Trip to Happiness*. Kino Culture in Weimar Germany, Part 2," *Jump Cut* 27: 56. Thus, in *Mother Krausen's Trip to Happiness*, which he calls a "high point in Weimar working-class culture," there are no signs identifying political allegiance at the demonstration that ends the film. However, *La Vie est à nous* repeatedly reminds the viewer of the importance of the Communist party.

130. C. Beylie, "Jean Renoir," *Cinéma d'Aujourd'hui* (Nouvelle série) 2 (May-June 1975): 26.

131. A. Sesonske, *Jean Renoir: The French Films, 1924–1939* (Cambridge, Mass.: Harvard University Press, 1980), pp. 187–88, 232.

132. C. Gauteur, Preface, in J. Renoir, *Ecrits*, ed. C. Gauteur (Paris: Belford, 1974), p. 8.

133. Ibid.
134. Renoir, *L'Avant-Garde*, March 13, 1937, reprinted in Gauteur, *Jean Renoir. La Double Méprise* (Paris: Les Editions Français Réunis, 1980), p. 42.
135. J. Renoir, *My Life and My Films* (New York: Atheneum, 1974), p. 126.
136. Ibid., p. 125.
137. Le Chanois, interview with author.
138. Cachin, *L'Humanité*, April 9, 1936.
139. Vaillant-Couturier, *L'Humanité*, April 10, 1936.
140. "We are not a party fallen from the sky. We are regular folks with firm roots in French soil." Vaillant-Couturier, *L'Humanité*, July 11, 1936, cited in N. Racine and L. Bodin, *Le PCF Pendant L'Entre-Deux-Guerres* (Paris: Presses de la Fondation Nationale des Sciences Politiques, 1972, 1982), p. 209.
141. J. B. Brunius, *En Marge du Cinéma Français* (Paris: Arcanes, 1954), pp. 130–32.
142. Renoir, URCJ Informations, 1961, quoted in P. Leprohon, *Jean Renoir* (Paris: Crown, 1971), pp. 84–85.
143. N. Sibirskaia, interview with Pierre Phillippe, *Cinéma 61* 60, quoted in *Premier Plan* 22–23–24 (May 1962): 190.
144. Sesonske, *Jean Renoir*, p. 233.
145. *Cahiers du Cinéma* 218: 45–51, quotes on 46, 47.
146. *Jeunesse nouvelle*, August 29, 1935, reprinted in Renoir, *Ecrits*, p. 93.
147. Renoir, "Souvenirs," *Le Point* 18 (December 1938), reprinted in Renoir, *Ecrits*, p. 42. Translation in A. Bazin, *Jean Renoir* (Paris: Delta, 1974), p. 154.
148. Bazin, *Jean Renoir*, p. 89.
149. Beylie, quoted in *Cahiers du Cinéma* 218, p. 46.
150. Many critics use the expression. Perhaps the earliest was Roger Leenhardt in *Esprit* (February 1937): "Unknown yesterday, everyone knows today that Renoir is the director of genius of the left." Reprinted in *la revue du cinéma. Image et Son* 315 (March 1977): 22.
151. *Commune* 39 (November 1936). "To Litvinov, Peoples' Commissioner for Foreign Affairs of the USSR. On two important occasions where the fate of justice and the rights of people were at stake, in Geneva and London, à propos Abyssinia and Spain, the USSR made heard the oppressed voice of the world conscience. The intellectuals grouped around the Maisons de la Culture want to express their gratitude to the USSR for having, in the present chaos and obscurantism, safeguarded the indestructible principles of justice, of dignity and of peace." Also in Gauteur, *La Double Méprise*, p. 38.
152. *Cahiers de la Jeunesse* 1 (July 15, 1937).
153. Renoir, *Cahiers de la Jeunesse* 2 (September 15, 1937), reprinted in *Image et Son* 315, p. 30.
154. Renoir, interview in *L'Avant-Garde* (January 2, 1937), reprinted in *Image et Son* 315, p. 34.
155. Renoir, *L'Humanité*, July 24, 1936, reprinted in Renoir, *Ecrits*, pp. 88–90.

156. Renoir, "Souvenirs."
157. Renoir, *Ciné-Liberté* 1 (May 20, 1936), and idem, *La Flèche* (May 30, 1936), reprinted in Renoir, *Ecrits,* pp. 80–82.
158. Renoir, *Ciné-Liberté* 1 (May 20, 1936), reprinted in Renoir, *Ecrits,* pp. 80–81.
159. Most of the articles are reprinted in *Ecrits.* The remainder can be found in *Image et Son* 315 and Gauteur, *La Double Méprise.*
160. Renoir, *Ce Soir,* March 25, 1937, reprinted in *Ecrits,* pp. 100–101.
161. Ibid.
162. Ibid.
163. Renoir, *Ce Soir,* April 14, 1935, reprinted in *Ecrits,* p. 163.

3

The Rise and Fall of
Left Filmmaking during
the Popular Front

The successful realization of *La Vie est à nous* transformed Left filmmaking activity from a hope to a reality. Just as the PCF had assumed primary responsibility for the political union of the Popular Front in the two years since the events of February 1934, so its leadership had borne fruit in the cultural field. The party effectively forced a choice on intellectuals and artists: for or against the Popular Front; opposition to or approval of fascism. PCF front organizations like the AEAR and its journal, *Commune,* invited writers to declare their sympathies for or against. The urgency of the situation afforded no political fence-sitting. With an extensive cultural apparatus already in place in the AEAR, the PCF easily found room for filmmaking in the Alliance of Independent Cinema. But only when the PCF placed an order for a propaganda film with the quasi-independent ACI did the group marshall antifascist filmmakers on the Left to enter production. The ACI promptly chose a more appropriate label for its militant stance, borrowing from its media relative Radio-Liberté to adopt the name Ciné-Liberté. In the following two years Ciné-Liberté led the struggle for an independent cinema. However, during this time the Popular Front suffered severe internal stress and eventual dissolution, and the activity of other independent filmmaking groups reflected the structural instability of the amalgam known as the Popular Front. Ultimately, as hopes waned and unity disintegrated, Left filmmakers were unable to sustain the innovations of *La Vie est à nous.*

Ciné-Liberté Takes Shape

Like the Popular Front itself, Ciné-Liberté required a gestation period. During that period scattered references in the press mentioned Ciné-Liberté but without any delineation of its precise goals or functions. At the end of January 1936, *L'Humanité* carried a short note on the organization, which existed "not in its own name" but under that of the ACI. In its two-month existence, the ACI had hardly galvanized the Left filmmaking world, having sponsored several screenings. The note, however, embroiders the modest reality with a more ambitious agenda:

> Ciné-Liberté groups already a large number of technicians and directors, etc. . . . and most of the technicians and directors who work at rescuing the French cinema from its present morass.
> The Maison de la Culture shelters the ACI, whose present task, between the production of films and the organization of meetings, is to group the spectators and help existing groups in the programming of their screenings.[1]

The text does not cite any illustrious names as evidence of legitimacy and breadth of support, nor does it list proudly the concrete accomplishments to that point of either Ciné-Liberté or the ACI. The inclusion of spectators is typical of the Popular Front's efforts to build mass organizations, but the initiative for the extension of this tactic to the mass media came from Radio-Liberté, which was publishing membership figures daily in *L'Humanité* and *Le Populaire*. By the end of February, Radio-Liberté had already signed up some 8,000 listeners.[2]

The numerical strength of Radio-Liberté probably convinced the leadership of the PCF to begin a sister organization. Thorez had just delivered his speech, "L'Union de la Nation Française," at the party congress in Villeurbanne, and the electoral alliance for the elections of the coming April (and May) had been completed formally only weeks earlier with the publication of the Programme of the Rassemblement Populaire. The PCF regularly published speeches and texts of prominent party figures, and a film would complement the dissemination of the PCF position on the elections: the premiere of *La Vie est à nous* did coincide with the opening of the election campaign. The PCF recognized as well that a new organization needed some tangible public demonstration of its efficacy. Gide and Malraux had presided at the founding meeting of the Maison de la Culture, but its first real achievement, several months later, was the International Congress of Writers for the Defense of Culture, which attracted a galaxy of stars including Barbusse, Rolland, Malraux, Gide, Aragon,

Heinrich Mann, Brecht, Ehrenburg, A. Tolstoy, Tretiakov, E. M. Forster, and Aldous Huxley. The PCF succeeded in getting Renoir to supervise the film project, but as the party had no experience with filmmaking, it probably preferred to look at the results before committing itself to publicity before the fact. Thus, there was no discussion of the production of the film in the press while it was being made, in contradistinction to the coverage of the production of Ciné-Liberté's best-known film, *La Marseillaise*, a year and a half later.

In February, when plans for *La Vie est à nous* were well underway, none of the Left publications had further information on Ciné-Liberté. *Vendredi*, the Popular Front journal par excellence, reported on the essential aims of the future organization but entirely in the framework of the ACI:

> Are we going to see finally some important "newsreels," some documentaries drawing their source from reality and not from a concern for propaganda? Without doubt, for after the founding of Radio-Liberté, now we have an "Alliance of Independent Cinema" formed, which has as its objective, on the one hand, to struggle against the poor present production and, on the other hand, to proceed itself to independent production of short films first, and some more important films when its first efforts have been crowned with success.
>
> The presence of G. Dulac, J. Painlevé, C. Aveline, Moussinac, Roger Desormières . . . at the head of ACI is a guarantee of probity and success.[3]

For a full month, during which *La Vie est à nous* was being completed, there was almost no word on the ACI or Ciné-Liberté. Only at the end of March, shortly before the release of *La Vie est à nous*, did news begin to dribble out, though still without a single mention of the film. The publicity effort mounted in *L'Humanité* at the beginning of April, when the official campaigning period for the election opened, indicates that the Left intentionally withheld any advance notice of the film, preserving the dramatic impact of its premiere. On March 27, 1936, *Le Populaire* informed its readers that "The ACI (Ciné-Liberté), which has as a goal the grouping of technicians and spectators to defend the cinema and to free it from its restrictions, informs its many members and sympathizers that information will be available every day from 3–6 P.M. and Saturday 2–7."[4] In this short item *Le Populaire* stresses once again the union of film workers with spectators, but it does not take the trouble to mention its predecessor, Radio-Liberté, even though the PS had participated fully in its constitution. Throughout the period, actually, the PS showed little interest in the use of the media. Pivert's group had a relatively autonomous existence within the PS, which remained suspicious of the mass media.[5] The same week Georges Sadoul, already a prominent Communist intellectual (he had represented France, with Aragon, at the Kharkov Writers Conference in 1930), also avoided any mention of *La Vie est à nous,* which he certainly knew about, but did point out the Radio-Liberté connection, after excoriating the censor in an article entitled "Liberté du Cinéma": "Just as a group Radio-Liberté was formed recently, the friends of the cinema have just created Ciné-Liberté. Among the first members of the new association are found the best French directors: Jean Renoir, Marc Allégret, and others. Such an organism, if it is supported by the thousands of spectators in the theaters, will have a great task to undertake and an efficacious role to play in resurrecting the French cinema."[6]

Although *L'Humanité* devoted considerable space to *La Vie est à nous,* with reviews, commentary by Vaillant-Couturier, and excerpts from an interview with Renoir (printed originally in *Canard Enchaîné*), neither the ACI nor Ciné-Liberté were given credit for the production. The PCF was fully justified in claiming credit itself for ordering the film, but it had contracted the ACI to see to the actual production. The extant version of the film awards production credit to "a crew of technicians, artists, and workers," which is the exact phrase used in the unsigned *L'Humanité* review of April 3, 1936.[7] Discussions probably took place in these first days of April to reach some agreement on both the institutional identity of Ciné-Liberté and future filmmaking plans, for *Le Populaire* printed a "Programme de Ciné-Liberté" on April 10, 1936:

> For a true cinema, for a human cinema, for a free cinema, the Alliance of Independent Cinema (12, rue de Navarin) has launched an appeal to all the active spectators and all the free cinéastes.
>
> Why?
>
> For a long time, the filmmakers most attached to their art, the most enlightened spectators, see in independent production the only force capable of regenerating the seventh art, of returning cinema to the people, to whom it belongs, in tearing it from the exclusive control of money, in setting an example of a production responding to the needs and aspirations of our epoch.
>
> How?
>
> Until now, spectators and cinéastes have been unconscious, caught up in their own activity, separated by the "wall of money." For an independent cinema to be possible, what was needed was for both to realize the necessity and the power of their union. They had to find the form of

their reciprocal support, of their effective collaboration. Now it has happened.

The alliance of filmmakers and spectators against the restrictions and defects of commercial production, for an independent production: the Alliance of Independent Cinema (ACI). The ACI is already making newsreels and documentaries meant to give an objective image of our time and organizing screenings of unreleased films and classic films, conferences where filmmakers will present their views on their art, their struggles for free expression, where eminent writers will share their ideas on the seventh art.

The ACI leads the campaign against the censor, against the stupidity, against the arbitrary decisions of the film merchants, for objective newsreels and for collaborating with the ciné-clubs, the free filmmakers, and all the personalities or organizations whose efforts converge with our own.

The ACI asks the public its opinion by referendum, petitions, etc. . . . It intends to publish a periodical, a free tribune for all members and rallying point for the renovation of the seventh art.[8]

Not only did the production of *La Vie est à nous* show the Left filmmaking community what could be done by working together, but also its banning provided a common focus for protest. Ciné-Liberté undertook plans to screen *La Vie est à nous* privately. In an article "For a Cinéma Populaire," *L'Humanité* announced private screenings of the film reserved for members of Ciné-Liberté; members would receive invitations for these events.[9] It was the police banning of some of these screenings that so angered Sadoul. This treatment of *La Vie est à nous* only revived the furor over the censor. While constant throughout the period, attacks on the censor increased in number and virulence at each new interdiction. Like Radio-Liberté and radio, Ciné-Liberté channelled this protest through a single tribune. On May 1, *L'Humanité* seconded in more terse form the aims of Ciné-Liberté, though without printing the text of the Programme that appeared in *Le Populaire:* "The technicians and artists grouped in Ciné-Liberté propose to struggle for an independent cinema, to produce themselves some films truly populaire, to group the spectators disgusted by the platitudes of bourgeois films, to support the independent productions, to fight the censorship which has axed *La Vie est à nous* and others of a high artistic, moral, and social interest."[10]

Still the leaders of Ciné-Liberté had yet to be identified, but the publication of the first issue of the monthly *Ciné-Liberté* (dated May 20, 1936) resolved any questions about the group's existence and the composition of the leadership. Just below the name of the magazine on the front page was the editorial committee: H. Jeanson, L. Moussinac, J. Renoir.[11] Opposite their names to the left was the organizational affiliation: "Organ of the Alliance of Independent Cinema." Also at the top of the page, beside the logo, the magazine left space for its most pressing concern: "Anastasia is persistent. Not as much as *Ciné-Liberté*."

More than any other single issue, the figure of the censor, Anastasia, preoccupied the contributors. Just below the comment on Anastasia next to the masthead, the political cartoonist Frick designed a drawing of "The Good Documentaries." A Roman warrior fires a cannon, a scroll marked *Ciné-Liberté* mounted on two reels of film serving as wheels. The target, feathers scattered in the air following the direct hit, is a bird with a large pair of scissors for a head, its eyes gazing anxiously down at the artilleryman. Of the four pages in the issue, the first three carried attacks on the censor. Below Frick's cartoon, Claude Aveline discussed "The Censor and Ciné-Liberté." After reviewing the sins of the censor, he faults the spectators for tolerating this suffocation of the cinema. Protests have yielded results on occasion, squeezing out a visa here and there, but to suppress censorship,

> it is not a handful of men who can bring it off. A mass movement is needed. There as elsewhere, what is impossible for some will be easy for all.
>
> Yes, the crowd of spectators in France is responsible for the present state of affairs. But it has its excuses. Each spectator feels there are too many intermediaries between the censor and him, between the producers and him. (Another problem, that of production, which should be debated without delay.) How many times have we heard, in Paris, in the country, our neighbors murmur at the end of a show, "It's too idiotic!" But their apathy, their apparent indifference comes from the fact that they had not found, up to this point, the means of demonstrating in a positive manner, in a common action. Ciné-Liberté offers this means to them today. It intends to gather all those who desire a cinema freed from all control, from all restriction, an untarnished cinema, a free cinema. It will make them judges of banned or mutilated films. It will establish a direct relationship between spectators and technicians. It will organize everywhere the screenings, the gatherings, the meetings necessary to put before public opinion all the questions to be resolved, the reforms to win. While waiting—I believe not a long time—it will create in turn. . . . The victories of Ciné-Liberté will be those of the cinema.[12]

Writing after the Popular Front had achieved political victory at the polls, Aveline has outlined exactly the same strategy for the cinema,

Cartoon in the first issue of *Ciné-Liberté:* "The Beautiful Documentaries.
Hunting the Censor—Anastasia." *Ciné-Liberté* 1, May 20, 1936

"Here, I'm returning your film to you . . . but I had to cut it a little."
Ciné-Liberté 2, June 20, 1936

joining forces in the struggle for a common goal. On the third page, P. J. Laspeyres articulated what Aveline left unsaid: "After the magnificent victory the Popular Front has just returned in the elections, to crush the censor should be written on the first line of the list of administrative tasks."[13]

Jeanson, also writing on censorship, began with two satirical anecdotes before taking issue with André Gide's position. The anecdotes lampooned the arbitrariness of the censor, who forces a director and producer to wait outside the screening room, where they nervously speculate on the possible cuts. When the film is in the middle of its second projection, the producer boldly walks into the screening room to discover the censor fast asleep. Upon waking him, the producer requests his visa. The censor agrees hurriedly but warns the producer not to disturb him again. In his commentary after the stories, Jeanson disagreed with Gide's claim that art grows from constraint and dies from liberty, though he admitted that French film had a healthy future in front of it if Gide was right. But then he read off a sampling of the censor's demands for past films, ridiculing the vast array of special interests protected by the Censorship Commission, from all the armed services through foreign affairs to fathers of large families objecting to seeing the thighs of chorus girls. In the name of Ciné-Liberté, he asks M. André Gide's pardon for not having created Ciné-Constraint.

While attacks on the censor dominated the issue, *Ciné-Liberté* did not neglect corollary subjects. Assorted distortions of newsreels were ridiculed: showing street urchins under the banner of the Popular Front; describing Mussolini's aggression in Ethiopia as "freeing" the slaves; presenting the bloody fighting in Spain under the sign of the Republic. In addition, faithful to its label as a grouping of technicians and spectators, *Ciné-Liberté* invited readers' queries on technical matters, including direction, editing, sound, photography, makeup, set design, projection, etc. Normally, curious spectators had no access to this information, but

> *Ciné-Liberté* proposes specifically to remedy this lack. Indeed, the hundred technicians in our organization are ready, each according to his own competence, to answer questions that spectators wish to pose.
>
> As for spectators, male and female, curious only to know the name of Mlle. Colette Darfeuil's lover or the brand of Jean Weber's depilatory cream, they are kindly asked to abstain.[14]

The "Technician Service" signed this offer and provided brief technical information on comparative running speeds and prices of 35 mm and 16 mm films.

On the same page, L. Lemare, writing for the "Technicians Corner," considered the still unresolved question of amateur formats. No standardization had been decided upon for nonprofessional equipment. Trade publications carried advertisements for several formats, including 9.5 mm, 16 mm, and 17.5 mm. Virtually all films, even those shot by marginal operations like the group under Pivert, were shot with the heavy 35-mm cameras unsuited to documentary and newsreel work. These groups offered projection prints of these films in reduced formats, at lower prices, but the lack of standardization of nontheatrical formats retarded the development of even reduced-format projection equipment, let alone production. The president of the League of Education addressed this problem at some length before the Renaitour inquiry at the end of 1936.[15] Teachers had often purchased equipment in various formats in earlier years, sometimes with their own money. Without standardization, they were understandably reluctant to risk replacement of obsolete equipment with new acquisitions that could soon become obsolete as well. Both Bremier and Lemare refer to an international film conference, held in Rome the previous year, which adopted 16 mm as the second standard format internationally (after 35 mm). Lemare recommends the 16-mm format as well for its reasonable cost, increased portability, and acceptable quality. He adds that sound filming is still difficult with the bulky cameras, so one should plan on postsynchronizing the films. "For these different reasons, the 16 mm is certainly the reduced format most favorable to the productions that we plan to execute for the spectators of 'Ciné-Liberté.'"[16] Despite this optimistic account of 16-mm possibilities and the prediction for future production, interviews with filmmakers indicate that actual use of 16 mm in France was rare.[17]

Regarding postsynchronization, the excellent results in *La Vie est à nous* proved that the prohibitive cost of sync shooting did not handicap effective and inventive solutions. In *La Vie est à nous*, the most powerful uses of sound occur precisely during the postsynchronized sequences. In fact, this very effectiveness of the postsynchronized sound may have been the primary reason for the rush of the departing government to pass the decree proscribing the use of postsynchronization in newsreels, a decree passed less than two weeks before Blum took office. The government no doubt was fully aware of the anger on the Left over the commercial newsreels and, after *La Vie est à nous*, feared the birth of a broad workers' newsreel network that would break the monopoly by the commercial newsreel houses and provide the Left with a powerful ideological tool. Even though the newsreels were theoretically exempt from the visa requirement before May 1936, the companies respected the wishes of the censors for the most part, an abdication of journalistic responsibility in the eyes of an infuriated Left.

Beside the predominantly militant rhetoric of the magazine in expressing its contempt of the censor and the commercial cinema, the tone of the lead article on the first page by one of the three members of the editorial committee was surprisingly restrained. In "A propos de *Modern Times*," Jean Renoir defended Chaplin against critics disappointed by Chaplin's latest film. He said nothing about Ciné-Liberté, its goals or future production plans, nor did he direct comments against his pet targets from his other writings, such as Mussolini and Goering. He did write in the essay style he was to perfect in his weekly pieces the following year for *Ce Soir*, moving from the personal to the general but without the political twist ending of so many of the later pieces. Though Renoir had just finished working on *La Vie est à nous*, a militant political film that fired its participants and sympathizers to form Ciné-Liberté, he chose to begin his contribution to Ciné-Liberté's magazine with the following passage:

> One beautiful spring morning, we were, several coworkers, seated around an editing table at the factory Léopold Maurice at Gennevilliers. We had spent the night further refining some work that we cared about deeply. The daylight crept stealthily through the large bay window and suddenly we could make out the trees in the garden and, in the middle, a large apple tree in bloom. It was abruptly like discovery of a new world. Of course we had all seen apple trees in bloom before, but it seemed to us that we had never seen them bearing such thick foliage. The flowers seemed to push against each other for space. We could not stop marvelling over their size, their lushness, their health. The bluish early morning colored them delicately. Then passing from the detail to the whole, as one does in the cinema, we looked at the whole garden as it awakened. . . . And, beyond this oasis, like a background, we could make out peeling houses, factories smoking tragically, the whole typical frame of the Paris suburb, otherwise the most beautiful countryside in the world, today wasted, soiled, dishonored by the greed and stupidity of industrialists and landlords.
>
> The film of Charlot is all that.[18]

The striking lyricism of this scene is far from the concrete political struggle of *La Vie est à nous*. One thinks, without question, of the highly personal project that Renoir was to work on next—*A Day in the Country*, which he began just over a month later—a film some have called "the most Renoir."[19] Does this mean that Renoir's relationship with the Popular Front was merely a passing dalliance? Was his commitment to Ciné-Liberté in name only?

The rest of the article helps in sorting through these questions, if not in resolving them conclusively. Renoir surveyed the critical reception of various Chaplin films. With film after film, the critics greeted the most recent film with coolness, lamenting that it was not up to the quality of the earlier "classics": "When *The Pilgrim* came out, this masterpiece, the connoisseurs claimed, with a gentle frown, 'It's very good, but it's not worth the first ones; the Essanay films, that was cinema, true, pure, the film for film's sake, the gag for gag's sake. In *The Pilgrim*, the puritan spirit showed through under the farce.'"[20] Renoir returned then to the image of the apple trees, familiar yet ravishingly new at the same time. So Chaplin, dressed as before in the same hat and wearing the same little mustache, appears to be the same character but takes off in new directions: "It's as if the ground were missing under our feet and only the great, the magnificent public populaire has the power to follow without dizziness an artist who leads it in such novel paths. This interior renewal, it is one of the marks of genius."[21] Renoir supported Chaplin's artistic choice to express his creativity as he saw fit. And this creativity is an interior one, the same creativity which Renoir discusses constantly throughout his autobiography almost forty years later and which in fact is a lesson he learned from his father, who taught him not to be distracted by externals. While some critics on the Left defended Chaplin's politics, seeking to claim him for the Left, Chaplin's screen character had only a vague political identity, certainly not one that conformed to any political party or coherent set of goals and tactics. Chaplin on screen took the side of the outsider. When he trundled off down the road at the end, he was neither following nor leading. Though taking an entirely different perspective, Renoir also delighted in presenting outsiders, the marginal characters that populate his films.

Renoir saw in Ciné-Liberté a chance to escape the creative restrictions of the commercial cinema industry. He had originally embarked on filmmaking as an independent, financing his own films. When he learned that he could not continue to make films on his own, he was forced to work in the commercial industry and even submitted to working on projects he considered puerile (*On purge bébé*) as necessary payment for the opportunity to make more personal films. Renoir did not specify what he liked in the Chaplin films themselves. Renoir no doubt envied Chaplin's ability to make films of his own choice, all financed independently. By avoiding any comment on partisan politics in his article, when the euphoria of the Popular Front's victory was at its height, Renoir propounded a program for Ciné-Liberté of aesthetic freedom, a program that would guarantee artistic freedom and independence for filmmakers, a freedom unavailable in the commercial industry. In this sense, it becomes perfectly understandable that, in that first exciting summer when law after law was passed restoring dignity to the working people of France, Renoir could walk away from the Popular Front, journey back to the village where his father had painted, and work on the ill-fated *A Day in the Country.*

The First Films of Ciné-Liberté

Shortly after the first issue of *Ciné-Liberté,* dated May 20, 1936, the great strike wave of May and June swept over France. As already noted in chapter 2, *La Vie est à nous* recounts a work action and offers an interesting view of the PCF's attitude toward strikes in the early spring, but it was completed more than a month before the strikes began. Ciné-Liberté, however, had declared its readiness and desire to make its own films ("newsreels and documentaries") after the release of *La Vie est à nous.* The sit-down strikes afforded an ideal opportunity, which it did not pass up. Although not referred to by name at the time, the resulting film now bears the title *Grèves d'occupation* (occupation strikes or sit-down strikes).

In considering this film, it is important to keep in mind the controversy discussed in the last chapter, about whether this wave of strikes constituted a revolutionary situation. Some of the historians take positions that correspond to their political affiliations of the time: both Lefranc and Guérin were participants in the events.[22] Guérin, following Trotsky, believes that there was a revolutionary situation. Trotsky proclaimed it at the time (from Norway), but as he was an unreconstructed proponent of international revolution ever imminent, his objectivity must be suspect.[23] Lacouture, on the other hand, observes that a revolutionary situation did not obtain, despite somewhat hysterical claims to the contrary by the likes of Guérin.[24] Though no definitive consensus can be found, the predominant view concerning the existence of a revolutionary situation seems to be, probably not.

Without question the workers were spurred by the astonishing electoral victory they had produced. The frustration pent up during the years of economic crisis and aggravated by the deflationary policies pursued by the previous governments could not await the formal transfer of power to the Popular Front government, so they occupied the workplaces as yet another demonstration of their combined power and initiative. For them, installation of the new government was just a formality that would as a matter of course recognize their just demands. The leaders, however, did not share the workers' confidence, for they knew that their entry into the government already was a delicate enough operation. Domestically, their main concern was to reassure business that its worst fears of wholesale governmental takeover of property had no foundation in fact. Such a fear in itself would lead forthwith to capital flight and destabilizing consequences for the economy. On the foreign front the Allies and the Soviet Union depended on the strength of France as the front line of defense against the rising menace of fascism. To have the Popular Front strategy backfire in such a catastrophic manner was the last thing the Soviet Union wanted. A weakened France would unravel the Soviet Union's plans of bilateral alliances, incarnated in the Franco-Russian pact of 1935.

But beyond fears of a disastrous alienation of capital, the spontaneous generation of the strikes meant that the leaders had no control over the workers. The strikes themselves were peaceful, with strict avoidance of the destruction of property, but they occurred erratically, without a clear, coherent set of initial demands. Thus, the organized leadership did not even understand what was happening, so they could in no way simply assume the reins of the movement as representatives of the workers. Obviously, forced evacuation of the factories would have eliminated any chance of channelling the demands of the workers and would have terminated the Popular Front before its inception.

For roughly six weeks, then, from the first takeovers until resolution, the government and authorities did nothing. Celebrations went on continuously during these weeks. Strikers in the film studios projected films. Theater troupes toured the factories. Workers sent out calls for accordions and other musical instruments to complete their bands. Seamstresses sewed material at hand for nightly fêtes.

The leaders of all the worker organizations debated what to do, which at least forestalled the need to take decisive action and bought time, indirectly perhaps in the hope that the situation would resolve itself. The PCF could not very well oppose the movement, but neither could it actively encourage its spread. And its militants were not necessarily in a position to do so anyway. Within the Socialist party, the pro-Trotsky Left wing (under Pivert and Zyromski) announced, in the words of Marceau Pivert, that "Everything is Possible,"[25] an appropriately vague battle cry, effectively acknowledging that it did not know how to proceed either. Of course Blum, about to head the government, avoided at all cost such inflammatory remarks and tried to pressure the factory owners into concluding an agreement for everyone's benefit so that the government could function. The PCF responded as well to Pivert's reckless enthusiasm with Thorez's famous

Worker celebrations in a factory, June 7, 1936, the date of the signing of the Mantignon Accords (*Grèves d'occupation*)

rejoinder that "everything is not possible. . . . It is necessary to know how to end a strike."[26]

It is interesting, then, to look at the Ciné-Liberté film shot during the strikes to examine its attitude toward them. The film includes shots from a variety of factories—in particular, film studios at Joinville and Billancourt, with Pathé even identified in one sign, but the voice-over mentions Renault as well. Thus, film must have been gathered from numerous Ciné-Liberté sources and completed shortly after the end of the strikes, for the enthusiasm of the workers pervades the film, an élan that was not to last for long, as the flush of victory soon turned to bitter resentment over subsequent developments, such as Blum's nonintervention policy during the Spanish Civil War decided on during the summer of 1936. The film that has survived lacks some of the footage described in contemporary accounts, but what remains does not contradict those early reports.

Without introductory titles, *Grèves d'occupation* opens with two shots from the inside of a factory office. Through the panes of a partition separating the office from the factory floor proper, one sees dancing in the background, postsynched to the popular music of an accordion. The leaf on the calendar hanging in the office fixes the date of June 7. Thus, the film opens on the date of the formal, legal signing of the

Matignon Accords by representatives of labor and management. This date was only the third day of the Popular Front government. Despite the extraordinary pressure of events, Léon Blum had pointedly refused an offer to take office before the officially scheduled time, because of both his long-standing and well-known strict observance of legalism as well as the need to tamp the volatile tensions of those days; he knew that he could not govern without at least some sympathy from the moderate wing of capital. He feared that irregularities in the installation of the government would only aggravate their fears and harden their anticipated intransigence. The country was virtually drifting without leadership during these first days of June, so the film takes pains in these first shots to enclose the strike activities within the bounds of the legally constituted government. As the papers had splashed either ominous or celebratory headlines on the front pages since the first strike publicity late in May[27] and the mass participation of workers guaranteed virtually universal familiarity with the exact chronology, this decision by the filmmakers could not have been casual, nor would viewers have mistaken its significance.

The opening, then, immediately announces the commitment of the film to the maintenance of order and to support of the government. It repudiates the more intemperate calls of the anarchists and Trotskyists for a revolutionary seizure of power. The placement of the camera in the factory office also indicates that the workers have taken over the direction of the factories, for the partition no longer represents a barrier between capital and labor. The filmmakers evidently are shooting from the domain of the bosses, and the music reinforces the suppression of this stratification. Similarly, the audible presence of the accordion—the iconic instrument par excellence of the working class—automatically signals worker occupation of the sound track.

Camaraderie and celebration continue in the film. An orchestra is seen, another vivid image, for local communities contributed instruments for these orchestras, extending the bond among the workers beyond the factory. A sign above another shot of dancing identifies the factory as an automobile works ("Culasses machines grève 1936"), and a banner carries the name of Henri Barbusse, the grand literary patriarch of the party. This early reference lightly introduces the presence of the PCF. Various shots of popular dances succeed one another in a minicatalogue of working-class leisure rites: la danse du bal, the farandole, billiards, les flèchettes (darts).

Afterward, the workers take chairs to listen to visiting singers and theatrical performers, as the narrator notes the performances of representatives from the Maisons de la Culture. Not only do neighboring communities lend their support, but also artists from the AEAR express their solidarity with these touring performances, a perfectly logical extension of their activities as itinerant troupes appearing at worker fêtes and soirées throughout the period. The performances also bear connotations of the Communist presence, for the Maisons de la Culture drew their inspiration and leadership from party intellectuals and faithful fellow travelers.

After the sequence illustrating the outside support of the artists, the bond between workplace and community is developed with a series of traditional ceremonies that now widen their orbit to include the factories: a sign in a factory announces that "On Sunday, at 4:00, the Cortège de la Rosière will stop here," after which a procession of young women dressed in white robes files by. A conductor leads an orchestra in a factory courtyard in the next shot, followed by a wedding procession on the street with several bars of marriage chords on the sound track, and finally several views of yet another local costume event.

The narrator usually introduces each new activity with "Ailleurs" ("Elsewhere") and a brief identification of the action. While most of the activities would probably be understood easily enough by the worker audiences, the repetition of "Ailleurs" rhetorically underlines the variety and scope of these activities in a long form of conceptual montage. This type of narrative intervention eliminates the need for spatiotemporal continuity in favor of implying more generally that this flood of activity and outpouring of popular enthusiasm is transpiring more or less at the same time. This rhetorical strategy is an effective solution to the probable paucity and scattered origins of the footage at hand. But although the narration does wrap the disparate scenes in a loose continuity, it does not distort the meaning of the individual shots with insidious juxtapositions to create inaccurate cause-and-effect shot chains or even a temporal linearity where none necessarily exists. The shots simply unroll one after the other as parallel events occurring "at the same time."

The next sequence also takes place, significantly, outside factory grounds, as men and women attend and execute a ceremony involving the burning of effigies bearing the demand "Death to 48 hours." Several shots here are edited in continuity, with low-angle camera placements as the figures are catapulted from the bridge matched with high-angle views as they plunge into the water. The care to match these shots implies at least some rudimentary familiarity with cinematic vocabulary.

The sequence, then, receives privileged treatment in the film and for understandable reasons. For the first time in the film, workers have massed around a demand—for reduction in the work week. There was probably conscious effort to insure more than one camera to record the event. Second, the demand fits firmly into a trade-union structure of desired reforms, clearly a repudiation of extremist or "adventurist" elements who wanted to confront the question of ownership. After the free rein given to the expression of pent-up worker discontent in the preceding sequences, this sequence tries to temper radical demands that would circumvent the established labor institutions. The heads of the labor establishment, having watched helplessly and powerlessly the spontaneous "explosion," eventually regained control by prudently letting the movement run its course until the energy subsided and then channelling the energy into a set of overdue demands that stopped short of a serious challenge to the system. Whatever the merits or motivations of this strategy, it restored the direction of the labor movement in the hands of the traditional labor directorate, namely the CGT, PCF, and the Socialist party. *Grèves d'occupation* reproduces this trajectory: it effectively marks the taming of the revolutionary threat with the date (June 7) in the first shot and seals it in the continuity editing of this symbolic interment of forty-eight hours.

The next shot displays a sign that proclaims "Victory, the 16th and last day of strike." Satisfaction of demands, in other words, defuses the defiance of the working masses. Appropriately, a headline from the CGT paper, *Le Peuple,* not only echoes this "Victory over Misery" but also focuses responsibility for the successful termination of the strikes on the apolitical CGT. Rather than using *L'Humanité* or *Le Populaire,* the film avoids such partisanship by choosing the organ of the CGT, which in the event did not take a line different from the PCF or the PS.

To cap this victory visually and to highlight the seal of the CGT, a lyrical camera movement tilts up and down the building of the Bourse de Travail, obviously now in the hands of the workers (i.e., the Popular Front government). A long series of superimposed industrial shots of factories and cranes, replete with exhilarating camera movements, prolongs this valorization of the workers. Though no one remarked on the similarities at the time, it is possible that the filmmakers had assimilated the lessons of Vertov's films on industrialization as a model for this sequence. The rush of movement, complexity of industrial gridwork meshing like giant erector sets, the assertive graphic designs

Photo in Communist illustrated weekly, showing striking workers hanging effigy of efficiency expert: "The struggle, the celebrations. . . . At Bennes Pillot, the strikers, beside a red flag, hanged a mannequin—a very humorous job—who represents the efficiency expert, a creature of management" (*Regards,* June 18, 1936)

"Death of Capital": workers celebrating the end of the strikes (*Grèves d'occupation*)

"Chrono" effigy dropping from bridge . . .

and drowning (*Grèves d'occupation*)

Superimposition of Léon Jouhaux, head of the re-unified CGT, over the facade of CGT headquarters and a factory (*Grèves d'occupation*)

of the shots themselves were unusual in French films of the 1930s, for the French Left extolled the virtues of camaraderie over the heady visions of industrialization.

This French bias reflects both the political and economic differences between France and the Soviet Union in their respective attitudes toward industrialization. Certain Soviet filmmakers were transported by these utopian visions of an industrialized Soviet Union, and Stalin's eventual historic decision to back the version of the First Five-Year Plan that committed the economy to heavy industry abetted this excitement with industrialization. France did not suffer from the same initial perception of industrial backwardness and perhaps had enough industrial experience behind it for the workers to recognize its more mixed rewards. In nonsocialist countries, Stakhanovism could hardly muster the same allure.

After this industrial celebration several speakers appear, the first being Léon Jouhaux, quickly followed by the Communist Duclos and several others. Jouhaux, of course, headed the CGT, just recently reunited with the Communist CGTU, and he pursued an independent line, essentially trade unionist, and resolutely avoided political alignment. Again, the PCF does not arrogate credit to itself here, and another headline from *Le Peuple,* "8 Million Salaried Workers Have Won," repeats the orientation given by the earlier headline.

The remainder of the film is given over to workers pouring out of the factories. However, before the workers leave, there is a shot of the negotiators carrying their briefcases, working their way through the corridor made for them in the knot of people outside. Once more, the film insists on the role of the leadership before ceding the screen to the workers. Presumably, these are the negotiators of the Matignon Agreements, although it is also possible that they may have completed one of the specific pacts that were concluded shortly afterward, for the Matignon Agreements provided only general guidelines to be followed in subsequent industry-by-industry and business-by-business pacts.[28] A long series of worker processions rounds out the film, again apparently strung more or less end to end, organized formally by matched camera movements panning in the same direction or paired opposites in one direction and then the other. Of course these formal editing practices only indicate once more a certain facility with film, the individual shots being selected obviously for the mix of banners carried by the celebrants. The "Alliance of the Unified CGT" heads this succession of icons, with the symbols of the PCF (hammer and sickle) and the Socialist party (three parallel arrows) adorning the corners. Many of the signs bear these insignia, with the Bonnet Phrygien of the French Revolution sometimes occupying a middle ground between them, as if mediating (for it is always between). Otherwise, one finds the expected names and faces mounted on the signs: Blum, Thorez, Barbusse.

The narrator names these figures as their images pass by, but the sound track consists primarily of a crowd singing the omnipresent Left song of the period, "Au devant de la Vie," and then a band playing the "Internationale." The song dots the sound track of many films from the era, often associated with youths as they march or file by. The "Internationale" of course was shared by the Socialists and Communists alike. However, the "Marseillaise" is conspicuous by its absence.[29]

The return of the national hymn to the inventory of Left symbols was much remarked upon in the press, and references to the resurrection of the tricolor in the speeches can be heard in the *Grand Rassemblement.* Still, the prominence of the Bonnet Phrygien on the banners assured this association in *Grèves d'occupation.* Furthermore, the strikes and their issue signalled a victory for labor, not the national electoral union of the Popular Front. The pride of place accorded the

Workers with raised fists celebrating the end of the strikes (*Grèves d'occupation*)

Workers celebrating the victorious end of the strikes: "All for one. One for all." Symbol of French Republic flanked by Communist (hammer and sickle) and Socialist (three arrows) symbols. The bottom line refers to the re-unification of the officially nonpartisan Confédération Générale du Travail with the Communist Confédération Générale du Travail Unitaire. (*Grèves d'occupation*)

leadership in the film had more to do with the containment of worker discontent than with reinvigoration of republicanism in the face of the fascists.

This interpretation of the function of the leadership in *Grèves d'occupation* is not proffered as an endorsement of an ultra-Left critique of the leaders selling out the workers and failing to heed the call of the workers for revolution. Quite the contrary. In the absence of a real revolutionary thrust among the mass of workers, the heads of the organizations acted prudently and responsibly in winning real gains for the workers, averting the Right's pressure for the use of force and convincing the Right of the need for a rapid resolution of a volatile situation. The reading of the film is simply an attempt to investigate the considerations facing the filmmakers at the time, consonant with the historical evidence, of which the film should be included as a part. The filmmakers probably sided with the predominant feeling among the strikers, which the leaders finally articulated in a form admissible of resolution and which they certainly took credit for, but only acting at the will of the workers.

Despite Ciné-Liberté's spirited calls for an alternative cinema, with the exception of *La Vie est à nous* the organization did little to publicize its subsequent production. Repeatedly, writers in the magazine (*Ciné-Liberté*) demanded the authorization by the censor of *La Vie est à nous*, but no one even reviewed Ciné-Liberté's production activity during the summer months after the election. Only Georges Sadoul remarked on the group's output, but not in *Ciné-Liberté*. Sadoul had just begun to concentrate his interests in film, taking over the cinema page in the illustrated Communist weekly (modeled after Münzenberg's AIZ) *Regards*. Moussinac had recommended him for his original position at *Regards*, and Moussinac also served on the editorial board of *Ciné-Liberté* and would have kept Sadoul informed of the independent filmmaking activity, in the event Sadoul did not know of it on his own. In August Sadoul congratulated Ciné-Liberté for "setting up a crew of young technicians who have made seven documentaries in several weeks."[30] Two months earlier he had reported on the filming of material on the strikes by a Ciné-Liberté crew "on the order of the CGT," which he predicted "will be more than a documentary, which will be a veritable historical document on the great period when we live." At that same time he praised the tightening of bonds between intellectuals and workers, "still extremely embryonic, the seeds of which will be the living culture of tomorrow."[31] Sadoul was also a regular contributor to *Commune*, the organ of the AEAR, which had set the popularization of culture as one of its central tasks. The par-

ticipation of artists and intellectuals at the very site of the massive
worker struggles, in the factories themselves, provided a dramatic
demonstration of its fulfilling that goal.

In his second article, when Sadoul elaborated on the strike film, he
reversed his emphasis. Rather than implying, perhaps somewhat
faintly, a degree of condescension toward the workers by commend-
ing the artists and intellectuals for deigning to sprinkle their cultural
largesse on the ignorant masses, Sadoul praised the film on the strikes
for showing that the workers had their own culture as well, which he
called folklore. Sadoul objected to the assertion by "the best folklorists
in the country" that folklore is uniquely a peasant phenomenon: "The
film of Ciné-Liberté proves the contrary. Worker energy has created,
in the thousand divertissements which took place beside the great
strike, some ceremonies which draw on popular traditions and which
are themselves part of these traditions. Thus, for example, the bur-
lesque 'funeral procession of the strike,' inspired, it seems, by the
traditional 'funeral procession of Père Cent,' in the barracks. These
facts prove right the young folklorists who are giving a new orientation to the science of popular traditions."[32] While Sadoul betrays a
somewhat academic tone here, he is responding to the exclusion of
the working class from the screens of French film, a frustration only
reinforced by the peasant tableaux in the films of Feyder and Pagnol.

This is not to say that the AEAR repudiated regional culture. In an
interview with Sadoul in *Regards,* titled "For a Living Culture," Aragon translates into cultural terms the political agenda set out by Duclos, to resolve the tricolor of the past with the red flag of the future:
" 'The Maison de la Culture' is in fact the real center of the intellectual
life of the country. In the new conditions made by the victory of the
Popular Front, our organizations will be at the disposition of the
government to work to return yesterday's culture to the people and to
create with the people the culture of tomorrow."[33]

As Aragon runs through the variety of activities of the Maison de la
Culture, including theater, architecture, music, painting, and literature, he cites a membership figure of 20,000 for Ciné-Liberté. It is
true that Ciné-Liberté did sell membership cards which entitled holders to reduced admission at Ciné-Liberté screenings, but the paucity
of screenings, advertising, and press coverage, even in the Left press,
suggests that this figure was pure fantasy, or at least not based on any
figures corroborated independently at the time. Even Radio-Liberté,
which did attain that figure, required several months of almost daily
publicity to reach 20,000, and it published its figures regularly.

The attempt to eliminate the barrier between the workers and intellectuals was not simply rhetoric, however. When the Fédération du Théâtre Ouvrier de France was founded at the beginning of 1931, during the "class-against-class" policy of the Comintern, its goal was to build a working-class theater movement. The split in the Prémices group reflected that dichotomy between amateur and professional, as the more politically militant members of Prémices broke away in protest against the "professionalism" of Legris. By the beginning of 1936, the wind had shifted with the rise of frontism and pressure for "a living culture." Thus, one of the officers in the FTOF, Jean-Paul Dreyfus (Le Chanois), a charter member of the Groupe Octobre and assistant on *La Vie est à nous*, announced the new orientation in *L'Humanité*.[34] The AEAR had recruited some of the most prestigious figures in French theater (Pitoeff, Jouvet, Dullin, and Baty), so some organizational change was in order. Dreyfus now said that the time had come to develop a better theater, and one would find in the new Union du Théâtre Indépendant de France "a concern for a better 'artistic' presentation, for an entertainment healthy and varied, for a spectacle worthy of the name."[35] As with former pariahs in the political arena, professional artists were now to be welcomed to the fold, even solicited. Several weeks later, at the same time that *La Vie est à nous* was being screened before the leaders of the three political parties of the Popular Front, Le Chanois assured readers in *L'Humanité* that no tendency would be discriminated against, whether "artistic, political, professional, amateur."[36]

Socialist Films

Ciné-Liberté may have taken a similar approach, but not everyone chose to cede autonomy to an organization that was at least Communist dominated, if not Communist controlled. Among the filmmakers Aragon listed in the *Regards* interview as belonging to Ciné-Liberté, in addition to the three members of the editorial board (Moussinac, Renoir, Jeanson), were Feyder, Jean Painlevé, J.-R. Bloch, Claude Aveline, and Germaine Dulac. Missing from this lineup were any members of Marceau Pivert's filmmaking organization, the Section Cinématographique of the SFIO (Socialist party). Although Pivert had long supported and lobbied for union with the PCF in common struggle, he guarded his filmmaking group's independence during this early period of Ciné-Liberté. In fact, his group had continued to produce films after the few films made in 1935.

On June 24, a week after Sadoul first spoke of the Ciné-Liberté CGT film on the strikes, Pivert ran an advertisement in *Le Populaire* for seven films available from his organization, the last five of which all covered events from 1936:

SOCIALIST CINEMA

MILITANTS! For your meetings, for propaganda, for your fêtes, here are some socialist films made by the section cinématographique of the Party.

1. La Commune. Demonstration at the Mur des fédérés. 25 m. 200 F rental.
2. Bastille 1789–Bastille 1935. The huge demonstration of July 14, 1935. 45 m. 350 F.
3. Boulogne socialiste. Municipal Socialist events. 15 m. 75 F.
4. The Attack on Léon Blum. Some evocations of the life and death of Jaurès; the fascist provocations, the demonstrations which preceded and followed the attack on Léon Blum.—Commentaries by Georges Monnet. 20 m. 150 F. This film is also available in reduced format. 17.5 m.
5. Le Deuxième Paris-Roubaix travailliste. Commentary by the director of the race, our comrade Boucherie. 20 m. 150 F.
6. Le Conseil National extraordinaire du 10 mai 1936. 35 m. 200 F.
7. La Manifestation triomphante du 7 juin au Vél d'Hiver. Les discours de Léon Blum, de Paul Faure, de Bracke, de Thorez, etc. la partie artistique socialiste.[37]

Unfortunately, only the first film on the list has survived (see chapter 1). To judge by the titles and the brief descriptions, the films deal with single events and constitute the only sustained effort on the Left to establish a Left newsreel service, in this case specifically a service provided by the Socialist party and presumably representing that party's political position. However, as already pointed out in the discussion of *Le Mur des fédérés*, Pivert argued for his own left-wing tendency within the PS, and as he saw film as a powerful propaganda tool, it would be interesting to examine the films to ascertain to what extent he allowed those views to inflect the films. *Le Mur des fédérés* resisted the more assertive nationalism of the Popular Front prompted by the PCF, but at the same time Pivert evidently did not make a film on the strikes, even though he wrote one of the most controversial articles in *Le Populaire* when the situation was still in flux and extremely volatile, an article that threatened to topple the Socialist Blum government even before it had taken office with its revolutionary battle cry, "Everything is possible!" Pivert's unofficial position in the Blum cabinet may have cooled, at least for a time, his revolutionary fervor. He accepted a post giving him responsibility for the press, radio, and motion pictures, but apparently he did not effect any significant changes or reforms.[38]

Actually, there had been some talk of nationalizing the film industry itself. In April 1936 a major industry journal, *La Cinématographie Française*, ran an article with a heading not likely to reassure the already beleaguered industry: "The Socialists Announce the Nationalization of the Cinema."[39] Paul Faure, one of Blum's closest associates and soon to become minister without portfolio in the Blum government, had given an interview in which he stated that the Socialists would nationalize the film industry.[40] The same magazine that had conducted the interview with Faure, *Cinémonde*, conducted an interview with Marcel Cachin the following week. Cachin edited *L'Humanité* at the time (the same role he plays in *La Vie est à nous*) and had some revealing comments when asked what he would do about film if he were head of the government.

> I would not leave it in the hands of the people who have made it what it is. I would make it a public service, obeying uniquely the joint interests of art and the public.
>
> Would you make film an instrument of propaganda?
>
> I believe yes, like everyone. Is there a single work of art, anywhere, which is not an instance of propaganda? The cinema which is given to us now tends only to make morons of the people and to glorify the domination of capitalism.
>
> Would you use newsreels for propaganda purposes?
>
> Each of the classes which are struggling has a tendency to present everything under the aspect which is most favorable to it. This is how Italian fascism floods our screens with images of war that harm the unfortunate Ethiopian people who are being massacred.
>
> One can imagine newsreels which cover all essential current events impartially. Do you subscribe to this idea?
>
> The class struggle is too powerful to permit the existence of purely objective newsreels. *The cinema is a combat weapon. We would know how to make use of it.*[41]

Of course the PCF refused to participate in the government, so these declarations had no practical consequences as official policy.[42] Cachin did summarize succinctly, however, the general attitude of the Left toward the commercial cinema and the newsreels produced by the various newsreel agencies. More significantly, his remarks conform precisely to the approach taken in *La Vie est à nous* toward the conception of objectivity in newsreels. All news reporting must have some interpretive grid for organizing the material. Given the opportunity, the Left would not disguise its own attitude under the camouflage of objectivity, and in *La Vie est à nous*, the filmmakers actively bent the newsreel footage for their polemical purposes. Hence, the reviewers had no reason to comment on the novelty of the political positions proffered in these sequences. The Left had always viewed Hitler as a demagogue and Mussolini as a deadly buffoon. What *La Vie est à nous* represented for them was the first major victory in the battle for access to the screen, for control over the means of producing films, and for freedom to exhibit the films as they wished, without having to submit to the political interventions of a reactionary censorship institution.

In contrast to the relatively extensive publicity given to *La Vie est à nous*, the more modest efforts of Pivert's group received almost no coverage. This observation may underestimate the dissemination of the group's films, for one of the principal cameramen of the group, M. Robert Talpain, has claimed that the group organized at least 4,000 screenings between 1936 and 1938 in France. Obviously, such a claim reveals the difficulties of writing the history of a popular movement, for published documents may provide only a pale trace of considerable activity at the grassroots. Pivert's political position at the extreme Left of the Socialist party did not enjoy wide support within the party as a whole. Neither did the Socialist party manifest great interest in film as a propaganda tool, though the party did engage in extensive propaganda activities. The PS had no cultural network even remotely comparable to the AEAR and the Maisons de la Culture of the PCF (to name only one organization in the PCF cultural arsenal). However, in a later account of the period by one of the members of Pivert's political following, Daniel Guèrin did make several observations on Pivert's filmmaking work.

Guérin described the way Pivert handled the presentation of *L'Attentat contre Léon Blum*, one of the films in the advertisement cited above. The blurb for this film gives more information on its content than the annotations on any of the other films, suggesting that Pivert wanted to put special emphasis on this film. The title of the film refers to a February 13, 1936, attack on Léon Blum by a group of young ruffians from one of the Fascist leagues (Action Française). They spotted Blum driving by one of their gatherings and proceeded to drag him out of the car and beat him, inflicting serious injury. Some workers nearby rushed to the rescue, but Blum had to retire to the country to recuperate for over a month. The timing of the attack and its violence provoked yet another large public demonstration to protest against the leagues and strengthened the Left's resolve to observe unity at all costs for the elections. Blum's recovery and eventual hero's return to the political arena for the official campaign only increased his personal stature. Pivert, who had great respect for Blum's personal integrity, even as he disagreed with him politically, realized the propaganda opportunities in these events and, according to Guérin, exploited those opportunities in a highly questionable manner:

> On the initiative of Marceau Pivert, the Socialist party devoted a film to the attack against "one of the best servants of the people of France, one of the best fighters for bread, for peace, for liberty." His features are reproduced on huge banners. When, the day after his appearance before the Parliament, June 7, he comes to the Vélodrome d'Hiver to swear to the French people to never surrender power without a struggle, an extraordinary mise en scène greets his arrival. Spotlights are pointed at him. An orchestra plays the "Internationale." The militants turn into a chorus. The Jeunes Gardes in blue shirts form an energetic double line. The faithful chant indefinitely and to the point of losing their breath: "Vive Blum!" or "Blum! Blum!"
>
> Who is the director of this cult? None other than Marceau Pivert. A little later, too late, he will request that the militants free themselves of a "certain religiosity" which prevents them from evaluating calmly the policies of "the most prestigious militants." But, in the meantime, he was the one who functioned as the high priest.
>
> Our leader believes in the techniques of totalitarian propaganda.[43]

Guérin explains that Pivert had fallen under the influence of a German social democrat who had studied the methods of German propaganda and advised Pivert that the PS should use the methods for humanistic ends: "Half-convinced, Marceau Pivert signs up the professor Flamm in the service of the Blum myth. During the month which passes between the victorious elections and the effective assumption of power by the government of the Popular Front under socialist direction, we march like sleepwalkers and react like drug addicts."[44] It is difficult to know if these methods were typical of the Pivert films, but from the brief descriptions of the films, it seems that they did not mix fictional and newsreel footage, nor did the group ever produce one major effort that would serve as an exemplary organizing tool for unity in the struggle against the censor and a formidable symbol of the possibilities for a Left independent cinema, both of which functions *La Vie est à nous* filled at the same time.

Not only did *Le Populaire* not set aside much space for Pivert's filmmaking activities, but also Pivert's Left extremism may have alienated other potential collaborators within the party. Shortly after the elections, another group arose within the Socialist party, taking the

name Mai 36. *Le Populaire* carried an announcement of the organization to be formed on July 31, 1936. Aside from specifying that it was to
be a Socialist organization, the note added little of its aims or functions, nor did it even say that the group would be concerned with
filmmaking.[45] Apparently Germaine Dulac headed the organization,
even though she was also listed as a member of Ciné-Liberté in a July
14, 1936, article on the various entities housed within the Maison de
la Culture.[46] Thus, despite all the publicity given to Ciné-Liberté
throughout the Left press, it did not succeed in centralizing all the
independent Left filmmaking, as the Socialists Pivert and Dulac made
their own films, and the filmmaker Renoir limited his contribution to
the articles of the journalist Renoir.

Dulac completed one film with the ephemeral Mai 36, *Le Retour à la
Vie*. Dulac's political ideas probably differed from Pivert's, but her
film also departed from the strictly newsreel format of Pivert's films.
Le Retour à la Vie mixes newsreel and fictional footage to propose a
solution to the economic crisis. Dulac herself had worked with both
types of films, having been a central figure in the avant-garde movement of the late 1920s and then producing newsreels during the
1930s.

The film essentially advocates a solution to the economic problems
of the country through a rise in purchasing power, an idea popular
with the Left at the time after the deflationary policies followed by the
Right had failed either to stimulate investment and production or to
stem the appalling spread of unemployment. Dulac illustrates this
thesis through the story of a simple peasant family. After an aerial
shot of farmland (taken from a plane), a peasant is seen inquiring
about purchasing a cow. A wipe then reveals a young mother pouring
milk into a bottle for her baby. The peasant, her father, returns home
and explains to his wife and daughter that he did not buy the cow
because no one would be able to buy the milk at the price he would
have to charge. The daughter immediately begins to lecture her parents about the need to increase the purchasing power of the people.
During the daughter's declamation, Dulac cuts in various graphics,
including bar graphs of the unemployment figures for the years
1930–36. The daughter then assures her parents that the young will
change the present situation through a massive reconstruction of
"houses, water, health, roads, schools, electricity," and Dulac again
inserts shots of all these visions of the future—new houses, highways,
and dams with power stations. The daughter immediately cites what
France has instead of this, as the shots accompanying her discourse
present half-finished construction, airless slums, idle machinery in a

factory, and a large crowd of unemployed. As her parents are shown listening, she places the blame on the lack of money circulating. The scene cuts away once again to an old man looking through a factory window from the outside at the still machinery inside. An owner sits down at his desk, and the gates of the factory close as the worker seen peering through the window walks off. Then a short sequence at a market shows a worker unable to purchase anything because he has no money, an obvious consequence of his having been denied work at the closed factory.

The culprits in this process are the "traitors" who refuse to invest in French industry, sending their money abroad. One of these "traitors" withdraws money from a bank, places it in his briefcase, and walks off. After a shot of a train sign designating the express train to Basel, an animated sequence shows the money leaving France for Basel. Dulac is indicting the industrialists here for the flight of capital that has ground French industry to a halt. This was a continual problem during the middle 1930s in France, to some extent perfectly understandable given the resistance to devaluation of the franc. Other currencies, notably the dollar, had been devalued earlier in the 1930s and were regaining stability, plunging France deeper into the crisis, for French goods had an increasingly difficult time competing on the world market. Business interests pushed for devaluation of the franc as well, but the parties of the Popular Front made opposition to devaluation one of the cornerstones of their joint program, for it would drive up prices of imported goods. Some of Blum's closest advisors insisted that devaluation was inevitable at some point, but Blum promised the people that he would not devalue.[47] This political intransigence only exacerbated the fears of capital, already apprehensive about the prospect of a Socialist-directed government, and the Bank of France suffered large drains of its francs in May and June. The Matignon Agreements, with their commitment to raise wages, hardly reassured business interests, as capital outflow continued. Higher wages would put pressure on French prices, which were already higher than those of its trade partners. Whether the electoral program of the Popular Front could have assuaged these fears at all and thereby have averted devaluation is debatable, but by the fall even Blum could put it off no longer.[48]

While Dulac's film does touch on the problem, it shows no sensitivity to the complexity of it. The daughter affirms that youth will change everything, and the animation shows the money traveling back to France from Basel. The vehicle of this change is unity, represented by a sign promising that "We will stay united" and a shot of a

demonstration. But then Dulac compares two paychecks of a cemetery worker, one from April 23, 1936, the other from July 10, 1936, or
after the Matignon Accords. The worker has put in forty-eight hours
in both cases, but the hourly wage has risen from 4.15 F to 5.75 F,
roughly 40 percent, and social security benefits have also increased.
The problem with this analysis in the film is that the rise in salaries
only put greater pressure on domestic prices, which in turn would
accelerate capital flight. In the film, however, there is no discussion of
such complications. With the rise of wages, a worker, with one arm,
picks up his paycheck and beams happily as he sees the raise. Now he
can purchase food at the market.

After the daughter repeats her incantation that "it is we who will
produce changes," the camera pans over a demonstration once more,
followed by a shot of *Le Populaire*, with the headline that the paper has
invested 100,000 F in treasury bonds. With the rise of purchasing
power taken care of, Dulac shows the factories operating once more,
smoke pouring out of chimneys, gates opening to admit the workers,
gears spinning, a row of tractors advancing. Converted by her daughter's exhortation, the mother retrieves the money that the father had
returned with at the beginning of the film and directs him once again
to purchase the cow, as the daughter observes, "A little stream to make
a great river." Dulac then literalizes this metaphor with shots of increasingly larger and more powerful streams and rivers, ending with
a superimposition of a demonstration with a large banner of the
Association Républicaine des Anciens Combattants held aloft (an ending obviously inspired by the final sequence in Pudovkin's *Mother*).

While exhibiting an undeniable political naiveté, this short, eleven-
minute film, like many of the films made before internal stresses
began to erode the unity of the Popular Front, conveys the early
optimism and inflated hopes of the power of the masses. The unemployed daughter, filled with the visions of the massive demonstrations,
projects these images for her discouraged parents. She intones the
recurring refrain of youth to combat the pessimism of her parents'
generation, an ideological call for rebirth which permeated the spirit
of the Popular Front but which was not by any means wholly illusory.
The strikes which had forced management to accept the Matignon
Accords were not the work of older, more conservative union leadership or rank and file but arose in the ranks of younger, unorganized
workers. The excellent animation in the film certainly grossly oversimplifies a complex economic situation, but the early enthusiasm that
produced the electoral victory and overflowed to the occupation of
the factories swept aside practical obstacles. As the enthusiasm sub-

sided, these persistent realities became more troubling, leading to the devaluation in the fall and the "pause" in the economic program of the Popular Front declared by Blum early in 1937.

Somewhat surprisingly, given Dulac's work with newsreels for several years, the film does not undertake any critique of newsreels or approach the use of newsreel and documentary footage in any type of dialectic. The newsreels function as simple illustrations of the declamatory statements of the daughter, whether of the operation of factories or the marching of demonstrators. The film does not question the dependability of newsreels or the distortions of commercial newsreels so often criticized by the Left. Coupled with its political simplicity, the banal alternation of fictional and newsreel material eliminates the possibility of any polemical thrust to the film, leaving as a result a film accomplished enough technically but basically anodyne politically and flaccid formally.

This combination may explain the surprisingly hostile reaction to the film in a Left film journal:

> A short film, but it would have been good to shorten it . . . completely. How is it that Mme. Germaine Dulac commits such errors? Propaganda, however it is done, is acceptable only when it is well disguised. But here, it is presented in such an infantile and ridiculous fashion that the most patient spectators respond aloud, "Do you take us for morons?"
>
> To ask the people to have confidence, to exhort them to put their money back in circulation, all fine, in principle. But to ask and exhort with images so badly put together and commented upon in such a stupid manner, is to harm the cause that one seeks to defend.[49]

The censor apparently had no objection to "infantilism," for it authorized a visa, and the following year Pivert even included the film in an advertisement for the films offered by his film section with the SFIO.[50] However, there is no evidence that Dulac attempted any further independent political films. At the same time, there was a general lull in independent production during the second half of 1936.

Ciné-Liberté and the CGT

Ciné-Liberté continued to publish its magazine through November 1936, but the political situation had already begun to change. On July 18, 1936, less than two months after Blum took office, the Spanish Civil War broke out, and the question of French (and Allied) intervention immediately inserted a wedge between the Communists and the

Socialists. Blum, a strong supporter of the Spanish Republic, was personally inclined to send aid to Spain and even directed his air minister, Pierre Cot, to arrange for the delivery of planes. In addition, France had a treaty with Spain that justified such action. However, the news of these shipments was leaked to the press by a Franco sympathizer, and a political furor erupted, forcing a public debate over French intervention. The facts surrounding this debate and the subsequent French policy are still the subjects of considerable debate by historians, but Blum quickly called a halt to official intervention.[51] The Communists pressed for the immediate resumption of aid and an active policy of support, citing the documented supplies of matériel and manpower from Hitler and Mussolini to Franco. Decisive action by France might have enabled the Spanish government to crush the rebellion quickly, but Blum worried about the possibility of touching off a civil war in France and could not convince England to support a joint intervention of some sort. Blum vacillated, eventually calling on the major powers to sign a pledge of nonintervention in Spain. This ostrich-like maneuver effectively locked France into a policy of nonintervention without having extracted any similar pledges from Germany or Italy.

The PCF, having refused participation in the government, attacked nonintervention throughout the summer. The issue introduced a serious strain on the already precarious balance of the Popular Front coalition, even though the PCF deputies did not risk toppling the government by voting against the policy in the chamber. In addition to this foreign problem, a similar situation was repeated in the fall with the devaluation of the franc, when the Communists abstained from the voting.

In this tense political atmosphere, it is not surprising that the earlier unity ebbed and independent film production declined as well. Most of the earlier films had taken that newfound unity as their virtual raison d'être, as can be readily seen in the titles and subjects of the films: Bastille Day, the demonstrations at the Mur des fédérés, at the Vélodrome d'Hiver. Nonetheless, throughout the summer and fall, Ciné-Liberté continued to publish its magazine, with repeated declarations to build an independent cinema:

> We want a healthy cinema.
> We want the films to be your films, written by you, produced by you, played by you.
> This independent production, in the true sense of the word, healthy, incorruptible, has been born. It is called:

Cooperative Ciné-Liberté

Our Cooperative of production, which is also yours, is the most democratic in the world. Every member has the right and the duty to express his ideas. All members will be consulted to learn their desires and particularly you, the representatives of the spectators, because it is for you that we are working.

Whether newsreels, films for the education of children, documentaries, fiction films, whether for private individuals, unions, municipalities, or our government.[52]

The only mention of films actually shot appeared in the October 1 issue, in which two articles referred to footage shot during the summer vacations. M. Hiléro describes shooting at a summer camp in Bernardoux for children who "only a few days earlier were wandering in the dirty streets, their only view being grey chimneys like prison bars in the sky, their only air being this mélange of dust, ashes, and foul kitchen odors which characterize the Parisian zone, these kids who just yesterday played with old tires among heaps of boxes, next to the old trailers that they live in and that some still dare to describe as 'picturesque,' were able in joy and liberty to find several weeks of happiness. What is striking at Bernardoux is the liberty."[53] This contrast between the dreary urban environment and the exhilaration of escape was only one of many accounts of that mythic summer when the French working class for the first time saw their own country on their paid vacations (a contrast captured before the summer in the early sections of *La Vie est à nous* with the shots of the countryside and the squalid milieu of the children as they walk home from school). On the same page of this issue, P. Lemare, writing again under the rubric of "La Technique," opened his article with his filming activity: "The vacation period has ended and we have returned with a certain amount of footage, souvenirs of hikes in the country, by the sea, or in the mountains, we have hunted images, most often at random in our travels."[54] The rest of the article recommended ways of editing such footage together, mixing close shots and long shots, shooting transitional shots in the city if necessary, controlling the rhythm through editing, timing the lengths of scenes in good professional films with a stopwatch, and so on. Perhaps films were completed from this footage, but Aveline failed to include them in his retrospective account of the Ciné-Liberté films at the end of 1936.[55] In his survey, he only repeated the praise for the seven documentaries that Sadoul had spoken of in July.

Aside from occasional screenings and the establishment of offices in various Parisian arrondissements and other cities (such as Lyon, Marseille, Rouen), the organization seems to have concentrated its work on the publication of the magazine. Five issues came out in 1936, the last one dated November 1, 1936. Despite the electoral victory of the Popular Front, the problem of censorship persisted. With the appointment of a liberal Radical, Jean Zay, to head the ministry of education, many had hoped for the elimination, or at least reform, of the censorship procedures of the previous years. Henri Jeanson, one of the directors of *Ciné-Liberté*, had harbored such hopes, but he revealed his disappointment in an "Open and Uncensored Letter to Jean Zay" in the July-August issue of *Ciné-Liberté*. Zay's refusal to issue a visa for *La Vie est à nous* or for the Ciné-Liberté film on the strikes provoked Jeanson's letter:

> "It is I," you explained to me, "who intervened in the Council of Ministers against the free distribution of *La Vie est à nous*. *La Vie est à nous* is a film of Communist propaganda. I find it inadmissable that this aural and visual tract be shown without any control to the general public. The screen should not serve as an electoral banner. I will give orders so that political organizations can project this film before their militants—in private screening, naturally. I will even go so far as to allow as an exception my visa if some exhibitor indicates the desire to show *La Vie est à nous* as part of its regular program. I will close my eyes, but I want it to be understood that it would be a matter of an exception, a favor and not a right. I refuse to create a precedent."
>
> Voila, some serious words which prove that liberalism is only a form of condescension, only a means of controlling, administering, making compromises with liberty.
>
> In one word as in ten, *La Vie est à nous* remains banned. The third of May [the second round of elections which secured the victory of the Popular Front] has meant nothing.[56]

Other writers joined in the attacks on the censor, advancing various arguments for its complete elimination, but to no avail. When Jean Zay spoke before the Renaitour Commission on February 3, 1937, he reiterated his reasons for not dispensing with censorship, citing the justification that public disorder could ensue.[57] Ciné-Liberté's long campaign for the dismantling of censorship met with no success. Just as the Popular Front government had failed to realize the political and economic hopes of the Left, the government also disappointed the Left filmmakers who saw censorship as the obvious and offensive residue of a reactionary cinema administration, a carry-over inhibiting the construction of a "free" cinema.

Censorship, of course, was not the only concern of the magazine. Brief reviews of feature films appeared, French and foreign, though no independent films were covered, not even any of the Ciné-Liberté films. A regular column dealt with the commercial newsreels, the critic normally bewailing their obsession with the fascist dictators and French reactionaries. Other recurring topics included technical information for beginning filmmakers, educational cinema, cinema and children, with an occasional contribution by Elie Faure (on Chaplin) or an interview with Marcel Carné (on *Jenny*, in which he complains of the demands made by the producers to circumvent potential objections by the censor).

Renoir laid out his views on the film industry in the second issue. On the whole, Renoir adopted an extremely even-handed and reasonable tone. He opposed the nationalization of the cinema but did think the government should support the film industry by taxing foreign films by an amount that would make their production costs equal the average production costs of a French film, thus insuring competition on a more equal footing. The problem of foreigners, principally refugees from the German industry working in the French film industry, upset many industry figures at the time, but Renoir typically saw no problem with the presence of foreigners. They offered possibilities for exchanges of technical information, and if French producers insisted on hiring foreign workers, they could pay a tax equal to the amount the producer would have paid a French writer, the tax being paid to the fund for unemployed cinema workers. Renoir obviously recognized that the government should have taken some measures to protect the French film industry, but any such steps should not have discriminated against foreign films or foreign workers, for "I think that a man no more than a film should be arbitrarily denied his day." Only at the beginning and end of the article did Renoir let some rhetorical excess seep into his prose. After taking his stand against nationalization, he claimed that such a "measure could have beneficial effects in a classless society and under the rule of the dictatorship of the proletariat," but he quickly added that "under the rule of money, it is better to recognize the power of money and to turn it to advantage." At the end of the article, after endorsing the program of Ciné-Liberté, he attacked the people currently running the industry as "idiots . . . illiterate and . . . dishonest."[58]

This was the last article Renoir was to write for *Ciné-Liberté* for the rest of the year, but he did collaborate on a satirical dialogue on "How One Makes a Film" that was printed in the July 1936 issue of *Commune*. Renoir, in the role of director, speaks with Jeanson, the author, about a film they are planning to make together. Jeanson outlines the subject for Renoir: "It concerns a story which begins during the Terror, continues during the Empire, and ends with the crowning of Louis XVIII." A long discussion follows on the complications involved in finding producers and distributors, but finally Renoir returns to the scenario:

RENOIR. I have to ask you a question: My producer likes Napoléon and I would like to know how you plan to represent him: as a great man? a bloodthirsty tyrant? or a sex maniac?

JEANSON. I show him just as he was. I treat him truthfully. He is a Corsican who made good, a Corsican who had a Corsican accent and who made France the Empire of friends [camarades].

RENOIR. Very unfortunate, your conception of Napoléon.

JEANSON. Why?

RENOIR. Because my distributor loves Napoléon and has a Corsican secretary.

JEANSON. You think that the Corsican would be upset if Napoléon had a Corsican accent.

RENOIR. Yes.

JEANSON. We'll cut Napoléon.

Renoir. Yes, we'll cut him. . . . Thus, we'll be able to avoid compromise on the rest.

JEANSON. Voila . . . I sacrifice Napoléon for the production.
. . . .
JEANSON. No Napoléon! No Revolution! Our film is taking shape. . . . All that's missing is the ambience.

RENOIR. I've got it! Let's use a time which hasn't been used in film. How about setting the Revolution at the time of the Gallic conquest?

JEANSON. There was no Revolution during the Gallic conquest.

RENOIR. I know, but we could easily make a producer believe that the Revolution took place in Gaul in 1789. . . . And then, no . . . impossible, the Revolution . . . forbidden, the Revolution . . .

JEANSON. By whom?

RENOIR. By the censor. The censor always suppresses revolution, nude women, and judicial errors.

JEANSON Louis XVI was an idiot. I've suspected it for a long time. If he had instituted the censor, there wouldn't have been a revolution. Gone, the Revolution!

RENOIR. What would we replace it with?

JEANSON. By the Cote d'Azur and a revolt of croupiers.

RENOIR. Yes . . . that's never been seen . . .

JEANSON. We'll make Robespierre the head croupier.

RENOIR. So, you're satisfied? We're going to make the film we want?

JEANSON. Listen: we don't always do what we want, but you've got to admit that it's nice to work finally freely, sincerely, without submitting to any outside influence! . . . No concessions!

RENOIR. You're right: no concessions![59]

This exchange must have pleased both of them, for Jeanson used the same dialogue format in an attack on distributors that he wrote for the November issue of *Ciné-Liberté*,[60] and Jeanson and Renoir made a joint presentation on "The Stupidities of the Censor" on an evening later that month under the auspices of Ciné-Liberté.[61]

In fact, the public activities of *Ciné-Liberté* did not begin again until after the last issue (November) of 1936 had appeared. After that fifth issue of 1936, *Ciné-Liberté* published only one special issue, on *La Marseillaise*, in March 1937, as the cleavages in the Popular Front probably began to take their toll on the organization. According to announcements in various Left papers in November and December, Ciné-Liberté scheduled a number of conferences and screenings at the end of the year. The four screenings were billed as a Retrospective of the History of Film:

November 22: America: A *travers l'orage.*
      29: Germany: *Variétés* and a fragment of *Lucretia Borgia.*
December 6: France: *Le Sire de Vinciglia, Entr'acte, La petite marchande d'allumettes,* color film of 1912. Commented on by Jeanson.
      13: Russia: *October.*

The conferences, which were probably panel discussions and question-and-answer sessions, were held during the same weeks:

November 25: Special Effects, explained and commented upon by specialists (Assola, Egros, Sacha, Dreyfus).
December 2: The Stupidities of the Censor (Jeanson, Renoir, Spaak, Godard).
      9: The Cinema and Actors (Lefèvre, Aznis, André Berley, Modot, Duvivier).

After this flurry of events, the energy and projects binding together Ciné-Liberté seemed to be exhausted. There were isolated attempts to revive the organization over the next year and a half, and several films were produced, but the concept of a vast organization of film workers and spectators united in the political struggle for an independent cinema did not last.

Part of the problem may have been the difficulty in turning the dream of an alternative, political cinema into a practical reality. Inexpensive equipment in reduced format was still rare, and audiences were not accustomed to attending noncommercial cinema. In this respect, the beleaguered state of the commercial cinema may have hindered the growth of an alternate network, for several of the leaders of Ciné-Liberté, such as Renoir and Modot, had worked in the commercial industry and depended on that work for their livelihood. Thus, the industry was ready to absorb, or at least finance, the work of new filmmakers; in other words, the barriers to entry into the commercial industry were not hard and fast, as in the monolithic American film industry. Even today, there is no independent cinema to speak of when compared to the experience of independent cinema in the United States.

In addition, the immediate circumstances that gave birth to Ciné-Liberté had changed. The electoral struggle had spurred many film workers to produce *La Vie est à nous* collectively, and the acceleration of events during the spring and early summer, the demonstrations and strikes, the dramatic victory of the Matignon Accords, accomplished a great deal in a short time. With so many demands satisfied, the popular will for change ebbed. By the end of the summer, the great days of the Popular Front were past. Furthermore, the political tensions that had been held in tenuous check through the elections resurfaced. For the municipal elections in the fall of 1937, the PCF did not call upon Ciné-Liberté but tapped filmmaking talent from its own ranks.

Finally, the very idea of Popular Frontism was probably not sufficiently coherent and focused to sustain a mass movement, particularly after its electoral victory. The eagerness of the PCF to enlist the Radicals forced the Socialist party to accept a highly diluted joint platform (the Programme of the Rassemblement Populaire). The massive strike movement by the workers, though almost exclusively reformist in nature, pried concessions from capital far beyond anything envisioned in the electoral program. In this sense the conclusion of the Matignon Agreements was more a victory of the workers themselves than of the Popular Front government. With that episode safely past, the government had no concrete agenda for struggle around which the workers could commit themselves en masse. Naturally, the government was unable to sweep aside in several quick strokes the domestic and foreign problems facing the country, and as the Blum government settled down to confront these problems, the political excitement subsided as well. No doubt many came to share a disillusion felt by Prévert even before the elections, when he complained of the Popular Front's new intoxication with the "Marseillaise," a revulsion that may explain his absence from the credits of *La Vie est à nous*.

At this point, the exact production history of Ciné-Liberté is difficult to establish with any certainty. Eisenschitz cites the following films from Ciné-Liberté's catalogue:

Grèves d'occupation (extant)
Espagne 36 (extant)[62]
Coeur d'Espagne (extant)
l'ABC de la liberté
L'aide au peuple catholique basque
Victoire de la vie (extant)
Le souvenir
Le temps des cerises (extant)
La vie d'un homme (extant)
Sur les routes d'acier
Les bâtisseurs (extant)[63]

This list, however, does not distinguish between films actually made by Ciné-Liberté and films simply distributed by Ciné-Liberté. For example, Alexander, in his recent book on American independent political films, calls *Heart of Spain* (*Coeur d'Espagne*) the first (and finest) film made by the American left group Frontier Films.[64] Of the other films that have been preserved (and that I have seen), only *Les bâtisseurs* carries production credits for Ciné-Liberté, and none of the six issues of *Ciné-Liberté* refers to a single one of these titles (though there is a reference to a film made on the strikes, clearly given the title *Grèves d'occupation* at some later date). Even the Communist press which covered film regularly, like the daily *Ce Soir* and the weekly *Regards* (with Sadoul writing every week on film), mentioned only *Sur les routes d'acier* and *Les bâtisseurs* as Ciné-Liberté films.

These latter two films, both completed at the end of 1937, indicate one of the changes in the development of Ciné-Liberté. Both films were made with the support of CGT member unions. But they are dedicated to valorizing the dignity of work, not building a militant class consciousness or exhorting viewers to participate in any type of political struggle. In March 1938, in *Commune*, Claude Aveline predicted, on the basis of these two films, that the collaboration of the Maison de la Technique ("younger sister of the Maison de la Culture") would produce a series of films which would eventually constitute "a veritable epic on work in France."[65] This prediction proved premature, for the series appears to have ended with these two films, but the orientation of the project is evident in Aveline's comments. Given that the films presented no pressing political demands, the critics concentrate on their technical accomplishments. Thus, Sadoul praises in *Sur les routes d'acier* the "beautiful images" of the director, Boris Peskine, the "beautiful music of Germaine Taillefer," and the animation of Griffoul—all of which mesh to "make of this documentary a true work of art."[66] Aveline is no less appreciative: "Everything in it is perfect: the images, the graphics, the text, without forgetting the score of Germaine Taillefer. The 'hardship of man,' naked and without grandiloquence. A masterpiece."[67]

During the summer of 1937, in its response to an inquiry on "Cinema and Youth," Ciné-Liberté had indicated this change of emphasis, from promoting a clear political engagement to illustrating the dignity of work. CGT membership had exceeded five million as a result of the strikes and the Matignon Accords, and some of the member unions sought to publicize the importance of their contributions through the production of films. Ciné-Liberte saw in this project the perfect opportunity to revive its production work:

> We wish to place the cinema in the hands of men. Ciné-Liberté endeavors, as much as possible, to develop an independent cinematic production. Today, there are many young directors who are extremely capable, but who are unable to "shoot" because of immense difficulties facing them.
>
> However, the emergence of these young talents is now favored by the large union organizations who want some films which exalt the national industry, the support provided by our workers, their talent, their art. These films have been assigned to some young directors who have not mastered their metier yet but who are beginning to work very well.[68]

Ciné-Liberté, then, welcomed the chance to hire itself out to the CGT, but this development suggested a more modest role for Ciné-Liberté than the more ambitious plans to build an alternative cinema with the support of millions of spectators who were ready to turn their backs on the hackneyed fare of commercial film. Of course this earlier idea had not died out completely, for plans were already well under way during the summer of 1937 to produce *La Marseillaise*, but this film was being handled by figures already well established, with considerable experience and success behind them, such as Renoir and Louis Jouvet. While it would have been perfectly reasonable for Ciné-Liberté to distinguish between major and minor productions, assigning its personnel accordingly, Jean Epstein, the director of the second union film, could not have been considered one of these "young talents."

Over the preceding fifteen years Epstein had made over thirty films, including some of the masterpieces of the French avant-garde during the 1920s. With the passing of the avant-garde in the late 1920s, Epstein withdrew from commercial filmmaking and concentrated on documentaries during the 1930s. This documentary work must have led to his choice as director of *Les bâtisseurs* by Ciné-Liberté, for there is no evidence whatsoever that he was involved in politics. None of the documentation from the period gives any indication that he was attached to Ciné-Liberté. However, as these films were to be dedicated to the dignity of work, Epstein may well have been the perfect choice because of his ability and aesthetic commitment to discover beauty in the world of men. Unfortunately, Epstein's talents do not shine in the film.

Les bâtisseurs was ordered by the Fédération des bâtiments (the construction union) in collaboration with the Maison de la Technique (like *Sur les routes d'acier*). The length of the film (fifty minutes) and the prominence of some of the collaborators (Robert Desnos and Arthur Honneger) indicate that it was not a minor film entrusted to amateurs to cut their teeth on.

The film has roughly four sections, with commentary of varying lengths bridging the separate parts. A long opening sequence presents a dialogue between two workers as they stand on the girders of a building under construction. Their discussion traces the history of building in France from the eleventh century to the Eiffel Tower. Then an architect, Perret, describes the strides made in building materials since the beginning of the twentieth century, in particular reinforced concrete. Le Corbusier then delivers an illustrated lecture on the principles behind his views on modern urban planning. Finally, Léon Jouhaux addresses a union meeting on the necessity for public and private investment in large public building projects. Presumably, Epstein gathered the images to match these texts.

The two workers, identified as unemployed construction workers in the credits, discuss the achievements of French construction workers over the centuries: the cathedrals, chateaux, the Versailles Palace, the Arc de Triomphe, and the hotels particuliers in the Napoleonic years, as well as the massive reconstruction undertaken by Haussmann, ending with the Eiffel Tower. As they reflect on their ancestors, they exchange stories about the historical epochs during which these monuments were built. For example, when marvelling at the craftsmanship of the stained glass windows in the cathedrals, one explains that they represented the scriptures on stained glass windows.

> But why?
> Because no one, or almost no one, knew how to read. Thus, so that everyone understand it, they made statues and windows. All you had to do was put your nose in the air and you taught yourself your catechism . . .[69]

They also tried to imagine their ancestors working on these cathedrals:

> What did they make as sculptors: holy virgins, gods, saints, devils, and then even some things which are not always very Catholic.
>
> I told you. They did it more or less as they wanted. Sometimes even, when they sculpted hell, for example, they put their bishop inside or some monks.
>
> They were jokers.
>
> They were like us, they liked a joke, no?
>
> Yes, like us.
>
> You see, I was wondering that perhaps eight hundred years ago, two guys were working here where we are, two construction guys, two guys who had perhaps the same names as we have.

The two workers continue in this elementary-school textbook style, showing obvious pride in the tradition of their trade, but only at the end do they think about their own housing:

> We've reached the twentieth century without having built anything for ourselves.
>
> It's true. I live still in a pathetic house, really shabby.
>
> Me too. You see, for centuries and centuries, the construction guys have built for gods, for lords, for kings, for emperors, for high bourgeois, for petits bourgeois, for nouveaux riches, and nothing for themselves. Nothing or almost nothing.
>
> Maybe it should be time for us to start now.
>
> It would be easy now with concrete.
>
> What are we waiting for?
>
> For you to get to work, lazybones.
>
> I see myself in a new house, with large windows, a little garden, flowers. . . . A house completely new, with air, light.

Throughout this long history lesson, images are intercut as testimony to the grandeur of the past. The material does not lend itself to the privileged techniques of slow motion and closeups that Epstein wrote about, but the images do sparkle nonetheless as the brilliant light pours through the massive cathedral windows or bounces off the stone facades of the chateaux and monuments. The aesthetic pull of these images justifies the pride felt by the two workers in the lasting achievements of their profession.

According to the commentary that follows, reinforced concrete will pave the way to the architecture of the future. Postwar inflation and easy money had financed a chaotic building boom, and archaic styles, such as "Art décoratif," persisted. Only a few voices of reason, the avatars of modernity—Perret, Malesteven, Le Corbusier, and Jenneret—"contributed truly some new elements to the architecture of to-morrow." In 1923 Perret provided a peek into that future with the construction of the first concrete church, Notre Dame du Raincy, "nicknamed the Holy Chapel of reinforced concrete. A style inspired by the possibilities of concrete. A style where the vertical is dominant and the rectangle was created." With this prelude, Perret appears on screen, delivering several self-evident platitudes on architecture ("Throughout time, by means of the construction systems, architects have met requirements both permanent and transitory") before tak-ing flight in a rapture of lyricism: "The architect is a poet. He is a poet who thinks and speaks in construction. I mean that construction should be like the natural language of the architect."

The filmmakers may have wanted to give credit to Perret for the popularization of modern building materials and construction meth-ods, but it was Le Corbusier who applied these ideas to the design of whole communities. Such projects would provide humane living envi-ronments for all the inhabitants. The commentary points out that "the needs of the collectivity are increasingly vital," and some towns, "for the most part Socialist or Communist," have begun to respond to these needs with bridges, hospitals, and schools. Among the commu-nities cited in the film, Villejuif was a standard example, for it was a Communist town and Vaillant-Couturier was the mayor. The film shows the 1933 foundation marker of a model school in Villejuif, with schoolchildren washing and playing in the spacious schoolyards. But the commentary finds these praiseworthy efforts insufficient: "But does the most beautiful hospital in the world resolve entirely the problems of social life? Isn't the central problem to build for healthy living in joy and light? Must the fate of the worker be to live in a slum and die in a palace? For years, practicable plans designed by various urbanists have remained in boxes. A builder of new cities, Le Cor-busier, is going to explain his conception of a town of light and verdure: the radiant city."

With the aid of graphics and shots of buildings he designed, Le Corbusier explains his ideas on urban design. Unlike Perret's short, summary presentation, Le Corbusier's talk is both theoretical and concrete, and lucid throughout. He begins by stressing the impor-tance of three natural factors which have affected the life of man since the beginning of time: the sun, space, trees. Apartment houses will be constructed to maximize the role of these factors. Thus indi-vidual apartments should have large windows to admit the light and allow a view of the landscape. The buildings should occupy only about 12 percent of the ground surface, leaving 88 percent to be used for parks. The vertical structures should rest on stilts to facilitate pedestrian traffic and preserve the openness of the ground space. Automobiles would be limited to parking lots on the perimeter of the park area.

The commentary then explains the political relevance of his plans. Aside from a general improvement in living conditions, new housing would also eradicate the slums that breed disease (tuberculosis) and depress the birthrate. Ever since the controversy over extending the term of military service to two years, the birthrate had become a national concern, and the filmmakers use that concern as a primary justification for supporting major new urban construction. In addition, even though the Popular Front government no longer held power (the first Blum government fell in June 1937), its humanitarian ideals still figured in the ideology of the workers, as the commentary concludes this section: "The fall in the birthrate will be effectively fought only by the execution of large projects and the application of social laws assuring the people of well being, and moral and material security—in sum, bread, peace, liberty."

The cultural offensive of the Popular Front brought with it a resurgence of French nationalism, and one of the great events of 1937 was the opening of the International Exposition. In his brief for a public-works program, Léon Jouhaux, head of the CGT, relates the success of this event to the great building tradition in France:

> When one contemplates the whole of the exposition of 1937–38 from the second level of the Eiffel Tower, it fills one with a feeling of joy and pride. A delight for the eye, this harmonious ensemble which rises boldly in the Parisian sky and is reflected in the waters of the Seine. Those who have constructed it are the worthy successors of the builders of the cathedrals. The same faith which filled their ancestors animated them and directed them in the battle against time, against the uncertainties of the production of materials, against the resistance to the social legislation that they have won. The exposition of 1937–1938 has a social significance which cannot be denied. It is the unquestioned grandeur and richness of work. The buildings of the exposition may be ephemeral in their duration, but they are eternal in their symbolism and significance. Those who have built them, one can say it now, under the worst difficulties, are they going to be thanked tomorrow, thrown on the sidewalk, reduced to depressing, demoralizing unemployment? Will misery for the skilled hands of these builders be the price for their efforts? This cannot be. The art of building, which is the foundation of all human evolution, cannot be condemned to idleness. Our nation, which can be proud of its exposition before which visitors from all over the world have received the shock of sacred emotion, owes it to itself to

permit its builders, its skilled workers, to pursue in their work their noble and useful trade. Through the great works which remain the order of the day of the activity of the CGT, unemployment can be effectively combated.

During Jouhaux's speech, as throughout the film, shots illustrating the discourse accompany the text—in this case, the pavilions and statues of the exposition and several large apartment complexes.

As the French economy had not recovered from the depression, even under the Popular Front government, the CGT advanced the solution of large public works. This tactic would not only reduce the immediate problem of unemployment but also would stimulate business nationwide by injecting money into the economy to raise purchasing power, an approach that had produced some success in the United States. Rather than ending with Jouhaux's speech, however, the film launches into a detailed description of the Fédération des bâtiments. In part, this description is meant to establish the importance of the union on the basis of the size of its membership (750,000 workers). But perhaps more significantly, the careful explication of the organizational structure of the union, again with flow charts to clarify the commentary, emphasizes the democratic procedures followed at every level, "from the base to the summit."

Though it is difficult to know exactly how to interpret this emphasis, in some way it must derive from internal stresses within the CGT. Once the PCF had decided to allow the CGTU to be reabsorbed into the CGT, the CGT experienced phenomenal growth, achieving a membership of five million. The greater part of this new membership was made up of young workers who were sympathetic to the PCF. Jouhaux tried to steer a course independent of specific political alignment, but traditionally the CGT was close to the Socialist party. Hence, despite the CGTU's acceptance of Jouhaux's demands before reunification could take place, Jouhaux understood that the PCF had not given up its struggle to wrest control of the labor movement from him, a struggle the PCF eventually did win after World War II. Before the reunification, the CGT had always charged that the PCF refused to abide by democratic procedures, and the appearance of this theme in the commentary may have been a reminder by the CGT of this principle. On the other hand, the PCF may have wanted this reminder as well to deflect the accusations that it repudiated democratic principles while it tried to gain positions of leadership within the CGT.

The film closes with a speech by the general secretary of the federation (Arachart) and some brief comments by several other speakers representing various special interests. Arachart calls for increased investment in the construction industry, the requisite funds to be supplied by both public and private capital. By that time, however, in the winter of 1937–38, the government did not have the funds available for public works, for it was already committed to substantial investment in the recently nationalized defense industries. The other short statements recalled the valuable contributions of skilled workers in traditional trades, such as painters and stone workers. These addenda appear tacked on at the end of the film to counterbalance the earlier exhilaration over the introduction of reinforced concrete, and the speakers warn against the cultural harm that would ensue if these crafts were to be eroded by unemployment.

The Left press applauded the film—a predictable response since the film had been made by workers, which the critics proudly noted. The production circumstances were at least as important as the film itself for Sadoul: "A new era of cinema is opened perhaps with these films no longer financed by a few investors but by the men who work with their hands. After *Sur les routes d'acier* of Peskine, ordered by the union of railroad workers, here is *Les bâtisseurs*, directed by Jean Epstein, ordered by the half million 'construction guys' who are members of the CGT. And without doubt it is one of the best films that Jean Epstein (maker of *Coeur Fidèle*, which was a landmark in the history of the cinema) has produced in many years. . . . The photography is almost always perfect, the montage is ingenious, the whole is a great, a very great success."[70] In *L'Humanité*, Louis Cheronnet was equally enthusiastic:

> Its greatest quality lies in the love of the métier that it explains. And in this love the filmmakers have drawn often lyrical accents of a beautiful and striking flight [envolée].
>
> On the other hand, how could it be otherwise since the maker of the film, one can say, is the Fédération nationale des travailleurs du bâtiment with the aid of Jean Epstein.[71]

Although Cheronnet went into greater detail than Sadoul about the substance of the film, both of them considered that the sponsorship of the union made the success of the film a foregone conclusion. In other words, the Left press understandably tended to view the independent production of the Left somewhat uncritically. As supporters of these fledgling independent efforts, the journalists felt it was inappropriate to apply the same standards and expectations for commercial cinema to these films made with limited financial and technical resources. When one sees these films fifty years later, the qualities hailed at the time of their release are not always apparent, as is the case with *Les bâtisseurs.*

There is no denying the aesthetic accomplishment of the photography, which does convey the beauty of French architecture from Chartres to the Eiffel Tower, but the film lacks the excitement and formal inventiveness found in many of the earlier films. *Les bâtisseurs* is constructed like an anodyne documentary. The union probably worked with the screenwriter (Jeander) on the text and then asked Epstein to supply the images because he had been working on documentaries throughout the decade. The result is a pleasant enough educational film which effectively evokes the links of French construction workers over the centuries and the dignity of their metier, but the élan of the workers who have joined together to forge the Popular Front is absent from the film, just as the Popular Front as a political force was moribund by then.

With the institutionalization of independent filmmaking on the Left and the formation of Ciné-Liberté, the absence of critical and theoretical reflection on the nature of Left filmmaking led to a certain compartmentalization in the conceptualization of Left filmmaking. With the few exceptions noted above, no one pursued the structural principles of *La Vie est a nous.* Even Ciné-Liberté, the direct offspring of *La Vie est à nous,* did not discuss the film in its own magazine. In the magazine's articles on its own filmmaking activities, it divided the projects into separate categories of documentary and newsreel, with no attempt to think through new categories. And when Ciné-Liberté came to make its best-known film, *La Marseillaise,* though based faithfully on historical events, the film was wholly fictional in terms of the footage.

Perhaps the very fragility of the Popular Front while it was still a reality was responsible for the formal diversity of *La Vie est à nous.* With many young filmmakers given their first chance to work on a feature film and with the responsibility for different parts of the film distributed among many participants, no one single person could impose a form that would fit into a traditional category. When the Popular Front government came to power, the unity began to come apart almost immediately, with the outbreak of the Spanish Civil War, devaluation, and the "pause" announced by Blum in January 1937. With the dissolution of the Popular Front, formalized by Blum's resignation in June 1937, the delicate balance that produced the innovative form of *La Vie est à nous* was upset, and the factions withdrew to their respective partisan camps. Thus none of the Communist filmmakers who had worked on *La Vie est a nous*—Le Chanois, Unik, Becker,

Modot—took part in the two CGT films made by Ciné-Liberté, *Sur les routes d'acier* and *Les bâtisseurs*.

The PCF Enters Production

As it happened, the PCF had already decided to produce its own films by then. In the winter of 1937–38, the PCF made three substantial films. Cine-Liberté was still working to complete *La Marseillaise* during that time, and the PCF supported that film, but it wanted to produce its own films independently. Whether its inability to control Ciné-Liberté more tightly motivated this course, or its resignation to the failure of unity, is not clear. The films certainly in no way renounced the PCF's endorsement of the Popular Front, and in 1938 the PCF even stated that it was prepared to participate in the government, an unprecedented accommodation to the bourgeois regime.

According to Jean-Paul Le Chanois, Jacques Duclos (head of the agitprop section of the party) asked Pierre Unik and him to write scripts for a film to be made for the local elections to be held in the fall of 1937.[72] Duclos chose Le Chanois's version and assigned him to direct the film, *Le Temps des cerises*. The title of the film is taken from the name of a popular song about the fall cherry harvest written in 1866 by Jean-Baptiste Clément. The film was made to publicize the PCF's program of benefits for the elderly, for those in "the autumn of their life," as Sadoul put it in his review of the film.[73] But "Le Temps des cerises" was more than simply a popular song; its author had also taken part in politics. As an official member of the Commune of 1871, he had been forced into exile in England for nine years, and upon his return he was the first of those formerly exiled to join the new Parti ouvrier of Jules Guesde, a party founded on a program of class struggle and socialization of the means of production.[74] The song thus carried political connotations reaching back to the nineteenth century.

The film follows the lives of two families from 1895 to 1937. After a montage of stills from the end of the nineteenth century, Gaston Modot and a friend enter the town hall on May 1, 1895, to register the birth of Modot's son. As they wait for the clerk, a well-dressed bourgeois father regards them with condescension as he walks out. In 1900 Modot is summoned to the office of the owner of the factory where he works to be congratulated for his work. At the end of this brief ceremony, a telephone call informs the owner that Modot's father has just died, and Modot then returns home with his father's body, but this section ends with Modot's son being served breakfast in bed, balancing the sadness of the past with the hopes for the future.

The film then skips to 1914, when Modot's family is staying in the country on vacation. The family and a friend discuss the possibilities of war, which Modot discounts. The men walk off to fish in the country as the son escorts his girlfriend on a stroll. After failing to catch any fish, Modot decides to choose another location. His friend warns him of a sign declaring private property and forbidding fishing without permission. Modot ignores the warning and promptly catches a fish. Immediately, the landowners appear, one of whom is the elderly owner of the factory where Modot works. They threaten him with prosecution, but their discussion is interrupted by the village church bells and a messenger announcing the declaration of war. Back at their home, Modot and his wife read in *L'Humanité* of the assassination of Jaurès. Jaurès, of course, was the great Socialist leader revered by Socialists and later Communists (the PCF did not exist before 1920). The film juxtaposes the beginning of World War I and the death of Jaurès to dramatize the latter's outspoken opposition to war, a stance that attracted great support in the postwar years.

A montage of flags of the countries drawn into the conflict introduces a long sequence on the war. After soldiers are shown marching, the film cuts to a shot of a cemetery as a statement on the ultimate futility of war, a view that many of the elderly of 1937 would share, for they had witnessed death and mutilation in the trenches. However, the film adds a more polemical sequence of a factory owner of an armaments plant directing his foreman to speed up production of the bombs and shells seen in the factory. Death awaits the working class, which supplies the human fodder; meanwhile, the arms merchants enrich themselves with the production of war matériel.

Soldiers then rush back and forth across a barren terrain amid steady bombardment. A small group of soldiers huddled together listens to one of their members passing on the news of the Russian Revolution and the victory of the Soviets, the only reference to revolution in the film. With the advent of the Popular Front, the Communists dropped their calls for revolution and demanded a strong national defense (a stance that, as we have seen, conformed to the foreign policy interests of the Soviet Union as well). This sequence also provides the structure for the rest of the film: the soldiers inscribe their names and occupations in a notebook, which is then discovered in 1937 among a pile of war memorabilia. The film resumes with the lives of several of these former trench partners.

A farmer, Dupuis, arrives at the gate of a country estate to meet his wife, who is pushing an empty wheelbarrow. She tells him that the family of the estate will no longer need her to attend to their laundry, and she wonders what will become of them with this loss of revenue. Dupuis is furious and rushes past the gate to confront the owners. As he marches grimly down the road, the camera tracks laterally with him as he passes by the wealthy members of this landed gentry sipping cool drinks at the outdoor tables: a young officer in elegant military dress, a couple clad in immaculate tennis attire complete with rackets, another group busily engaged in playing cards. Before he reaches his destination, we see the owner bundled up in a chair set apart from the others; a servant hovering over him hands him a hunting rifle, which he then fires at a rabbit. At that moment, Dupuis charges up to the man, grabs the gun, and asks the bewildered old man about the laundry. The owner is either too senile or too astonished to say anything, and during the silence Le Chanois cuts in several shots of the rabbit still twitching in its death throes. His fury spent, Dupuis retraces his steps, as the others watch with distaste the departure of the rude intruder. As he rejoins his wife outside the gates, a group of bicyclists ride by singing "Au devant de la vie."

While the sequence is obviously designed to dramatize the plight of older agricultural workers, the climactic scene with the rabbit holds special interest, for it is a dry run, in abbreviated fashion, of the famous hunt sequence in La Règle du jeu. Many of the elements are identical: the close shots of the twitching rabbit, the servant standing by to hand the gun to the owner, the idle self-absorption of the wealthy in their country habitat. Even in Le Temps des cerises, which, it must be admitted, is a rather stodgy work, this metaphor of the hunt used to indict the landed gentry stands out as an effective idea well executed. Whether Renoir took the idea from this film is unimportant, for the sequence in La Règle du jeu blends brilliantly with the whole of the film. Furthermore, it is even possible that the target-practice episode in La Vie est à nous actually suggested the idea to Le Chanois (though who thought up that scene is probably impossible to ascertain).

In the next sequence a bill collector visits another veteran, Dufour, a carpenter. Dufour has no money, so the creditor inspects his miserable lodgings in a decaying neighborhood on the outskirts of Paris. He notices a beautiful handcrafted wooden chest, which he says he will have to seize, but on hearing this, Dufour throws the visitor out. After a fade, we see the son of the factory owner from earlier in the film admiring the craftsmanship in the cabinet, which has found its

The dry run of the *Rules of the Game* hunt sequence (*Le Temps des cerises*)

The farmer Dupuis confronts the landowner (*Le Temps des cerises*)

way to the home of the factory owner. The son, played by Brunius in the same role he played in *La Vie est à nous,* is now running the factory, but the father is still active. Other members of the family and friends assemble in the room with the cabinet to hear the old man read his will. The contrast is clear. In his old age, Dufour cannot even guard the products of his own skilled labor. The capitalists protect their wealth over time through the institution of inheritance.

The last sequence takes up the story of Modot's son, now a grown man. On an outing with his girlfriend, he gazes proudly over the Exposition grounds at the Trocadero, as the Eiffel Tower rises in the background. He recalls that his grandfather worked on the Eiffel Tower, and they both look up at the massive statue commemorating Soviet workers, a man with a hammer and a woman with a sickle. As they sit down at a bench near the Sacre-Coeur, Dufour appears and sings the title song of the film. Later, the son, apparently a member of the PCF, puts up a poster supporting aid to retirees.

Meanwhile, the girl has returned home, where she lives with her mother, sister, and grandfather. As she serves coffee to her mother and grandfather, she sees that the sugar box has only one cube of sugar left. That evening, as the rest of the family sleeps, her sister sits at a sewing machine late into the night. The next day, the son takes her to a fair and wins a prize. From the array of prizes, he chooses a puppet, but the girl's attention is arrested by a large box of sugar, also offered as a prize. After he sees her home, she sneaks back to the booth with the intent of exchanging the puppet for the sugar but is too embarrassed to ask for the sugar.

In the next scene Modot, who still works at the same factory, questions the girl, Gilberte, who also works at the factory, about her refusal to marry his son. We realize that she believes she is too poor and cannot desert her family, but before she can respond, Modot is called to the office. The director (Brunius) has summoned him to honor his years of service with a medal and 100 francs and at the same time to notify him of his dismissal, owing to the need for cutbacks. Dumbstruck, Modot throws the money and the medal on the desk and wanders out of the room in a daze, as the director and his assistants shrug their shoulders in consternation. Modot stumbles through the street, reaches a bridge, contemplates suicide as the shots of the shimmering water capture his disorientation (as in Ruttmann's *Berlin*), but eventually finds his way home.

Soon his son enters with Gilberte, who is carrying flowers, for they have just been married. After congratulating the couple, Modot laments the plight of the elderly, and as he speaks the film cuts in many

Inspired by the Communist party's program for retirees, Gilberte (Svetlana Pitoëff) explains the party's plans for the future (*Le Temps des cerises*)

shots of old men and women on the street, some crippled. In a low-angle shot, Gilberte begins a speech on the effort of the PCF to care for these lost people, and during her talk we see shots of the elderly in a packed arena listening to Jacques Duclos express the solidarity of the party with their needs. Stirred by Gilberte's enthusiasm, the family members and friends toast the elderly workers, and the film ends with a montage sequence of Gilberte and the son framed against the sky, intercut with extreme long shots of Paris.

With the exception of Modot and Brunius, the acting in the film is wooden, and the didactic finale clashes with the strictly fictional scenes through the rest of the film. However, within the fiction the shots of the elderly at the end and of Duclos at the rally were not staged for the camera, and their documentary appearance clearly stands out from the fiction. The PCF (or the filmmakers) still believed in the power of these images, feeling that in certain ways they were more realistic than the fiction. As the film was made to campaign for the elderly, they wanted to show at least some views of the elderly as they really lived, whether hobbling about the streets with nowhere to go or gathering together at a political meeting in the hope that their years of hard work would not be forgotten by the younger workers.

Again, it is impossible to gauge the political effectiveness of the film, but the PCF did consider it important enough to seek a commercial release. Thus, despite the typical attacks on the censor in the Left press, Le Chanois made the cuts required by the censor and the film received a visa permitting its commercial distribution.[75]

Reviewers acknowledged that the film slipped into didacticism at times, but otherwise they liked it. Sadoul called the discourses of the couple at the end "a sort of oratorical prosopopoeia," but he excused it because "it expresses the deepest real desires of a mass to which they belong." He also approved of the film's realism, a crucial category for Sadoul, even if it remained only vaguely defined. For Sadoul, the realism of Le Temps des cerises was summed up by the comment that "all the details are true, faithfully observed, incontestable."[76] Writing in Pour Vous, Claude Vermorel was more specific: "We liked the documentary views which bathe the action—landscapes of factories and fields, worker streets, traveling fairs, faces of the elderly—and give an atmosphere real and nicely populaire to this film very distant from 'studio reconstruction.'"[77] Shooting in a studio would have inflated the cost of the film, but the filmmakers may have preferred shooting on location for exactly the reasons noted by Vermorel. The audience would recognize their own world on the screen, not the artificial studio world of vapid melodrama.

The last two films made by the PCF during this Popular Front period were both documentaries, also made in the winter of 1937–38. The first, La Vie d'un homme, was a peculiar biography of the most popular and best-known ideologue of the party, Paul Vaillant-Couturier, who died in 1937 at the age of forty-five. What is strange in the film, which is composed for the most part of a wide range of documents, is the inclusion of fictional scenes with actors to dramatize parts of his life. The massive turnout of some 500,000 mourners at his funeral may have generated the idea of making a film on Vaillant-Couturier, for it was probably intended as a tool to retain the allegiance of fellow travelers brought into the orbit of Communist influence by the PCF's ablest builder of ties with non-Communists.

Le Chanois directed this film also, but many of the most prestigious cultural figures in the party aided in the production. Moussinac and Aragon worked on the script; Modot acted in the film; and Georges Auric, Arthur Honegger, and Henry Sauveplane composed the sound track. The film assembles a great number of documents, arranges them chronologically, and interpolates footage shot for the film for transitions.

The film opens with a reconstructed sequence at the house where Vaillant-Couturier first lived. During the planning of the film, Le Chanois tracked down this first home in Paris and found that the apartment was vacant.[78] He transported the memorabilia that he had collected of Vaillant-Couturier's early years and tried to recreate the interior. He placed photographs of Vaillant-Couturier as a baby and pictures of his parents on the walls, sheet music on the piano, and some of his paintings elsewhere. A commentary identifies and describes these details as Beethoven's *Eroica* Symphony reverberates on the sound track. When the commentary describes the boy's daily path to school, the camera tracks behind a schoolboy carrying his briefcase on his back along the banks of the Seine and past the school building.

A jarring and facile visual rhetoric creeps into many of these effects. Before seeing the sensitive young man's first book of poetry, we see picturesque shots of the countryside, one with a lonely silhouette of a tree framed against the sky. At the end of his adolescence, when he faces a career choice, the film cuts to a crossroad marker. On the eve of the war, storm clouds gather. When a man in a cart races down a country road with the news that war has been declared, the shot of the crossroad marker reappears, followed by a large cross on a tombstone and then a long superimposition of graveyard crosses over a field of wheat. This whole sequence is remarkably similar to the same incident in *Le Temps des cerises,* which Le Chanois had just completed. However, Le Chanois was a beginning filmmaker working on command of the party without previous models to study, so it would be surprising not to encounter infelicities of one sort or another, which is not to ignore their obvious ineptitude.

Wounded in the war and scarred by the carnage, Vaillant-Couturier dedicates himself to politics and cultural work. Modot, sitting by the fireplace in Vaillant-Couturier's boyhood home, relates the formative factors in this progression: the Russian Revolution, the examples of Karl Liebknecht and Rosa Luxembourg. Modot rises, as if illustrating Vaillant-Couturier's discovery of purpose, and solemnly declares that "A new hope" is born: *Clarté.* A shot of the magazine follows, inserted among shots of the sky, fields, wheat, the crossroads, and finally a large Popular Front demonstration (taken from *Grand Rassemblement*). After the commentary recounts his founding the ARAC with Barbusse, an excerpt from Vaillant-Couturier's speech at the end of *La Vie est à nous,* in which he defends the rights of veterans, is shown, as well as several other shots of a procession of crippled veterans also seen in that film. Shots of Lenin speaking, with clouds racing by above, and scenes of the fighting in the Russian Civil War complete these decisive influences which were to guide the young man's actions until his death. In this political biography there is not a single reference to his activities during the 1920s, after his founding of *Clarté*, or to the early 1930s. The film tries to identify Vaillant-Couturier's memory with the Popular Front, thereby expunging the period of bolshevization of the PCF and the "third period" of the Comintern, a period the PCF avoided after the great turn to the Popular Front.

The remainder of the film recounts in similar fashion the dedication of the indefatigable Vaillant-Couturier to the cause of antifascism. He traveled to Shanghai to report on the Chinese struggle against the Japanese in articles for *L'Humanité*. From Spain, he wrote on the bombing of children, and then he traversed France, raising funds for the Spanish government; a rapid montage of these speeches and superimpositions of trains speeding back and forth across the screen represent these activities. Then the exhausted freedom fighter's poor health forces him to seek rest. During his recuperation, he paints some frightful pictures. Even after his death, however, his inspirational voice is not silent. A hand places a phonograph needle on a record of one of his speeches, as the film reviews some of the projects he has sponsored as mayor of Villejuif, including the school and hospital seen in *Les bâtisseurs*. When the record finishes, in an acted scene a telephone call brings news of his death, and the film ends with the funeral cortège and the tributes paid by the PCF leaders Thorez and Duclos, ribbons of the tricolor draped across their breasts, at the bier of Vaillant-Couturier. The inspiration of his life does not die with him, however, as superimpositions of Communist Youth marching close the film.

As biography, the film is hagiography, to be sure. Non-Communists would find the excision of his consistent support of party policy throughout the period before the Popular Front a serious problem. His unquestioning acceptance, at least publicly, of the zigzags of the party in the 1920s and early 1930s could be cited as a lack of principle, an opportunism characteristic of an apparatchik. While such charges cannot be dismissed, they probably oversimplify the reality, for they imply that the party did not tolerate dissension within its ranks. On political matters, members could not question official policy openly, but there were inevitably disagreements over tactics and policy in the decision-making process.

However, on cultural matters demands for unanimity were certainly less rigid. French Communist literary policies took an independent course, even during the "third period," and the party did not reprimand Barbusse after his censure at the Writers' Conference of

Maurice Thorez at the funeral of Paul Vaillant-Couturier (*La Vie d'un homme*)

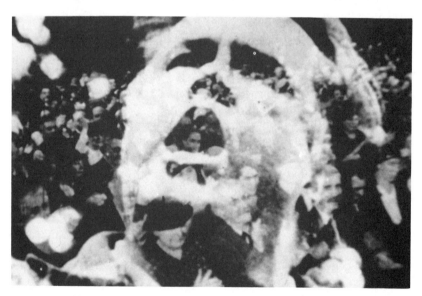

Paul Vaillant-Couturier, popular chief spokesman for the French Communist Party, in the film about his life, made following his death in 1937 (*La Vie d'un homme*)

1930 in Moscow. Similarly, Vaillant-Couturier's recommendation of Prévert to the future members of the Groupe Octobre does not reflect a cultural practice narrowly subservient to political affiliation. Obviously, Vaillant-Couturier maintained ties to the non-Communist cultural world before the Popular Front. With the change, Vaillant-Couturier was the logical choice to spearhead the cultural drive to enlist fellow travelers in the cause of antifascism.

Furthermore, although the film can be classified as political biography, it was made for political purposes. The party wanted to capitalize on the popularity of Vaillant-Couturier to revive and prolong the sagging spirit of the Popular Front and implicitly associate itself with the man Vaillant-Couturier in the hope of attracting to itself the admiration given to the man, not the party, by fellow travelers.

Finally, the film employs once again the mixture of document and fiction characteristic of a number of films from the period. The interrelation between the two does not approach the complexity of their use in *La Vie est à nous,* but the retention of the fiction at all appears strange today (the crudeness of the execution aside). As a rule, film biographies take the form of either fiction *or* documentary. In a documentary fiction is thought to contaminate the collection of documents, and in fictional biographies the documents would clash with the premises of the fiction. In *La Vie d'un homme,* the fictional scenes are used sparingly but, it seems, unnecessarily. Were they simply eliminated, the outline of Vaillant-Couturier's life would not be changed in any factual or political sense. The film would lose several moments of drama emphasized by the fictional shots. The commentary describes the importance of *Clarté* for Vaillant-Couturier, but the film has Modot stand up gravely so that the light of the idea can hit him full in the face. The phone call that tells of his death is even less understandable, except perhaps as a type of dramatic caesura held for this special moment in the film. Whether these scenes bothered audiences at the time is not clear. Aveline does not mention them in his review, though he does say that he does "not know how to label [it], documentary, homage, legend, funeral song: it is all at the same time."[79]

Whatever the reasons for the juxtaposition of fiction and document, the decision to shoot fictional scenes which seem entirely inappropriate suggests that the filmmakers working for the PCF used the idea often as a structural device because of some commitment to the form. Its success in *La Vie est à nous,* which several critics noted, may have led them to view the combination of fiction and document as a basic principle of the new Left filmmaking. The fact that the form resisted classification made it uniquely their own.

The last of the PCF films to be made during these years forms a fitting coda to their filmmaking experience. At the end of January 1937, the party held its last national congress before the war, at Arles. Historians cannot agree on how to characterize this event, whether "happy,"[80] and the "apogee"[81] of the party or "held in a mood of increasing pessimism after the fall of the first Blum cabinet,"[82] but the title of the film leaves no doubt about the attitude of the party at the time: *La Grande Espérance* (*The Great Hope*). As the reality of the great hope for the possibilities of the Popular Front faded almost from the start, and certainly after the summer of 1936, the party's embrace of the idea of the Popular Front became progressively more impassioned, for the idea by that point persisted more in the rhetoric of the party than in its political accomplishments. Thus the PCF had moved from a "ministry of the masses" that refused ministerial posts in the Blum government, to acceptance of its ministerial "responsibility" in a Socialist government when it was too late (in June 1937, when the fall of the Blum government was certain), and finally to an offer of participation in a Radical government.

At a time when Stalinist purges were being carried out to eradicate all opposition to Stalin, not only in Russia but also in Spain, and the Comintern was being stripped of all semblance of autonomy from the CPSU, *La Grande Espérance* shows the PCF eagerly exploring the rich and ancient culture of the Camargue in the countryside of Arles. In the film the work of the Congress alternates with passages on the local customs and the architectural remnants of the past. After the arrival of the delegates, everyone meets at the bullfighting ceremony, the delegates seated beside their hosts. Thorez smiles as the crowd is treated to displays of horsemanship by the local "cowboys" and dancers outfitted in traditional costumes. Then the crowd sings the "Internationale" as the long shots taken from the top of the stadium pan across the sea of people. Marcel Cachin thanks the people of Arles for their warm welcome, praising the area's past and its beauty, the camera illustrating these qualities with a sequence of old monuments, buildings, and ancient ruins. The music of *Sheherezade* on the sound track underlines the exoticism of these sites.

The next morning, Thorez addresses the opening session, as delegates and stenographers work furiously to transcribe his words. In this excerpt from the speech, Thorez quotes Mussolini's attacks on the great French intellectual tradition of the encyclopedists and Hitler's scorn for democracy and parliamentarism, before recalling to his listeners the great theme of the Popular Front: "We are pleased, Communist proletarians, sons of the people of France, heirs of the thought of the materialists of the eighteenth century, continuing in the tradition of the revolutionary action of the Jacobins, we are pleased that the question is posed thus: 'Democracy or fascism.'"[83] Even though the former enmity between the Communists and the Socialists had been rebuilding for over a year and a half, Thorez avoids any breach with the Socialists, for he was still trying to rally his party to the Popular Front. While this hope had little chance of surviving, the PCF did continue its identification with the French Republic, a bond that solidified their patriotic image.

After Thorez sketches the ideological rationale behind the Popular Front, Jacques Duclos enumerates the platform of the PCF more specifically. With the fall elections past, Duclos spoke first of the pressing issue that the Communists could claim proudly as their own—support for the Spanish Republic. Nonintervention had triumphed largely through the dissension in the ranks of the Socialists and Radicals, but the PCF had consistently advocated aid for Spain (though not military intervention). Footage of the war in Spain is cut in here during this section of Duclos's speech. Duclos proceeds to the PCF's domestic program, which could not be differentiated as clearly from the general political orientation of all the members of the Popular Front: the retired and elderly, small businesses (i.e., the middle classes), and the peasants. Throughout this resumé of party positions, images are inserted of elderly people, small shops, and picturesque landscapes, as well as several shots from earlier films, such as the marching veterans from *La Vie est à nous*, demonstration footage from *Grande Rassemblement*, and countryside views from *Le Temps des cerises* and *La Vie d'un homme*. Duclos concludes with an appeal for unity as a graphic of France fills with the heads of demonstrators.

Following the simple structure of the film, which alternates brief excerpts from the speeches at the congress with scenes of the delegates sightseeing, groups from the congress visit the surrounding hills, gazing at the battlements from the tenth century and the horsemanship of the Camargues. On returning to the proceedings of the congress, the commentary notes the presence of intellectuals, such as Jean-Richard Bloch, who asserts that the congress deserves to be called the Congress of the French People. The presence of non-Communist intellectuals of course contributes to the image of a party which has risen above a narrow and divisive sectarianism. So widely shared is the will for unity that, as the commentary points out, all the motions and elections at the congress are carried unanimously.

As in *La Vie est à nous,* Thorez, the general secretary of the party, has the last word (though in fact this excerpt is actually the conclusion of the speech heard earlier in the film). He surveys briefly the success of the PCF in recommending and applying the only correct policy for procuring new advantages for the workers of the country, and he stresses the unflinching role of the party in building hope and confidence for the future. As soon as he broaches this theme of the future, shots of youth unroll on the screen, from babies in cribs to children leaving school and a parade of the Union des Jeunes Filles de France. According to Thorez, critics may carp at the utopian goals of the PCF and Marxism, but the reality of the 180 million men and women of "the great country of the victorious Soviets" gives the lie to these "ideological 'arguments.'" Furthermore, Thorez goes on, the Soviet Union has just completed its new constitution, which

> Stalin has said . . . will be a document attesting that what millions of honest men in the capitalist countries have dreamed of and continue to dream of has already been realized in the USSR.
> The Bolshevik party of Lenin and Stalin has made the Socialist dream of yesterday the reality of today.
> Lenin, Stalin, the Bolsheviks were able to inspire themselves with the glorious example of our Paris Commune.
> The Communists of France will be able to inspire themselves with the victorious example of the great Soviet Commune.
> They cry with more force and resolution than ever:
> *Long live the power of the Soviets!*
> Forward, comrades! Forward, workers and peasants of France, to complete the destiny of our people!
> Long live the French Communist party! Long live the Communist International!
> Long live France—free, strong, and happy, faithful to its mission of progress, liberty, and peace![84]

With this rousing finale the camera pans over a graphic of the Soviet Union and Europe, stopping as it reaches France, which then lights up, while a long dissolve superimposes a drawing of the (winged) République Française. The sound track makes the same point, starting with the "Internationale" and fading into "La Marseillaise."

In political terms the film clearly places a reformist nationalism above the international proletarian revolution. The program of the PCF embraces the middle classes and refrains from attacks on the Socialists. The new constitution of the Soviet Union proves that country's realization of true democracy and will inspire workers and peasants in the capitalist countries driven by a love of liberty, not an implacable desire for the toppling of the capitalist regime. In short, the film is a perfect distillation of the PCF vision of the Popular Front, a less militant vision even than the one that animated the previous congress at Villeurbanne before the great electoral victory only two years earlier.

In retrospect, one might find the invocation of Stalin and the Soviet constitution at the end of the film particularly offensive. Similarly, the stand of the Communists as the only true defenders of the Spanish Republic would seem to have been severely compromised by the elimination of the POUM in Spain by the Communists. However, the importance of the Soviet Union as a symbol for the Left in the West, particularly in France, exerted a powerful attraction as the first and only prototype of a Socialist society. That the society should experience problems and growing pains did not mean that it should be denied support. If this resulted in a double standard, and the reaction of the Left to the case of Gide and his *Retour de l'URSS* is a classic example, the Left felt the enormity of the task of transformation deserved a more generous and flexible set of standards. Furthermore, many saw the Soviet Union as the only state willing to promote an active resistance to fascism (whatever its reasons), while the Western powers practiced a realpolitik that not only made a mockery of their purported defense of democracy but also failed in its ultimate design of preventing war, or at least war between Germany and the Allied Powers. Retrospective judgment only strengthens this view.

In addition, historians who could not be accused of sympathy for Stalin or Communism caution against indicting the pro-Communist Left too quickly for a conscious duplicity in their hesitation and reluctance to denounce the trials and the purge of the POUM. David Caute shows that even bourgeois observers at the trials accepted the confessions as true, even "the God-fearing, Republican U.S. Ambassador to Moscow, Joseph Davies, who was convinced that those who confessed and the generals tried *in camera* had been conspiring with Germany and Japan."[85] Regarding the persecution of the POUM by the Communists in Spain, Hugh Thomas indicates that there was (and is) considerable confusion about what actually happened and that the Spanish Communists themselves did not necessarily know about abductions and deaths of POUM members.[86] As Caute remarks in his discussion of the trials, the lack of information prevented expressions of protest and perhaps defection among the Communist and non-Communist Left.[87] Thus the popularity of the PCF during this period cannot be dismissed simply as endorsement of Stalinism by party members and Communist and non-Communist intellectuals, and it would be wrong therefore to see *La Grande Espérance* as Stalinist propaganda. The film shows that the PCF built its program around antifascism and that the PCF was a *French* party. In the film the few references to Stalin and the Soviet Union are basically pro forma nods to the inspiration of the Soviet Union, far more muted in tone than those in *La Vie est à nous,* which was made long before the revelations of the trials and the Spanish Civil War. *La Grande Espérance,* however, suffers from a similar institutionalization of form that characterized the CGT films of Ciné-Liberté. That is, although the film employs footage from other films in the PCF Ciné-Liberté group of productions, there is no fictional or dramatic material shot specifically for the film, or at least not identifiably so as in the dramatized sequences from the previous PCF film, *La Vie d'un homme.* The film resembles a typical, well-crafted, inoffensive documentary film, which just happens to have been sponsored by the Communist party.

The End of Political Filmmaking: *La Marseillaise*

There is one other film with which the PCF was associated, even though it had its premiere long after the PCF opted to make its own films outside the organizational framework of Ciné-Liberté: *La Marseillaise. La Marseillaise* provides an instructive companion piece to *La Vie est à nous* because of its similarities to and differences from the earlier film. Ciné-Liberté was born with the success of *La Vie est à nous* and died with the completion of *La Marseillaise.* The PCF had sponsored *La Vie est à nous* for a particular use in an historic election campaign. *La Marseillaise,* produced and released with much greater fanfare, had no concrete raison d'être. It was an exclusively ideological project conceived as a celebration of the Popular Front, and its opening was originally planned to coincide with the Paris Exposition scheduled to begin on May 1, 1937. A mass subscription drive organized by Ciné-Liberté in the unions supplied only partial funding for the film, and the CGT contributed a substantial amount to make up the shortfall. While many of the same filmmakers worked on both films, *La Vie est à nous* was truly a "film d'équipe," as the credits accurately noted; *La Marseillaise* is unquestionably a Renoir film, from the construction of the script, through the distribution of the roles, to the stylistic consistency of the film. *La Vie est à nous* was made in roughly two months; *La Marseillaise* required more than one year. And perhaps most significantly, *La Marseillaise* does not take contemporary historical reality as its subject, but rather presents a Frontist interpretation of the greatest symbol for the Popular Front, the

French Revolution. As Renoir remarked at the time: "It would be impossible for us to make a film on the present political situation; this would risk provoking polemics and being disagreeable to a public which goes to the cinema simply for distraction."[88]

The film covers the period from the storming of the Bastille in 1789 to the arrest of Louis XVI in 1792, on the eve of the battle of Valmy. The formation of the battalion of Marseillais and their march to Paris supplies the narrative organization for the central portion of the film. Scenes of the royal court and the aristocracy form brackets around the story of the Marseillais. French audiences, of course, understood the relevance of the soldiers from Marseille, for they were the troops who marched from Marseille to Paris to defend the newly founded republic, singing the "Battle Song of the Army of the Rhine," later known as the "Marseillaise." The song was written by the otherwise undistinguished composer, Rouget de l'Isle, who wrote it on the night of April 25, 1792, in Strasbourg. No one knows how the song travelled across France to Marseille—a character in the film maintains that a Jewish merchant was the conduit—but its fame dates from the march of the Marseillais to Paris.

The film opens on the changing of the royal guard and proceeds to the bedroom of Louis XVI (Pierre Renoir, Renoir's older brother). A messenger arrives to inform the king of the taking of the Bastille, which he calls a revolt, but the messenger corrects him by calling a revolution. With the popular uprising thus announced, the scene shifts to Marseille, where a noble observes and arrests a pigeon poacher, thereby broaching the issue of seigneurial rights. At the trial, the breach between the nobility and the third estate is suggested, before the accused escapes out the window to the approval of most of the spectators.

The poacher seeks refuge in the hills and meets up with two other fugitives from the city, establishing a familiar Renoir association between man and nature, though in this case the cause of the common people is allied with nature, rather than used to oppose civilization and nature. This natural state contrasts sharply with the rigid, entirely man-made order which reigns at the Court. A friendly country priest arrives with provisions and complains of the corruption of the local bishop, thereby opening up a class division within the clergy as well.

Soon the nature dwellers depart for Marseille to defend the Revolution, eventually joining the Marseille battalion that effects a bloodless takeover of the Marseille fort from the confused aristocrat St. Laurent. This battalion of artisans then marches the 500 miles across

France from the Mediterranean to Paris, bivouacking from time to time, discussing politics and slowly learning the "Marseillaise." In Paris, they participate in and attend popular entertainment as they battle outraged aristocrats on the Champs Elysées in mock serious swordplay which appears to leave few casualties. Following the King's release of the Brunswick Manifesto, the revolutionary army, whose battle cry above all seems to be the preservation of order, enters the palace, quickly convinces the National Guard to join their cause, overcomes the Swiss Guard that rejects these entreaties, and finally escorts the royal family into captivity. All of this transpires in an atmosphere of bonhomie and generosity, with little rancor and not the slightest hint of revolutionary excesses (such as the massacre at the palace).

Several scenes of the nobility interrupt this narrative trajectory of historical inevitability. In Coblenz, the nobles living in exile discuss the future, most welcoming the support of the Duke of Brunswick and anticipating a swift dispatch of the Revolution. Saint-Laurent questions both the propriety of accepting the Protestant Duke as their savior and the self-evidence of victory. Rather than tarring these exiles as traitorous villains covetous of restoring their privilege, Renoir actually presents them sympathetically, in particular by introducing the scene with Mme. Saint-Laurent at the piano singing a beautiful song, "Toujours, Toujours, O Mon Pays, Soit Mes Amours, Toujours," a feeling that clearly moves everyone in the room. During the song, the ever courteous Saint-Laurent circles the room to thank his wife for her performance, one that expresses marvelously their love and nostalgia for their native land. Later, the king voices reservations about signing the Brunswick Manifesto, but his strong-willed wife, Marie Antoinette, manipulates him coquettishly into approving it.

The idea for making a film on the French Revolution, a subject of considerable appeal to Popular Front supporters, arose early in 1937, and the film was produced by Ciné-Liberté personnel. The last issue of Ciné-Liberté, which appeared in March 1937 as a special issue, was devoted to the film and contained an outline of its scenario. In the film, the Marseillais represent the people who made the Revolution, and Renoir and his collaborators took great pains to assure the historical fidelity of these simple artisans (as they did for the whole film). They combed archives and history books in this effort, and based events of the film on those records. Even some of the dialogue in the film is taken verbatim from those contemporary accounts. What Renoir wanted was an historical film peopled with ordinary Frenchmen—the mason, the custom's clerk, the artist—who answered the call of history by marching with the battalion to Paris to found the Republic. As he had done in *Toni,* Renoir chose actors with authentic regional accents, of the Marseille region for the later film (the aristocrats were played by professionals drawn from the Comédie Française).

Renoir had demonstrated his interest in regional culture in *Toni* in 1934, and certainly must have enjoyed working with Prévert on the

Madame de Saint-Laurent (Irène Joachim):
    How many of these memories I have
    Of that beautiful region where I was born.
    My sister, how beautiful were those days in France.
    Forever, forever,
    Oh, my country, be my beloved forever.
    Oh, who will return to me my Helene
    And my mountain and the big oak tree.
    Their memory saddens me every day.
    Forever, forever,
    Oh, my country, be my beloved forever.

Saint-Laurent (Aimé Clariond): Madame, this song moves me deeply. It reminds me of our Provence.

Madame de Saint-Laurent: Excuse me, but I cannot sing this song without tears welling up in my eyes. (*La Marseillaise*)

popular culture aspects of the Arizona Jim feuilletons in *Le Crime de M. Lange,* but this legitimation of popular culture was an important goal of the Popular Front. The Maisons de la Culture not only sought to disseminate high culture to working people, but also wanted to draw popular cultural forms into the orbit of serious culture. Of course this latter thrust coincided with the resurgence of nationalism promoted actively by the Popular Front, particularly by the Communists, who controlled the Maisons de la Culture. In *La Marseillaise,* then, authenticity may have been important to the filmmakers, especially Renoir, but at the same time it corresponded felicitously with a political desideratum of the Popular Front.

A similar correspondence may explain the incorporation of forms of historical representation in the film. One of the Marseillais is a painter, who comments throughout the film on the way he would depict various historical events. The film provides a glimpse of his style on occasion, which turns out to be vast neoclassical tableaux, a prevailing academic style of the period. When the battalion arrives in Paris, in the festive atmosphere a disgruntled "citoyen" must wait to mount the stage while a troupe of Breton actors dressed in regional costumes insist on their right to complete their turn before ceding the stage. And later, when the soldiers take time out for entertainment, they take their girlfriends to a performance of a shadow play recounting the veto of the king and the Manifesto of Brunswick.

Clearly, it was the cultural program of the Popular Front that chose these details for inclusion, rather than a simple concern for historical accuracy. Despite Renoir's public concern with the minutiae of historical truth, many critics saw the film as a representation of the French Revolution seen through the prism of the contemporary Popular Front. Aragon and Sadoul claimed to hear the voice of the 1930s archreactionary Henri de Kerillis in the dialogue of the film,[89] and others were struck by similar echoes. When one patriot rebukes a fellow soldier for assuming that priests are reactionary, Popular Front viewers recognized "la main tendue" of Maurice Thorez extended to the church. Jeanson rightly enumerated—derisively—the full panoply of the PCF platform: " 'main tendue' to the Catholics, retirement for the elderly, antifascist war, open the Spanish frontier, and make us fight at the borders to defend paid vacations! . . ."[90] That is, although the filmmakers built the film out of historically verifiable facts, their principle of selection was based on the prevailing political ideology of the Popular Front.

King: Madame, Madame la Nation. Please come into my arms that I may embrace you.

The Nation: Monsieur the King, impossible to come into your arms. Between us the bridge is broken and an abyss separates us.

King: What is this, this abyss?

The Nation: The Manifesto of Brunswick. (Shadow play in *La Marseillaise*)

As has already been noted, by the time *La Marseillaise* was released in February 1938, not only was the government of the Popular
Front no longer in power, but also the mass popular support that had
forced the political parties to unite had all but disappeared. The
momentum driving the Popular Front forward had abated. By 1938,
the leaders of the political parties, so hesitant to seek unity in 1934,
pretended that the unprecedented mass movement was still a reality.
But that reality did not survive the disillusionment with nonintervention in Spain in the summer of 1936, devaluation of the franc in the
fall, the "pause" in the spring, and the persistence of economic difficulties. As these hopes evaporated, the ideology of the Popular Front
was all that remained as the leaders sought vainly to rally the people
to the cause, the cause that the people had driven the reluctant leaders to adopt after February 1934.

Thus, while the political leaders at the time may have heralded *La
Marseillaise* as the cinematic summa of the Popular Front, and since
that time it has come to be known as "*the* film of the Popular Front,"[91]
it should be understood rather as the expression of the Popular Front
emptied of any political relevance. At the time of *La Vie est à nous*,
before the elections of May and June, battle lines were drawn between
Frenchmen and tensions were high. Anxiety over civil war was in the
air as political divisiveness had triggered outbreaks of violence in the
preceding years. *La Marseillaise* reveals none of this. The Marseillais
occupy the fort without firing a shot, and the fighting at the end pits
the foreign Swiss Guard against the popular national army, as the
king walks resignedly, without bitterness, to bow to the will of the
Assembly. At the end, the Revolutionary Army prepares to meet the
foreign aggressor at Valmy. The historical supporters of this foreign
threat, the aristocracy, are not even shown as traitors among the ranks
of the Prussians, for the nobles were last seen in the film toiling away
at retrieving the errant third step of the gavotte. Among those left in
France, with the exception of the obsolete aristocracy, all belong to the
unified nation of "peasants, workers, shopkeepers, soldiers, priests,
the ordinary people."[92] As Ory comments on the inclusiveness of this
list, "Effectively, the 'main tendue' is extended in all directions."[93]
Thus, as the masses abandoned the Popular Front, depriving it of its
political efficacy and strength, *La Marseillaise* symbolizes the passing
of the Front's former militancy, and in this case, does justify Fofi's
verdict that the Popular Front of *La Marseillaise* "was a politics of
renunciation. This updating of the Revolution is a sweetening, a cas-
tration. Confused, tired, uncertain, good-natured, sometimes in-
sipid."[94]

Roederer (Louis Jouvet), in the presence of the queen (Lise Delamare), warns the king: Sire, your Majesty hasn't a minute to lose. Your only refuge is the Assembly. Right now it is the only thing the people respect. The considered opinion is that you should go there without delay. (*La Marseillaise*)

"At Versailles, during the third step of the gavotte, did we look right when going to the right or rather to the left? But it's very simple. Look . . . but it's inconceivable; I have forgotten." (*La Marseillaise*)

All the foregoing is not meant to conclude that *La Marseillaise* is a film to discard as one devoid of interest. As a bland embodiment of Popular Front ideology it has no rival. As well, the filmmakers consciously tried to avoid the cliches of the Hollywood historical film, or its sometimes hysterical French analogues, as in a film like Abel Gance's *Napoléon*.[95] Thus, the film intentionally elides the storming of the Bastille and the French victory at the battle of Valmy. Several critics objected that the film did not succeed in banishing the traces of history according to Hollywood ("As for the attack on the Tuileries, it is conceived in the exact style of the old silent Hollywood films on the Civil War"[96]), but the distinction remains nonetheless, particularly in the treatment of the ordinary people of Marseille, whom Renoir referred to as "the people of the street."[97]

However, whatever virtues one might find in the film today, few considered the film a success when it opened. Not only did audiences stay away in droves, but also, with several exceptions, the critics had difficulty generating enthusiasm for the film. Predictably, speaking as semi-official party critics, Sadoul and Aragon applauded the film. Sadoul repeatedly sang the praises of the film's humanism, calling it "one of the most free, most direct, most vibrant, most human films ever made."[98] Aragon was even more unreserved in his praise. He compared Renoir and his film ("so magnificent, so human") with Michelangelo, Courbet, Flaubert, Malraux, and Charlot.[99] But these party critics aside, a surprising number of sympathetic critics wrote only lukewarm reviews. Roger Leenhardt, who, after *Le Crime de M. Lange*, had dubbed Renoir "the director of genius of the Left" called *La Marseillaise* "a mediocre film."[100] But once again, as with his comments on *La Vie est à nous,* the remarks of Pierre Bost struck a reasonable note amid an often partisan critical fray:

> I confess that, for my taste, these huge, dramatic, bloody events seem here a little too human. The film lacks cruelty. A revolution has never happened in such a way, and never will. Picturesque imagery is always too seductive; in a battle painting there is always more painting than battle. Already, in *La Grande Illusion*, there was a lack of hardship in the life of the prisoners. It is thus that M. Renoir treats conscientiously, with love, each episode, each scene. Every moment of the work is for him a perfect universe, without past or future. It is, precisely, a painter's view.[101]

What Bost was pointing to was Renoir's failure to portray the social conflicts underlying the Revolution in the film. Virtually all the critics noted that the most sympathetic character was Louis XVI, played by Renoir's brother, Pierre. As in *La Grande Illusion, Le Crime de M. Lange,*

Nobility bowing to the king and singing, "O Richard, O Mon Roi" (*La Marseillaise*)

and *La Règle du jeu*, Renoir could not avoid imparting the feeling expressed by Octave in the latter film that "the most terrible thing is that everyone has his reasons." Hence the sympathy given to the terrified aristocrats of the Court as they spontaneously kneel to express their fealty to the king, chanting "O Richard. O mon roi."

Consequently, as Ory later wrote, the only villains in the film are the foreigners: Marie-Antoinette and the Duke of Brunswick. In *La Marseillaise*, the aristocracy do not recognize that the world is changing and cannot understand the new concept of "the people." In fact, they are presented as the last of a dying race, bypassed by the emergent Republic. Thus, in the bloodless takeover of the Marseille fort, the articulate patriot Arnaud tries to explain the ideas of the Revolution to the commander, but St. Laurent cannot comprehend. He knows only that he serves the king. Sensitive to the bewilderment of St. Laurent, instead of taking him prisoner, Arnaud politely advises him to seek exile, as if assuming that his allegiance to the king was entirely irrelevant to the victory of the Revolution at that point. The later scene of the aristocrats in exile reinforces this view that the nobility is obsolete, when none of them is able to recall the sequence of steps of the gavotte.

There is little disagreement over the verdict: *La Marseillaise* was a

The king's appreciation of the situation:

Queen: Sire, how can you eat at a time like this?

King (Pierre Renoir): Why not? The stomach is an organ which knows nothing about the subtleties of politics. I ordered some tomatoes. We have heard much about this vegetable since the arrival in Paris of this troupe of Marseillais. I wanted to taste them also. Madame, would you like my opinion? It is an excellent dish which we have been wrong to neglect.

Saint-Laurent (right): You justify acts that I view as a rebellion with words that I don't understand. *The Nation, Citizens,* what does that all mean?

Arnaud (Andrex): The nation is the fraternal union of all French people. It is you. It is I. It is the people who pass by in the street. It is that fisherman over there in his boat. The citizens are the people that make up this nation. (*La Marseillaise*) failure. The critics didn't like it, spectators did not support it, and historical judgment has not redeemed it. Yet few films began with greater promise of success, from production by some of the most prominent actors, screenwriters, and the greatest director of the day, to distribution and exhibition, initial costs raised from contributions of working people and actively supported by the Socialist-led government of the Popular Front and the French equivalent of the AFL-CIO, the CGT. How is this failure explained?

Perhaps the most common complaint about the film upon its release in February, 1938 was boredom. Critics across the spectrum, with the Communist critics such as Sadoul and Aragon notable exceptions, found the film dull, boring, mediocre, fatiguing. Admittedly, some partisan criticism was aired, with extremes of right and left carping over political biases, but by and large, even in these reviews, boredom was the dominant objection.

To a large degree, I believe this objection was directly proportional to the inflated hopes with which the project had been inaugurated; probably no film could have fulfilled those hopes. For *La Marseillaise* was to be the cinematic monument to the French people who had elected the first Socialist government in France in 1936. The film was to reflect that achievement as a film made by the people and for the people, a film that would usher in a new era of French filmmaking, an era liberated from the venality of capitalist swindlers and crooks. But not only did the film face great expectations, it also had to extend and even intensify the popular unity that had brought the Popular Front to power in June of 1936. Furthermore, the announcement of the film preceded its release by almost one full year, long after the first Popular Front government had fallen. Under all of this pressure, and with articles on the production appearing periodically during the long months of gestation and production, with internal quarrels and bitter personal feuds, it is little wonder that the film fell short of these expectations.

But the (great) expectations in themselves did not *cause* the failure. Rather, they were symptomatic of a denial of a reality that no one wanted to recognize: the Popular Front had ended effectively even *before the announcement* of the film. The very scope of the project for the film reveals the ambition of the endeavor. An outline for a script published in that last issue of *Ciné-Liberté* contains twelve parts, which was quickly acknowledged to be far too unwieldy, since its projected length would run to several days. Similarly, the rhetoric attending the announcement of the project clearly generated expectations out of all proportion to reality. In fact, the novel plan of financing the film by public subscription did not succeed, and the CGT and the government itself had to invest funds to cover production costs.

The participation of the CGT is also revealing, for the CGT, under the strong leadership of Léon Jouhaux, carefully avoided overt political activity. Blum had offered ministerial participation to Jouhaux when he formed his government in May 1936, but Jouhaux had refused, preferring to retain his independence outside the government, and perhaps to exercise greater political leverage. Thus, the involvement of the CGT augured a retreat from politics in the film. That is, in a sense, the CGT represented the lowest common political denominator on the Left, eschewing any political stance that could be identified with any political party.

From the very inception of the film, then, one sees a withdrawal from political engagement. With the political coalition becoming increasingly unstable, no one wanted to risk tipping a balance in one partisan direction. Renoir acknowledged as much when he remarked in an interview that making a film about the contemporary situation was out of the question. Clearly, no one working on *La Vie est à nous* could have made a similar remark. Yet the organizers of *La Marseillaise* did want to make a film to celebrate the Popular Front, so they had to find some idea that would meet with broad, even unanimous approval on the Left. The ideal choice for a Popular Front France, a Popular Front which came to power with full, one might say even excessive, respect for democratic procedures, was the very birth of the Republic—the French Revolution.

What I am emphasizing, then, was the importance of suppressing all threats of controversy in this project. Unlike other potential candidates for events drawn from French history—the uprising of 1830, the revolution of 1848, the Commune, all of which still today provoke spirited debate—the importance and complexity of the French Revolution allowed the entire Left to support at the very least certain parts of the Revolution. For the Revolution, contrary to the impressions of many Americans, was not simply the storming of the Bastille and the overthrow of the monarchy. Two hundred years of historiography of the Revolution have produced many interpretations and controversies, with many disagreements on the Left. What is curious about *La Marseillaise* in this respect is the almost complete elimination of any references to the standard controversies about the Revolution, and this is another crucial reason for the failure of the film, its failure to arouse passionate discussion of any sort. It skirted controversy so successfully that there was little to argue about. Probably no other event in French history has attracted as much attention, debate, and acrimony, yet *La Marseillaise* managed to escape controversy altogether.

One can gauge the importance of this consideration by comparing the script printed in that last issue of *Ciné-Liberté* with the completed film (which is probably a fairly accurate reconstruction of the original). There are a number of incidents that have been eliminated in the final version, but most significant is the long conversation between Robespierre and Brissot, which Renoir referred to in an accompanying article as the "principal scene" of the film. The script indicates that the entire emphasis would be on the spoken text, with no distractions of action or decor. Thus, aside from a quantitative paring of material, the core of the work has been excised.

Keeping in mind the concern to eliminate controversy, one can see that controversy is exactly what the conversation between Robespierre and Brissot would have brooked. As it is, with the exception of the king and the nobility, there are no renowned historical figures representing the republicans in the film, for that is where controversy would erupt on the Left in discussions of the Revolution. The film was not being made for the Right after all, but to rally the Left yet again to the banner of the Popular Front. Introducing the formidable historical figures on the Left, Danton and Robespierre in particular, would only have aggravated tensions already eating away at the coalition.

Notice that the film ends before the battle of Valmy, in 1792, before the famous struggle between the Girondins and the Jacobins. But as with so many aspects of *La Marseillaise*, the very periodization of the Revolution is fraught with disagreement. The last great historian of the Revolution from the nineteenth century, Aulard, had ended the revolutionary period with 1804. Mathiez, the most important historian of the interwar period, had taken issue with Aulard, his mentor, and saw the fall of Robespierre as the end of the Revolution. Furthermore, the Communist Mathiez was the first modern historian to take the side of Robespierre, whom previous writers tended to view as a murderous fanatic.[102] Mathiez took the view that Robespierre was the hero of the Revolution for his courage and incorruptibility in struggling against the counterrevolution.

La Marseillaise was to have none of this. "No enemies on the Left" was its (effective) motto/cry. Consequently it forfeited in advance any chance for critical engagement: the film broached no critical issues, and critics took little issue with the film. One might even say that the film provides the ultimate illustration of the derisive account of the duplicity and cravenness of the commercial French cinema provided by the satirical dialogue cited above between Renoir and Jeanson, published at the height of Popular Front enthusiasm in July 1936, which concluded with the mutual congratulation for having accepted "No Compromises!" Yet this is exactly what happened to *La Marseillaise,* albeit with far less amusement, no doubt. The fear of offending any partners on the Left, like the fear of displeasing producers and distributors in the dialogue, resulted in the remarkable disinterest met by the film.

In view of this flight from volatile realities, it may be surprising to learn that Renoir and his crew constantly spoke of the historical research that went into the film. Perhaps the care exercised in avoiding certain issues found more positive outlet in the material culled from archives about the battalion of Marseillais which provided the narrative armature of the film. Perhaps they viewed such archival work as part of the new historiography of the Revolution, concentrating on local records, looking at history from the bottom up. After all, those years were the early years of the *Annales* historians, and the new historians of the Revolution—Albert Mathiez, George Lefebvre—diverted the study of the Revolution from political histories to social and economic histories. According to Jacques Godechot, Lefebvre himself worked as an advisor to Renoir.[103]

But here again, though following the appealing group of Marseillais from Marseille to Paris may seem like a felicitous device for approaching the Revolution—personalizing it, giving the heady ideas flesh and blood, deflecting the historical focus from Paris, salting the discourse with the provincial accents of the Midi—an additional factor must have applied, and that was the battle for the national anthem, the "Marseillaise."

For those of us weaned on *Casablanca,* we know that the "Marseillaise" stirs the patriotic heart and larynx of every freedom-loving French person, as it always has. Except that the song did not always stir the same hearts. Today one may associate the "Marseillaise" with the struggle for liberty and perhaps think of it as the anthem of the French people in 1789, rising up to claim the freedom that rightfully belonged to them. But the "Marseillaise" has a checkered past, and only after the ideological battles of the Popular Front period did the song become an institution embraced by all French people and probably the only such national anthem embraced by struggling people in other countries as well. Through most of the nineteenth century, for royalists and reactionaries lamenting the passing of the *ancien régime,* the song conjured images of the Republican rabble storming various barricades and committing unending atrocities. Though the Convention had formally passed a resolution establishing the "Marseillaise" as the national hymn in 1794 (July 14), the song was not officially recognized as the national anthem until 1879, and even then there was spirited debate in the Assembly, for its most recent association at that time was with the bloody days of the Commune of 1871.

But lest such historical arcana seem a bit esoteric for the latter day republicans of 1937, it should be pointed out that the song continued to elicit partisan passion through the interwar years. Specifically, the song evoked memories of the carnage of the First World War, a carnage that scarred a whole generation of survivors and offspring after the war. Subsequently, the Left repudiated the song for its militarist and chauvinist overtones—overtones officially sanctioned with the transfer of the ashes of its composer, Rouget de L'Isle, to the Invalides instead of the Pantheon. The Left committed itself instead to internationalism, and the anthem of both Socialists and Communists was the "Internationale."[104] For most of the years before the Popular Front, the Left, or to be more precise, the Socialists and Communists alike, were militant pacifists and internationalists. For them, French nationalism and patriotism, incarnated in the tricolor and the "Marseillaise," represented French imperialism and the enemy of all the working classes of Europe. Throughout the postwar years, Socialists and Communists voted against war credits for the French military, and systematically renounced the singing of the "Marseillaise." For the French working class, the "Internationale" was the anthem of liberty. Only when the working class began to sense the real danger of fascism in France, after the decimation of the working class in Germany, did the French working class rediscover nationalist sentiments. At that point, it tried to recapture national symbols from the monopoly of the Right, raising the tricolor beside the red flag and singing the "Marseillaise" in tandem with the "Internationale."

Not everyone on the Left marched to this new tune. Probably the most important artist who bristled at this new embrace of nationalism and the "Marseillaise" was Jacques Prévert. One may wonder why his name does not appear in the credits of La Marseillaise. After all, he had been excoriating reaction for years as a member of the Groupe Octobre, the most important left-wing theater troupe of the period, composing attacks on militarism and fascism, performing constantly at left-wing political gatherings. He collaborated with Renoir on Le Crime de M. Lange which came out during Christmas of 1935, just before the electoral agreement among the parties on the Left that formalized the Popular Front as an electoral coalition. Yet Prévert himself dated the end of the Groupe Octobre to the height of popular enthusiasm for the Popular Front, and specifically attributed his own political withdrawal to the rehabilitation of the "Marseillaise": "I quit [the Front Populaire] . . . when it became fashionable to replace 'The Internationale' by 'La Marseillaise.' I wasn't happy about this, for I knew 'La Marseillaise' from the time I was little, and I had rejected it in all its forms. And I liked 'The Internationale.' Thus it ended there for me." In fact, Prévert's withdrawal probably coincided with the official PCF endorsement of the "Marseillaise" when Thorez travelled to Choisy-Le-Roix to honor the centenary of Rouget de L'Isle's death in June 1936.[105]

But how could Prévert, or anyone on the Left for that matter, not support the Popular Front, the "Marseillaise" or no "Marseillaise"? Actually, few did reject the Popular Front. Some, however, from the far Left, attacked the failure of the Left to seize power in a revolutionary takeover during the massive strike wave that swept France during May and June of 1936, just before and after Blum took office. But this highly sectarian criticism of the Popular Front was not Prévert's. One must understand that Prévert's politics were essentially anarchist, not part of any formal political organization. He recoiled from any political dogma. As one can see quite clearly in his films, his preferred characters were outsiders, such as M. Lange the dreamer. What he saw as the saccharine politics of the Popular Front were temperamentally anathema to him, just as were the rigid policies of Breton's surrealism. There is no indication that Prévert opposed the Popular Front; he simply could not muster any enthusiasm for it, and we do know that his work with the Groupe Octobre ended roughly with the victory of the strikers in June of 1936.

But if Prévert, prolific composer of Groupe Octobre skits hurling epithets of "social fascism" at social democrats in the first half of the decade and heaping praise on the great strides of the Soviet Union, that is, following the notorious ultra-left line of the Comintern's "third period," if Prévert was unable to throw in with the Popular Front, how is it that Renoir emerged as the leading filmmaker on the Left? After all, many of Renoir's characters were outsiders as well, and we can observe the degree of Renoir's identification with that role in his brilliant creation of Octave in *Rules of the Game*. In fact, Renoir's very remoteness from political activity made him a perfect choice of the Left, as he would not provoke partisan infighting. Having not taken part in any political activity in the first half of the 1930s, he would not cause controversy. Why, he didn't even come from the working class. So much the better.

What's more, the prestige of his name was a valuable commodity for the Communists, who were the first to "turn" Renoir into a leftist.

Catching their foes on the Left, the Socialists, continually on the defensive throughout the years of the Popular Front, the Communists led the struggle to patch together the Popular Front. For the non-Communist Left, the irony of the rigidly doctrinaire French Communist party suddenly reversing its position on social democracy and casting all principle aside in its efforts to build the coalition kept the Socialists off guard, for the Socialists proved less flexible in their response to the threat of fascism. The Socialists were deeply suspicious of the Communists from earlier years and appeared to drag their feet in joining the Popular Front.

Like the film *La Marseillaise,* Renoir avoided partisanship. Despite his embrace by the Communist party at the time of *La Vie est à nous,* he certainly never joined the party, nor was he affiliated with any other party. Renoir was swept up in the mass popular movement, but never chose sides within the ferment, and that reticence shaped the form of *La Marseillaise.*

I have concentrated on the political emptiness at the center of *La Marseillaise* for understanding that aspect of the film explains a great deal about its failure, and unlike Renoir's limited role in *La Vie est à nous,* which proffered many explicit political demands, Renoir's political position was mirrored far more clearly/accurately in *La Marseillaise.* One might say that *La Marseillaise* was a purely formalist exercise for Renoir. Challenged to walk a political tightrope with critics ready to snipe at him from all sides, bound by his own political sympathies to exclude the Republicans from criticism, Renoir extended the formal experiments which he had been working on throughout the decade, but there was no content to the film. Ironically, the very overload of content inherent in the material left no room for the particularity of Renoir's vision. Consequently, the tragic view of Renoir which culminated in *Rules of the Game* had no place in *La Marseillaise,* for he could not refer to the fate that had already befallen the Popular Front by the time the film was completed. An honest and perceptive view of the time would have acknowledged divisions among the Republicans, conflicting attitudes toward the monarchy, the clergy, war with Prussia. Unlike *Rules of the Game,* there is no criticism of the lower classes allowed in *La Marseillaise,* and that directed toward the nobility is sympathetic, as if hostility toward a soon-to-be-obsolete class would be taking unfair advantage.

As it is, the plan to make a film paid for by the people, and made for the people, did not succeed, and the hopes of charting a new direction for French cinema died with *La Marseillaise,* and perhaps we can see some of the gloom that set in after the anticlimax of *La Marseillaise* in

La Bête Humaine. The film that was to establish Ciné-Liberté as a viable enterprise for the production of popular films was in fact the last production of Ciné-Liberté.

While *La Marseillaise* has come down to us as *the* film of the Popular Front, and I have tried to indicate the particular way that such an assessment is accurate, it is also important to keep in mind its relation to the relatively unknown production of independent political films by both the political parties and Ciné-Liberté, for those films specifically addressed contemporary political realities. Only *La Marseillaise* departed from this pattern, resorting to an entirely fictional form, in fact a form resembling the fictional spectacles of the commercial cinema. The aspiration to attract a mass audience entailed a return to costume drama, for according to Renoir, that audience was "a public which goes to the cinema simply for distraction."[106]

The films made by the political parties were for the most part documentaries but even when a political film adopted fiction, such as *Le Temps des cerises* by Jean-Paul Le Chanois, there were still documentary images included. What I am suggesting is that all of the independent political films, whether made by the political parties or by Ciné-Liberté, without exception, always included documentary material. The significance of this is that those films attempted to respond to the immediate political realities, and contemporary images were crucial in establishing some claim to that reality, as if the filmmakers consciously avoided fiction, contaminated as it was by associations with the vapid melodramas which were the staple of the French industry, an industry which manifested remarkable indifference in their films to the lives of working people.

When critics on the Left expressed their dissatisfaction with the French industry, they also called for the production of Left newsreels, newsreels which would combat the version of reality offered by commercial newsreels. They criticized the commercial companies for their failure to document the rapid growth of the Popular Front easily observed at the massive public demonstrations during those years. As many historians have noted, the Popular Front was a truly popular movement, formed in response to desires of the working class. During those years, the political leaders and parties on the Left were reacting to the masses, and those masses were not given adequate coverage for the critics on the Left. In what turned out to be the last issue of *Ciné-Liberté*, the importance attached to this self-representation is clear in the demand at the top of the list of future projects for "popular newsreels," for they would allow millions of spectators to learn "to see themselves at the cinema, to know themselves, to recognize each other."

From this point of view, La Marseillaise becomes an anomalous film, the only one fully enclosed within fiction, and a fiction in which the French working class could not recognize itself. The filmmakers who planned La Marseillaise, working with the support of the CGT, probably were conscious of tailoring the film for a mass audience, and adopted the costume drama model from the commercial cinema as the most likely way of attracting that audience.

In a way, the very success of the Popular Front in France may have contributed to the demise of a distinct independent filmmaking movement on the Left. The concrete achievements of the Popular Front were real and lasting ones. Though faced with formidable opposition, the Popular Front government did secure gains for the workers, and the building of an oppositional cultural movement, such as the Maisons de la Culture (which exist to this day spread over the entire country), did succeed in reclaiming national symbols for the Left. Having repulsed the domestic fascist threat and having improved tangibly the lot of the workers, what struggles were left to pursue? There had been setbacks to be sure, but La Marseillaise chooses to celebrate the unity of real French working people. It is they who are the true "enfants de la patrie," and their ancestors were the forefathers of the Republic. If La Marseillaise was predicated on restoring the lineage of the national anthem to the working people of France, should it at the same time repudiate the conventions of French commercial cinema?

Whether La Marseillaise could have realized its aims in another form is impossible to say, but critics at the time certainly noticed that the pulse of struggle no longer beat in this democratic revolution. Rather than extending the mobilization of the masses which was responsible for the victory of the Popular Front, as La Vie est à nous certainly did, La Marseillaise looked backward, thematically and formally, basking in the glow of victory instead of examining and extending the agitational successes of films such as La Vie est à nous.

As the last film produced by the Left during the years of the Popular Front, La Marseillaise provides a fitting conclusion for this discussion of political films made during the period, for, despite all its failings, it too must be read as a political intervention at an eventful historical moment. Such a claim may seem obvious. But a recent writer on La Marseillaise specifically rejects the value or relevance of a political reading of the film. In Sesonske's study of Renoir's French films, the author writes that

> in evoking the union that had created the nation in 1792, *La Marseillaise* sought to sustain a union which would save the nation in 1939. Of course! Yet a remark about the film often repeated since it appeared in a fascist journal in 1938, that when a Marseillais asserts that a priest is not necessarily a reactionary this refers to Maurice Thorez' hand extended to the Catholics, now seems ridiculous, or at least irrelevant. It diminishes the film by diverting attention from it—which was perhaps its original intent.[107]

While Sesonske is by no means insensitive to the historical and political context of *La Marseillaise* (as he is not insensitive to the context of *La Vie est à nous*), the auteurist thrust of his approach would omit from discussion contemporary political references, one of the crucial determinants of its construction and meaning. For example, the PCF's "extended hand" to the Catholics was one of the most famous and remarked upon phrases of the epoch. Though the reference to it in the film appears only in an almost casual remark, it bore a highly significant resonance at the time. The filmmakers undoubtedly included this line for that very reason. Not to attend to the political meaning and importance of this line is equivalent to not understanding one of the fundamental correspondences between *La Marseillaise* and the political environment from which it drew its financing, its script, its inspiration, and its particular construction.[108]

La Marseillaise, then, relies on an exclusively fictional form. Every scene is an historial reconstruction with actors playing the roles of others, historical figures or characters patched together from historical documents. Formally, the film represents a retreat from the dialectic of document and fiction used so effectively in *La Vie est à nous*. Rather than combining documentary and fiction modes within the same film, Ciné-Liberté now chose either one (*Sur les routes d'acier*) or the other (*La Marseillaise*). After the decision of the PCF to produce films on its own, Ciné-Liberté moved closer to the shelter of the CGT. In so doing, Ciné-Liberté's production ended with Renoir's *La Marseillaise*. Despite all the expectation and publicity accompanying the long production history of *La Marseillaise*, as Renoir acknowledged later,

> Yes, along the way the film became an absolutely normal enterprise and was distributed normally.[109]

NOTES

1. *L'Humanité,* January 31, 1936.
2. *Le Peuple,* March 4, 1936.
3. *Vendredi,* February 21, 1936.
4. *Le Populaire,* March 27, 1936.
5. According to one writer, the Socialist party reduced its budget for film propaganda by half in the belief that film was "a bad agent of politics." G. Guillaume-Grimaud, *Le Cinéma du Front Populaire* (Paris: L'Herminier, 1986), p. 48.
6. G. Sadoul, "Liberté du Cinéma," *Regards,* March 20, 1936.
7. *L'Humanité,* April 3, 1936.
8. *Le Populaire,* April 10, 1936.
9. "Pour un cinéma populaire," *L'Humanité,* April 21, 1936.
10. *L'Humanité,* May 1, 1936.
11. *Ciné-Liberté* 1 (May 20, 1936).
12. C. Aveline, "La Censure et Ciné-Liberté," *Ciné-Liberté* 1.
13. P. J. Lespeyres, "Une Enquête Sur La Censure. Sens Interdit," *Ciné-Liberté* 1.
14. "Les Techniciens Répondent," *Ciné-Liberté* 1.
15. Renaitour, et al., *Où va le cinéma français* (Paris: Editions Baudinière, n.d., [1937]), p. 194.
16. Lemare, "Le Coin des Techniciens," *Ciné-Liberté* 1.
17. Yves Allégret, interview with author, Paris, August 19, 1981, and Jean-Paul Le Chanois, interview with author, Paris, July 22, 1981.
18. J. Renoir, "A propos de *Modern Times,*" *Ciné-Liberté* 1.
19. Beylie quotes this expression without giving its source, though he may be quoting himself. Beylie, "Jean Renoir," "Anthologie du Cinéma," in *l'Avant Scène Cinéma* 251/252 (July 15, 1980): 149.
20. Renoir, "A propos de *Modern Times.*"
21. Ibid.
22. Among those that consider that the strikes did present an opportunity for revolution, see the following: F. Claudin, *The Communist Movement: From Comintern to Cominform. Part One. The Crisis of the Communist International* (New York: Monthly Review Press, 1975); D. Guérin, *Front Populaire. Revolution Manquée* (Paris: François Maspero, 1963; 1970). For those who disagree, see the following: G. Lefranc, *Histoire du Front Populaire (1934–1938)* (Paris: Payot, 1965); F. Goguel, *La Politique des partis sous la IIIe République* (Paris: Editions du Seuil, 1946).
23. "L'Etape Decisive," June 12, 1936, *La Lutte ouvrière* (issue seized by the police); "La Révolution Française a Commencé," June 9, 1936, *La Lutte ouvrière.* Both reprinted in *Le Mouvement Communiste en France (1919–1939),* ed. P. Broué (Paris: Les Editions de Minuit, 1967), pp. 571–83.
24. J. Lacouture, *Léon Blum* (Paris: Editions du Seuil, 1977), p. 279.
25. M. Pivert, "Tout est possible," *Le Populaire,* May 27, 1936.

26. *L'Humanité*, June 12, 1936. The text is the transcription of a speech given by Thorez in the evening of June 11, 1936, at the Jean Jaurès Gymnasium.

27. According to Kergoat, the beginnings of the strike movement did not receive extensive coverage in the press. Kergoat, *La France du Front Populaire*, pp. 100–101.

28. For a discussion of the Matignon Agreements, see J. Colton, *Léon Blum: Humanist in Politics* (Cambridge, Mass.: M.I.T. Press, 1966), pp. 149–55; A. Sauvy, *Histoire Economique de la France entre les deux guerres, Tome 2 (1931–1939)* (Paris: Fayard, 1967), pp. 202–12.

29. Kergoat relates two revealing incidents about this struggle over symbols. "The demonstration which ended the occupation marched symbolically behind the busts of Cachin, of Blum, and of Costes, Communist deputy from Billancourt and the CGT's director at Renault. But the PCF officials notice that this unity allegory is incomplete: it lacks a Radical! So they hastily make a poster symbolizing Herriot that is carried beside the three busts" (p. 125). On another occasion, during a strike in September of the same year, "The red flag blew above the factory, but the strikers refused to accompany it with the tricolor. Every morning, one arose to the sound of the 'International': some militants of the PCF wanted to follow it with the 'Marseillaise' but the strike committee confiscated the record" (p. 205).

30. Sadoul, *Regards*, August 27, 1936.

31. Sadoul, *Regards,* June 18, 1936.

32. Sadoul, *Regards,* August 27, 1936.

33. Aragon, quoted by Sadoul, *Regards,* May 28, 1936.

34. J.-P. Dreyfus, "Vers une Théâtre de France," *L'Humanité*, February 16, 1936; "L'Union du Théâtre de France," *L'Humanité*, March 8, 1936; "Les Théâtres de la Liberté," *L'Humanité*, April 4, 1936.

35. Dreyfus, *L'Humanité*, February 16, 1936.

36. Ibid., March 8, 1936.

37. *Le Populaire*, June 24, 1936.

38. Lefranc, *Histoire du Front Populaire*, p. 153.

39. "Les Socialistes Annoncent l'Etatisation du Cinéma," *La Cinématographie Française*, April 11, 1936.

40. Ibid. The interview appeared in an issue of *Cinémonde* from the same week.

41. *Cinémonde*, April 16, 1936, emphasis in original.

42. Despite indications before the elections that the PCF might be prepared to participate as members of the Blum government, the PCF refused Blum's invitation. Vaillant-Couturier explained that the PCF would support the government of the Popular Front in the Chamber and that it would "exercise from outside a ministry of the masses." Lefranc, *Histoire du Front Populaire*, p. 135.

43. Guérin, *Front Populaire*, pp. 112–13. For Talpain, see Grelier, *Mémoires*, pp. 101–4.

44. Ibid. According to Guérin, the man referred to as Professor Flamm is Chakotin, who wrote *Le Viol des Foules* (Paris: Gallimard, 1939), translated as *The Rape of the Masses* (London: The Labour Book Service, 1940).

45. *Le Populaire,* July 29, 1936.

46. *Cinémonde,* July 14, 1936.

47. Lefranc, *Histoire du Front Populaire,* p. 200.

48. The franc was devalued on October 1, 1936. As with so many of the historical problems posed by this period, scholars disagree about both the real attitudes toward and the real import of devaluation. Classically, capital flight can be curbed in two ways. Strict controls can be imposed to halt the movement of funds abroad, but such a policy entails a strong govermental intervention in the capital market and obviously risks alienating financial interests. Conversely, the government can devalue in an attempt to induce capital holders to invest in newly competitive French industries. This measure raises domestic prices of foreign goods for French consumers, thereby placing the burden of addressing the currency problem on working people. As a party ostensibly representing the working class, the Socialist party, and more particularly Léon Blum, promised in the Popular Front electoral program not to devalue. Some of Blum's closest advisers informed him before the election that devaluation was inevitable and that, economically, the sooner the better. The problem with untangling this issue is that Blum made no attempt to impose currency restrictions as a possible way of averting devaluation, thereby effectively guaranteeing the inevitability of devaluation as the only solution to halting the galloping depletion of the national treasury. Whatever position one takes on the merits of devaluation—my own sense is that it was not necessarily unavoidable, though I recognize the delicately compelling reasons for it—the Left, broadly speaking, opposed devaluation as an article of faith and devaluation unquestionably opened yet another disaffecting fissure in that coalition. For discussion, see R. Girault, "La Trahison des possédants," *L'Histoire* 58 (July-August 1983): 85–93; R. Girault, "Léon Blum. La Dévaluation de 1936 et la conduite de la politique extérieure," *Rélations Internationales* 13 (Spring 1978): 91–109; E. Bonnefous, *Histoire Politique de la Troisième République,* Tomes 5, 6 (Paris: Presses Universitaires de France, 1962; 1965); G. Lefranc, *Histoire du Front Populaire (1934–1938)* (Paris: Payot, 1965; 1974); A. Sauvy, *Histoire Economique de la France entre les deux guerres 1931–1939* (Paris: Fayard, 1967); Colton, *Léon Blum,* pp. 177–95.

49. *Comoedia,* August 8, 1936.

50. *Le Populaire,* May 16, 1937.

51. For discussions of the French actions regarding nonintervention in Spain, see the following: Colton, *Léon Blum,* pp. 234–69; Lacouture, *Léon Blum,* pp. 330–87; H. Thomas, *The Spanish Civil War* (New York: Harper, 1961; 1981), pp. 334–69, 387–99.

52. *Ciné-Liberté* 3 (July-August 1936).

53. M. Hilero, "En tournant la colonie des vacances des Bernardoux," *Ciné-Liberté* 4 (October 1, 1936).

54. P. Lemare, Ibid.

55. *Almanach Ouvrier-Paysan*, 1936.

56. H. Jeanson, "Lettre Ouverte et non censurée à Jean Zay," *Ciné-Liberté* 3 (July-August, 1936).

57. Renaitour, *Où va le cinéma français?*, p. 129.

58. Renoir, "Suggestions," *Ciné-Liberté* 2 (June 30, 1936).

59. J. Renoir and H. Jeanson, "Comment on fait un film," *Commune* 35 (July 1936).

60. Jeanson, "Il faut en finir avec . . . Messieurs les Distributeurs," *Ciné-Liberté* 5 (November 1, 1936).

61. *Comoedia*, November 22, 1936.

62. According to Aranda, a copy of this film exists in the Filmoteca Nacional Española in Madrid, but considerable ambiguity surrounds the film. First, Aranda claims there are four- and nine-reel versions. Second, production credits have never been established with certainty, including the role of Luis Buñuel. Buñuel helped advise Le Chanois on the editing of the compilation material, but their respective contributions have not been clarified. Third, Aranda refers to the film as *España 1936* in the body of his book yet lists the film as *España 1937* in the filmography. F. Aranda, *Luis Buñuel: A Critical Biography*, ed. and trans. by D. Robinson (New York: Da Capo, 1976), pp. 119, 291. While this discrepancy may have been simply an error, documentation from the period also indicates that both titles were advertised in newspapers, including one notice announcing that *both* films ("actualités espagnols") would be shown. *Ce Soir*, October 2, 1937. On April 11, 1937, *Ce Soir* ran an interview with "L. Brunel" [*sic*] by Karl Obermann, in which Buñuel declared that "the task of the Spanish film had to be reproducing the simple reality of facts." I have not seen any of the versions. It is possible, then, that either two versions were made, a later one corresponding to changes in the development of the war, or that *Espagne 36* was cannibalized for footage used in *Espagne 37*.

I have chosen not to discuss the Spanish films that Ciné-Liberté was involved in for several reasons. First, I have not seen all of them. Second, it is not clear what role Ciné-Liberté played in the production of these films. As with *Coeur d'Espagne*, Ciné-Liberté may have only distributed the film(s). Third, as indicated above, the status of the extant material is problematic. I might add that "reproducing the simply reality of facts" was an extremely difficult, even impossible, task. Accounts of the Spanish Civil War emphasize the confusion and lack of information throughout the war, in particular the internecine struggles on the Left among anarchists, Socialists, Communists, and Trotskyists. Yet the films that I have seen, such as *Coeur d'Espagne* and *Victoire de la Vie*, give no indication of this complex "reality of facts." Naturally, the filmmakers wanted to mobilize support for the Republican effort, and my impression is that, intentionally or not, the films provide no information on the political conflicts on the Left. Joris Ivens has responded recently to criticism leveled at his film, *Spanish Earth*, for its failure to address some of these problems, a failure shared by the other Spanish films I have seen:

> France and England let Spain fight alone against the fascists of Mussolini and the legions of Hitler. Following that, we looked for explanations; it said that there were confrontations between the Communists and the Trotskyists, or between the Socialists and the anarchists, but I never saw it, nor heard of it. Never. If not, I would not have accepted it. Certainly, there were tensions and oppositions, between Catalan and the government, between the parties or within the parties, but this was normal. The Spanish government was a government of the Popular Front, where all the tendencies of the Left were able and had to express themselves. For the rest, it was most often simple rivalries within the group. When we reached the front, if we were crossing an abandoned truck by the side of the road, for the Communists, it was always the POUM or the anarchists. They joked about it, saying "they don't know how to drive." For their part, the men of Durruti said the same of the Communists. Today, the young people are certainly right to look at history with a magnifying glass to try to understand the aberrations, but at the time it was not possible; I was unable to do it. No one was able to do it, unless they were enemies of the Republic. If now they wish the truths, there are other documents than my film; there are other books, and each gives a part of the truth. My film is not a document of history, it was the human truth; it shows a people which fights against fascism. It was not possible to be otherwise.

J. Ivens and R. Destanque, *Joris Ivens ou la Mémoire d'un Regard* (Paris: Editions BFB, 1982), p. 140. Noam Chomsky, relying on an unpublished 1967 paper (W. B. Watson and B. Whaley, "The Spanish Earth of Dos Passos and Hemingway"), claims that "a striking example of the distortion introduced by the propaganda efforts of the 1930s is the strange story of the influential film *The Spanish Earth* . . . a project that was apparently initiated by Dos Passos. . . . For the libertarian Dos Passos, the revolution was the dominant theme; it was the antifascist war, however, that was to preoccupy Hemingway. The role of Dos Passos was quickly forgotten, because of the fact (as Watson and Whaley point out) that Dos Passos had become anathema to the Left for his criticisms of Communist policies in Spain." Chomsky, "Objectivity and Liberal Scholarship," *American Power and the New Mandarins* (New York: Pantheon, 1969), excerpted in *The Chomsky Reader*, ed. J. Peck (New York: Pantheon, 1987), p. 431 n. 77. Because the Ciné-Liberté films and the British films do not allow these political differences to surface, they tend to take a similar view of the events, hence the French films have little to offer of a specifically French interpretation of the events. As well, humanitarian organizations were often responsible for funding the films, such as the sponsorship of *Victoire de la Vie* by La Centrale Sanitaire Internationale, not the French Communist party or Ciné-Liberté. I think that a careful discussion of films made on the Spanish Civil War should be pursued in a special study devoted to those films. Since this book has gone to press, an excellent article by Ben Hogenkamp has appeared on this subject, "Le film de gauche et la Guerre Civile d'Espagne, 1936–39," *Revue Belge du Cinéma* 17 (Autumn 1986): 3–27.

63. B. Eisenschitz, "Front Populaire et Idée de Cinéma Militant de France (1928–1937)," Publication of the International Federation of Film Archives and Bulgarska Nacionalna Filmoteka, Varna, 1977.

64. W. Alexander, *Film on the Left* (Princeton: Princeton University Press, 1981), p. 162.

65. C. Aveline, "De Ciné-Liberté à *La Marseillaise*," *Commune* 55 (March 1938).

66. Sadoul, *Regards*, December 16, 1937.

67. Aveline, "De Ciné-Liberté."

68. *Cahiers de la Jeunesse* 4.

69. A transcription of the sound track has been prepared by Claude Thibault, to whom I would like to express my thanks for providing me with a copy. I would also like to thank the late Martine Loubet, who helped me obtain the copy.

70. Sadoul, *Regards*, February 10, 1938.

71. Cheronnet, *L'Humanité*, February 9, 1938.

72. Le Chanois, interview with author.

73. Sadoul, *Regards*, September 30, 1937.

74. *Regards*, June 24, 1937.

75. *Ce Soir*, November 22, 1937.

76. Sadoul, *Regards*, September 30, 1937.

77. Vermorel, *Pour Vous*, February 2, 1938.

78. Le Chanois, interview with author.

79. Aveline, "De Ciné-Liberté."

80. J. Fauvet, *Histoire du Parti Communiste Français*, Tome 1 (Paris: Fayard, 1964), p. 213.

81. P. Robrieux, *Histoire intérieure du parti communiste. 1920–1945* (Paris: Fayard, 1980), p. 483.

82. R. Tiersky, *French Communism, 1920–1972* (New York: Columbia University Press, 1974), p. 74.

83. The relevant passages from the speech of Thorez can be found in his *Oeuvres Choisies*, Tome 1, *1924–1937* (Paris: Editions Sociales, 1967).

84. Ibid.

85. D. Caute, *Communism and the French Intellectuals, 1914–1960* (New York: Macmillan, 1964), p. 129.

86. Thomas, *The Spanish Civil War*, pp. 701–9.

87. Caute, *Communism and the French Intellectuals*, pp. 128–29; N. Werth, *Les Procès de Moscou* (Bruxelles: Les Editions Complexe, 1987).

88. Renoir, "La Marseillaise," *Les Cahiers de la Jeunesse* 7 (February 15, 1938), reprinted in *la revue du cinéma. Image et Son* 135 (March 1977): 23. As *La Marseillaise* is the only film from this episode of Left filmmaking to have been discussed at any length by commentators, I have kept my own remarks on the production history brief. For additional background see Faulkner, *Jean Renoir;* Fofi, "The Cinema of the Popular Front in France"; Gauteur, *Jean Renoir,* and the articles from *La Revue du Cinéma, Image et Son* cited in the Bibliography below; Ory, "De Ciné-Liberté à *La Marseillaise*"; Serceau, *Jean Renoir, l'Insurge;* Sesonske, *Jean Renoir: The French Films.*

89. See the reviews cited in notes 98 and 99 below.

90. H. Jeanson, "La Marseillaise ou les Fourberies de Stalin [La Marseillaise or the Deceitfulness of Stalin]," *La Flèche de Paris,* February 2, 1938, reprinted in Gauteur dossier, "La Marseillaise," *La Revue du Cinéma, Image et Son* 268 (February 1973): 69.

91. Ory, "De 'Ciné-Liberté' à *La Marseillaise,*" p. 163.

92. Article by André Seigneur, a member of the PCF, *L'Avant-Garde,* August 14, 1937, cited in Ory, "De 'Ciné-Liberté'," p. 169.

93. Ibid.

94. Fofi, "The Cinema of the Popular Front," p. 37.

95. Sadoul referred specifically to two earlier films on the French Revolution, one by Griffith (*Orphans of the Storm,* 1921), the other by Gance (*Napoléon,* 1927) in his review of *La Marseillaise:* "The taking of the Tuileries would have been for Griffith a counterpoint of ingeniously orchestrated crowds, for Abel Gance a thunder of romantic music played on the organ, interwoven with false notes. . . . With Renoir, there are no formal effects; we are in a real palace, at the siege of a real palace, with its disorder and its sandbags, the letters that were burned, the parliamentarians clothed in black, the dauphin who is scolded, and soon the aristocrats who will be shot en masse, in the great, gilded corridors. We are inside this palace, now destroyed, face to face with History, as truly as we were in the misty night of February 9, assaulted by black cars and gunshots." *Regards,* February 10, 1938, reprinted in Gauteur, "Dossier," p. 42. Leger Grindon discusses some of the earlier films on the French Revolution in an unpublished paper, "The Politics of History in *La Marseillaise,*" 1981.

96. Article by Jean Galtier-Bossière, in *La Flèche de Paris,* March 5, 1938, reprinted in Gauteur, "Dossier," p. 62.

97. Phrase used by Renoir in interview with Jean Kress, *L'Avant-Garde,* March 13, 1937, reprinted in part in Gauteur, "Dossier," p. 21.

98. *Regards,* February 10, 1938, reprinted in Gauteur, "Dossier," p. 41.

99. *Ce Soir,* February 10, 1938, reprinted in Gauteur, "Dossier," pp. 39–40.

100. *Esprit,* February 1937, March 1, 1938, reprinted in Gauteur, "Dossier," p. 55.

101. *Vendredi*, February 18, 1938, reprinted in Gauteur, "Dossier," p. 60.
102. Mathiez wrote for *l'Humanité* until 1923 and broke with Stalin in 1931. His *French Revolution*, published in several volumes during the 1920s, was the most influential Left interpretation during the 1930s. For a discussion of the major historians of the Revolution, see J. Godechot, *Un Jury Pour la Révolution* (Paris: Editions Robert Laffont, 1974).
103. Godechot, *Un Jury*.
104. See note 135, chap. 1, p. 81.
105. See note 136, chap. 1, p. 81. For the speech of Thorez, June 27, 1936, see his *Oeuvres Choisies*, pp. 348–53. Robrieux included this date in his chronology of the PCF, claiming that "beginning with this speech the militants of the party truly begin to get used to singing 'La Marseillaise.'" Robrieux, *Histoire intérieure* 4:669.
106. Renoir, "La Marseillaise."
107. Sesonske, *Jean Renoir*, p. 334.
108. This exclusion of the political dimension as *the* most valuable way of understanding *La Vie est à nous* allows Sesonske to write of that film that "A report by Maurice Thorez to the Eighth Congress of the Parti communiste français *purportedly* supplied the outline for a script. . . ." [my emphasis] Sesonske, *Jean Renoir*, p. 223. The most cursory glance at the speech of Thorez reveals that the speech was absolutely crucial to the conception of the whole film; it also provided passages used verbatim for the film, as was shown above in chapter 2. Thus, while Sesonske discusses at length the work of Marivaux, Musset, and Beaumarchais in his consideration of *Le Régle du jeu*, he fails to examine the "purported" source for the script of *La Vie est à nous*. This omission illustrates the dangers of imposing traditional blinders on criticism (in this case, auteurism), which consequently fails to register the centrality and complexity of politics in political films (though I would maintain also that a political reading can often enrich the understanding of many films that are not necessarily overtly political).
109. Interview with Renoir by J. Rivette and F. Truffaut, *Cahiers du Cinéma* 78 (Christmas 1957), reprinted in *Jean Renoir. Entretiens et Propos* (Paris: Editions de L'Etoile-Cahiers du Cinéma, with the assistance of the National Center of Letters, 1979), p. 62.

Conclusion

Left political filmmaking in France ended with the production of *La Marseillaise*. The worker enthusiasm that swept the Popular Front to victory in 1936 and the production of *La Vie est à nous* catalyzed the formation of a political filmmaking organization on the Left, Ciné-Liberté, committed not only to establishing an alternative filmmaking community but also to extending the mobilization of the people. But less than two years later, as *La Marseillaise* "along the way became an absolutely normal enterprise," Ciné-Liberté dissolved. Were these two events related? How did the episode of Left filmmaking in France conclude so abruptly and disappointingly with the film that was supposed to be its greatest success?

To begin with, despite all the publicity that *La Marseillaise* benefited from in the Left press during production and the mass subscription drive to raise money from workers, the film fared poorly, both with its intended worker audience and with critics who might have been expected to be sympathetic. It may be easy today to look back on *La Marseillaise* and wonder how the film could be considered as a political intervention, but that was its principal goal.

In fact, as we have seen, commentators viewed it as a conventional film. Instead of bearing the transformative stamp of the Popular Front, a film by and for workers to commemorate their earlier role in the birth of the French Republic and their newfound role in the rescue of the Republic from the fascist threat, *La Marseillaise* failed to distinguish itself from the familiar costume dramas of the commercial industry, for these French films consistently set events in foreign venues. Admittedly, viewers had no difficulty deciphering contemporary references in the film—Prussian military = Hitler Germany's fascists, the French aristocracy = French Fascist leagues, the silencing of attacks on the church = the PCF's "extended hand" to the Catholics— but the sobriety of this defense of the Republic hardly captured the élan that galvanized the workers when they claimed their rights after the 1936 elections by occupying their factories. *La Marseillaise* presents the aristocracy as the enemy of the Republic, but in the 1930s the aristocracy was not responsible for unemployment, scientific management, and repression of the labor movement. That labor movement had suddenly awakened and seriously shook the French bourgeoisie, and its success attracted ever greater numbers of workers.

The phenomenal growth of the labor movement probably influenced the particular filmmaking form of *La Marseillaise*. Though filmmakers certainly hoped that the earlier films would reach large audiences, their resources were limited and they did represent specific constituencies within the Left. The electoral coalition of the Popular Front did not eliminate divisions on the Left, and those divisions became more pronounced in fact as the Blum government had to make difficult decisions and faced the counteroffensive of the bourgeoisie. The filmmakers who planned *La Marseillaise,* working with the support of the CGT, probably were conscious of tailoring the film for a mass audience and adopted the costume-drama model from the commercial cinema as the most likely way of attracting that audience.

By choosing a period piece for its most ambitious undertaking, Ciné-Liberté removed the single most recurrent characteristic of the earlier political films: embedding the action in the reality of 1930s France. Whether making newsreels to document the growth of the Popular Front or constructing dramatic situations to illustrate real events, those films challenged the portrait of France presented in commercial theaters. As political interventions they protested against the exclusion of workers from the screen. For many the mere appearance of working people on the screen represented a victory. The images alone spoke eloquently of the power of the people united. When workers on the factory floor in *La Vie est à nous* discussed the repression of management and demanded redress or construction workers atop a scaffold in *Les Bâtisseurs* admired the craft of their ancestors, millions of new union members could hear the dramatized echo of their own militant organizing activity.

La Marseillaise captured none of this resonance. The pre-industrial artisans bore little resemblance to the poor French workers of the 1930s who stood up to management as they sat down in the factories for the first time. Like their American counterparts, the French workers of the Popular Front organized the unorganized, and if the French owners did not send in goon squads to battle the workers, the workers did not view their employers with the same fraternal bonhomie found in *La Marseillaise,* politely inviting the aristocracy to leave the country. *La Marseillaise* chides the nobility for its pursuit of idle distractions but does not attack it for the hypocrisy of forcing workers to subsidize the irresponsible profligacy of management. Oblivious to the wave of republicanism, the French nobility in the film were anachronisms, not class enemies who gambled with the security and future of the country.

However, rather than indicting the film for these similarities with commercial filmmaking, it may be more instructive to consider in what ways the filmmakers thought *La Marseillaise* was going to be *different* from an "absolutely normal enterprise." Here the contemporary accounts that appeared during the production of the film are consistent. The French Revolution was an ideal choice for a subject, for the entire Left drew inspiration from the founding event of the Republic, a Republic the Popular Front had mobilized to defend. Only a few isolated voices spoke of a revolutionary overthrow of the Republic. Furthermore, what would distinguish the Ciné-Liberté production from commercial costume dramas was the attention to realistic detail in the film, the use of real Marseillais with authentic accents, for example, and the archival research which would guarantee the authenticity of the filmed events. True, there would be characteristics shared with the commercial cinema, but those similarities were perhaps acceptable dramatic techniques which would contribute to the success of the film with the intended mass audience. After all, *La Vie est à nous* and subsequent films of both Ciné-Liberté and the PCF included fictional scenes and episodes. With the Left press devoting considerable coverage to the project during its production and building anticipation for its release, perhaps the filmmakers of *La Marseillaise* did not realize the degree to which they were retreating from the formal and political experiments of the preceding films. Perhaps more significantly, they apparently did not consider the potential consequences of that retreat.

In this respect the abrupt foundering of Ciné-Liberté may underline the importance of theoretical activity in ensuring the longevity of alternative cultural production. There is no evidence that the formal innovations of the earlier films, pre-eminently *La Vie est à nous*, elicited significant and ongoing theoretical reflection during the period. Pierre Bost's incisive criticism about the "film essay" stands out as a lone and allusive attempt to think through a formulation of radical political film, an alternative practice with which the Left would speak with its own voice and its own point of view. Only in the films themselves can one discern theoretical reflections, as the films experimented with various hybrids of fictional and documentary material. As I have suggested, the dual dissatisfaction with commercial fictions and newsreels animated these political experiments.

What is crucial to keep in mind when looking back over this first experience of political filmmaking in France is that it was an oppositional movement. Politically, it was an attempt to contribute to the struggle against fascism in France. Economically, the filmmakers wanted to establish an alternative cinema, one which defined itself in opposition to the commercial cinema. Hence the repeated invocations of a "cinema populaire," a cinema that would address topical concerns of working-class audiences. One might call this aspiration a search for a populist cinema.

At the same time, this was to be a *French* political cinema. It may seem strange, when considering the writing on film in France during this period, and on *La Vie est à nous* in particular, that the Left did not simply adopt the models of the much-admired Soviet films. Yet the great Soviet films, rather than seeking an effective oppositional stance, celebrated the state—a state in which the proletariat had seized power. Sadoul insisted on this salient difference when, in an article in *Commune,* he rebuked Rene Clair for suggesting that intervention by the French government might improve the French film industry: "Rene Clair . . . should understand that if, in the USSR, the problems of cinema have been resolved by an intervention of the state, it is because this state is the state of the workers, the antithesis of the bourgeois state." Presumably, so long as France remained a bourgeois state, Left filmmaking in France had to maintain its oppositional stance.

Coincident with these aims, the filmmakers sought forms which would speak to popular audiences at a particular historical moment about that historical moment. Documentary and newsreel images offered the most direct route to that goal. The most politicized filmmakers concentrated on this approach. Marceau Pivert, the ultra-Left Socialist politician, saw the function of film in a narrowly propagandistic view, and from the fragmentary evidence available—the few films that have survived and written records—he worked exclusively with newsreel material which chronicled participation of the masses in large public demonstrations. But unlike other Left filmmaking activity, there was nothing novel formally in his project. Not only did he fail to examine reflexively the newsreel form, to demonstrate and criticize the limitations of commercial newsreels, which might lead to some theoretical analysis of the newsreel form, but he also avoided fiction altogether.

Most of the other Left filmmaking projects searched for novel cinematic structures which would occupy a position somewhere between the poles of fiction and document. Even the earliest and in some ways the most crude films, such as *La Crise* and *Prix et Profits*, exhibit this characteristic. *La Crise* is a polemical documentary propounding the argument and rhetoric of the Comintern's "third period," but it includes a fictional sequence to dramatize the problem of farm foreclosures. Later films made by the PCF—*La Vie d'un homme*—though taking an entirely different political position, also use short fictional anecdotes to dramatize the documentary. Alternatively, *Prix et Profits* inserts documentary images at times into the fiction, as if insisting that the fiction has its source in contemporary events. Documentary images somehow validate the claims of the fiction. After the victory of the Popular Front, the Socialist Dulac and the Communist Le Chanois used documentary images similarly in *Retour à la Vie* and *Le Temps des cerises* respectively.

As I have tried to show, *La Vie est à nous* offers the most interesting and successful realization of and reflection on these ideas. Rather than simply and uncritically having documentary/newsreel images validate assertions of the fiction, the film changes those images and re-edits them to demonstrate their power to dissimulate, to mislead, to distort some hypothetical reality. The film postulates such a putative cinematic "reality" as a field of struggle, ever subject to manipulation. Furthermore, the film refuses to accept any simple boundary between fiction and document, as the very opening sequence of the film defies and challenges the categories themselves. In addition, instead of simply oscillating between fiction and document, there are multiple fictions, and the final one merges with nonfiction, further confounding the boundaries between them.

But why and how did *La Vie est à nous* attain this success? It was not the result of theoretical debate from the period, for we find no evidence of such discussions in published sources. Like the other films, *La Vie est à nous* was an attempt to make an oppositional statement, but why was its result more theoretically engaged? I think that there are several answers. First, of all the political films made during the period, *La Vie est à nous* had a clear and specific purpose: mobilization for the electoral campaign. Second, it was made at an important moment, just before the upsurge of the great strike wave, a time that coincided with the first days of the Blum government, the first paid vacations, and before the outbreak of the Spanish Civil War, the first and perhaps most tragic fissure in the Popular Front coalition. At that moment, *La Vie est à nous* was at once riding the crest of the popular wave and propelling it. With no precedents for such films in France but knowing well what they objected to in the commercial cinema, the filmmakers experimented freely with both fiction and document. And the collective nature of the enterprise must have reinforced the variety of experiment in the film, each collaborator eager to make a significant contribution. In such an atmosphere, Renoir was the perfect choice to oversee the project, free as he was of either political or aesthetic dogma and confident enough of his own vision as an artist to elicit the best from the participants in the collective. None of the other films shared this confluence of circumstances.

The reticence of critics on the Left to address the theory of political filmmaking is surprising, given all the attention paid to the establishment of mass cultural organizations, including Ciné-Liberté itself. For all the talk about the openness of the PCF to varied forms of cultural production, perhaps developments in the Soviet Union did have repercussions in France, at least in the film community. I have already referred to the vigorous debates among Soviet filmmakers in the 1920s, specifically over the relative importance of documentary and fiction, with Vertov and Eisenstein arguing over the respective merits of the Kino-Eye versus the Kino-Fist, two metaphors for political filmmaking, but those debates ceased during the 1930s. The 1935 Moscow film conference provides evidence of the change. While there was no attempt to impose a doctrine of Socialist Realism on French cultural production, the pall that settled over cultural debate in the Soviet Union at the very moment of the rise of the Popular Front in France may have discouraged theoretical inquiry in France.

Whatever the origin and influence of its aesthetic strategies, *La Vie est à nous* did provide the impetus for the formation of an independent organization on the Left dedicated to film, Ciné-Liberté. This organization, formed during the days of hope raised by the success of *La Vie est à nous* and the electoral victory, sought for the first time in France to forge a viable film community which would not serve the commercial industry. Instead it devoted itself to films funded by political parties, trade unions, and other groups on the Left. Once the urgency of struggle subsided, however, French militant filmmaking abandoned its agitational agenda and did not renew that agenda on a comparable scale until May 1968.

Appendix—The Films

1. *Prix et Profits* 1931 Silent
Director: Yves Allégret
With Jacques Prévert, Pierre Prévert
Produced for Célestin Freinet
Length: 18 minutes

When I began my research, this film was considered lost. However, in my interview with Yves Allégret, he told me that he had deposited a copy at the Centre National de la Cinématographie (CNC). When I inquired at the CNC, Mme. Nicole Schmitt informed me that the CNC had a copy of the film, but only in negative, which the Centre was barred by law from screening. However, she kindly arranged for me to look at the film at the Pathé studios at Joinville-le-Pont, on the Marne, outside of Paris. I viewed the film on a flatbed editor with the image shown on a video screen with the polarities reversed so that I could see the film in positive. Since that time, a positive copy of the film has been struck and is available for screening at the Centre.

2. *La Crise* 1931(?) Silent
Produced by the French Communist Party
Length: 17 minutes

3. *Le Mur des fédérés* 1935
Produced by the Cinematographic Service of the Federation of the Seine, Socialist Party, Section Française de l'Internationale Socialiste (SFIO, official name of the French Socialist Party). The Service was headed by the left-wing Socialist Marceau Pivert.
Camera: H. Champion, M. Fredetal, A. Thomas
Length: 15 minutes

A copy of this film is preserved in the Cinémathèque Suisse in Lausanne.

4. *Grand Rassemblement** 1935
Probably produced by the Alliance du Cinéma Indépendent, part of the
Maison de la Culture
Length: 9 minutes

5. *La Vie est à nous* 1936
Directors: Jean Renoir, Jean-Paul Le Chanois, Jacques B. Brunius, Jacques
Becker
Script: Jean Renoir, Pierre Unik, Jean-Paul Le Chanois, Paul Vaillant-
Couturier
Assistants: Henri Cartier-Bresson, Marc Maurette, Maurice Lime
Camera: Louis Page, Jean-Serge Bourgoin, Jean Isnard, Alain Douarinou,
Claude Renoir, Nicolas Hayer
Script-girl: Renée Vavasseur
Sound: Robert Teisseire
Editing: Marguerite Renoir
Cast: Jean Dasté (schoolteacher), Jacques B. Brunius (industrialist), Jean Re-
noir (bistro owner), Simone Guisin (a lady at casino), Teddy Michaux (a fascist
exercising), Pierre Unik (Cachin's secretary), Max Dalban (Brochard, the
"chrono," or efficiency expert), Madeleine Sologne (a factory worker), Fabien
Loris (a worker), Emile Drain (the elderly Gustave Bertin), Charles Blavette
(Tonin), Madeleine Dax (secretary at cell meeting), Roger Blin (a metalworker), Sylvain Itkine (accountant), Georges Spanelly (factory manager),
Fernand Bercher (a secretary), Eddy Debray (usher), Henri Pons (M. Lecocq,
the farmer), Gabrielle Fontan (Mme. Lecocq), Gaston Modot (Phillippe,
farmer's nephew), Léon Larive (a customer at farm auction), Pierre Ferval
(second customer), Julien Bertheau (René, the unemployed engineer), Nadia
Sibirskaia (Ninette, René's girlfriend), Marcel Lesieur (garage owner),
O'Brady (Mohammed, the north African garage worker), Marcel Duhamel
(M. Moutet, the Volontaire-National), Tristan Sevère (an unemployed man in
the line at soup kitchen), Guy Favières (the old unemployed worker), Muse
Dalbray (an unemployed woman), Jacques Becker (the young unemployed
man), Claire Gérard (a bourgeois woman in the street), Jean-Paul Le Chanois
(P'tit Louis), Charles Charras, Francis Lemarque (singers at the Communist
club), Maurice Marceau. In the final group of marchers: Vladimir Sokoloff,
François Viguier, Yolande Oliviero, Madeleine Sylvain, etc. As themselves:
Marcel Cachin, André Marty, Paul Vaillant-Couturier, Renaud Jean, Martha
Desrumeaux, Marcel Gitton, Jacques Duclos, Maurice Thorez
Length: 62 minutes

Available in the United States through Unifrance Film USA, 745 5th Avenue,
New York, New York (212) 832-8860

6. *Le Retour à la vie* 1936
Director: Germaine Dulac
Produced by the group "Mai 36"
Length: 11 minutes

A copy is preserved at the Centre National de la Cinématographie.

7. *Grèves d'occupation** 1936
Filmed by Ciné-Liberté
Length: 6 minutes

8. *Le Temps des cerises** 1937
Director: Jean-Paul Le Chanois
Script: Jean-Paul Le Chanois
Produced by the French Communist Party, with technical assistance of the Société "La Marseillaise"
Camera: Jean Bourgoin, Alain Douarinov, Jacques Lemare
Decors: G. Wakevitch
Make-up: S. Schleifer
Producers: Barryel, S. Guesin
Cast: Gaston Modot (Gaston Ravaux), Svet. Pitoëff (Gilberte), Loris (Pierrot), Jeandeline (peasant), Spanelli (director), Jean Dasté (director's son), Brunius (director's grandson), Camille Corney (decorator), Delferrière (engineer), Claire Gérard (the affected woman), Gabrielle Fontan (Antoinette), and Madame Varennes, Marizier, Uruchona, Friant, Madeleine Sologne, Madeleine Gaillard, Mm. Vény, Raphael Cailloux, Roger Blin, Roger Maxime, Eddy Debray, Lesieur, Amy Dalaize, Guy Dacombe, Ferval, Forney, Maxel, Malbert, Roussel, Dumontier, Marceau Barryel, Rosen, Courquin, the Marc Brothers
Length: 81 minutes

9. *La Vie d'un homme** 1937
Director: Jean-Paul Le Chanois (uncredited)
Produced by the French Communist Party
Contributors: Guy de la Batut, Léon Moussinac, Aragon, Jandeline, Gabrille Fantin, Gaston Modot
Camera: Jacques Lemare-Isnard, Maillot, Verdier
Montage: Laure Sejour
Decors: Barsacq
Graphics: Griffoul
Music: Auric, Arthur Honegger, Henry Sauveplane
Length: 42 minutes

10. *Les bâtisseurs* 1938
Director: Jean Epstein
Producer: La Fédération des Cheminots, with the Confédération Générale du Travail
Cast: Le Corbusier, Jenneret, Léon Jouhaux
Length: 51 minutes

I originally saw a videotape of the film obtained by Claude Thibault. The film had badly deteriorated. It is now available at the Centre National de la Cinématographie.

11. *La Marseillaise*

Director: Jean Renoir
Produced by the Société "La Marseillaise"
Script: Jean Renoir, with Carl Koch, Nina Martel-Dreyfus (wife of Jean-Paul Le Chanois), Jean-Paul Le Chanois
Assistants: Jacques Becker, Claude Renoir, Jean-Paul Le Chanois, Louis Demazure, Marc Maurette, Antoine and Francine Corteggiani
Shadow Theater: Lotte Reiniger
Camera: Jean-Serge Bourgoin, Alain Douarinou, Jean-Marie Maillols, Jean-Paul Alphen, Jean Louis
Decors: Léon Barsacq, Georges Wakhévitch, Jean Périer
Sound: Joseph de Bretagne, Jean-Roger Bertrand, J. Meméde
Editing: Marguerite Renoir, assisted by Marthe Huguet
Music: Lalande, Grétry, Mozart, Johan Sebastian Bach, Rouget de l'Isle, Joseph Kosma, Sauveplane
Cast:
The Court: Pierre Renoir (Louis XVI), Lise Delamare (Marie-Antoinette), Léon Larive (Picard, king's valet), William Aguet (La Rochefoucauld-Liancourt), Elisa Ruis (Mme. de Lambelle), Germaine Lefèbvre (Mme. Elizabeth), Marie-Pierre Sordet-Dantès (le dauphin), Yveline Auriol (la dauphine), Pamela Stirling, Genia Vaury (two members of court)
Civil and Military Figures: Louis Jouvet (Roederer), Jean Aquistapace (mayor of the village), Georges Spanelli (La Chesnaye), Pierre Nay (Dubouchage), Jaque-Catelain (Capitaine Langlade), Edmond Castel (Leroux), Werner Florian-Zach (Westerman)
Aristocrats: Aimé Clariond (Monsieur de Saint-Laurent), Maurice Escande (the village lord), André Zibral (Monsieur de Saint-Méry), Jean Ayme (Monsieur de Fougerolles), Irène Joachim (Mme. de Saint-Laurent), Jacques Castelot
The Marseillais: Andrex (Honoré Arnaud), Charles Blavette, then Edmond Ardisson (Jean-Joseph Bomier), Paul Dellac (Javel), Jean-Louis Allibert (Moissan), Fernand Flament (Ardisson), Alex Truchy (Cuculière), Georges Péclet (Lieutenant Massugue), Adolphe Autran (drummer), Edouard Delmont (Anatole Rous, called Cabri, a peasant)
The People: Nadia Sibirskaia (Louison), Jenny Helia (woman speaking at Jacobin Club), Gaston Modot and Julien Carette (two volunteers), Séverine Lerczinska (a peasant), Marthe Marty (mother of Bomier), Odette Cazau (Thérèse), Edmond Beauchamp (the priest), Blanche Destournelles (Clémence)
And Roger Prégor, Pierre Ferval, Fernand Bellan, Jean Boissemond, Lucy Kieffer, Raymond Pélissier, Paul Lambert
Length: 130 minutes

The film is distributed in the United States by Corinth Films.

12. *La Grande Espérance** 1938
Produced by the French Communist Party
Length: 28 minutes

In this film on the PCF Congress at Arles, December 25–29, 1937, many party luminaries appear, include Maurice Thorez, Jacques Duclos, Marie Politzer, Daniella Casanova, Georges Politzer, Pierre Semard, Jean-Richard Bloch.

*I saw these films initially at UNICITE, the film and television office of the French Communist Party. When UNICITE closed, the films were given to the Centre National de la Cinématographie.

Bibliography

Abel, R. *French Cinema: The First Wave: 1915–29.* Princeton: Princeton University Press, 1984.

A la rencontre de Jacques Prévert. Saint Paul: Fondation Maeght, 1987.

Alexander, W. *Film on the Left.* Princeton: Princeton University Press, 1981.

Altman, G. "Ça, c'est du Cinéma." In *Paris, les Revues.* 1931.

———. "La Censure contre le Cinéma." Parts 1–3. *La Revue du Cinéma* 17 (1 December 1930), 19 (1 February 1931), 20 (March 1931).

Amengual, B. *Prévert, du cinéma.* Algiers: Travail et Culture, 1952. Reprinted by La Cinémathèque Québécoise, Montréal, 1978.

Amey, C., et al. *Le théâtre d'agit-prop de 1917 à 1932.* Tome 3. *Allemagne, France, U.S.A., Pologne, Roumanie. Recherches.* Tome 4. *Allemagne, France, Pologne, U.S.A. Ecrits théoriques et pièces.* Lausanne: L'Age D'Homme/La Cité, 1978.

Anderson, M. "The Myth of the 200 Families." *Political Studies* 13:2 (1965).

Anquetin, A. "Symboles, Mythes et Stéréotypes Nationaux dans les Cinémas Français et Allemands 1933–1939." *Rélations Internationales* 24 (Winter 1980).

Aragon, L. *L'Homme Communiste.* Tome 2. Paris: Gallimard, 1963.

Aranda, F. *Luis Buñuel. A Critical Biography.* Edited and translated by D. Robinson. New York: Da Capo, 1976.

Armes, R. *French Cinema.* New York: Oxford University Press, 1985.

Auriol, J.-G. "La Censure Peut Tuer le Cinéma." *La Revue des Vivants* 10 (October 1931).

Badie, B. "Les Grèves du Front Populaire aux usines Renault." *Le Mouvement Social* 81 (October/December 1972): 69–109.

Bardèche, M., and R. Brassilach. *Histoire du Cinéma.* Vol. 2. *Le Cinéma Parlant.* Paris: André Martel, 1953–54.

Bazin, A. *Jean Renoir*. Edited by F. Truffaut. Translated by W. W. Halsey and W. H. Simon. New York: Delta, 1973.

Beloff, M. "The Sixth of February." In *Decline of the Third Republic*. Edited by J. Joll. London: St. Anthony's Paper No. 5, 1959.

Bernard, J.-P. A. "Le Parti Communiste Français et les Problèmes Littéraires (1920–1939)." In *La Revue Française de Science Politique* 17:3 (June 1967).

———. *Le Parti Communiste français et la question littéraire (1921-1939)*. Grenoble: Presses Universitaires de Grenoble, 1972.

Berstein, S. *Le 6 février 1934*. Paris: Gallimard, 1951.

Beylie, C. "Jean Renoir." *Anthologie du Cinéma* 105. In *L'Avant scène Cinéma* 251/252 (July 1980).

———. "Jean Renoir." *Cinéma d'Aujourd'hui*. Nouvelle série, no. 2 (May-June 1975).

Blin, R. *Souvenirs et Propos Récueillis par Lynda Bellity Peskine*. Paris: Gallimard, 1986.

Bodin, L., and J. Touchard. *Front Populaire: 1936*. Paris: Armand Colin, 1972.

Bonnefous, E. *Histoire Politique de la Troisième République*. Tomes 5, 6. Paris: Presses Universitaires de France, 1962, 1965.

Boussinot, R., ed. *L'Encyclopédie du Cinéma*. Paris: Bordas, 1967.

Bradby, D. "The October Group and Theatre under the Front Populaire." In *Politics and Performance in Twentieth-century Drama and Film*. Edited by D. Bradby, L. James, and Bernard Sharratt. London: Cambridge University Press, 1980, pp. 231–42.

Braucourt, G. "Jean Renoir et Jean-Paul Le Chanois. Petite histoire de *La Vie est à nous*." *Les lettres françaises* 1308 (November 12, 1969).

Braudy, L. *Jean Renoir: The World of His Films*. New York: Doubleday, 1972.

Brower, D. *The New Jacobins: The French Communist Party and the Popular Front*. Ithaca: Cornell University Press, 1968.

Brown, E. J. *The Proletarian Episode in Russian Literature, 1928–1932*. New York: Columbia University Press, 1953.

Brown, J. A. C. *Techniques of Persuasion: From Propaganda to Brainwashing*. London: Penguin, 1963.

Brunet, J.-P. "Un Fascisme Français: Le Parti Populaire Français de Doriot (1936–1939)." *Revue Française de Science Politique* 33: 1 (February 1983).

Brunius, J. *En Marge du Cinéma Français*. Paris: Arcanes, 1954.

Buñuel, L. *Mon Dernier Soupir*. Paris: Editions Robert Laffont, 1982.

Cacérès, B. *Allons au-devant de la vie. La naissance du temps des loisirs en 1936*. Paris: Maspero, 1981.

Cahiers de L'Institut Maurice Thorez. c.v. de la Conférence d'Ivry. October 1966.

Campbell, R. *Cinema Strikes Back: Radical Filmmaking in the United States, 1930–1942*. Ann Arbor: UMI Research Press, 1982.

Capdenac, M. "Réalisme Polémique, Réalisme Poétique." *Les lettres françaises* 1308 (November 12, 1969).

Carr, E. H. *Twilight of the Comintern, 1930–1935*. New York: Pantheon, 1982.

Caute, D. *Communism and the French Intellectuals, 1914–1960*. New York: Macmillan, 1964.

————. *The Fellow Travelers.* New York: Macmillan, 1973.

Chakotin, S. *The Rape of the Masses: The Psychology of Totalitarian Political Propaganda.* London: The Labour Book Service, 1940.

Chardère, B. "Jacques Prévert et le Groupe Octobre." In *Jacques Prévert, Premier Plan* 14 (November 1960).

Chrystal, W. "Nazi Party Election Films 1927–1932," *Cinema Journal* 15:1 (Fall 1975).

"Cinema/Sound," *Yale French Studies* 60 (1980).

Claudin, F. *The Communist Movement: From Comintern to Cominform.* Part 1. *The Crisis of the Communist International.* New York: Monthly Review Press, 1975.

Colton, J. *Léon Blum: Humanist in Politics.* Cambridge: M.I.T. Press, 1966.

Courtade, F. *Les Malédictions du Cinéma Français.* Paris: Editions Alain Moreau, 1978.

Danos, J., and M. Gibelin. *Juin 1936.* Paris: Editions Ouvrières, 1952.

Daudelin, R., ed. *Cinéma de France, 1930–1939.* Montréal: La Cinémathèque Québécoise, June 1976.

Deak, I. *Weimar Germany's Left-Wing Intellectuals: A Political History of the Weltbühne and Its Circle.* Berkeley: University of California Press, 1968.

Drachkovitch, M., and B. Lazitch. *The Comintern: Historical Highlights.* Hoover Institute on War, Revolution, and Peace. New York and Washington: Praeger, 1966.

Dupeux, G. "L'Echec du premier Gouvernement Léon Blum." *Revue d'Histoire Moderne et Contemporaine* 10 (January-March 1963).

Durgnat, R. *Jean Renoir.* Berkeley: University of California Press, 1974.

Earle, E. M. *Modern France: Problems of the Third and Fourth Republics.* Princeton: Princeton University Press, 1951.

Eisenschitz, B. "Front Populaire et Idée de Cinéma Militant de France (1928–1937)." Publication of the International Federation of Film Archives and Bulgarska Nacionalna Filmoteka. Varna, 1977.

————. "Who Does the World Belong To? The Place of a Film." *Screen* 15:2 (Summer 1974).

Ellul, J. *Propaganda: The Formation of Men's Attitudes.* Translated by K. Kellen and J. Lerner. New York: Random House, 1973.

Este, P. "Les Actualités." In *Le Cinéma par ceux qui le font.* Présenté par Denis Marion. Paris: Fayard, 1949.

Estier, C. *La gauche hebdomadaire, 1914–1962.* Paris: Armand Colin, 1962.

Farmer, *France Reviews Its Revolutionary Origins.* New York: Columbia University Press, 1944. Reprinted New York: Farrar, Straus and Giroux, 1973.

Farnoux-Reynaud, L. "De la censure cinématographique." *Crapouillot* (February 1930).

Faulkner, C. *Jean Renoir: A Guide to References and Resources.* Boston: G. K. Hall, 1979.

————. *The Social Cinema of Jean Renoir.* Princeton: Princeton University Press, 1986.

Fauré, M. *Le Groupe Octobre.* Paris: Christian Bourgeois, 1977.

Fauvet, J. *Histoire du Parti Communiste Français*. Tome 1. Paris: Fayard, 1964.

Fofi, G. "The Cinema of the Popular Front in France (1934–38)." Translated by the editors of *Screen*. *Screen* 13:4 (Winter 1972/73).

La France des Années Trente vue Par Son Cinéma. Catalogue of Exposition organized by the Cinémathèque de Toulouse, la Bibliothèque de Toulouse, and the Musée des Augustins. May-June 1975.

Freinet, E. *Naissance d'une pédagogie populaire*. Paris: Maspero, 1981.

———. *L'Itinéraire de Celestin Freinet*. Paris: Payot, 1977.

Furet, F. *Interpreting the French Revolution*. Translated by E. Forster. New York: Cambridge University Press, 1981.

———. *Penser la Révolution française*. Paris: Gallimard, 1978.

Furhammer, L., and F. Isaksson. *Politics and Film*. Translated by K. French. New York: Praeger, 1971.

Garçon, F. *De Blum à Pétain. Cinéma et Société Française (1936–1944)*. Paris: Les Editions du Cerf, 1984.

Gaudibert, P.: "Front Populaire et Arts Plastiques." *Politique Aujourd'hui* (October-December 1974).

Gauteur, C. "Dossier sur *La Marseillaise*." *La Revue du Cinéma. Image et Son* 268 (February 1973).

———. "Jean Renoir de *Nana* à *la grande illusion*." *La Revue du Cinéma. Image et Son* 296 (May 1975).

———. *Jean Renoir. La Double Méprise*. Paris: Les Editeurs Français Réunis, 1980.

———. "Sept documents 'inédits.' Renoir 1937–1938. Suite. Et fin?" *La Revue du Cinéma. Image et Son* 315 (March 1977).

Gérard, A. *La Révolution française, mythes et interprétations (1789–1970)*. Paris: Flammarion, 1970.

Girault, R. "Léon Blum. La Dévaluation de 1936 et la conduite de la politique extérieure." *Rélations Internationales* 13 (Spring 1978).

———. "Réalités et images des crises extérieures chez les Français des années trente." In *Opinion Publique et Politique Extérieure*. Vol. 2. *1915–1940*. Colloque de l'Ecole française de Roma. 1982. Rome: Ecole Française de Rome, 1984.

———. "Les Rélations Internationales et L'Exercise du Pouvoir Pendant le Front Populaire, Juin 1936-Juin 1937." *Cahiers Léon Blum* 1 (May 1977).

———. "Le Trahison des possédants." *L'Histoire* 58 (July-August 1983).

Girault, R., et al. *Le PCF, Etapes et Problèmes*. Paris: Editions Sociales, 1981.

Godechot, J. *Un Jury pour la Révolution*. Paris: Editions Robert Laffont, 1974.

Goguel, F. *La Politique des Partis sous la IIIe République*. Paris: Editions du Seuil, 1946.

Greene, N. *Crisis and Decline: The French Socialist Party in the Popular Front Era*. Ithaca: Cornell University Press, 1969.

Grelier, R. *Mémoires d'en France, 1936–1939*. Paris: Editions AIMO, 1986.

Grindon, L. "The Politics of History in *La Marseillaise*." Unpublished paper, 1981.

Gross, B. *Willi Münzenberg: A Political Biography.* Translated by M. Jackson. Lansing: Michigan State University Press, 1974.

Gruber, H. "Willi Münzenberg: Propagandist For and Against the Comintern." *International Review of Social History* 10:2 (1965).

———. "Willi Münzenberg's German Communist Propaganda Empire, 1921–1933." *Journal of Modern History* 38:3 (September 1966).

Guérin, D. *La Révolution Française et Nous.* Brussels: Editions la taupe, 1969.

———. *Front Populaire Révolution Manquée.* Paris: Maspero, 1963; 1970.

Guillaume-Grimaud, G. *Le Cinéma du Front Populaire.* Paris: Lherminier, 1986.

Hainsworth, R. "Les Grèves du Front Populaire de mai et juin 36." *Le Mouvement social* 96 (July-September 1976).

Hardy, F., ed. *Grierson on Documentary.* New York: Faber and Faber, 1971.

Haudiquet, P. "La Vie est à nous." *La Revue du Cinéma. Image et Son* 235 (January 1970).

Hogenkamp, B. "Film and the Workers Movement in Britain, 1929–1939." *Sight and Sound* 45:2 (Spring 1976).

———. "Le film de gauche et la Guerre Civile d'Espagne, 1936–39." *Revue Belge du Cinéma* 17 (Autumn 1986).

———. "Worker's Film in Europe." *Jump-Cut* 19 (December 1978).

———. "Worker's Newsreels in the 1920's and 1930's." *Our History* 68 (1977).

Horak, J.-C. "German Communist Kinokultur, pt. 1: Prometheus Film Collective (1925–1932)." *Jump-Cut* (December 1981).

———. "Kino-Culture in Weimar Germany, Part 2. *Mother Krausen's Trip To Happiness.* 'Tenements Kill Like an Ax,'" *Jump-Cut* 27 (1982).

Interview with Raymond Bussières. *Critique Communiste* (Summer 1982).

Ivens, J., and R. Destanque. *Joris Ivens ou la Mémoire d'un Regard.* Paris: Editions BFB, 1982.

Jacques Prévert et ses amis Photographes. Lyon: Fondation Nationale de le photographie, 1981.

Jacques Prévert. Premier Plan 14 (November 1960).

Jean Renoir. Premier Plan, numéro spécial 22–23–24 (May 1962).

Jean Renoir Entretiens et Propos. Paris: Editions de l'Etoile–Cahiers du cinéma, 1979.

Jeancolas, J.-P. *Le Cinéma des français. 15 ans d'années trente.* Paris: Stock, 1983.

Jeander. "Les Ciné-Clubs." In *Le Cinéma par ceux qui le font.* Présenté par Denis Marion. Paris: Fayard, 1949.

Jeanson, H. *Soixante Ans d'Adolescence.* Paris: Stock, 1971.

Joll, J. "The Front Populaire—After Thirty Years." *Journal of Contemporary History* 1:2 (1966).

———. "The Making of the Popular Front." In *Decline of The Third Republic.* Edited by J. Joll. London: St. Anthony's Paper No. 5, 1959.

Kergoat, J. *La France du Front Populaire.* Paris: La Découverte, 1986.

Kiefé, R. "Le Cinématographe et le Droit." *La Revue des Vivants* 16 (November 1931).

———. "Pour Une Réforme de la Censure." *La Revue du Cinéma* 21 (1 April 1931).

Koestler, A. *The Invisible Writing.* New York: Macmillan, 1954.

Kriegel, A. *Le Congrès de Tours (1920). Naissance du Parti Communiste français.* Paris: Collection Archives, 1964.

———. "Le Parti Communiste français sous la Troisième République (1920– 1939). Evolution de ses Effectifs," *Revue Française de Science Politique* 16:1 (February 1966).

———. *Aux Origines du Communisme Français.* Paris: Flammarion, 1969.

———. *The French Communists.* Chicago: University of Chicago Press, 1972.

Lacouture, J. *Léon Blum.* Paris: Editions du Seuil, 1977.

Lazitch, B. "Le Komintern et le Front Populaire." *Contrepoint* (Spring 1971).

Lazitch, B., and M. Drachkovitch. *Biographical Dictionary of the Comintern.* Stanford: The Hoover Institution Press, Stanford University Press, 1973.

Lefranc, G. *June 36. "l'explosion sociale" du Front Populaire.* Paris: Julliard, 1966.

———. *Le Mouvement Syndical sous la Troisième République.* Paris: Payot, 1967.

———. *Histoire du Front Populaire (1934–1938).* Paris: Payot, 1965; 1974.

Leglise, P. "Censure et presse filmée sous la Troisième République." *Etudes de Presse,* nouvelle série 12:22–23 (1960).

———. *Histoire de la Politique du Cinéma Français. Le Cinéma et la IIIe République.* Tome I. Paris: Pierre Lherminier, 1970.

Leprohon, P. *Jean Renoir.* Translated by B. Elson. New York: Crown, 1971.

Leyda, J. *Kino.* New York: Collier Books, 1960.

Losfeld, E. *Les Français et leur Cinéma, 1930–1939.* Paris: Creteil, 1973.

Lottman, H. *The Left Bank.* Boston: Houghton Mifflin, 1982.

Manevy, R. *Histoire de la presse, 1914–1939.* Paris: Corréa, 1945.

Marcus, J. *French Socialism in the Crisis Years, 1933–1936.* New York: Praeger, 1958.

Mathiez, A. *The French Revolution.* Translated by C. A. Phillips. New York: Alfred A. Knopf, 1928.

McPherson, D., ed. *Traditions of Independence: British Cinema in the Thirties.* London: British Film Institute, 1980.

Miquel, P. *Histoire de la Radio et de la Télévision.* Paris: Editions Richelieu, 1972.

Mitry, J. *Histoire du cinéma.* Tome 4. *Les années 30.* Paris: Jean-Pierre Delange, 1980.

Modot, G. "La Censure au cinéma." *Les Vraies Richesses* 3 (April 1939).

Monaco, P. *Cinema and Society: France and Germany during the Twenties.* New York/Oxford/Amsterdam: Elsevier, 1976.

Monnerot, J.-M. "*La Vie est à nous.*" *Commune* (May 1936).

Murray, B. "*Mutter Krausens Fahrt ins Glück:* An Analysis of the Film as a Critical Response to the 'Street Films' of the Commercial Film Industry." *enclitic* (1982).

Ory, P. "La Politique Culturelle du Premier Gouvernement Blum." *La Nouvelle Revue Socialiste* 10–11 (1975).

———. "De Ciné-Liberté à *La Marseillaise:* Espoirs et limites d'un cinéma libéré (1936–1938)." *Le Mouvement social* 91 (April-June 1975).

Oury, F., and A. Vasquez. *Vers une pédagogie institutionelle?* Paris: Maspero, 1967.

———. *De la classe coopérative à la pédagogie institutionelle.* Paris: Maspero, 1971.

Pettifer, J. "Against the Stream—*Kuhle Wampe!*" *Screen* 15:2 (Summer 1974).

Piaton, G. *La Pensée pédagogique de Celestin Freinet.* Toulouse: Edition Privat, 1974.

Pinel, V. *Introduction au Ciné-Club.* Paris: Editions Ouvrières, 1964.

Pithon, R. "La Censure des films en France et la crise politique de 1934." *Revue historique* 258 (1977).

———. "Le Scandale Stavisky et La Censure du Cinéma: L'Affaire *La Banque Nemo* (1934)." *Etude de Lettres.* Série III. Tome 8. no. 2 (April-June 1975).

Pivasset, J. *Essai sur la Signification Politique du Cinéma.* Paris: Cujas, 1971.

Prédal, R. *La Société Française 1914-1945 à travers le Cinéma.* Paris: Armand Colin, 1972.

Pronay, N., and D. W. Spring, eds. *Propaganda, Politics and Film, 1918–45.* London: Macmillan, 1982.

Prost, A. *La CGT à l'epoque du Front Populaire.* Paris: F.N.S.P., 1964.

———. *L'Enseignement en France, 1800–1967.* Paris: Armand Colin, 1968.

Prouteau, H. *Les Occupations d'Usines en Italie et en France (1920–36).* Paris: Librairie Technique et Economique, 1938.

Rabaut, J. *Tout est possible.* Paris: Denoël, 1974.

Racine, N. "L'Association des Ecrivains et Artistes Révolutionnaires (A.E.A.R.)" *Le Mouvement social* 54 (January/March 1966).

———. "Une revue d'intelectuals communistes dans les années vingt: '*Clarté*' (1921–1928)." *La Revue Française de Science Politique* 17:3 (June 1967).

Racine, N., and L. Bodin. *Le Parti Communiste Français pendant l'Entre Deux-Guerres.* Paris: Armand Colin, 1972.

Razdac, P. "Un Théâtre d'agit-prop." *Critique Communiste* (Summer 1982).

Reberioux, M. "Théâtre d'agitation: Le Groupe 'Octobre.'" *Le Mouvement social* 91 (April-June 1975).

Rémond, R. *Les Droites en France.* Paris: Audier Montaigne, 1982.

Rémond, R., and J. Bourdin, eds. *Edouard Daladier, Chef de Gouvernement.* Paris: F.N.S.P., 1977.

Renoir. J. *Ecrits, 1926–1971.* Edited by C. Gauteur. Paris: Belfond, 1974.

———. *My Life and My Films.* Translated by N. Denny. New York: Atheneum, 1974.

"Résolution sur les questions de la littérature prolétarienne et révolutionnaire en France." *La Littérature de la révolution mondiale.*

"Résolution sur la revue 'monde.'" *La Littérature de la révolution mondiale.*

Robert, F. "Genèse det destin de *La Marseillaise.*" *La Pensée* 221/222 (July-August 1981).

———. "Maurice Thorez et *la Marseillaise.*" *Cahiers de l'Institut Maurice Thorez* 6:25 (January-February 1972).

Robrieux, P. *Histoire intérieure du parti communiste français, 1920–1945.* Tomes 1, 4. Paris: Fayard, 1980.

Rudé, G. *Interpretations of the French Revolution.* London: Routledge and Kegan Paul, Pamphlet 47 of Historical Association, 1961.

Sadoul, G. *Chroniques du cinéma français, 1939–1967.* Edited by B. Eisenschitz. Paris: 10/18, 1979.

————. *Dictionary of Filmmakers.* Translated by P. Morris. Berkeley: University of California Press, 1972.

————. *French Film.* London: Falcon Press, 1953. Reprinted edition, New York: Arno Press and the New York Times, 1972.

————. *Histoire Générale du Cinéma.* Tome 5. Paris: Denoël, 1975.

————. *Rencontres 1. Chroniques et entretiens.* Paris: Denoël, 1984.

Samuels, S. "The Left Book Club." *Journal of Contemporary History* 1:2 (1966).

Sauvy, A. *Histoire Economique de la France entre les Deux Guerres 1931–1939.* Paris: Fayard, 1967.

Schumann, P. "Le Cinéma prolétarien Allemand (1922-1932)." Translated by I. Schroeder. *Ecran* 73:20 (December 1973).

Schwartz, S. "Les Occupations d'usine en France de mai et juin 36." *International Review for Social History* 2 (1937).

Serceau, D. "The Communist Party and *La Vie est à nous:* Document and Fiction, Poetics and Politics." In *"Show Us Life": Toward a History and Aesthetics of the Committed Documentary.* Edited by T. Waugh. Metuchen, N.J. and London: The Scarecrow Press, 1984.

————. *Jean Renoir, l'Insurgé.* Paris: La Sycamore, 1981.

Sesonske, A. *Jean Renoir: The French Films, 1924–1939.* Cambridge: Harvard University Press, 1980.

Shattuck, R. "Writers for the Defense of Culture." *Partisan Review* 3 (1984): 393–416. Reprinted as "Having Congress: The Shame of the Thirties." In *The Innocent Eye.* New York: Farrar, Straus and Giroux, 1984.

Sherwood, J. *Georges Mandel and the Third Republic.* Stanford: Stanford University Press, 1970.

Short, K. R. M., ed. *Feature Films as History.* Knoxville: University of Tennessee Press, 1981.

Short, R. S. "Contre-attaque." In *Entretiens sur le surréalisme.* Paris: Mouton, 1968.

————. "The Politics of Surrealism, 1920–1936." *Journal of Contemporary History* 1:2 (1966).

Spitzer, S. "Prévert's Political Theatre: Two Versions of *La Bataille de Fontenoy.*" *Theatre Research International* 3:1 (October 1977).

Strebel, E. G. "French Social Cinema of the Nineteen-thirties: A Cinematic Expression of Popular Front Consciousness." Unpublished doctoral dissertation, Princeton University, 1974.

————. "Renoir and the Popular Front." *Sight and Sound* (Winter 1979–80).

Sussex, E. *The Rise and Fall of British Documentary.* Berkeley: University of California Press, 1975.

Talon, G. "Regards critiques sur la production et la réalisation des films au temps du Front Populaire!" *Cinéma 75* 194 (January 1975).

Taylor, R. *Film Propaganda: Soviet Russia and Nazi Germany.* New York: Harper and Row, 1973.

———. *The Politics of the Soviet Cinema, 1917–1929.* Cambridge: Cambridge University Press, 1979.

Thirion, A. *Revolutionaries without Revolution.* New York: Macmillan, 1975.

Thomas, H. *The Spanish Civil War.* New York: Harper and Bros., 1961; 1981.

Thompson, K. *Exporting Entertainment: America in the World Film Market 1907–34.* London: British Film Institute, 1985.

Tiersky, R. *French Communism, 1920–1972.* New York: Columbia University Press, 1974.

Touchard, J. *La Gauche en France depuis 1900.* Paris: Editions du Seuil, 1977.

———. "Le Parti Communiste Français et les Intellectuels (1920–1939)." *La Revue Française de Science Politique* 17:3 (June 1967).

"Trois films invisibles." *L'Avant-Scène Cinéma* 99 (January 1970).

Trotsky, L. *Le Mouvement Communiste en France (1919–1939).* Edited by P. Broué. Paris: Les Editions de Minuit, 1967.

Tudesq, A.-J. "L'Utilization Gouvernementale de la radio." In *Edouard Daladier, Chef de Gouvernement.* Edited by R. Rémond and J. Bourdin. Paris: F.N.S.P., 1977.

Tudesq, A.-J., and E. Cazenave. "Radiodiffusion et politique: les élections radiophoniques de 1937 en France." *Revue d'histoire moderne et contemporaine* 23 (October-December 1976).

Unir, *Histoire du PCF.* Tome 1. Paris: Editions Veridad, 1964.

"*La Vie est à nous.* Film Militant." *Cahiers du Cinéma* 218 (March 1970).

Vincendeau, G., and K. Reader. "Community, Nostalgia and the Spectacle of Masculinity: The Jean Gabin Persona in films from the Popular Front Period." *Screen* 26:6 (November-December 1985).

Vincendeau, G., and K. Reader, eds. *"La Vie est à nous!" French Cinema of the Popular Front 1935–1938.* London: British Film Institute, 1986.

Wall, I. "The Resignation of the First Popular Front Government of Léon Blum." *French Historical Studies* 6:4 (Fall 1970).

———. "French Socialism and the Popular Front." *Journal of Contemporary History* 5:3 (1970).

Walsh, M. "The Complex Seer: Brecht and the Film." *Sight and Sound* 26:3 (Autumn 1974).

Walter, G. *Histoire du Parti Communiste Français.* Paris: Somogy, 1948.

Wegg-Prosser, V. "The Archive of the Film and Photo League." *Sight and Sound* 46:4 (Autumn 1977).

Weill, S. *La Condition Ouvrière.* Paris: Gallimard, 1951.

Welch, D. "The Proletarian Cinema and the Weimar Republic." *Historical Journal of Film, Radio, and Television* 1:1 (1981).

Werth, A. *Whither France.* Translated by J. G. Wright and H. R. Isaacs. New York: Pioneer Publishers, 1936.

Willard, C. "Les Intellectuels Français et le Front populaire." *Cahiers de l'Institut Maurice Thorez* 3–4 (1967).

Wright, G. *France in Modern Times.* New York and London: W. W. Norton, 1960; 1981.

———. *Rural Revolution in France.* Stanford: Stanford University Press, 1964.

Index

Page numbers for photographs are in italics.